P9-CJV-226

RENEWALS: 691-4574

DATE DUE

MAY 0 4			
MAY 1 2			
SEP 1 3			
3/28			
4/11/96			

WITHDRAWN
UTSA LIBRARIES

Demco, Inc. 38-293

The Chronic Mental Patient
Five Years Later

The Chronic Mental Patient
Five Years Later

Edited by
John A. Talbott, M.D.
Professor of Psychiatry
Cornell University Medical College
Associate Medical Director
Payne Whitney Clinic
New York, New York

Grune & Stratton, Inc.
(Harcourt Brace Jovanovich, Publishers)
Orlando   San Diego   San Francisco   New York   London
Toronto   Montreal   Sydney   Tokyo   São Paulo

Library of Congress Cataloging in Publication Data
Main entry under title:

The Chronic mental patient.

Includes bibliographical references and index.
1. Mentally ill—Care and treatment—United States.
2. Mental illness—Research—United States. 3. Mental
health services—United States. I. Talbott, John A.
[DNLM: 1. Mental Disorders. 2. Chronic Disease. WM 100
C5567]
RC443.C495 1984   362.2′0973   84-6672
ISBN 0-8089-1649-1

©**1984 by Grune & Stratton, Inc.**
All rights reserved. No part of this publication
may be reproduced or transmitted in any form or
by any means, electronic or mechanical, including
photocopy, recording, or any information storage
and retrieval system, without permission in
writing from the publisher.

Grune & Stratton, Inc.
Orlando, Florida 32887

Distributed in the United Kingdom by
Grune & Stratton, Ltd.
24/28 Oval Road, London NW 1

Library of Congress Catalog Number 84-6672
International Standard Book Number 0-8089-1649-1
Printed in the United States of America
84 85 86 87   10 9 8 7 6 5 4 3 2 1

LIBRARY
The University of Texas
At San Antonio

Contents

Contributors

WILLIAM A. ANTHONY, PH.D.   Professor, Department of Rehabilitation Counseling, Boston University; Director, Center for Rehabilitation Research and Training in Mental Health, Boston, Massachusetts

PAUL S. APPELBAUM, M.D.   Co-Director, Law and Psychiatry Program, Western Psychiatric Institute and Clinic; Assistant Professor of Psychiatry and Law, University of Pittsburgh, Pittsburgh, Pennsylvania

LEONA L. BACHRACH, PH.D.   Research Professor of Psychiatry, Maryland Psychiatric Research Center, University of Maryland School of Medicine, Catonsville, Maryland; Senior Consultant to the Maryland Division of Mental Hygiene in Deinstitutionalization and Community Support Planning, Baltimore, Maryland

JAMES T. BARTER, M.D.   Professor of Psychiatry and Chief, Division of General Psychiatry, University of California at Davis School of Medicine, Sacramento, California

ELLEN BAXTER, M.P.H.   Research Associate, Community Service Society, New York, New York

ALLAN BEIGEL, M.D.   Professor of Psychiatry, University of Arizona College of Medicine, Tucson, Arizona; Chairman, APA Joint Commission on Government Relations, Washington, DC

CAROL L. M. CATON, PH.D.   Associate Professor of Social Sciences, Department of Psychiatry, School of Public Health, College of Physicians & Surgeons, Columbia University; Research Scientist, New York State Psychiatric Institute, New York, New York

BARRY F. COHEN, PH.D. Director of Special Projects, Center for Rehabilitation Research and Training in Mental Health, Boston University, Boston, Massachusetts

MIKAL R. COHEN, PH.D. Director of Training, Center for Rehabilitation Research and Training in Mental Health, Boston University, Boston, Massachusetts

DAVID CUTLER, M.D. Associate Director of Community Psychiatry Training Program; Chief of Emergency Services, Oregon Health Sciences University, Portland, Oregon

TEDDI FINE, M.A. Assistant Director, Division of Government Relations, American Psychiatric Association, Washington, DC

HOWARD H. GOLDMAN, M.D., M.P.H. Associate Professor of Psychiatry, Langley Porter Institute, University of California, San Francisco, California; Assistant Director for Mental Health Financing, National Institute of Mental Health, Rockville, Maryland

AGNES B. HATFIELD, PH.D. Associate Professor of Education, Department of Human Development, College of Education, University of Maryland, College Park, Maryland; Past President, National Alliance for the Mentally Ill, Washington, DC

DOUGLAS W. HEINRICHS, M.D. Assistant Professor, Department of Psychiatry, University of Maryland; Chief, Outpatient Programs, Maryland Psychiatric Center, Baltimore, Maryland

GRETA S. HERMAN, M.D. Instructor, Department of Psychiatry; Associate Director of Residency Training, Department of Psychiatry, The Mount Sinai School of Medicine, New York, New York

MARVIN I. HERZ, M.D. Professor and Chairman, Department of Psychiatry, State University of New York at Buffalo School of Medicine; Director, Department of Psychiatry, Erie County Medical Center, Buffalo, New York

KIM HOPPER, M.A. Research Associate, Community Service Society, New York, New York

JOHN M. KANE, M.D. Director, Psychiatric Research, Long Island Jewish-Hillside Medical Center, Glen Oaks, New York; Associate Professor of Psychiatry, School of Medicine, Health Sciences Center, State University of New York at Stony Brook, Stony Brook, New York

SAMUEL J. KEITH, M.D.   Chief, Center for Studies of Schizophrenia, National Institute of Mental Health, Rockville, Maryland

H. RICHARD LAMB, M.D.   Professor of Psychiatry, University of Southern California School of Medicine, Los Angeles, California

ROBERT E. LOVE, PH.D.   Independent Consultant, Washington, DC

SUSAN M. MATTHEWS   Research Analyst, Center for Studies of Schizophrenia, National Institute of Mental Health, Rockville, Maryland

ARTHUR T. MEYERSON, M.D.   Associate Professor and Vice Chairman, Department of Psychiatry, The Mount Sinai School of Medicine; Clinical Director, Department of Psychiatry, The Mount Sinai Hospital, New York, New York

BERT PEPPER, M.D.   Director, Rockland County Community Mental Health Center, Pomona, New York; Clinical Professor of Psychiatry, New York University School of Medicine, New York, New York

JUDITH RABKIN, M.P.H., PH.D.   Associate Professor of Clinical Psychology, College of Physicians and Surgeons, Columbia University; Research Scientist, New York State Psychiatric Institute, New York, New York

JEFFREY RUBIN, PH.D.   Associate Professor of Economics, Department of Economics, Rutgers—The State University of New Jersey, New Brunswick, New Jersey

HILARY RYGLEWICZ, Clinical Assistant to the Director, Rockland County Community Mental Health Center, Pomona, New York

JOHN A. TALBOTT, M.D.   Professor of Psychiatry, Cornell University Medical College; Associate Medical Director, Payne Whitney Psychiatric Clinic, The New York Hospital, New York, New York

KENNETH TARDIFF, M.D., M.P.H.   Associate Professor of Clinical Psychiatry, Associate Dean, Cornell University Medical College, New York, New York

The Chronic Mental Patient
Five Years Later

John A. Talbott

Introduction

The process of depopulating state hospitals in the United States began in 1955, but it was not until 20 years later that both governmental and professional organizations began to study the issue seriously. In turn, the Government Accounting Office,[1] the National Institute of Mental Health,[2] the President's Commission on Mental Health,[3] the Group for the Advancement of Psychiatry (GAP),[4] and the American Psychiatric Association,[5] analyzed the problems arising from this depopulation process and published their findings.

It is now only a little over five years since these studies were conducted and their findings became available. In the meantime, there has been a veritable explosion of information concerning the objects of this depopulation—the chronically mentally ill. Several specialty journals have concentrated on therapeutic, programmatic, and systems issues—*Hospital and Community Psychiatry, New Directions in Mental Health Services,* and *Schizophrenia Bulletin.* In addition, several major texts have appeared that detail treatment,[6,7] service,[8,9] and administrative[10] issues.

It is our intent in this volume to cover the entire range of issues involving the chronically mentally ill. In so doing, we will provide the reader with an update on most of the areas of concern about these patients, supplying most of the information we now know, that we did not know five years ago, as well as spelling out areas of needed work.

THE CHRONIC MENTAL PATIENT
ISBN 0-8089-1649-1

Copyright © 1984 by Grune & Stratton.
All rights of reproduction in any form reserved.

Overview

The volume is divided into four parts, representing the major areas of the field: Research and Education, Treatment and Rehabilitation, Community Treatment, and Systems Issues. In many respects the divisions are arbitrary, since almost every chapter contains new knowledge and research, provides information about therapeutic modalities (such as treatment), and has implications regarding the future of mental health service delivery (e.g. systems).

Samuel Keith provides an introductory overview of the field of research. His chapter is followed by five more that chronicle the expanding areas of knowledge: Howard Goldman's on the numbers of the chronically mentally ill; Bert Pepper's on the exploding numbers of young (ages 18–35) chronically mentally ill persons; Ellen Baxter's on the epidemic of street people, or homeless individuals, many of whom are seriously or chronically mentally ill; Marvin Herz's, on newer attempts to define the course of chronic mental illness and its relapse, and thereby teach patients and their families how to seek earlier effective intervention; and Kenneth Tardiff's, which uses newly acquired data from several diverse sources to gain a better hold on the question of how violent the chronic mentally ill are. Finally, I summarize the state of knowledge about what education psychiatrists and nonpsychiatric physicians need to treat and care for this population better.

The second section is concerned with treatment and rehabilitation issues. It begins with a chapter by John Kane on one of the most important areas in the treatment of the chronically ill—medication. An area of equal importance, that of psychosocial treatment, is covered in the next chapter by Douglas Heinrichs; and the final area of importance, rehabilitation, is discussed by William Anthony. Carol Caton reviews the consistent but still unimplemented research on lengths of hospital stay. Leona Bachrach then discusses the principles of programs for the chronically ill. Finally, James Barter discusses one of the most dynamic and potentially effective modes of intervention—psychoeducational approaches with both patients and their families.

The third section of this work focuses on community treatment of the chronically mentally ill. The largest federal initiative for this population, the NIMH's Community Support Program, is examined by Robert Love, five years after its inception. Richard Lamb then covers many areas where the chronically ill reside—prisons, board and care homes, etc.—not usually considered ideal therapeutic alternatives to hospitals. Arthur Meyerson discusses the entire world of what used to be called "after care," but now is more appropriately viewed as the outpatient part of a lifetime of care and treatment. Finally, David Cutler discusses the many types of social networks needed by the chronically ill, thus giving us a practical as well as theoretical model of intervention into the everyday lives of these individuals.

The fourth and concluding section discusses the implications of the prior chapters from a broader perspective. Jeffrey Rubin gives us an update on the economics of care of the chronically ill; Allan Beigel and Teddi Fine discuss developments at the federal level to care for this population; Paul Appelbaum covers the emerging legal issues; Agnes Hatfield, the views of and involvement of families of the chronically ill in their care; and Judith Rabkin, the attitudes of average Americans toward the chronically ill.

It is apparent from the impressive display of information contained in this work that we certainly know more now than we did five years ago, and a great deal more than we did 29 years ago, when the depopulation movement began. We know more about the demographics of the population, their number and location, and emerging groups of young and elderly chronically ill; the differential diagnosis of chronic mental illness and therefore successful treatment of entities such as primary affective disorders and pseudodementia; the course of chronic illness and signs of relapse; elements common to successful treatment, followup, and rehabilitation programs; community support systems; housing and alternatives to institutions; economic factors; public attitudes; personnel and training issues; legal issues, including violence among the chronically mentally ill; and systems issues.

There is still more, however, that we do not know. Not surprisingly, we still do not know the cause (or causes) of mental illness and, by inference, how to prevent chronicity. We do not know what specific treatment and care elements work for which patients in what settings (e.g. medication, psychotherapy, vocational and social rehabilitation, and case management), including their cost versus benefit, treatment and program effectiveness, and quality-of-life determinations; and we do not know how many of each kind of service unit we need per population unit (numbers of beds or slots in asylum care, active treatment, emergency care, private proprietary housing, nursing homes, supervised apartment living, and independent living).

The progress we have made in the past five years is impressive, not only in the amount of information, but in the correction of widely held beliefs. We know, for instance, that schizophrenics do relapse, despite the best care, and the causes of relapse are symptomatic, not institutional. We also know that community care is as successful, if not more so, on a number of outcome indicators than institutional or institutional plus traditional followup care. We still need hospitals, however, for many acute episodes. Finally, we know the principles of good treatment, of effective work with families, of proper locating of community residences, of effective training of personnel, of cost efficiencies, and of community support systems. The task of the next five years will be to translate this knowledge into action, to make our certain knowledge work. And in five more years I hope we can present the reader with more progress toward these ends achieved.

REFERENCES

1. Returning the mentally disabled to the community: Government needs to do more. US General Accounting Office, 1977
2. Bachrach LL: Deinstitutionalization: An analytical review and sociological perspective. Rockville, MD, DHEW, 1976
3. Talbott JA: Report to the President from the President's Commission on Mental Health, Sup. of Documents, Washington, DC, 1976
4. GAP Report: The chronic mental patient in the community. New York, Group for the Advancement of Psychiatry, 1978
5. Talbott JA (ed.): The chronic mental patient in the community. New York, Recommendations for a Public Policy. Washington, DC, American Psychiatric Association, 1978
6. Lamb HRH: Community survival for long-term mentally ill. San Francisco, Jossey-Bass, 1976
7. Lamb HRH: Treating the long-term mentally ill. San Francisco, Jossey-Bass, 1982
8. Stein LI, and Test, MA: Alternatives to mental hospital treatment. New York, Plenum, 1975
9. Segal AP, and Aviram U: The mentally ill in community-based sheltered care. New York, Wiley, 1978
10. Talbott JA: The chronic mentally ill: Treatment, programs, systems. New York, Human Sciences Press, 1981

PART I

Research and Education

Samuel J. Keith
Susan M. Matthews

1

Research Overview

More than two million Americans will have their lives altered, some irreparably, by the tragic mental disorder of schizophrenia. The tendency toward chronic disability in a disorder that removes people from a functional existence early in their career or late in their education explains why 40 percent of our nation's mental hospital beds are now occupied by schizophrenic patients. This dramatic utilization of inpatient beds, however, tells only a small part of the overall extent of the problem. With the increasing emphasis on community care for the chronically mentally ill, a far larger number of former hospitalized patients are now being cared for in the community. It should be clear, however, that unless treatments also continue to improve, what has changed is the location of the suffering, not the amount. The treatments available for disorders such as schizophrenia, while important in alleviating some of the suffering for some of the people afflicted, are not yet sufficient to prevent the wasteful denouement seen all too frequently. Of those initially affected by schizophrenia, it is estimated that 50 percent will experience some form of disability in an intermittent course of the illness throughout their lifetime; an additional 25 percent will never recover from this initial episode and will require life-long care. For these hundreds of thousands of Americans the only hope lies in expanding our research data base in order to provide a better understanding of the causes, treatments, and preventions for schizophrenia. With a disorder as complex and probably as heterogeneous as schizophrenia, the challenge is to find meaningful and useful constructs to integrate the accumulating knowledge about the illness. Unfortunately, the field of research has had a tendency to polarize around certain issues: neuroscience research versus social-psychological research; pharmacologic treatment versus

THE CHRONIC MENTAL PATIENT
ISBN 0-8089-1649-1

psychosocial treatment. Although we find that the pursuit of goals in discretely defined areas is absolutely essential for research progress, it is also essential to remember that the overall goal is to relieve the suffering in fellow human beings. Suffering occurs in both biological and psychosocial forms.

One possible means to integrate these elements is to develop a conceptual model that can encompass both the biological and psychosocial aspects of schizophrenia. It would also be helpful if this same model could help us to understand the problems encountered in chronic mental illness. What is it that we are really discussing when we are talking about chronic mental illness? Is it the chronic presence of florid symptomatology? Is it the disability resulting from the manifest illness? Is it something about the illness itself that causes disability as an integral part of the illness?

The past five years have fortunately provided some answers that are quite significant in that they supply a context in which we can better understand the disorder and apply rational treatment strategies. The approach that comes the closest to this perhaps too idealistic solution was first presented well over five years ago, in 1974. The recently renewed interest in it, however, has been due to the development of new means of assessment and the understanding of the interface with our available clinical armamentarium. There is, in addition the beginning of a suggestion that some biologic variables may have a distinct relationship to this conceptualization.

An approach to schizophrenia that may be helpful in understanding the current research data base was first presented by Strauss, Carpenter, and Bartko.[1] Drawing from the Hughlings Jackson evolution/dissolution theory, they developed a rather compelling base of evidence from precursors and prognostic factors supporting three groupings of problems associated with schizophrenia: positive symptoms, negative symptoms, and disorders of interpersonal relationships. By positive symptoms, they refer to symptoms of schizophrenia that characterize it by their presence—hallucinations and delusions—or, as defined in DSM III, the Category A symptoms of schizophrenia; by negative symptoms, they refer to those symptoms of schizophrenia that characterize it by their absence—lack of goal-directed behavior, blunting of affect and verbal paucity, reflective of DSM III schizophrenia symptom categories B (deterioration from a prior level of functioning) or C symptoms (prodromal or residual characteristics); by disordered interpersonal relationships, they are referring to patterns of asociality, withdrawal, and lack of close personal ties (a further refinement of the DSM III dysfunction criteria for schizophrenia). Their data supported the following conclusions: positive symptoms develop over a short period of time, are state specific, represent a reaction to either biological or socioenvironmental factors, and account for little in terms of overall prognosis. Negative symptoms develop over an extended period of time prior to or following the appearance of the syndrome-defining positive symptoms, represent either the source of chronicity (e.g., poor premorbid adjustment) or the result of chronicity (deteriorating course), and account for considerable contribution to overall outcome. Disordered interpersonal relationships develop over an extended period of time (frequently in the premorbid state) but may appear acutely with the onset of positive symptoms or their prodrome or may deteriorate over the life course of the disorder, represent an interactive process between inherent social skills of the patient, the destructive impact of the positive symptoms, and the environmental response patterns, and account for important aspects of outcome in terms of social functioning, but also interact with the outcomes in the areas of positive and negative symptoms.

Significant in this report is the focus on the development of negative symptoms and the impaired interpersonal relationships. The importance of identifying the presence of negative symptoms and disordered relationships in the "premorbid" or "prepositive symptom" stage is to establish them as independent of the florid psychosis. This separation creates the possibility of identifying the negative symptoms that precede the onset of the diagnosable disorder from the defect state that may result as a consequence of the florid psychosis. The defect state could then be conceptualized as a gradual withdrawal from the spectrum of functioning, creating an essentially residual category of symptoms.

At this point in our understanding of schizophrenia and of the needs of people afflicted with this potentially disabling disorder, it is possible to apply this conceptual framework to our available treatment armamentarium and to propose realistic treatment expectations and develop rational delivery mechanisms. In addition, it is possible to identify the gaps in our knowledge and to propose strategies to reduce these gaps.

The general approach to the treatment of schizophrenia most frequently involves some combination of pharmacologic and psychosocial modalities. Indeed, combined advances in psychopharmacology and psychosocial treatments produced a major revolution in the treatment of schizophrenia in the 1950s. The ensuing three decades, however, have seen a parallel, but until recently distinctly separate, development of knowledge about these two elements of treatment. The well designed, rigorous clinical trials of neuroleptics have produced an imposing body of data that points to their control of the initial positive symptoms of schizophrenia in approximately 80 percent of the population. In addition, well designed studies of maintenance chemotherapy demonstrate a decided advantage of those assigned to receive drugs as compared with those assigned to placebo treatment.[2] It must be borne clearly in mind, however, that this "decided advantage" is in the prevention of the recurrence of positive symptoms and not in overall outcome, an area clearly more dominated by the persistence of negative symptoms than by the elimination of positive ones. The issue of safety versus relative efficacy must also be considered. In a review of 56 studies presenting data on tardive dyskinesia (TD) in cases exposed to neuroleptics, Kane and Smith[3] reported an average TD prevalence of 20 percent as compared with 5 percent prevalence of "spontaneous" dyskinesia in 19 samples of untreated individuals. What becomes clear in summarizing these findings is that the neuroleptic treatment of schizophrenia provides a potential for establishing a baseline of freedom from positive symptoms for most patients. At this point in our understanding of schizophrenia and its effective treatment, this reduction of positive symptoms approaches a *sine qua non* or necessary first step for any treatment directed at the negative symptoms or disordered interpersonal relationships. We take this position even though we acknowledge fully and accept our earlier point that positive symptoms are the least enduring and the least prognostic aspect of schizophrenia. They are its most characteristic, dramatic, and perhaps most significantly, its most frightening aspect, because such symptoms as hallucinations and delusions are discontinuous with normal behavior and expectations. While there are a few dedicated and talented clinicians working in settings where regressed behavior and florid symptomatology are accepted as relevant to therapeutic recovery (e.g. Mosher [4]), most of us find it difficult to address issues of negative symptoms and social competence in the presence of florid positive symptoms. In reducing positive symptoms and maintaining this remitted status, the prevention of side effects and the potential for interference with negative symptom recovery from the inhibiting aspects of neuroleptics must also be included in the treatment planning. Several new strategies have been developed to offset the development of the potentially undesirable aspects of pharmacologic treatment; all involve the reduction of dosage. Kane and coworkers[5] have tested a one-fifth standard dosage; Carpenter and associates[6] are testing an approach called targeted medication and Herz[7] is using a strategy called intermittent medication. All are exploring the potential benefits of lowering the overall level of medication in an attempt to find the best interface between the prevention of relapse, the reduction of side effects, and the improvement in negative symptoms and interpersonal relationships. The next several years will provide us with data from these studies that will permit us to make the greatest use of pharmacologic treatment.

Studies of the impact of psychosocial treatments have not developed the same type of data base over the past three decades. Given the long and rich history of psychosocial treatment including individual, group, and family therapies for schizophrenia, going back well before the advent of neuroleptics, there is a serious lack of availability of reported studies evaluating its utility. In searching for explanations for this, we have identified two recurring themes in the literature. The first is perhaps most eloquently expressed by Carpenter and Heinrichs.[8]

Psychotherapy was the most prestigious form of psychiatric treatment, and the need for testing the therapeutic efficacy was not readily appreciated by those who presumed a treatment effect. We looked to the philosopher, the essayist, the metapsychologist, and the indoctrinated clinician for new knowledge. Many leading psychiatrists came from the ranks of those who had prolonged educational experience which stressed the inculcation of beliefs, with neglect of scientific principles of hypothesis testing and theory disproof. Arrogance is no friend of science and we now face the consequences of having failed to establish a data base suitable for testing therapeutic efficacy of social treatments in general, and psychotherapy of schizophrenia in particular."(p. 242).

The second theme recurring in the literature is that psychotherapy as we have traditionally defined it may not be the most effective form of treatment for schizophrenia. It becomes essential, at this point, to distinguish between psychotherapy and psychosocial treatment. By psychotherapy, we refer to the traditional format of placing the emphasis on the patient with the implication that the patient will be able to take corrective steps outside of therapy based on what he or she has learned inside the therapeutic situation. For many patients with disorders other than schizophrenia, this certainly occurs. For some exceptional patients with schizophrenia, this may yet turn out to be a successful approach if we are able to identify who these patients will be prior to treatment assignment. Further, there are no doubt times during the course of the schizophrenic disorder where the timely intervention by psychotherapeutic techniques would prove exceedingly useful. We hope that in this regard the current generation of psychotherapy studies will examine both the specificity and timing issues of this kind of treatment in schizophrenia. For the majority of patients suffering from schizophrenia, however, the reliance on psychotherapy as the sole psychological intervention would appear to be unsupported by research evidence.[9]

Where then should we turn for treatments that will address the needs of our patients and will interface with our current pharmacologic strategies? The answer has been developing in the field of psychosocial treatments. By psychosocial we refer to those approaches which integrate the psychological/psychiatric knowledge of schizophrenia with the social environment or milieu in which the person suffering from schizophrenia lives. In a disorder as all-pervasive as schizophrenia, the failure to consider the interaction of the disordered process with the environment is to invite treatment failure. Whether one gains total environmental control to reverse the most severe and pervasive schizophrenic symptoms as Paul and Lentz[10] have done, or whether it should be done in the community as have Stein and Test,[11] or whether one can utilize a significant component of the person's environment (the family, for instance) for the delivery of effective treatment as reported by Goldstein and associates,[12] is not as crucial as is the basic principle which underlies all of these—the consideration of the impact of the schizophrenic patient on his or her environment and in turn the impact of the environment on the patient. We should be aware, however, that the power of a milieu or environment has been demonstrated both in beneficial and detrimental ways. Initial evidence for the impact of institutionalism[13] and impoverished social environments[14] showed a dramatic impact of the nonstimulating milieu on the production of negative symptoms. Interest in environmental impact has recently been stimulated by those looking to explain the substantial relapse rates found in patients for whom medication compliance could be guaranteed. The answer could still relate to medication: individual differences in rapid metabolism, clearance, or other as yet unspecified phenomena which prevent medication from having its desired effect. Several groups of investigators, on the other hand, have now reported on the specific phenomenon of expressed emotion (EE) initially described by Brown and associates[15] as being an overinvolved, critical environmental interaction seen in families of patients who have been prospectively found to be at high risk for relapse. What these studies have generally found is that patients in families with high EE relapse at significantly higher rates than those from low EE families, and that medications, while reducing the rate of relapse, can by no means offset it. Others have also reported on the potential for a detrimental impact of a forceful, overstimulating milieu in generating unexpectedly high rates of relapse from a total push rehabilitation program.[16] Indeed, the initial treatment failure seen in many studies and the high attrition rates from intensive therapy in others can possibly be explained in this manner. We are now in the fortunate position, however, of being able to identify specific psychosocial strategies, particularly in the area of family management strategies, which have been shown to alter the potential negative outcome. Goldstein et al.,[12] Leff et al.,[17] and Falloon et al.,[18] in separate studies of different styles of family management, have all reached similar conclusions: relapse can be significantly reduced through the use of these strategies in conjunction with medication, and negative symptoms and social functioning improved and family burden (in those studies which examined this variable) was reduced.

It would appear that a data base relevant to specific psychosocial interventions is developing. The family management strategies are emphasizing practical approaches to the treatment of schizophrenia and enlisting the aid of the major source of emotional and psychological support for this group of patients—the family. Once relegated to the position of being blamed as a possible cause of the disorder, families can now be seen as active partners in a rational treatment approach to schizophrenia. This progress alone will contribute to the relief of much suffering on the part of family members who have long endured the dual burden of having an ill person in their family as well as being accused of causing the illness.

Further, the practical and teachable nature of the family management strategies may signal the end of attempts to replicate charisma or technologies that are so specialized that only a handful of highly trained professionals can implement them. We have no doubt that there is a difference in the outcome based on charisma, skill, level of training, and technique, but if we cannot identify strategies that have general applicability and can be taught effectively in training programs, our contribution to the overall state of the schizophrenic condition will be minimal.

Clearly, we have not reached a comfortable status on our knowledge of schizophrenia and its effective treatment: too much suffering still exists. The next steps in this process will involve studying the enhancement of innovative pharmacologic treatment with the psychosocial strategies. We can now establish the type of data base Carpenter and Heinrichs have called for in their seminal article. We are indeed past the time when our confidence in and enthusiasm for the power of our treatments can carry the day. We are also cognizant that humanitarian goals and the logic of a treatment approach are becoming less compelling factors in our increasingly fiscally accountable society. Assessing the impact of the treatment of schizophrenia is a complex, frustrating task. The disorder itself is also complex and frustrating. Overcoming the challenge of schizophrenia will not be easy; overlooking it is not acceptable.

REFERENCES

1. Strauss JC, Carpenter WT, Bartko JJ: Part III. Speculations on the processes that underlie schizophrenic signs and symptoms. *Schizophr Bull* 1974;2:61–69
2. Davis JM, Schaffer CB, Killian GA, et al: Important issues in the drug treatment of schizophrenia. *Schizophr Bull* 1980;6:70–87
3. Kane JM, Smith JM: Tardive dyskinesia: Prevalence and risk factors. *Arch Gen Psychiatry* 1982;39:473–481
4. Mosher LR: Research design to evaluate psychosocial treatments of schizophrenia, Rubenstein D, Alanen YO (eds): *Psychotherapy of Schizophrenia.* Amsterdam, Excerpta Medica Foundation, 1972, pp 251–260
5. Kane JM, Rifkin A, Woerner M, et al: Low-dose neuroleptics in outpatient schizophrenics. *Psychopharmacol Bull* 1982;18:20–21
6. Carpenter WT, Stephens JH, Rey AC, et al: Early intervention vs. continuous pharmacotherapy of schizophrenia. *Psychopharmacol Bull* 1982;18:21–23
7. Herz MI, Szymanski HV, Simon J: An intermittent medication for stable schizophrenic outpatients; an alternative to maintenance medication. *Am J Psychiatry* 1982;139:918–922
8. Carpenter WT, Heinrichs DW: The role of psychodynamic psychiatry in the treatment of schizophrenic patients, in Strauss JS, Bowers M, Downey TW, Fleck S, Jackson S, Levine I (eds): *The Psychotherapy of Schizophrenia.* New York, Plenum Publishing Co, 1980, pp 239–255
9. Keith SJ, Matthews SM: Schizophrenia: A review of psychosocial treatment strategies. Paper presented at the Annual Meeting of the American Psychopathological Association, New York, New York, 1983
10. Paul GL, Lentz RJ: *Psychosocial Treatment of Chronic Mental Patients: Milieu vs. Social Learning Programs.* Cambridge, Harvard University Press, 1977
11. Stein LI, Test MA: Training in community living: One year evaluation. *Am J Psychiatry* 1976; 133:917–918
12. Goldstein MJ, Rodnick EH, Evans JR, et al: Drug and family therapy in the aftercare of acute schizophrenics. *Arch Gen Psychiatry* 1978;35:1169–1177
13. Goffman E: *Asylums: Essays on the Social Situation of Mental Patients and Other Inmates.* New York, Doubleday-Anchor, 1961
14. Wing JK (ed): *Schizophrenia: Towards a New Synthesis,* London, Academic Press, 1978
15. Brown CW, Monck EM, Carstairs GM, et al: Influence of family life on the course of schizophrenic illness. *British Journal of Preventive and Social Medicine* 1962;16:55–68
16. Wing JK: Social factors in schizophrenia. Paper presented at the Annual Meeting of the National Alliance for the Mentally Ill, Rosslyn, Virginia, 1982
17. Leff J, Kuipers L, Berkowitz R, et al: A controlled trial of social intervention in the families of schizophrenia patients. *Br J Psychiatry* 1982;141:121–134
18. Falloon IRH, Boyd JL, McGill CW, et al: Family management in the prevention of exacerbations of schizophrenia: A controlled study. *New Eng J Med* 1982;306:1437–1440

Howard H. Goldman

2

Epidemiology

Five years ago, the problem of the chronic mental patient was an emerging issue in national mental health policy. The problem had been apparent for nearly 150 years, and the social conscience of America had again turned its attention to the plight of the chronically mentally ill in the mid-1970s. The American Psychiatric Association's publication, *The Chronic Mental Patient*,[1] was one of several important documents that addressed concern for the mentally disabled.[2-4] It provided a comprehensive overview of data, service concepts, models, plans, and programs relating to the chronically mentally ill, including an excellent chapter by Minkoff on the scope of the problem.[5] Since publication of *The Chronic Mental Patient* additional work related to the epidemiology of chronic mental disorder has been completed. Most notably, the National Plan for the Chronically Mentally Ill (NP/CMI),[6] based on recommendations and data presented by the President's Commission on Mental Health (PCMH),[4] developed a definition of the target population and provided an unduplicated count of the chronically mentally ill.[7]

This chapter reviews those studies in the epidemiology of chronic mental disorder published after 1978 that are national in scope or inform the process of delimiting, defining, locating, counting, and characterizing the chronically mentally ill. This work follows the conceptual and organizational framework developed for the NP/CMI, borrowing text and supplementing it with new findings and new approaches to defining and counting the chronically mentally ill. Several other chapters in the monograph discuss related material on special populations and on the course of chronic disability that will not be detailed in this chapter.

THE CHRONIC MENTAL PATIENT
ISBN 0-8089-1649-1

Copyright © 1984 by Grune & Stratton.
All rights of reproduction in any form reserved.

WHO ARE THE CHRONICALLY MENTALLY ILL?

Sylvia Frumkin is chronically mentally ill[8]; so are Jim Logue and the Duck Lady from Don Drake's, "The Forsaken."[9] Al, Luther, Agnes, Morning Star, and Angelita are five patients who introduce the NP/CMI.[6] The Box Lady and her tragic death are the subjects of a report in the New York Times. They are all chronically mentally ill, as are approximately two million others we designate by this broad term. The term *chronically mentally ill* presents several problems and it has been difficult to define operationally. It stigmatizes individuals with connotations of hopelessness and inevitable deterioration, and it obscures the heterogeneity of the population, grouping together a diversity of individuals under a single pessimistic rubric which some fear may become a self-fulfilling prophecy.[1,6,10,11] In spite of these limitations, we continue to use the term because of its widespread acceptance.

Prior to the era of deinstitutionalization, the chronically mentally ill were easier to identify and count; they were the long-term residents of psychiatric hospitals. These institutions are today no longer home to the majority of persons disabled by chronic mental illness. One consequence of the shifts in the pattern and locus of mental health care arising from deinstitutionalization is a lack of definitive information on the scope of the problem of chronic mental illness. Sources of data, like the affected individuals and their services, have been dispersed and decentralized. The difficulty is compounded by the absence of consensus on a definition that would delimit the target population.

Broadly speaking, a chronic condition is characterized by an illness of long duration, which may include periods of apparent wellness interrupted by flareups of acute symptoms, and secondary disabilities. This simple characterization is applicable to chronic mental illness, but the task of identifying persons who are chronically mentally ill is not at all straightforward. Although it is true that most such persons "are, have been, or might have been, but for the deinstitutionalization movement, on the rolls of long-term mental institutions, especially state hospitals,"[12] any attempt to specify the attributes of state hospital patients must take into account the dynamic nature of clinical judgements about these patients.

Perceptions about the appropriateness of the placement of patients in state hospitals and other psychiatric facilities have been changing rapidly in recent years,[13] and there is every reason to think that they will continue to change in the future. As knowledge about the heterogeneity of the needs of patients increases, the formulation of appropriateness should evolve. As the number and variety of community-based services expands, however, clinical judgments about appropriateness change. This variability in the assessment of needs is to be expected and encouraged in a dynamic service system.

DELIMITING THE TARGET POPULATION

Assessing the prevalence of chronic mental illness is complicated by the dynamic, episodic course of severe mental disorders. Von Korff and Parker,[14] who propose several models for determining the prevalence of chronic episodic disease, conclude that "The prevalence of episodic disease is not solely a function of incidence and duration . . . [It] is a function of incidence, average episode duration, and average number of episodes" (p. 84). Some individuals recover; some have histories marked by exacerbations and remissions; others have a persistent, deteriorating course.

Chronic mental illness encompasses more than episodic disorder; it implies impairment and disability. Minkoff's[5] attempt to define and count the chronically mentally ill distinguished persons who are severely mentally ill (defined by diagnosis), those who are mentally disabled (defined by level of disability), and those who are chronic mental patients (defined by duration of hospitalization).

These three dimensions—diagnosis, disability, and duration—are sufficiently operationalizable to serve as criteria for delimiting the target population (Figure 2-1). We can begin with the following general description: the chronically mentally ill population encompasses persons who suffer severe and persistent mental or emotional disorders that interfere with their functional capacities in relation to such primary aspects of daily life as self-care, interpersonal relationships, and work or schooling, and that often necessitate prolonged hospital care.

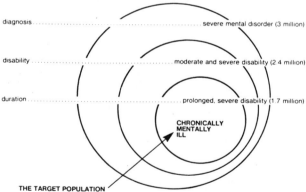

Fig. 2-1. The dimensions of chronic mental illness (diagnosis, disability, and duration), with population estimates. From *National Plan for the Chronically Mentally Ill,* final draft report to the Secretary of Health and Human Services. Washington, DC, 1980. With permission.

Diagnosis

There is general agreement that the psychotic and other major disorders predominate among this population, that is, organic mental disorders, schizophrenic disorders, major affective disorders, paranoid disorders, and other psychotic disorders.[15] Other disorders may also lead to chronic mental disability—some of the personality disorders, for example, especially those designated as "borderline disorders." Furthermore, alcohol- and drug-abuse disorders and mental retardation may complicate the course of severe mental disorders (occasionally becoming designated as the primary diagnosis) or may become chronically disabling conditions themselves. Among children, schizophrenia, childhood autism, and some behavior disorders may lead to chronic disability; the same may be said of nonpsychotic organic mental disorders, or "senility without psychosis"[16] among the elderly.

Disability

Most definitions of disability center on the concept of functional incapacity, for example, "partial or total impairment of instrumental (usually vocational or homemaking) role performance."[5] One statutory definition refers to a condition that "results in substantial functional limitations in three or more of the following areas of major life activity: (i) self-care, (ii) receptive and expressive language, (iii) learning, (iv) mobility, (v) self-direction, (vi) capacity for independent living, and (vii) economic self-sufficiency."[17] Objective measures of these "functional limitations," however, are not in widespread use.

In contrast, chronicity of disability may be operationally defined. Insofar as receipt of Supplemental Security Income payments (SSI) implies that the beneficiary has been unable to engage in any substantial gainful activity because of a disorder which has lasted or can be expected to last for a continuous period of not less than 12 months, there is general agreement that approval of SSI eligibility is a measure of chronic disability for noninstitutionalized persons. Similar vocational criteria are common to other definitions of disability, such as those used in the Survey of Disabled Adults (Social Security Administration) and the Survey of Income and Education (Bureau of the Census). Chronicity may also be inferred from the need for extended hospitalization or other forms of supervised residence or sheltered work.

Duration

To infer disability from the need for extended hospitalization or supervised residential care requires specifying some duration of residence. Most would agree that one year of continuous institutionalization in a state mental hospital or of residence in a nursing home would qualify as a measure of chronic mental disability. At least half of the population of chronically mentally ill, however, are not continuously institutionalized. (See Figure 2-2.) Although these individuals reside in the community, many of them were hospitalized in the past or are hospitalized during the course of the year. Some formula is necessary for determining what duration of hospitalization to use as a criterion for chronicity for the chronically mentally ill living in the community.

Treated prevalence estimates may be obtained by reference to the national reporting program of the NIMH Division of Biometry and Epidemiology, which uses a three-month period of follow-up for providing data on extended hospitalization. Eighty percent of all patients admitted to state and county mental hospitals and virtually all patients admitted to private psychiatric hospitals and general hospital psychiatric units are discharged within 90 days.[18,19] Likelihood of release diminishes after this point; hence, we may consider that these unreleased patients represent a chronic intermediate-stay (3–12 months) population of the chronically mentally ill. (See Figure 2-2.)

It should be noted that some persons with characteristics fitting the diagnosis and disability criteria have received short-term (less than 90 days) inpatient care, solely outpatient care from a medical or mental health professional, or no care at all except what their families or other natural support groups have provided. Although we are unable to locate definitely or enumerate such individuals, we include them in the target population. Prolonged functional disability caused by or aggravated by severe mental disorders, and not former hospitalization, is the chief distinguishing characteristic of chronic mental illness.

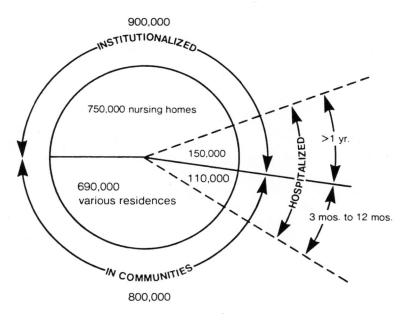

Fig. 2-2. The location of the chronically mentally ill in the United States, 1977.

DEFINING THE CHRONICALLY MENTALLY ILL

There have been several recent attempts to define operationally the chronically mentally ill. The definitions reviewed here were all developed to provide estimates of the size of the population. They are not conceptual definitions; they are practical definitions designed to identify mentally disabled individuals who are eligible for services and to estimate the scope of the problem of chronic mental illness.

The Community Support Program (CSP) of the National Institute of Mental Health developed the following parameters for eligibility for its target population of noninstitutionalized chronically mentally ill. "Severe mental disability [must satisfy at least one of the following]: A single episode of hospitalization in the last five years of at least six months duration; or two or more hospitalizations within a 12-month period".[20] This definition includes individuals with non-chronic conditions who may have required two brief hospitalizations in one year and excludes multiple-admission chronic patients who have been kept out of the hospital for 12 months. Furthermore, it is difficult to obtain national data estimates by using the CSP formula.

The CSP continues to change its definition of program eligibility in order to ameliorate problems associated with earlier definitions. CSP has recently attempted to focus on assessing functional disabilities and to minimize reliance on a history of prior institutionalization. This opens eligibility to the mentally disabled who may not have been hospitalized due to current deinstitutionalization efforts (see Chapter 3 on the Young Chronic Patient). Unfortunately, preliminary field tests of the reliability of these new eligibility criteria were disappointing.[21] In addition, CSP sponsored a needs-assessment project conducted by John Ashbaugh and the Human Services Research Institute. This project developed a series of models for estimating the needs and size of the chronically mentally ill in the community.[22] National data from this project will be discussed later.

Szymanski and his colleagues[23] described three methods for estimating the local prevalence of the chronically mentally ill who might need community support programs. The first method identifies patients who require outpatient care and who were hospitalized in the past. The second identifies patients who require rehospitalization during a specified period of time following a prior hospitalization. The third identifies outpatients who have a diagnosis of schizophrenia. These approaches to estimating the size of the population are all derived from treated prevalence data which tend to underestimate true prevalence. Such data, however, are readily available at low cost for regional planning. Other methods for local needs assessment have been described by Warheit and coworkers,[24] and more recently by Ashbaugh.[25]

The National Plan for the Chronically Mentally Ill[6] adopted the following definition of its target population based on the dimensions of diagnosis, disability, and duration:

The chronically mentally ill population encompasses persons who suffer certain mental or emotional disorders (organic brain syndrome, schizophrenia, recurrent depressive and manic depressive disorders, paranoid and other psychoses, plus other disorders that may become chronic) that erode or prevent the development of their functional capacities in relation to (three or more of) such primary aspects of daily life as personal hygiene and self-care, self-direction, interpersonal relationships, social transactions, learning, and recreation, and that erode or prevent the development of their economic self-sufficiency. Most such individuals have required institutional care of extended duration, including intermediate-term hospitalization (90 days to one year in a single year), long-term hospitalization (one year or longer in the preceding five years), nursing home placement on account of a diagnosed mental condition or a diagnosis of senility without psychosis. Some such individuals have required short-term hospitalization (less than 90 days), others have received treatment from a medical or mental health professional solely on an outpatient basis, or—despite their needs—have received no treatment in the professional-care service system. Thus included in the target population are persons who are or were formerly "residents" of institutions (public and private psychiatric hospitals and nursing homes), and persons who are at high risk of institutionalization because of persistent mental disability (p 2-11).

LOCATING THE POPULATION

Bearing in mind the caveat concerning the dynamic nature of any definition of this population, we propose to outline a series of separate segments of the population of the chronically mentally ill. The numbers of chronically mentally ill persons in each of these segments may be determined by a number of methods, and the size of the population in each segment or location is subject to change because of the movement of people from one location to another (see Figure 2-2).

Institutional residents

For purposes of this report, the institutionalized chronically mentally ill are those individuals with any psychiatric diagnosis in mental hospitals for more than one year and those individuals in nursing homes (as defined by the National Center for Health Statistics) with a diagnosed mental condition or a diagnosis of senility without psychosis. The latter are included because simple senility, either alone or in a combination with other chronic medical conditions, was a reason for admission to a state mental hospital prior to policies encouraging deinstitutionalization and the transfer or diversion of the elderly into nursing homes.

Community residents

Within communities, the chronically mentally ill are those individuals in a variety of residential settings (e.g., with families, in boarding homes, in single occupancy hotel rooms) who are considered to be disabled by any one of several criteria (e.g., SSI eligibility, episodic or prolonged hospitalization, inability to work). This community-dwelling segment may be subdivided into several groups on the basis of their location, their utilization of mental health facilities, and the level and type of their disability.

COUNTING THE CHRONIC POPULATION

Having defined the target population in terms of disability and location, we now turn to determining their number. As Table 2-1[6] indicates, estimates of the number of the chronically mentally ill range from 1.7 million to 2.4 million, including 900,000 who are institutionalized. Table 2-2[6] presents estimates of the

Table 2-1.
Estimates of the Number of the Chronically Mentally Ill
in the United States, 1975–1977.

Institutionalized Population		Community Population	
Location		Level of disability	
Mental health facilities*	150,000	Severe[||]	800,000
Nursing homes[†]		Moderate[#] and severe	1,500,000
Residents with mental disorder[‡]	350,000	Subtotal (as a range)	800,000–1,500,000
Residents with senility without psychosis[§]	400,000		
Subtotal	900,000		
		Total**	1,700,000–2,400,000

* Residents for one year or more in the following facility types: state and county hospitals, Veterans Administration in-patient facilities, private psychiatric hospitals, residential treatment centers, community mental health centers. (Estimates provided by Division of Biometry & Epidemiology, NIMH, 1975.)

[†] Universe of 1,300,000 residents of skilled nursing and intermediate care facilities sampled by the National Center for Health Statistics, National Nursing Home Survey, 1977.

[‡] Residents with a diagnosis (primary or nonprimary) from Section V of the International Classification of Diseases–9. (National Nursing Home Survey, 1977.)

[§] Residents with a diagnosed condition (primary or nonprimary) coded 797 in the International Classification of Diseases–9. (National Nursing Home Survey, 1977.)

[||] Includes individuals with a mental disorder unable to work at all for one year and those who could work only occasionally or irregularly. (Estimates provided by the Urban Institute, Comprehensive Needs Survey, 1973, and Social Security Administration, Survey of Disabled Adults, 1966.)

[#] Includes so-called "partially disabled" individuals whose work (including housework) was limited by a mental disorder. (Urban Institute, Comprehensive Needs Survey, 1973.)

** For purposes of the National Plan, the lower figure (1,700,000), representing the severely disabled chronically mentally ill, will be used as the size of the target population.

types of disabilities suffered by persons with chronic illness and their utilization of mental health facilities. These estimates of the total number of chronically mentally ill are derived from a number of sources, including true prevalence estimates of chronic mental disorders, community estimates of chronic mental disability, and treated prevalence data on chronic mental patients.

Chronic mental disorders—True prevalence estimates

The field of psychiatric epidemiology has expanded dramatically since the publication of the President's Commission on Mental Health,[4] *The Chronic Mental Patient*[1] and the other seminal works on the chronically mentally ill written in the late 1970s. Robins[26] and Weissman and Klerman[27] herald the advances of the field and their promise for reliable and valid community estimates of the incidence and prevalence of specific mental disorders. The National Institute of Mental Health's Epidemiology Catchment Program is currently sponsoring a five-site field study of the epidemiology of mental disorder in the United States. It will be several years before data from this study will be available to guide estimates of the prevalence of severe and chronic mental disorder.

In the absence of such data, the National Plan for the Chronically Mentally Ill relied on data estimates from the PCMH[4] based largely on a review paper by the Dohrenwends.[28] The NP/CMI also used data reported in Minkoff's secondary

Table 2-2.
Estimates of the Number of the Chronically Mentally Ill
by Type of Disability and Utilization of Mental Health Facilities
(Duplicated Counts) in the United States, 1975–1977.

Type of Disability		Utilization of Mental Health Facilities[§]	
Receiving SSI/SSDI[*]	550,000	Admissions (length of stay	
Complete work disability[†]	350,000	≥ 90 days)	150,000
Activity limitation[‡]	700,000	Readmissions[‖]	650,000

[*] Estimates from JR Anderson: Social Security and SSI benefits for the mentally disabled. Hosp Community Psychiatry 1982;33:295–298.

[†] Prevalence of disability in the 18-64-year-old population. (Source: Digest of Data on Persons with Disabilities, Bureau of the Census, Survey of Income and Education, 1976, DHEW 1979.)

[‡] Prevalence of disability in population three years old or older. (Digest of Data on Persons with Disabilities, Survey of Income and Education, 1976.)

[§] Facilities include state and county mental health hospitals, private psychiatric hospitals, psychiatric units in general hospitals, and residential treatment centers. (Estimates provided by the Division of Biometry and Epidemiology, NIMH, 1975.)

[‖] Readmission counts will overestimate chronic patients. Some patients with less severe disorders are admitted many times for brief periods. (Division of Biometry and Epidemiology, NIMH, 1975.)

analysis.[5] This section will review the prevalence estimates developed for the NP/CMI and mention some newer sources that would modify these estimates.

According to the Report of the President's Commission on Mental Health,[4] there are approximately 2,000,000 people in the United States who could be given a diagnosis of schizophrenia. Approximately 600,000 of them are in active treatment during a given year, accounting for more than 500,000 admissions in the specialty mental health sector. Any individual given a diagnosis of schizophrenia is at risk of becoming chronically mentally ill. Because of the existence of other acute syndromes that mimic the overt symptoms of schizophrenia but do not invariably become progressive or chronic (e.g., schizophreniform psychosis, brief reactive psychosis), however, not all are to be counted among the chronically mentally ill. Estimates of the number of chronically mentally ill individuals with a diagnosis of schizophrenia would range from 500,000–900,000. There is considerable controversy in the literature concerning the prevalence of schizophrenia. Researchers such as Taylor and Abrams[29] and Pope and Lipinski[30] have been questioning reported rates of schizophrenia, asserting that they are overestimates which confuse schizophrenia with psychotic manifestations of affective disorders. Carpenter, Bartko, Strauss, and their collaborators[31,32] have emphasized the difficulty in predicting chronicity from symptomatology in the schizophrenic disorders unless diagnostic criteria are based on duration of symptomatology. They assert that chronic deterioration is overestimated. Further, they find that only prior disability and chronicity predict future disability and chronicity.

Serious depression has a prevalence rate ranging from 0.3 percent to 1.2 percent.[4] Assuming that the lower end of the range represents the population at highest risk of chronicity, there are perhaps 600,000–800,000 chronically and severely depressed individuals in the United States. Since publication of the PCMH,[4] several reviews of the epidemiology of affective disorders have been published.[33-35]

None of these papers, however, deals directly with the issue of severity or chronicity. In a forthcoming publication, Prien[36] reviews the data on the prevalence of chronic affective disorder, concluding that about 20 percent of individuals with affective disorders have a chronic course. However, not all such patients suffer persistent disabilities.

Psychoses in the elderly (primarily organic mental disorders, predominantly chronic) are estimated to account for between 600,000–1,250,000 individuals.[4] These estimates are sustained by recent reviews of the epidemiology of senile dementia.[37,38]

All authors stress the expected increases in this population as the large cohort born during the post-war baby boom survive into the senium. This aspect of chronic mental illness may be the single most critical problem for the future.[39]

Other more prevalent disorders, such as personality disorders (7.0 percent prevalence), alcoholism and alcohol abuse (5–10 percent), and drug abuse and misuse (1–10 percent, depending on the type of drug), may become chronic or may be complicated by chronic mental disorder. Only a small minority of these individuals, however, are part of the target population.[6]

Chronic mental disability—community estimates

Currently there are four major sources of national data on chronic mental disability in the community: the Bureau of the Census Survey of Income and Education in 1976,[40] the National Center for Social Statistics[41] Survey of Disabled Adults in 1966, a 1973 Comprehensive Needs Assessment Study conducted by the Urban Institute for the Department of Health and Human Services,[42] and a 1978 Social Security Administration Household Survey of Disabled Adults. These studies indicate that there are between 350,000 and 800,000 individuals severely disabled by emotional disorder in the community and perhaps an additional 700,000 people with moderate disability.

According to data published by the Bureau of the Census, based on 1976 estimates of disability in the community, approximately 700,000 persons three years of age or older (2.5 percent of a total of 28,000,000) have an "activity limitation" due to severe mental disturbance.[41] A total of 350,000 individuals between the ages of 18 and 64 have some work disability secondary to severe emotional disturbance.[16]

Extrapolations from the Urban Institute study indicates that approximately 800,000 individuals in the community have a severe mental disability, and 700,000 more are moderately or partially disabled.[42] These data are corroborated by the most recent Social Security Administration survey (1978), which estimated that approximately 1.07 million adults living in households were disabled by emotional disorder (unpublished data provided by John Ashbaugh, Human Services Research Institute, Boston, Massachusetts). Further estimates from the Social Security Administration suggest that 550,000 of the severely disabled are receiving Supplemental Security Income or Social Security Disability Income.[43]

Chronic Mental Patients—Treated Prevalence Data

Estimates of the number of chronic mental patients may also be derived from two sources of treated prevalence data. The first source is national data from the reporting program of the NIMH Division of Biometry and Epidemiology, the Veterans Administration, and the Long-Term Care Statistics Branch of the National Center for Health Statistics. The second is the Monroe County (NY) case register. Both data sources suggest that the number of chronic mental patients is approximately 1.7 million.

The Monroe County figure is derived (by Carl Taube of the National Institute of Mental Health Division of Biometry and Epidemiology) by extrapolation from the 10-year follow-up experience of a cohort of state mental hospital patients from Rochester State Hospital in 1962. Although generalization from these data is problematic, this estimate provides a useful verification of the estimates derived from the national data.

The national data provide the following estimates: the institutional population totals 900,000, and includes two major subdivisions of chronic mental patients based on place of residence: specialty mental health sector facilities and nursing homes. Approximately 150,000 chronic mental patients are in the specialty mental health sector. Based on a 1973 study of resident patients in an unrepresentative sample of state mental hospitals in 13 states (and confirmed by a 1979 survey of a representative sample), an estimated 60 percent of the patients had been in continuous residence for 1 year or more. Applying this estimate to the 1977 resident census of 160,000 patients in state and county mental hospitals, we can conclude that there are approximately 100,000 chronic mental patients institutionalized in these facilities. An additional 50,000 (crude estimate) are long-term (greater than 1 year) residents of other specialty facilities. Approximately 20,000 are in VA hospitals; approximately 10,000 are in residential treatment centers; and approximately 20,000 are in other facilities, including private psychiatric hospitals and CMHC inpatient units.[5]

There are an estimated 750,000 chronic mental patients in nursing homes, out of a total nursing home resident population of 1.3 million. This figure, which may be a slight overestimate, encompasses three groups of individuals: those with a primary mental disorder (approximately 250,000), those with a diagnosed mental condition that is not the primary cause of institutionalization (approximately 100,000), and those with senility without psychosis (approximately 400,000). The two former categories are clearly part of the target population; the latter group probably represents a population of elderly individuals who would have been admitted to the state mental hospitals in the pre-deinstitutionalization era. For this reason, all three subpopulations of nursing homes are considered chronic mental patients.

Data on prior care in a state mental hospital indicate that in 1977 perhaps only 100,000 nursing home residents were transferred directly from a state mental hospital. Although this number strikes many as implausibly low, several explanations are possible—under-reporting, successful diversion programs barring the elderly from public long-term care hospitals in recent years, and transfers from other nursing homes rather than directly from state and county mental hospitals. Data suggest that nursing homes may indeed be the new "back wards in the community."[44]

The community population of chronic mental patients with severe disability numbers approximately 800,000. An additional 700,000 individuals have a partial disability due to a mental condition. The patterns of service utilization of this population are more difficult to estimate because the population is more dynamic, possibly using several facilities during the course of a year. They are also more mobile, living in a wide variety of residential treatment settings—with their families, for example, or in other congregate care, in single-room-occupancy residences, or in board and care homes. The use of treated prevalence data alone will present an undercount of the community population, some of whom receive no treatment or receive care exclusively in other sectors, such as the general health care, social welfare, or criminal justice systems.

The severely disabled community population may be divided into two subgroups on the basis of utilization of specialty mental health services. The first is the intermediate-length-of-stay hospitalized population, composed of approximately 110,000 individuals who remained in the hospital for more than three months following admission to state and county mental hospitals (about 80,000), private psychiatric hospitals (about 10,000), residential treatment centers (about 15,000), and general hospital psychiatric units (about 5,000).

The second severely disabled community group is the ambulatory population of approximately 700,000 chronic mental patients. The estimates of the service utilization of this ambulatory population are less reliable than the other estimates. Of these chronic patients, at least 200,000 are readmissions to state and county mental hospitals for brief hospitalization (less than 90 days), another estimated 100,000 are chronic patients in community mental health centers, and the balance are chronic patients being cared for in other specialty facilities in the community. The 700,000 figure represents a very conservative estimate, since it is based on treated prevalence data and therefore does not account for the chronic ambulatory population in other sectors, such as primary care and social welfare, or the number of untreated individuals.

Criticism of the role of community mental health centers in the care of chronic patients[2,45,46] has led to several studies of the prevalence of patients with severe and chronic disorder in such facilities.[47,21] Abt Associates, under contract to the National Institute of Mental Health, is examining this issue in detail. Unpublished preliminary data indicate that community mental health centers continue to see a significant number of chronic patients even if this is not their primary target population. As Langsley[48] reminds us, we need more than biometric data to answer the critical question: "Do community mental health centers treat patients?"

Data on the quality and appropriateness of services are limited. Data on service utilization, however, are plentiful. We do know that in 1975 there were approximately 650,000 patient readmissions to state and county mental hospitals, private psychiatric hospitals, and psychiatric units in general hospitals. All of these readmitted patients are not chronic mental patients; they may, however, be counted among the 800,000–1,500,000 individuals moderately and severely disabled by mental disorder who spend most of the year in the community.

These chronic mental patients live in a variety of community residences. A service delivery assessment in HHS Region 3 estimated that 300,000–400,000 of these chronic mental patients reside in board and care facilities. These domiciliary care residences and single-room-occupancy hotels often are criticized as substandard, isolating, and a form of "transinstitutionalization" and continued neglect.[1,44]

Not all chronic patients are transinstitutionalized, however. Some return to their families. Although approximately 65 percent of discharged mental patients return home,[49,50] not all of these are chronic. Several studies report that approximately one in four chronic patients are discharged to their families' care.[5] Ashbaugh's unpublished analysis of data from the Social Security Administration Survey of Disabled Adults (1978) indicates that 59 percent of the 1.07 million mentally disabled Americans living in households were married and residing with a spouse.

THE CHALLENGE FOR THE FUTURE

The technical criteria described in this paper for defining the chronically mentally ill establish the objective boundaries of the target population; these criteria are vital to the activities of planners and policy-makers. But they do no more than hint at the clinical, socioeconomic, ethnic, and cultural heterogeneity of this population. Data from several national surveys are currently being analyzed and a few reports on the characteristics of chronic patients in national programs have been published.[51-53] Data, however, cannot convey any sense of the individual people referred to, their frailties and strengths, their suffering and that of their families, their hope and striving, however falteringly, for normalcy.

The chronically mentally ill population includes persons whose clinical conditions and functional disabilities vary widely at any point in time and, moreover, change over time. Kramer's projections for the year 2005 indicate that chronic mental disability will increase dramatically.[39] Variability makes an accurate determination of the size and nature of the population extremely difficult. At best we can provide an estimate to guide national policy-makers in a more scientific assessment of needs. Suffice it to note here that, although our definition encompasses persons with prolonged moderate-to-severe disability, a significant proportion possess the capacity to live in relative independence if adequate community-based services, social supports, and life opportunities are provided.

ACKNOWLEDGMENT

The author wishes to acknowledge the help of Robert C. Larsen, M.D., Robert Woods Johnson Clinical Scholar, University of California, San Francisco Department of Psychiatry for his help in reviewing the literature.

REFERENCES

1. Talbott JA: *The Chronic Mental Patient*. Washington, DC: American Psychiatric Association, 1978
2. *Returning the mentally disabled to the community: Government needs to do more.* US Government Accounting Office. US Government Printing Office, 1977
3. Group for the Advancement of Psychiatry. *The Chronic Mental Patient in the Community.* New York, GAP, 1978
4. *Report to the President from the President's Commission on Mental Health,* Vol 1. Washington, DC, 1978
5. Minkoff K: A Map of Chronic Mental Patients, in Talbott JA: *The Chronic Mental Patient,* Washington, DC: American Psychiatric Association, 1978, pp 11–37
6. *National Plan for the Chronically Mentally Ill,* final draft report to the Secretary of Health and Human Services. Washington, DC, 1980
7. Goldman HH, Gattozzi, AA, Taube CA: Defining and counting the chronically mentally ill. *Hosp Community Psychiatry* 1981;32(1): 21–27
8. Sheehan S: The patient, I: Creedmoor Psychiatric Center. *The New Yorker* May 25, 1981, p 49
9. Drake D: The Forsaken. Reprinted from *The Philadelphia Inquirer* series, July 18–24, 1982
10. Olson WA: Chronic mental illness, what it is and what it means. *Wis Med J* 1981;80:28–29
11. Denver Research Institute: *Factors Influencing the Deinstitutionalization of the Mentally Ill: A Review and Analysis.* Denver, CO: University of Denver, 1981
12. Bachrach LL: *Deinstitutionalization: An Analytic Review and Sociological Perspective.* Rockville, MD, National Institute of Mental Health, 1976
13. Faden VB, Goldman HH: *Appropriateness of Placement of Patients in State and County Mental Hospitals,* Statistical Note 152. Rockville, MD, National Institute of Mental Health, 1979
14. Von Korff M, Parker RD: The dynamics of the prevalence of chronic episodic disease. *Journal of Chronic Disease,* 1980;33:79–85
15. American Psychiatric Association. *Diagnostic and Statistical Manual of Mental Disorders,* 3rd Edition. Washington, DC, 1980
16. US Department of Health, Education and Welfare. *International Classification of Disease,* 8th Edition. Washington, DC: US Government Printing Office, 1966
17. Public Law 95–602. Rehabilitation, Comprehensive Services, and Developmental Disabilities Amendments of 1978
18. Goldman HH, Adams N, Taube CA: Deinstitutionalization: The data demythologized. *Hosp Community Psychiatry,* 1983;34(2):129–134
19. Goldman HH, Taube CA, Regier DA, et al: Multiple functions of the state mental hospital. *Am J Psychiatry* 1983;140(3):296–300
20. Community Support Program: *Guidelines* (mimeographed). Rockville, MD, National Institute of Mental Health, 1977
21. Naierman N: *The Chronically Mentally Ill in Community Mental Health Centers* (mimeographed). Washington, DC: Abt Associates, Inc, January 29, 1982
22. Ashbaugh JW, Hoff, MK, Bradley V: *Community Support Program Needs Assessment Project: A Review of the Findings in the State CSP Reports and Literature.* Boston, MA, Human Services Research Institute, 1980
23. Szymanski HV, Schulberg HC, Salter V, et al: Estimating the local prevalence of persons needing community support programs. *Hosp Community Psychiatry* 1982;33(5):370–373
24. Warheit GJ, Buhl JM, Schwab JJ: *Need Assessment Approaches: Concepts and Methods,*

Department of Health, Education and Welfare Publication No. (ADM) 79-472. Rockville, MD, Public Health Service, National Institute of Mental Health, 1977

25. Ashbaugh JW: Assessing the need for community supports, in Tessler RC, Goldman HH (eds): *The Chronically Mentally Ill: Assessing Community Support Programs.* Cambridge, MA, Ballinger (Harper & Row), 1982, 141–158
26. Robins LN: Psychiatric epidemiology. *Arch Gen Psych* 1978;35:697–702
27. Weissman MM, Klerman GL: Epidemiology of mental disorders. *Arch Gen Psychiatry* 1978;35:705–712
28. Dohrenwend BP, Dohrenwend BS, Gould MS, et al: Scope of the problem. Working paper prepared for the President's Commission on Mental Health, 1978
29. Taylor MA, Abrams R: The prevalence of schizophrenia: A reassessment using modern diagnostic criteria. *Am J Psychiatry* 1978;135(8):945–948
30. Pope HG, Lipinski JF: Diagnosis in schizophrenia and manic-depressive illness. *Arch Gen Psychiatry* 1978;35:811–827
31. Carpenter WT, Bartko JJ, Strauss JS, et al: Signs and symptoms as predictors of outcome: A report from the international pilot study of schizophrenia. *Am J Psychiatry* 1978;135(8): 940–944
32. Strauss J: Assessment in outpatient settings: The prediction of outcome, in Mirabi M (ed): *The Chronically Mentally Ill: Research and Services.* New York, SP Medical and Scientific Books, in press
33. Clayton PJ: The epidemiology of bipolar affective disorder. *Compr Psychiatry* 1981; 22(1): 31–43
34. Boyd JH, Weissman MM: Epidemiology of affective disorders. *Arch Gen Psychiatry* 1981; 38:1039–1046
35. Hirschfeld RMA, Cross CK: Epidemiology of affective disorders. *Arch Gen Psychiatry* 1982; 39:35–46
36. Prien R: Affective disorders, In Mirabi M (ed): *The Chronically Mentally Ill: Research and Services.* New York, SP Medical and Scientific Books, in press
37. Mortimer JA, Schuman L: *The Epidemiology of Dementia.* New York City: Oxford University Press, 1981
38. Brody JA: An epidemiologist views senile dementia—Facts and fragments. *Am J Epidemiol* 1982;115(2):155–162
39. Kramer M: The increasing prevalence of mental disorder. Paper presented at Langley Porter Psychiatric Institute, San Francisco, CA, August, 1981
40. Bureau of the Census Survey of Income and Education: *Digest of Data on Persons with Disabilities.* Washington, DC: Department of Health, Education, and Welfare, 1979
41. National Center for Social Statistics: *Findings of the 1970 APTD Study.* Washington, D.C.: Social and Rehabilitation Service, 1972
42. Urban Institute: *Report of the Comprehensive Service Needs Study.* Washington, D.C.: Department of Health Education and Welfare, 1975
43. Anderson, JR: Social Security and SSI benefits for the mentally disabled. *Hosp Community Psychiatry* 1982;33:295–298
44. Schmidt W, Reinhardt AM, Kane RL, et al: The mentally ill in nursing homes: New back wards in the community. *Arch Gen Psychiatry* 1977;34:687–691
45. Gruenberg E, Archer J: Abandonment of responsibility for the seriously mentally ill. *Milbank Mem Fund Q* 1979;57:485–506
46. Winslow WW: Changing trends in community mental health centers: Keys to survival in the eighties. *Hosp Community Psychiatry* 1982;33(4):273–277
47. Goldman HH, Regier DA, Taube CA, et al: Community mental health centers and the treatment of severe mental disorder. *Am J Psychiatry* 1980;137(1):83–86

48. Langsley DG: The community mental health center: Does it treat patients? *Hosp Community Psychiatry* 1980;31(12):815–819

49. Goldman HH: Mental illness and family burden: A public health perspective. *Hosp Community Psychiatry* 1982;33:557–560

50. Goldman HH: The post-hospital mental patient and family therapy: Prospects and populations. *Journal of Marital and Family Therapy* 1980;6:447–452

51. Tessler RC, Bernstein AG, Rosen BM, et al: The chronically mentally ill in community support systems. *Hosp Community Psychiatry* 1982;33:208–211

52. Tessler RC, Goldman HH: *The Chronically Mentally Ill: Assessing Community Support Programs.* Cambridge, MA, Ballinger (Harper & Row), 1982

53. Tessler RC, Manderscheid RW: Factors affecting adjustment to community living. *Hosp Community Psychiatry* 1982;33:203–207

Bert Pepper
Hilary Ryglewicz

3

The Young Adult Chronic Patient:
A New Focus

When the light of professional attention was first turned on the plight of the chronically mentally ill in the community, the focus of that attention was the deinstitutionalized patient who had been discharged after decades of state institutional care. Pioneering efforts were begun five years ago by John Talbott and others—through the APA Board of Trustees and the APA Task Force on the Chronic Mental Patient—to explore and improve the condition of this chronically mentally ill population, and to examine and expose the inadequacies of their care in communities which were ill-prepared and ill-equipped to receive them. This population was clearly deserving of top priority in the wake of the most massive change in professional and social policy toward the mentally ill that has occurred in this century.

During the past five years, however, even as our central vision was directed at the neglect of the shopping bag men and women in our city streets (and their unmet needs for decent housing, support, and rehabilitation), our peripheral vision was beginning to be captured by the furtive, lurking young man or woman in the doorway, who now has come to occupy the foreground of our attention: the young adult chronic psychiatric patient in the community. This new population of mentally ill young adults is a transitional generation which is not *de*institutionalized but *un*institutionalized. It is composed of young men and women between the ages of 18 and 35, who have grown to chronological adulthood and into adult mental and emotional disorders while living in the community. This new generation of young adults who are severely and persistently impaired in

THE CHRONIC MENTAL PATIENT
ISBN 0-8089-1649-1

Copyright © 1984 by Grune & Stratton.
All rights of reproduction in any form reserved.

their psychological and social functioning, yet live most of their lives outside the walls of institutions, has presented distinctive problems in mental health treatment and has become a most pressing concern for mental health agencies today.

WHENCE THE YOUNG CHRONIC PATIENT?

The young adult chronic patient population can be seen as the fruit not of deinstitutionalization per se but of its corollary policies of admissions diversion and short-stay hospitalization, which keep most mentally ill people in the status of community outpatients most of the time. The first of these policies, admissions diversion, means that patients continue to live in the community in mental and emotional states which in the past would have brought about their hospitalization. Although they are diverted to alternative programs such as day hospital, they may or may not follow through on such alternatives, and in most states they are under no legal constraint to do so. In some communities appropriate programs are simply not available, so that the burden of care is placed upon family members, if any, or the patient is simply "discharged" to the street.

The second corollary to deinstitutionalization, the increasing brevity of hospitalization, often results in patients being discharged into the community in a state of incomplete remission, with their most obvious, threatening, and troublesome symptoms reduced, but with their mental/emotional state still severely compromised.[1] They go out of the hospital, often into very inadequate and stressful living conditions, while they are still unusually vulnerable to the vicissitudes of community and family life. And again, they are generally under no legal requirement to remain in outpatient treatment; therefore even the most carefully-laid discharge plans are often not followed through.

These policies also have an impact, of course, on the older generations of chronically mentally ill, deinstitutionalized persons. But the condition peculiar to the younger generation of the mentally and emotionally ill is that they have grown up as members of the community. This circumstance strongly colors their life experience, their self-perception, their expectations, and the problems encountered in their treatment. Many young adults whose mental disorders are manifest in their social functioning do not perceive themselves as psychiatric patients, nor are they so perceived by others, except when their disorders take the overt form of an acute psychotic episode. They mingle with the general population, share in the recreational drug use commonly practiced by their generation today, carry the burden of the normal life expectations of their age group—school, work, love relationships, marriage—without being able to attain their goals in any of these areas, and suffer repeated failures without the forgiving public identity of a handicapped person, which may be onerous but at least operates psychologically and socially as an explanation of limited functioning and as a curb for unrealistic expectations.

If policies associated with deinstitutionalization are in large part responsible for the problem in community psychiatry presented by this new generation of chronically mentally ill young adults, the growing magnitude of the problem has its source in demographic factors. Bachrach[2] has pointed out that the uncommonly high birth rate of the post-World War II years has increased the proportion of our total population which has now aged into young adulthood.

Today the 64 million babies born between 1946 and 1961 are between the ages of 21 and 36. . . . They represent nearly one-third of the nation's population. Because of their overrepresentation in the population, the absolute number of young persons at risk for developing schizophrenia and, later, other chronic mental disorders is very substantial. As predicted by Kramer . . . the coming of age of children born after World War II is now having a marked impact on the psychiatric service system (p 190).

Talbott, commenting upon this demographic phenomenon as a key factor in an "emerging crisis" in the public mental health system, adds that "this trend is occurring concomitantly with new moves to abolish state mental hospitals . . . The entire mental health system now seems designed to care for the acutely ill (p 1).[3]

THE GROWTH OF PROFESSIONAL AWARENESS
OF THE YOUNG ADULT CHRONIC PATIENT

These two major factors—the one demographic and the other a massive change in social policy and in the system of care—have led in the past few years to new pressures and concerns for mental health professionals. Like most problematic trends, this one first emerged at the two extremes of the vertical continuum of professional awareness: the level of psychiatric epidemiology[4] and the grass-roots level of everyday clinical experience.

By the mid-1970s mental health agencies across the country were beginning to feel the pressure of this new breed of young adult psychiatric patients—at that time, a species without a name. Hospital units which had previously been left unlocked were forced to lock their doors because of the frequent presence of young, psychotic, and violent males and females who required a restricted environment for the duration of intensive treatment of an acute episode. There was much talk about the rise in the level of violence in general hospital psychiatric units. It was observed that the violent psychosis was often precipitated by one of a variety of hallucinogenic drugs, making it difficult to distinguish young schizophrenic patients from drug abusers.

Many professionals also noted that the "revolving door" phenomenon no longer involved solely the older chronic mental patients, discharged from state hospitals. There were now some young adults who were passing in and out of general hospitals and community mental health center inpatient units with remarkable, depressing frequency. Many of these young adults had never been long-term state hospital patients. They were young men and women who in the past might well have been members of a new generation of long-stay institutionalized patients. Instead, they were being treated—or left untreated—in communities that were and are extremely variable in their capacity to provide any care, let alone coordinated, continuous care.

These young adults were typically agitated and disruptive (if not overtly violent), and rejecting both of treatment and of the very identity of psychiatric patient. They were frequently remarked upon anecdotally as being extremely difficult to treat, either refusing or not following through on referral to aftercare programs, or else creating disruption in an otherwise smooth-running rehabilitation or day hospital program. Many of these young adult patients were denied further treatment, either formally or informally, and were written off as having had "maximum hospital benefit" when they reappeared, again needing admission to an inpatient unit.[5]

Published accounts of these phenomena began to appear, addressing, like the blind men the parts of the elephant, disparate aspects of the emerging problem. Segal and Baumohl, studying young vagrants in Berkely in 1973, found that 22 percent of them had histories of mental illness.[6] Robbins and others, studying inpatient charts at Bellevue Hospital in 1978, found that a group of "unwelcome patients" were typically young men with few skills "who responded to stress with rage, augmented by alcoholism or drug abuse."[5] Young adult patients were also discussed by Klein with regard to the problems and limitations of drug therapy[7] and by Lamb in terms of their psychiatric rehabilitation needs.[8] Haley published a book on treatment of disturbed young adults as a cross-diagnostically defined group from a strategic family therapy perspective.[9] But the needs of the mentally ill young adult usually were addressed in terms of specific diagnostic categories—most commonly schizophrenia, which has been the appropriate subject of a wealth of literature, and more recently the diagnostic category of borderline personality.

From a community psychiatry perspective, a major accomplishment in the past three years has been the introduction and spread of the concept of the young adult chronic patient population as a whole, as a pressing contemporary public mental health problem, having meaningful dimensions which cut across diagnostic lines. To our knowledge the first major effort to address this population as such was a conference held in 1980 by the Rockland County (New York) Community Mental Health Center in an effort to focus professional attention upon this patient group. This conference, which presented a definition, overview, and initial research by Pepper and associates,[10] additional research by Caton[11] and by Sheets and associates,[12] and policy, epidemiologic, and psychopharmacologic perspectives on the population by Talbott,[13] Gruenberg, Klein, Bachrach and others,[14] marked the beginning of a groundswell of professional attention to the special nature, needs, and characteristics of the young adult chronic patient. This conference and a second held in Albany were soon followed by two special sections in *Hospital & Community Psychiatry* [13] and an edited sourcebook in the *New Directions for Mental Health Services* series,[14] which presented papers from the two conferences and from other sources; as well as a third annual conference and innumerable programs and presentations around the country on the subject of this young adult patient group.

These early efforts have essentially served to affix a generic label to what had become an increasingly urgent and troubling problem to mental health professionals; and the use of this label has opened up discussion, has raised the level of awareness of the problem, has brought many perspectives to bear upon the needs of this generically-identified patient group, and has inspired research and program planning efforts that are addressed to the young adult chronic population as a whole. This broad conceptualization of the problem has given professionals the advantage of a public health, community, and family perspective on a large group of patients who ultimately have more similarities in their long-term problems and needs than would be predicted by their initial differential diagnoses. This broader perspective is essential for clinicians, administrators, and program planners, because the problems presented by today's mentally ill young adults are more similar than different for the various diagnostic groups. This is especially true of those problems that are new and distinctive for this population—problems in continuity of care, medication compliance, family intervention and support, substance use and abuse, and appropriate expectations, as well as the more common problems of employment, housing, and social and vocational rehabilitation as they have an impact upon young adults. The definition of the young adult chronic patient as a community population has given clinicians, administrators, and program designers a unifying concept for a mixed caseload. In addition to widespread professional and public attention to this population, and the relief of professionals and parents as they learn that they are not alone, perhaps the most significant sign of progress in this consciousness-raising process was a working conference on the young adult chronic patient that was sponsored in October 1982 by the federal alcohol, drug abuse, and mental health administration and its three components—NIMH, NIAA, and NIDA—which addressed (for the first time at the federal level) the problem of these young adults as an inter-agency concern calling for new and coordinated efforts.[15]

RESEARCH ON THE YOUNG ADULT CHRONIC PATIENT

Research into the nature, numbers, characteristics, and needs of the young adult chronic patient as a total population is in its early stages because this population is itself newly identified. Until three years ago epidemiological studies treated the mentally ill young adult merely as a portion of the larger population of chronic mental patients, and research in treatment and etiology has been addressed to specific diagnostic categories. Conceptualization of the young adult chronic patient as a total and discrete population has opened the way to research efforts with a new focus in the context of community psychiatry.

Bachrach[2] has published an analytical review of research reports and other relevant published and fugitive literature. As already noted, some of the literature addresses the chronically mentally ill population as a whole, from which material on the young adult population may be abstracted. Research on the young adult chronic patient population per se has been reported by Pepper et al.,[10] Sheets et al.[12] Egri and Caton,[16] and Woy and et al.,[17] in addition to the work by Caton[11] on the young adult schizophrenic population. Further statistics on service utilization have been reported by Schwartz and Goldfinger,[18] Bassuk,[19] Pandiani,[2] and others.

The initial work by Pepper et al.[10] dealt with a small exploratory study of a segment of the young adult population (ages 18–30) treated in Rockland County CMHC outpatient clinics during a three-month period in 1980. Nearly one third of the 900 young adult clinic patients seen during that period were identified by clinicians as young adult chronic patients, based on the severe and persistent nature of their disabilities and their dysfunctional use of mental health treatment. Of these nearly 300 persons: 55 percent were male, 55 percent had mental health treatment before age 18, 25 percent had never been hospitalized, 60 percent were unemployed, 30 percent were receiving federal social security income based on disability, 27 percent were on public assistance, 19 percent were receiving support from their families, 24 percent were self-supporting, 24 percent were known to have been in trouble with the law, 37 percent had a known history of alcohol abuse, 37 percent (not necessarily the same 37 percent) had a known history of marijuana abuse, 28 percent had a known history of other drug abuse, and for 42 percent of these persons, suicide had been an issue addressed in treatment.

Sheets and associates[12] examined a population served at Hutchings Psychiatric Center in Syracuse, New York in 1979. They selected, from 966 patients judged to be chronic by functional criteria alone, 369 (36 percent), between the ages of 18 and 35. The researchers used their statistics to develop contrasting profiles for the prototypical young adult chronic patient and the prototypical older chronic patient in their population. The young adult chronic patient was profiled as a single white male, age 27, residing in the city, diagnosed schizophrenic, first hospitalized at age 22 (and subsequently hospitalized slightly less than once a year for periods averaging less than 30 days, with frequent admissions or transfers between inpatient, outpatient, and day treatment services), and some use of either a supervised residence or a supervised day program. The incidence of problems in community functioning in the young adult chronic patient sample was reported as significantly higher than in the older chronic patient group in the areas of psychiatric symptoms, daily living skills, behavior problems, social isolation, and alcohol or other drug abuse.

Sheets and associates also interviewed 22 informants from state, county, and voluntary agencies in order to identify similarities and differences among groups of patients within the young adult chronic patient population as a whole. From these data they hypothesized three subgroups with identifiable characteristics which they called the System-Dependent Group, the High-Energy/High-Demand Group, and the High-Functioning Group, each with identifiable characteristics in terms of their self-perception, functional levels, and attitude toward mental health services.

Supplementing these initial explorations of the young adult chronic patient population per se, Caton[11] highlighted the issue of suicide risk within this population by reporting for a New York City cohort of 119 discharged patients (most of them young adults) five successful suicides within a one-year follow-up period. Unpublished results of follow-up studies over a longer period indicated an even higher suicide rate, concentrated in the lower range of the 18 to 30 age group of young male adults.[20]

Other data reported have been in the areas of service utilization in the general hospital,[16,18,19,22] the community mental health center,[2] the state psychiatric center,[12,2] the community support center,[2] and the board-and-care home[21]; and, in addition, the self-perception of mentally ill young adults in the streets[23] and the incidence of mental illness among young adults in shelters for the homeless.[24]

Pepper and associates have, since their initial study, undertaken a more extensive and detailed survey of the numbers, characteristics, and needs of the young adult chronic patient population within the Rockland County CMHC service system. From 1200 young adults age 18–35 who had at least one contact with RCCMHC treatment services in 1980 and at least one contact two years or more before, 800 were identified by their most recent clinicians through a screening questionnaire as having the characteristics which have been used to define this patient group: severe and persistent social disability, and indications of a need extending over two years or more for mental health services. The extensive data gathered in this study are currently under analysis. Preliminary data on a sample of 152 of the chronic patient group have been reported as suggesting that

48.5 percent of the "chronic" sample are known by their clinicians to have used or abused alcohol and/or other drugs, 7 percent are known to have been involved in a criminal offense involving violence, 11 percent are known to have been involved in a nonviolent criminal offense, 31 percent are still living with their families, only 16 percent are self-supporting, 34 percent have made suicide attempts, 45 percent have rejected specific mental health services recommended by their clinicians, and 51 percent have never been hospitalized.[25]

CURRENT STATE OF KNOWLEDGE OF THE YOUNG ADULT CHRONIC PATIENT

It has been established that the young adult chronic patient is a discrete population with commonalities which transcend the diversity of clinical profiles and functional levels. As has been pointed out by Pepper and associates, these patients share "two overarching characteristics"—their severe deficits in social functioning and their "tendency to use mental health services inappropriately, in ways that drain the time and energy of clinicians, yet do not conform to viable treatment plans (p 463).[10] Bachrach has documented through her review of the literature that these patients are "pervasive users of the service system"; yet "at any given time a substantial portion of young adult chronic patients are *not* enrolled in psychiatric facilities and are essentially unserved by the psychiatric service system." (p 192).[2] For those patients who are known to, and to some degree served by, the service system

[their] existence . . . is typically associated with severe system stress. This situation is at least partially explained by the widespread absence of community supports for these patients. Young adult chronic patients generally alienate family, friends, and other crisis resources, and the psychiatric service system must assume a major support role during the recurrent crises in their lives. (p 192).[2]

As clinical observations and data on the young adult chronic patient have accumulated, characteristics of the population and its subgroups are being clarified, and guidelines for programming and treatment are beginning to emerge. Some reports have confirmed and documented initial clinical impressions of the population, while others have challenged a stereotype of the "typical" young adult chronic patient. While Sheets and associates found the prototypical patient at Hutchings Psychiatric Center to be a young male, diagnosed schizophrenic, with a history of multiple psychiatric hospitalizations,[12] data from other settings suggest an alternate prototype who is female, dually diagnosed as bipolar disorder (manic-depressive) or borderline personality with alcohol or other substance abuse.[25,26]

Experience in the Rockland County CMHC setting, where the DSM-III was adopted as the standard diagnostic instrument between the initial 1980 study and the present study, indicates that a smaller proportion of patients in the post-DSM-III sample have been diagnosed as schizophrenic, while multiple diagnoses are emerging for a significant proportion of this more recent sample. The majority of the sample (some 60 percent) are now identified as having a personality disorder with affective symptoms and/or alcohol or other substance abuse.[25] This observation has also been made in other settings[26] and may reflect in part a more precise diagnostic framework and an increasingly conservative use of the diagnosis of schizophrenia, which had been frequently applied to institutionalized patients as the basis for hospitalization. It is in any case increasingly clear that diagnosis, despite its important implications for some aspects of treatment, is only the beginning of an adequate portrayal of the clinical and functional characteristics of a "typical" young adult chronic patient; that there is no one "typical" diagnosis but different mixes of diagnostic groups in different settings and populations; and that the difficulty in diagnosis and the presentation of a multiplicity of functional problems are features frequently encountered in this young adult population.

The wide spectrum of hospitalization histories is equally significant. In contrast to the multiply-hospitalized prototypical patient at Hutchings, who is certainly representative of a large segment of the population, an even larger proportion (slightly more than half) show up in the Rockland County "chronic" sample as never hospitalized. Obviously the proportions of never-hospitalized and frequently hospitalized persons identified in a patient sample in a specific locality and setting may be assumed to be strongly affected by such factors as the nature of the community, the process of patient identification, and, perhaps most important, the range of alternative services available, as documented by Stein and Test.[27] A range of appropriate and integrated alternative services does not in itself eliminate problems of noncompliance, inappropriate termination, rejection of referral, and the common tendency of these young adults to accept only episodic treatment and to rely heavily on emergency and crisis units (or to use other services as if they were crisis services). But the problem of the young adult chronic patient in the community is obviously most serious in those localities where hospitalization or weekly outpatient therapy—and possibly a day hospital populated with older deinstitutionalized patients—are the only options. In such localities and especially in our large cities, the problems of system stress are felt most keenly, and the buildup of a large untreated and underidentified population of seriously disabled young adults carries the highest potential for human tragedy, placing heavy pressure on other social systems.[24] An additional problem impinging upon systems and also fragmenting even the possibility of treatment is the high geographic mobility of many adult chronic patients, which has been noted by Segal and associates[23] and by Bachrach.[2]

At this point in our collective knowledge of the young adult chronic patient, we can say that the population includes ample representation from both sexes and from all socioeconomic groups. It appears in a great variety of settings and includes patients with a variety of diagnoses (and, for some samples, a high proportion of non-psychotic diagnoses). It includes in at least some settings a high proportion of never-hospitalized persons and also a large segment of "revolving door" patients, with a range of hospitalization histories between these extremes; it is characterized by a high incidence of alcohol and other drug use and abuse, suicide and suicide attempts and/or risk, disruptive social behavior, total or partial financial dependence on public assistance programs or on family, and rejection and/or inappropriate use of mental health services. Except for financial dependency, all of these characteristics significantly distinguish the young adult chronic patient population from the population of chronically mentally ill persons over the age of 35.[12,17]

Additional concerns regarding the young adult chronic patient have been suggested by the Rockland County CMHC research and by clinical experience in various settings. Recent data from Rockland County suggest that the majority of the young adult chronic sample have had mental health treatment before age 18; 44 percent of the sample have had outpatient treatment before that age, and 26 percent have had inpatient treatment before 18. Further data from a subsample of the young adult chronic population suggest a sizable number of children being raised by parents who are young adult chronic patients: in a group of 100 such patients, 22 persons had among them 44 children ranging in age from 2 to 17 years old, who were being raised by the patients.[28]

Finally, the impact of these young adult patients upon their families, and the hazards presented to them by family conflict, have received particular attention, both in the form of rapid growth of family support and advocacy groups at both the local and the national level (e.g., National Alliance for the Mentally Ill) during the past few years. New developments in family education, intervention programs, and evaluation research are further evidence of this attention. The frontier of family intervention programs is represented by programs on the psychoeducational model which are designed specifically for families of schizophrenic patients, growing out of the research by Brown and Birley[29] and by Leff [30] on the role of expressed emotion in the course of schizophrenia; and the family systems approach to therapy of disturbed young adults described by Haley.[11] The importance of further development of effective family intervention programs is highlighted by favorable data on psychoeducational programs and by current Rockland County data suggesting that some 30 percent of a suburban sample of young adult chronic patients are living with their families.[25]

DIRECTIONS FOR FUTURE RESEARCH

Because of the attention now focused on the young adult chronic patient population, we can anticipate an explosion of information on this patient group in the next five years. Such information will include further statistics on service utilization, data from planned research, and evaluations of new program initiatives tailored to the needs of young adults. In view of the importance of such data, a new national organization, *The Information Exchange on Young Adult Chronic Patients* (TIE), has been initiated by Pepper and colleagues with the intent of serving as a nationwide clearinghouse to facilitate the exchange of such information and ideas.

Future research initiatives might profitably be focused on the following areas:

1. Review of agencies' current caseloads of young adults to identify chronic patients; gathering data on diagnoses, time and nature of onset, functional history and current level of functioning patterns, utilization of mental health services, reasons for treatment failures, and the role of family dynamics and family burden.
2. Delineation of subgroups of the young adult chronic patient population based on past current functional characteristics. Attention should be directed not only to diagnostic subgroups but to such categories as have been suggested by Sheets and associates[12] with relation to social functioning and service utilization characteristics, and by Pepper[36] with relation to age of onset (childhood, adolescent, or young adult).

3. Attention to similarities and differences in patterns of treatment history and service utilization for young adult chronic patient populations in different settings and with relation to availability and range of services.
4. Investigation of the relationships between chronic mental disorders and other chronic conditions such as physical disability, alcohol and substance abuse, antisocial behavior, mental retardation, and learning disabilities, and of special needs of multiply disabled young adults.
5. Investigation of the relationships among such etiological factors as genetic, organic, or developmental problems, and family and community stress, in terms of both family and developmental history and the current young adult life situation.
6. Studies of the life and treatment course of persons receiving inpatient and/or outpatient treatment before age 18, and especially in mid- or late adolescence, directed toward developing indices of risk factors to be used in prognosis and in initiating programs of early intervention.
7. Evaluative research for program initiatives, especially in the areas of day treatment programs, family intervention programs, educationally and vocationally oriented programs, and nontraditional mental health services such as drop-in centers and hostels and with attention to cost/benefit studies for specially staffed and tailored programs with regard to relapse, rehospitalization, and indices of rehabilitation.

DIRECTIONS FOR TREATMENT AND PROGRAMMING

Experience and the accumulating data on the young adult chronic patient have taught clinicians and administrators a great deal about the difficulties of treatment. We have noted elsewhere that the functional characteristics of these patients result from the interaction of intrapsychic process, developmental determinants, and the current community environment. Similarly, the difficulties in treating young adult chronic patients today result from their own dysfunctional ways of relating to mental health services; the present state of psychiatric service development in the community; the social policies, treatment principles, and legal safeguards which have resulted in placing most mental health treatment on a voluntary outpatient basis; and finally, the conditions of the community itself, which requires a high degree and frequency of individual choice, self-direction, impulse regulation, and processing of stimuli.

Noting the difficulty of maintaining continuity of care with these patients, we find sources of the discontinuity both in their own characteristics and in the structuring of services. Discontinuity in our service delivery system springs from the fragmentation of agencies, in communities which have not integrated a unified service network, presenting a need to develop effective links for communication, referral, and consistency of attitude between services. This discontinuity is also the result of the difficulty of providing a constant relationship with a particular clinician or treatment team in a system which offers comprehensive and variegated services, and in which patients therefore may experience multiple transfers from one treatment team to another; and of the difficulty, in communities which lack a range of services, of maintaining treatment when the total burden of clinical response rests on the shoulders of a single clinician, such as a private outpatient practitioner.

The problem of providing and maintaining care which is both comprehensive and continuous often becomes unmanageable in combination with the common tendency of these young adult patients to be physically mobile, emotionally labile, and to have difficulty in forming stable relationships (including those with clinicians). Our major task in providing effective treatment programs is to find ways of compensating for, rather than mirroring, the intrapsychic difficulties of our patients.

Based on what we now know of the young adult chronic patient, the following may be expected to foci of professional thinking in developing treatment programs.

1. *Continuity vs. discontinuity of treatment.* This continuity may be provided by improvement of service integration, the use of treatment teams, and the use of case managers in a flexible range of capacities as constant helpers.
2. *Treatment teams vs. individual therapeutic relationships.* The demanding, yet help-rejecting behavior of young adult chronic patients, the extensiveness of their needs and the generally erratic course of their treatment and progress makes them exceptionally draining for any one individual. Concern with continuity and the management of multiple crises also makes it essential to have clinical backup from more than one individual who is familiar with the patient.
3. *Day (and evening) programs vs. either hospital-based programming or traditional weekly outpatient therapy.* Even for these young adults who are repeatedly hospitalized, such hospitalization (while a potentially useful opportunity for evaluation, engagement and treatment planning) is generally too brief to permit even the beginning of therapeutic management. Traditional psychodynamically-oriented outpatient therapy, on the other hand, is grossly inadequate to the needs of these young adults. Day programs must be developed which are non-stigmatizing in their format and specifically tailored to the needs of this age group.
4. *Group vs. individual treatment modalities,* in order to offer, through peer involvement, the most promising opportunity to engage patients and to address fundamental problems in interpersonal behavior.[37,38]
5. *Family intervention vs. exclusive concern with individual patients* in view of increasing awareness of the family burden and of the actual or potential influence of family dynamics upon the course of treatment.[29-35,39]
6. *Problems in social functioning vs. intrapsychic process as a focus of treatment,* through programs designed to develop coping skills, modify behavior, and enhance self-esteem and self-awareness.[37,38]

7. *Flexible, informal, and very accessible mental health services vs. traditional, formal mental health services,* in order to engage that portion of the young adult chronic patient population that currently evades treatment.[23]
8. *Programs tailored to the young adult age group vs. age-heterogeneous programs* that attempt to meet the needs of older, deinstitutionalized persons as well as the special needs of young adults, since the heterogenous programs are frequently either rejected or disrupted by younger patients and are not geared to the developmental and goal-oriented needs of the younger age group.[38]
9. *Residential programs vs. the present unsatisfactory options* of transient hotels, proprietary homes inhabited by older, deinstitutionalized patients, the childhood homes of overburdened and conflict-ridden families, and last and worst, the street.[23]

Among all of these foci for future programming for the young adult chronic patient, the development of community residences for this population stands out as an urgent need. The types of residences that are needed may vary with the functional characteristics of subgroups of the population, as well as with a patient's functional status at a given time. Types of residences to be considered are:

1. *Crisis residences* to serve as viable alternatives to hospitalization.
2. *Long-term or lifelong residences,* on the model of community residences for the mentally retarded, for those young adults who can be expected to require specialized and supportive housing for their entire lives.
3. *Developmental residences,* on the model of the adolescent group home, which could function as a locus of treatment and support—including educational and vocational help and family treatment facilitating separation—over a period of perhaps one to three years. Such residences might provide an opportunity to work intensively and with continuity, over an adequate period of time, on developmental tasks which the young adult chronic patient (like the troubled adolescent) has not been able to accomplish through the usual course of development. This would be a preferred choice of residence for Sheets' "High-Energy/High-Demand" group[12] and might enable us to learn more about the role that a depriving, insufficiently supportive, and overstimulating environment—the community—plays in the apparent chronicity of these patients, by providing corrective measures for its deficits.

DIRECTIONS FOR ADVOCACY

It is obvious that these guidelines for more effective treatment of the young adult chronic patient cannot be realized without a dramatic increase in the level of support for community-based programs. As is the case for the older population of chronically mentally ill persons, the unmet needs of the young adult chronic patient place an urgent demand for advocacy not only upon groups of citizens already engaged in that work but upon professionals as well. The mentally ill are at a unique disadvantage in the political arena: most are unable to advocate their cause on their own behalf, either individually or collectively. Many of their families have been reluctant to "come out of the closet" and make their needs known, although with the growth of such organizations as the National Alliance for the Mentally Ill, their voices are now beginning to be heard. The neglect and lack of support from services for mentally ill young adults is particularly hazardous because of their special needs and characteristics, and the ease with which they can be perceived as socially unacceptable deviants rather than as impaired persons in need of treatment. The size and nature of this population, if not adequately handled by the psychiatric service system, will make them an increasingly unmanageable problem for all social agencies, including the courts and prisons, with staggering human and economic costs.

Advocacy efforts for this population must focus upon ensuring adequate funding for community service systems as a whole, encouraging programs specially-tailored for the young adult, developing funding eligibility criteria based on functional disability rather than on the obsolete criterion of hospitalization history, and developing appropriate community housing which can accommodate this volatile population and its needs.

As professional attention to the young adult chronic population grows ever more widespread and more precisely focused, our knowledge will grow; but the value of this increasing knowledge will depend entirely upon our ability to put it into practice. That ability to create the necessary services will depend, in turn, on our ability to make the needs known, and to press the case of the young adult chronic patient with vigor, devotion, and persistence.

References

1. Crabtree L: Disability at discharge in young adult chronic patients at discharge from a private psychiatric hospital, in Pepper B, Ryglewicz H: *New Directions for Mental Health Services: Advances in Treating the Young Adult Chronic Patient, No. 21.* San Francisco, Jossey-Bass, 1984, pp 000–000
2. Bachrach LL: Young adult chronic patients: An analytical review of the literature. *Hosp Community Psychiatry* 1982;33:189–197
3. Talbott J. The emerging crisis in chronic care, in Talbott J (ed): The Young Adult Chronic Patient: Collected Articles from H & CP. Washington, DC, American Psychiatric Association, 1982, p 1
4. Kramer M: Psychiatric Services and the Changing Institutional Scene, 1950–1985. Rockville, MD, National Institute of Mental Health, 1977
5. Robbins E, Stern M, Robbins L, et al.: Unwelcome patients: Where can they find asylum? *Hosp Community Psychiatry* 1978;29:45–56
6. Segal SP, Baumohl J, Johnson E: Falling through the cracks: Mental disorder and social margin in a young vagrant population. *Social Problems* 1977;24(3):387–400
7. Klein DF: Psychopharmacology: Special considerations, in Pepper B, Ryglewicz H (eds): *New Directions for Mental Health Services: The Young Adult Chronic Patient, No. 14.* San Francisco Jossey-Bass, 1982, pp 51–56

8. Lamb HR: Structure: The neglected ingredient of community treatment. *Arch Gen Psychiatry* 1980;37:1224–1228
9. Haley J: Leaving home: The therapy of disturbed young adults. New York, McGraw-Hill, 1980
10. Pepper B, Kirshner M, Ryglewicz H: The young adult chronic patient: Overview of a population *Hosp Community Psychiatry* 1981;23:463–469
11. Caton CLM: The new chronic patient and the system of community care. *Hosp Community Psychiatry* 1981;32:475–478
12. Sheets JL, Prevost JA, Reihman J: Young adult chronic patients: Three hypothesized subgroups. *Hosp Community Psychiatry* 1982;33:197–203
13. Talbott J (ed): The young adult chronic patient: Collected articles from H & CP. Washington, DC, American Psychiatric Association, 1982, p 1–37
14. Pepper B, Ryglewicz H: *New Directions for Mental Health Services: The Young Adult Chronic Patient, No. 14.* San Francisco, Jossey-Bass, 1982
15. Glass J: Summary of proceedings: The Young Adult Chronic Patient, an ADM working conference, October 21–22, 1982, pp 1–19
16. Egri G, Caton CLM: Serving the young adult chronic patient in the 1980s: Challenge to the general hospital, in Pepper B, Ryglewicz H (eds): *New Directions for Mental Health Services: The Young Adult Chronic Patient, No. 14.* San Francisco, Jossey-Bass, 1982, pp 25–31
17. Woy JR, Goldstrom ID, Manderscheid RW: The young chronic mental patient: report of a national survey. NIMH–OP–79–0031, National Institute of Mental Health, 1982, pp 1–17
18. Schwartz SR, Goldfinger SM: The new chronic patient: Clinical characteristics of an emerging subgroup. *Hosp Community Psychiatry* 1981;32:470–474
19. Bassuk EL: The impact of deinstitutionalization on the general hospital psychiatric emergency ward. *Hosp Community Psychiatry* 1980;31:623–627
20. Caton CLM: Personal communication, November 1981
21. Lamb HR: Young adult chronic patients: The new drifters. *Hosp Community Psychiatry* 1982;33:465–468
22. Bristol JH, Giller E, Docharty JP: Trends in emergency psychiatry in the last two decades. *Am J Psychiatry* 1981;138:623–628
23. Segal SP, Baumohl J: Engaging the disengaged: Proposals on madness and vagrancy. *Social Work* 1980;25:358–365
24. Hopper K, Baxter E, Cox S: Not making it crazy: The young homeless patients in New York City, in Pepper B, Ryglewicz H (eds): *New Directions for Mental Health Services: The Young Adult Chronic Patient, No. 14.* San Francisco, Jossey-Bass, 1982
25. Pepper B, Ryglewicz H, Kirshner M: Unpublished data
26. Crabtree L: Personal communication, October 1982
27. Stein LI, Test MA: Alternative to mental hospital treatment. *Arch Gen Psychiatry* 1980;37:392–397
28. Pepper B, Ryglewicz H, Kirsher M: The uninstitutionalized generation: A new breed of psychiatric patient, in Pepper B, Ryglewicz H (eds): *New Directions for Mental Health Services: The Young Adult Chronic Patient, No. 14.* San Francisco, Jossey-Bass, 1982, pp 3–14
29. Brown GW, Birley JLT, Wing JK: Influence of family life on the course of schizophenric disorders: A replication. *Br J Psychiatry* 1972;121:241–258
30. Leff JP: Developments in family treatment of schizophrenia. *Psychiatr Q* 1979;51
31. Anderson CM, Hogarty F, Reiss DJ: The psycho-educational family treatment of schizophrenia, in Goldstein MJ (ed): *New Directions for Mental Health Services: New Developments in Interventions with Families of Schizophrenics, No. 12.* San Francisco, Jossey-Bass, 1981, pp 79–92
32. Berkowitz R, Kuipers L, Eberlein-Frief R, et al: Lowering expressed emotion in relatives of schizophrenics, in Goldstein MJ (ed): *New Directions for Mental Health Services: New Developments in Interventions with Families of Schizophrenics, No. 12.* San Francisco, Jossey-Bass, 1981, pp 27–48

33. Falloon IRH, Boyd JL, McGill CW, et al: Family management training in the community care of schizophrenia, in Goldstein MJ (ed): *New Directions for Mental Health Services: New Developments in Interventions with Families of Schizophrenics, No. 12.* San Francisco, Jossey-Bass, 1981, pp 61–78

34. Goldstein MJ, Kopeikin HS: Short- and long-term effects of combining drug and family therapy, in Goldstein MJ (ed): *New Directions for Mental Health Services: New Developments in Interventions with Families of Schizophrenics, No. 12.* San Francisco, Jossey-Bass, 1981, pp 5–26

35. Snyder KS, Liberman RP: Family assessment and intervention with schizophrenics at risk for relapse, in Goldstein MJ (ed): *New Directions for Mental Health Services: New Developments in Interventions with Families of Schizophrenics, No. 12.* San Francisco, Jossey-Bass, 1981, pp 49–60

36. Pepper B, Ryglewicz H: Treating the young adult chronic patient: From crisis toward maturation. Keynote address at Third Annual Conference on the Young Adult Chronic Patient, Concord, New Hampshire, 1982

37. Neffinger GG, Schiff JW: Treatment by objectives: A partial hospital treatment program, in Pepper B, Ryglewicz H: (eds): *New Directions for Mental Health Services: The Young Adult Chronic Patient, No. 14.* San Francisco, Jossey-Bass, 1982, pp 77–83

38. Schacter M, Goldberg W: GAP: A treatment approach for the young adult chronic patient, in Pepper B, Ryglewicz H: (eds): *New Directions for Mental Health Services: The Young Adult Chronic Patient, No. 14.* San Francisco, Jossey-Bass, 1982, pp 85–89

39. Ryglewicz H: Working with the family of the psychiatrically disabled young adult, in Pepper B, Ryglewicz H: (eds): *New Directions for Mental Health Services: The Young Adult Chronic Patient, No. 14.* San Francisco, Jossey-Bass, 1982, pp 91–97

Ellen Baxter
Kim Hopper

4

Troubled on the Streets:
The Mentally Disabled Homeless Poor

The single most critical factor which prevents effective service coordination and implementation of rational discharge planning is the lack of provision for adequate specialized housing for the chronically disabled.[1]

—Committee Report to the
Commissioner of Mental Health,
Albany, New York

As 1984 dawns, more people in New York City are seeking refuge in public shelters (some 6,000 men and women), voluntary shelters, and church basements than at any time since the worst days of the Depression. Nor is this a phenomenon restricted to New York City. As many as 2,500,000 people are thought to be homeless nationwide.[2] They crisscross the country in a futile search for work, they scavenge dumpsters for food, and bind scrap material together for shelter. Nobody knows the exact numbers, but it is clear that the homeless today are legion.

Thousands find haven in privately run hostels, missions, Salvation Army facilities, Catholic Worker Houses, and drop-in centers. Untold numbers remain on the street, subject to the assaults of cold, rain, and the occasional vicious passer-by. The tales of the homeless poor now make up part of the daily tabloid of urban life: the mother and two small children found living in an elevator equipment room on top of a housing project in New York City; the two men who died (one in Denver, the other in Chicago) while asleep in trash compactors

THE CHRONIC MENTAL PATIENT
ISBN 0-8089-1649-1

Copyright © 1984 by Grune & Stratton.
All rights of reproduction in any form reserved.

which began operating; the Manhattan woman returned to the street because a judge found her fears of mistreatment in a mental hospital to be justified; a Commissioner in Fort Lauderdale who proposed spraying public trash cans with poison to prevent "real scum" or "dirt bags" from picking through garbage for food; 550 white crosses driven into the ground of Lafayette Park across from the Capitol to commemorate known deaths of homeless people in 11 cities. It strains the meaning of the term to see these as tokens of a civilized society.

Among the homeless poor are thousands of former psychiatric patients (again, the exact number is unknown) whose precarious arrangements for "community living" have fallen apart. There are also multitudes of others, mentally disabled (sometimes cripplingly so), who (although in obvious need of assistance) do not meet the restrictive admitting criteria in effect at public psychiatric facilities since the late 1960s. They are ubiquitous; rare is the city street that does not play host (at least on occasion) to an obviously disturbed homeless man or woman.

It must be emphasized that the population of the homeless poor is heterogenous; it defies categorization under any single heading of disability, mental or otherwise. The homeless men, women, and children who now reside on urban avenues, in encampments on the outskirts of Sunbelt cities, and in abandoned buildings, public parks, and emergency shelters wherever available, represent a diverse cross-section of the citizenry. They come from varied social, economic, and personal backgrounds. The one thing they share is privation.[2-4] The great majority have neither history of hospitalization nor debilitating symptoms. Still, the loss of a home, the sudden entry of insecurity and fear as daily companions, and the constant struggle to meet the basic needs of people with no place to go, can all weigh heavily on one's capacity to cope.

Much of the information in this chapter relies on data of admittedly uneven quality, collected by both public and nonprofit mental health and social welfare agencies in New York City. The volume of material available here is no accident. Several class action suits brought before the New York State Supreme Court under the auspices of the Coalition for the Homeless (*Callahan v. Carey; Klostermann v. Carey; Eldredge v. Koch*), intensive advocacy efforts on behalf of the homeless and the needs of low-income housing residents in general, a dramatic shrinkage of low-rent dwellings in the city, and the well-documented failure of deinstitutionalization efforts in the area, have focused political and media attention on the issue. Substantial allocations of public funds,* a number of publicly and privately commissioned studies of the homeless population, extensive out-

---

*The annual operating budget for the New York City public shelter system currently stands at $48 million. In 1982, the State Legislature appropriated $5 million in direct capitalization funds available to nonprofit groups committed to providing low-income residences or shelters for the homeless. In January 1983, the newly elected governor pledged $50 million to provide 6,000 permanent housing units for the homeless.

reach efforts, and the development of several low-barrier alternatives to the streets and shelters (drop-in centers), all serve to indicate the relatively advanced nature of New York's policies toward the homeless. The information store makes it a rich (if atypical) case for consideration. At the same time, the fact that New York, along with California and Massachusetts, was considered to be in the forefront of the nationwide deinstitutionalization movement[5,6] makes it an instructive one. And while the focus of this chapter will be on New York, the proposals and policy questions addressed throughout are relevant to other urban areas.

EMPTY HOSPITALS, FULL STREETS

In the last decade, British,[7-9]; Canadian,[10] and American[11,12] studies have all attested to the growing numbers of psychiatrically disabled among the homeless poor. To date, few attempts have been made to collect systematic data on the mental health status of emergency shelter recipients, let alone the street-dwellers. And, indeed, at a time when armories, warehouses, churches, and schools everywhere are being pressed into service as places of refuge, it makes little sense logistically to expend scarce resources on time-consuming intake and assessment procedures. Nevertheless, the yield of what few studies have been performed is telling.

A study in Phoenix found that 21 percent of a random sample of 150 homeless men and women had "serious mental health problems—they are either psychotic, possibly psychotic or severely depressed."[13] An additional 9 percent were found to be physically handicapped "with serious emotional problems." Fully 22 percent of the sample reported having been hospitalized for psychiatric reasons, and this was thought to be an underestimate. In 1980–81, 10 percent of all out-patients in county mental health clinics had no address.[14]

A survey of 165 men staying at an emergency shelter in St. Louis found that 40 percent of them were former psychiatric patients, the majority of whom had histories suggestive of "chronic, serious mental health disorders." An additional 15 percent of the sample examined were found to have a "current, serious level of psychopathology."[15,16]

In San Francisco, 13 percent of the street population served by five shelters and drop-in centers said they had been hospitalized for psychiatric reasons since becoming homeless.[17] A sample of one such drop-in center revealed that 50 percent of its clients were chronically mentally ill; citywide, at least 25 percent of the homeless population are thought to fall within this category.[18]

Of approximately 200 homeless people seen over a three month period in a Philadelphia emergency shelter, roughly 35 percent were found either to have psychiatric histories or to suffer from current disabilities.[19] Of those referred to a specialized shelter for the psychiatrically disabled, 84 percent were found to have a DSM-III disorder (nearly 40 percent were judged schizophrenic)–but only 35 percent had histories of psychiatric hospitalization.[20]

Dr. Roger Farr, of the Los Angeles County Department of Mental Health's "Skid Row Project," estimates that 50 percent of the county's homeless poor (numbering as many as 30,000) are chronically mentally disabled.[21]

A study of nearly 300 homeless individuals seen over a 4 month period in Albany, New York found that 38 percent of the adults show signs of significant and continuing psychiatric disability, most of whom had histories of hospitalization within the past year.[22]

Spot checks with advocates elsewhere confirm three general impressions: the psychiatrically disabled are a significant subgroup of the ranks of the homeless; the response of mental health officials to this development has been meek where it has been acknowledged at all; and the community mental health networks in place are almost universally ill-equipped or unwilling to deal with homeless clients. The critical issue at stake—in both espoused policy and actual practice—remains an entrenched separation of service delivery and the meeting of basic survival needs,[23] the most important of which is housing.

LACK OF HOUSING IN THE COMMUNITY

It has become evident that any effort to salvage a policy of community care will require that an array of supportive living facilities—emergency, transitional, and long-term—be made available to the chronically disabled. Evidence of formal recognition of this imperative is ubiquitous. At the federal level it is expressed that in the 1975 Amendment to the Community Mental Health Centers Act, the 1977 Comptroller General's Report to the Congress, the 1978 President's Commission on Mental Health, the Mental Health Systems Act of 1980, the Community Support System Programs, and the HUD/HEW demonstration grants. Yet despite the fact that the development of supportive housing had been a priority issue throughout the 1970s, and the fact that the literature of this period is replete with descriptions and evaluations of a variety of forms of community residential care which demonstrate that the chronically disabled can fare reasonably well in community settings if given sufficient support,[24-29] the supply of such alternative programs remains highly limited.

So enduring is the gap between the demonstrated need for and the actual availability of decent housing alternatives that it is difficult to attribute it simply to administrative inefficiency or casual neglect on the part of policy-makers. A willful refusal to engage the issue—except in low-risk experimental forays—appears to be at fault. In part, this may be owing to some dim appreciation of the true scale of need. Whatever the reasons, the effects are clear. While housing development is a largely unfamiliar and potentially costly venture for mental health authorities, its absence effectively undermines even the most energetic of therapeutic efforts for the severely disabled in the community.

As is the case with other large urban centers, the shortage of housing for the chronically mentally disabled in New York City is acute.[30,31] Between 1965 and 1977, New York State records show 126,000 discharges from state hospitals to the New York City area. This figure does not include the estimated 8000 a year who were denied entry to state hospitals under the tightened admitting criteria in effect since 1968.[31] By conservative estimates, 47,000 chronically mentally disabled people are thought to reside in the metropolitan area.[32] Various surveys of their whereabouts indicate that tens of thousands are in nursing homes, single-room occupancy hotels (SROs), adult homes, and family care facilities, with the largest numbers residing in nursing homes.[33-35]

The search for housing theoretically begins while an individual is still an inpatient—as part of "discharge planning." Throughout the late 1960s and early 1970s, such planning was in many cases limited to giving the released patient the address of the local Department of Social Services and a subway token to get there.[36] There, referrals to SROs were made so long as the supply of rooms lasted. The dramatic shrinkage of the low-income housing stock in New York City, including but not limited to the SROs,* has forced people living in these generally substandard environments to even poorer settings—emergency shelters or the streets.[38,39]

OFFICIAL POLICY

By 1978, psychiatrists had christened the Bowery one of the newly emerging "dumping grounds" for discharged psychiatric patients,[40] although local residents had noticed this and registered their protest some time earlier.[41] A year later, a report from the Office of the City Council President compared the Men's Shelter to a nineteenth century asylum.[42]

To be sure, state mental health officials have not been oblivious to the crisis. The regional director of the State's Office of Mental Health recently characterized homelessness as "the single greatest problem in New York City today."[43] Recognition of the problem, however, has not extended to assuming primary responsibility for the fate of the chronically mentally disturbed who have found themselves homeless. The 1981 Five-Year Plan of the Mental Health Department, for example, insisted that "the basic needs of the 'street people'—food, shelter, bath, clothing, medical care—are the responsibility of the social welfare system" (p 49).[44] At the same time, assertions that careful planning for placement outside the hospital is now standard practice,[45] declarations that deinstitutionalization policies have been ended,[46] and acknowledgments of past mis-

*Between 1970 and the present, over 110,000 low-rent SRO units were lost in New York City, representing 87 percent of the total stock. Nor is this decline restricted to New York City. In the same decade, 1,116,000 units nationwide—47 percent of the total supply—disappeared.[37]

takes[47] are more common. The intended message is clear: the present is not the past, nor need the present assume responsibility for the errors of the past.

Admittedly, from an administrative point of view—with people rather than problems assigned to categories of concern—difficulties do arise owing to the nature of homelessness itself. To take only the most obvious instance, the route from a psychiatric ward to the streets is not always a direct one. Ex-patients resort to welfare offices, mental health clinics, emergency rooms, and family members, sometimes repeatedly. But cracks open, thresholds of tolerance are crossed, resources exhausted—and suddenly the ex-patient may have no place to go. Once housing has been lost (as, for example, when brief hospitalization results in nonpayment of rent, or when rent increases outstrip one's ability to pay, or when eviction action is taken), it is virtually impossible to find again.

In New York, the acute shortage of psychiatric beds in city hospitals[48] make them inaccessible to all but the most disturbed and dangerous, criteria that exclude most of the disabled. Overburdened emergency room staff tend to be quick to assume (sometimes correctly) that homeless people are simply there to get off the street. The executive director of one such hospital was quoted as saying:

The criteria for admission now have become suicidal and homicidal criteria. We are rationing medical health care. Our average length of stay is ten days, which is just about getting them stabilized.[46]

Matters have worsened in certain quarters owing to newly intensified review procedures initiated by the federal government and directed at Supplemental Security Income (SSI) recipients. As many as 350,000 nationwide have lost their benefits as a result.[49] More to the point, mental disability is overrepresented in successful review cases (those that are discontinued) by a factor of three: roughly 11 percent of all disability checks go to the mentally disabled, but nearly a third of the closed cases are psychiatrically impaired.[50]

SURVEY FINDINGS

Much dispute surrounds discussion of the proportion of the homeless who have psychiatric histories and/or ongoing disorders. The New York State Office of Mental Health's estimates have varied considerably in recent years—the range is between 5,200 and 18,000.[51,52] No one knows for certain how many there are, for the simple reason that most of these individuals have long since been lost to service providers.

Surveys of public shelters show that by 1976, psychiatric problems rivaled alcoholism as the predominant disorder of homeless men: over half were found to show some indication of psychiatric problems; nearly 31 percent had prior histories of psychiatric hospitalization.[53] More recent examinations conducted by mental health teams in a shelter facility showed that of the 219 men referred for evaluation in the first sixteen days of operation, 25 percent were so disturbed as to require immediate hospitalization.[54] Subsequent on-site examinations of 840 men and 62 women at three public shelters by the same teams, for the period February–June 1981, found that 74 percent of the individuals interviewed had histories of psychiatric hospitalization, over half of which were in New York State, and that 8 percent had come directly to the shelter from a mental hospital. In over 200 instances (18 percent), hospitalization was the recommended "service disposition."[55] It should be noted that the 902 individuals examined constituted a selected minority of the total sheltered population.

A random sample study by the State Office of Mental Health found that of the 107 men interviewed, 33 percent had histories of psychiatric hospitalization and 22 percent had been hospitalized in a New York State facility.[56] These findings corroborate those of the city in a study of "long-term" residents of one shelter site. Out of the total of 169 men interviewed, 33 percent reported past psychiatric hospitalizations. Forty-one percent of those with psychiatric histories, however, had never been referred to the on-site mental health teams,[57] lending further weight to the observation already made that the casualties of deinstitutionalization are really two: those inappropriately discharged and those who were never hospitalized.

While survey data on homeless women is sparser, a 1975 study did find 58.5 percent of clients at a women's shelter to have histories of at least one hospitalization.[58] A more recent survey of 100 first-time women's shelter applicants found that 32 percent reported psychiatric hospitalizations; five had been referred by the hospital to the shelter upon discharge.[59] Impressionistic evidence from voluntary shelter providers and drop-in centers that serve women who do not use public shelter facilities suggests that the proportion of homeless women who suffer from mental instabilities is somewhat higher than that of homeless men.

Project Reach-Out, a van program which approaches people who are in apparent need of help in the streets and parks, has estimated that from a one-third to one-half of the homeless individuals they encounter are psychiatrically disabled.[60] These people generally do not utilize the public shelters and thus would not be represented in any of the surveys mentioned above. If anything, the built-in deterrent features of the public shelter system—the dirt, danger, and degradation that have traditionally been part and parcel of the city's offer of relief—are even more powerful for people with a heightened sensitivity to even a hint of menace in their environment.* As a result, an unnatural selection process operates that ensures that those most in need of a protective setting are those least likely to secure it. The public shelters, in effect, winnow for the younger, more resourceful, and resilient among the homeless poor. The streets retain the rest. This alone may help explain the difference sometimes noted between official

*Conditions in recent years have improved somewhat owing to the ongoing monitoring by the Courts of the City's compliance with the Callahan Consent Decree signed in August, 1981.[61]

surveys of the captive homeless population, and the reports of outreach workers. The latter consistently yield a picture of a more elderly and disabled population on the streets.

LIFE ON THE STREETS

To be hungry, cold, deprived of sleep, and socially isolated for even a short period can be mentally and physically wearing. The symptoms of those with mental disabilities are easily exacerbated on the streets, often taking on a character and severity that are frightening to the homeless themselves. While bizarre behavior and appearance are partially a product of the hardship of street life, they can also be assumed as protective techniques. Some women, for example, describe their filth and odor as a necessary defense against strangers, particularly against sexual predation.

The charitable institutions (churches, missions, Salvation Army, etc.) which have traditionally served the destitute are generally ill-prepared or unwilling to handle the needs of the increasing numbers of mentally disabled people who arrive at their doors in search of help. Where food and shelter are provided on a "first-come first-served" basis, however, mentally disabled people do gain access—so long, that is, as their behavior is not too disruptive.

Though many may be entitled to income assistance of some kind (SSI, Welfare, VA), the procedures for obtaining it are beyond the reach of the majority of the homeless. Managing such money, when secured, can also be beyond the capacity of some, without outside assistance. Among the many papers and completed forms required to show eligibility are a birth certificate and social security card. The systems are inaccessible to those without the necessary documents or an address to which they might be sent.

Homeless people have acquired a peculiar reputation for purportedly refusing all forms of assistance offered them. Refusal is described in psychiatric terms as symptomatic of illness, paranoia, or as a "flight syndrome."[12] The homeless are commonly depicted by human service professionals as noncompliant and "hard to reach." It is assumed that help is accessible and attentive to the needs of homeless people. Examination of existing shelters and services for the homeless reveals the shortsightedness of this assumption. The demand on all public and private shelters, drop-in centers, soup kitchens, and food pantries exceeds their capacities.[62] Where decent, accessible refuge has been made available, homeless people—regardless of what claim to sanity they can make—have shown themselves eager to take advantage of it.

BASIC NEEDS AND MENTAL HEALTH SERVICES

Attempts by the New York State and City Offices of Mental Health to better the circumstances of the chronically disabled in emergency shelters have taken the form of on-site service teams who, in addition to gathering survey data, conduct assessment and referral and offer medical and psychiatric back-up services. While these efforts may assist residents to a degree, therapeutic gains are severely checked by the deplorable physical conditions of the shelter settings themselves.[13,63] The scale, conditions, and routine of emergency shelters are oppressive in ways that are strikingly similar to state mental hospitals prior to the deinstitutionalization movement. When staffing levels in shelters cannot even ensure security, it may appear premature to consider the shortage of social and mental health services afforded homeless men and women. This is not to say that services are not needed, if only to ease the daily existence of those requiring emergency shelter. It is, rather, to insist that the value of offering clinical attention must be questioned when basic needs for food and shelter remain unmet. Conversely, it would appear that the fulfillment of basic needs would greatly aid rehabilitative or therapeutic efforts.

Present staffing levels in shelters preclude genuine assistance with the securement of entitlements, a prerequisite for obtaining a residence elsewhere. Given the extreme shortage of decent, affordable housing, moreover, the goal of appropriate residential placement elsewhere has been virtually abandoned by service staff. In two years of operation, a Community Support System team in the Men's Shelter managed to place only fifteen men in residences off the Bowery. Similarly, outreach workers are repeatedly stymied in their efforts by the lack of placement alternatives for people whose "re-engagement" may be quite tenuous.

Genuine responsibility for mentally disabled homeless people will require official acknowledgment and development of the essential missing resource in community care—supportive housing. For the homeless, therapeutic and survival imperatives are inextricably linked. Wing and Olsen[64] put it neatly when they argued that

there is always an interaction between clinical and social problems. It is rarely possible to separate the two in any way that would be convenient for the development of independent medical and social services (p 172).

Supportive housing is a basic mental health provision, without which outreach, assessment, and referral services simply cannot function effectively.

DISCUSSION

The disturbing presence of the deinstitutionalized homeless has sparked and maintained public and official attention with more intensity than the placement of discharged patients in notorious, substandard, and inappropriate housing ever did—largely, we suspect, because the latter are well-hidden from public view. The wrenching plight of the homeless also has its own persuasive power. And while it can be said that visibility itself can serve a socially useful purpose, we must be careful not to carry such a conclusion too far. The presence of the homeless on city streets can evoke reactions of repulsion as often as pity. The timeworn connotation of the streets as the abode of "bums," "derelicts," and "transients"—each class disreputable in its own distinctive way—does little to elevate concern for the majority of the homeless who do not fit such labels. Nor does the history of this country's efforts on behalf of the mentally disabled offer uncompromised grounds for hope—surely this constitutes no heresy today.

The public and professional tendency to point to the obviously disoriented ex-patients on the streets as a defense for the traditional functions of mental hospitals is worrisome. It is a Hobson's choice which depicts the options as either mental hospitalization or a life on the streets. The regularity with which mentally disabled homeless people express a strong preference for getting by as they do rather than submitting to hospitalization (where a bed and three meals are, at the least, assured) says much about human resistance to institutionalization. The high cost of in-patient care would indicate that this option will not be carried out, at least not under current state budget constraints, among which accreditation standards weigh heavily.

Given the slow rate at which mental health agencies appear to be able to develop housing, and given the scale of the need, there is little doubt that thousands of mentally disabled people will continue to reside in the streets and in emergency shelters for many years to come, unless other types of less costly facilities which ensure confinement should emerge. Perhaps some will be relegated to the criminal justice system; others have already arrived.[65,66] According to a study by the Department of Corrections, 10 percent of the prisoners in New York City jails are either former psychiatric patients or are in need of hospitalization for severe psychoses.[67]

Surely the courts will play a part in the outcome. Judge Gartenstein in *People v Spagna* made a rather special effort. He refused to convict an eighty-year-old man arrested for arson (the man had lit a fire on the floor of his flat to avoid freezing to death); he also refused to sentence him to psychiatric confinement for observation. The judge, prosecutor, and defense attorney joined forces to find the accused a suitable residence.[68] In May of 1982, a class-action suit (*Klostermann v Carey*) was filed in New York State Supreme Court on behalf of homeless men and women with histories of state psychiatric hospitalization. The suit sought community-based residences appropriate for such persons. The suit was dismissed on the grounds that

in the allocation of the state's financial resources, resulting in the unavailability of community based residences for the mentally ill, may indeed have some merit, but the forum for their presentation is not a court of law (p 8).[69]

The judge referred the homeless plaintiffs to "the voting machine" as the ultimate public remedy against poor government management. A first appeal by plaintiffs was denied; a second is being prepared.

How the expanding ranks of the "new poor" homeless will affect the position of the mentally disabled—a stigmatized but clearly deserving subgroup of the population—remains to be seen. A clear opportunity exists for demanding that common needs for decent, low-cost housing be satisfied. Meeting essential needs is essentially a political question, one of social justice, whereas the provision of services is commonly reduced to a technical or administrative problem. The domain of mental health practice cannot be restricted to the latter: decades of research and service provision have demonstrated intimate relationships between poor social environments and mental instability. Service providers cannot be expected to compensate for elemental scarcities in resources; they can, however, join a growing constituency of demand in an organized effort to challenge the official priorities which have created homelessness and which prevent its solution.

ACKNOWLEDGMENT

This work was supported in part by the Ittleson Foundation and the Van Ameringen Foundation.

REFERENCES

1. Committee Report to the Commissioner of Mental Health, Albany, New York: Office of Mental Health, 1982
2. Hearings before the House Subcommittee on Housing and Community Development of the House Committee on Banking, Finance, and Urban Affairs, No. 97-100. Washington, DC, December 15, 1982
3. Hombs ME, Snyder M: *Homelessness in America: A Forced March to Nowhere.* Washington, DC: Community For Creative Non-Violence, 1982
4. Leepson M: The Homeless: Growing national problem. Washington DC: Congressional Quarterly, October 29, 1982
5. Scull A: *Decarceration: Community Treatment and the Deviant—A Radical View.* Englewood Cliffs: Prentice-Hall, 1979
6. Castel R, Castel F, Lovell A: *The Psychiatric Society.* New York: Columbia University Press, 1982
7. Tidmarsh D, Wood S: Psychiatric aspects of destitution: A study of the Camberwell Reception Centre. In *Evaluating a Community Psychiatric Service*: The Camberwell Register 1964–1971. London: Oxford University Press, 1972
8. Cook T: *Vagrancy: Some New Perspectives.* New York: Academic Press, 1979
9. Leach J, Wing J: *Helping Destitute Men.* New York: Tavistock, 1980
10. Freeman SJ, Formo A, Alampur AG, et al: Psychiatric disorder in a skid-row mission population. *Compr Psychiatry* 1979: 20:454–462
11. Segal S, Baumohl J: Engaging the disengaged: Proposals on madness and vagrancy. *Social Work* 1980; 25:358–365
12. Baxter E, Hopper K: *Private Lives/Public Spaces.* New York: Community Service Society, 1981
13. Brown C, Paredes R, Stark L: *The Homeless of Phoenix: A Profile.* Phoenix: Phoenix South Community Mental Health Center, 1982

14. *Safety Network*, New York: Coalition for the Homeless Newsletter, July 1982
15. Morse G: "A Conceptual Paper to Develop a Comprehensive System of Care for Chronically Mentally Disturbed Homeless Persons in St. Louis, Missouri." St. Louis: Community Support Program, 1982
16. Morse G: *Homeless Men: A Study of Service Needs, Predictor Variables and Subpopulations*. St. Louis: Department of Psychology, University of Missouri, 1982
17. Central City Shelter Network: "San Francisco Homeless Survey: Preliminary Results." San Francisco, September 1982
18. Conant House: "San Francisco Support Services: A Comprehensive Approach to Services for the Chronically Mentally Ill." San Francisco, 1982
19. Arce A: "Emergency Shelters for Street People: A Psychiatric Perspective." Paper presented at the 34th Institute on Hospital and Community Psychiatry, Louisville, KY, October 10–14, 1982
20. Vergave M: "Roundtable on the Homeless". Presentation to the Administration on Drug, Alcohol and Mental Health. Rockville, MD, March 31, 1983
21. Farr R: "Roundtable on the Homeless". Presentation to the Administration on Drug, Alcohol and Mental Health. Rockville, MD, March 31, 1983
22. Council of Community Services, "Research and Program Evaluation Report on the Centralized Emergency Shelter Intake Service." Albany, NY, February 1983
23. New York Mental Health Discussion Group. Disorders in Mental Health: A Critique of the President's Commission on Mental Health. *Health/Pac* Bulletin, 12(6), July/August 1981
24. Stein LI, Test MA: *Alternatives to Mental Hospital Treatment*. New York: Plenum Press, 1978
25. Sandall H: Ex-patients Succeed in Community Living. *Innovations* 3(2), 1976
26. Cohen CI, Sichel WR, Berger D: The use of a mid-Manhattan hotel as a support system. *Community Ment Health J* 1977;13(1):76–83
27. Dubin WR, Ciavarelli B: A positive look at boarding homes. *Hosp Community Psychiatry* 1978;29(9):593–595
28. Carling P, Perlman L, eds. *Readings in Housing and Mental Health*. Prepared for HUD/HHS Technical Assistance Workshop: Demonstration Program for Deinstitutionalization of the Chronically Mentally Ill. Washington, DC: National Institute of Mental Health, 1980
29. Burger AS, Kimelman L, Lurie A et al: Congregate Living for the Mentally Ill: Patients as Tenants. *Hosp Community Psychiatry* 1978;29(9):590–592
30. State Communities Aid Association (SCAA): "Housing for the Chronically Mentally Ill." Report No. 2 of the Mental Health Action Network. New York: February 1982
31. New York City Office of the Comptroller: *Performance Analysis of Programs of New York State Assistance to New York City Agencies Serving Deinstitutionalized Psychiatric Patients*, September 21, 1979
32. Jurow GL: "Financing Long Term Care for the Chronically Mentally Impaired in New York State: An Issue Analysis." Paper delivered to the State Communities Aid Association Institute on Care of the Mentally Impaired in the Long Term Care System, June 4, 1979
33. Final Report of the SRO Project: "Survey of the Needs and Problems of the Single Room Occupancy Hotel Residents on the Upper West Side of Manhattan, New York City." New York: State Department of Social Services, May 7, 1980
34. Trends and Forecasts: *Community-Based Services and Housing for Chronically Mentally Ill Adults*. New York City: Community Council of Greater New York, May 1981
35. New York State Office of Mental Health: *Five Year Comprehensive Plan for Mental Health Services*. Albany, New York, 1981
36. Christmas J: "Final Report of the Interagency Task Force on Problems of Deinstitutionalization and the Chronically Mentally Ill." Department of Mental Health, Mental Retardation, and Alcoholism Services, New York City, July 17, 1978
37. Green CB: "Housing Single, Low-Income Individuals." Paper presented at the Conference on New York State Social Welfare Policy (Setting Municipal Priorities), New York, October 1–2, 1982

38. Crisis Intervention Services: "The Diminishing Resource: Lower-Priced Hotels in New York City, 1979." New York: Human Resources Administration, 1979

39. New York State Mental Hygiene and Addiction Control Committee: "Single Room Occupancy Hotels: A Dead-End in the Human Services Delivery System." Albany, New York: 1980

40. Reich R, Seigal L: The emergence of the Bowery as a psychiatric dumping ground. *Psychiatric Q* 1978; 50(3):191–201

41. Senate Democratic Task Force on the City of New York: *Shelter Care for Men*. Albany: The State Senate of New York, 1976

42. Bellamy C: "From County Asylums to City Streets." Office of the New York City Council President, July 1979

43. Carmody D: New York is Facing 'Crisis' on Vagrants. *New York Times*, June 28, 1981

44. New York State Office of Mental Health: Five year comprehensive plan for mental health services, 1981. Albany, NY, 1980, p 49

45. Haveliwala Y: Community Help for the Homeless. *New York Times*. Letter to the Editor, October 8, 1981

46. Herman R: New York City psychiatric wards overflow as Albany changes its mental health role. *New York Times*, December 8, 1980

47. Connell S: Letter to the Editor, *New York Times*, October 27, 1982

48. Robbins ES et al: Psychiatry in New York City: Five systems, all overwhelmed. *Psychiatric Annals*, 1979;9(5):237–246

49. Mental Health Law Project: "Arbitrary Reductions of Disability Roles." Washington, DC, March 3, 1982

50. Pear R: Fairness of Reagan's Cutoffs of Disability Aid Questioned. *New York Times*, May 9, 1982

51. New York State Office of Mental Health: *Five Year Comprehensive Plan for Services to Mentally Ill Persons in New York State: 1980*. Albany, New York, October 1, 1979

52. New York State Office of Mental Health: Internal Memo, "Level of Care Distribution of Resident Patients in State Psychiatric Center Adult Units." Albany, New York, March 31, 1980

53. Family and Adult Services: "An Investigation of the Shelter Care Center for Men (SCCM) Operations and Clientele." New York: Human Resources Administration, 1976

54. New York State Office of Mental Health: Who are the Homeless Mentally Ill? *This Month in Mental Health*. Albany, New York, 1981

55. New York State Office of Mental Health: "Shelter Outreach Project. Statistical Report, February to June, 1981." New York City: Regional Office of Mental Health, 1981

56. New York State Office of Mental Health: "Who are the Homeless? A Study of Randomly Selected Men Who Use the New York City Shelters." Albany, New York, May 1982

57. Human Resources Administration, City of New York: *Chronic and Situational Dependency: Long Term Residents in a Shelter for Men*. New York, May 1982

58. Schwam K: *Shopping Bag Ladies: Homeless Women*. New York. Manhattan Bowery Corporation, 1979

59. Vera Institute of Justice: "First Time Users of Women's Shelter Services: A Preliminary Analysis." New York City, 1981

60. Lovell A, Makiesky-Barrow S: "Psychiatric Disability and Homelessness: A Look at Manhattan's Upper West Side." Paper presented at the Conference on "The Community Support Population: Designing Alternatives in an Uncertain Environment." Syracuse, New York, November 19, 1981

61. Hopper K, Cox LS: Litigation in advocacy for the homeless: The case of New York City. *Development: Seeds of Change, Village through Global Order* 1982;2:57–62

62. Coalition for the Homeless: "Cruel Brinkmanship: Planning for the Homeless—1983." New York City, August 16, 1982

63. Hopper K, Baxter E, Cox S, et al: *One Year Later: The Homeless Poor in New York City 1981*. New York. Community Service Society, 1982

64. Wing JK, Olsen R: *Community Care for the Mentally Disabled*. New York. Oxford University Press, 1979
65. United States General Accounting Office: *Prison Mental Health Care Can Be Improved by Better Management and More Efficient Federal Aid*. (GGD-80-11) Washington, DC: 1979
66. United States General Accounting Office: *Jail Inmates, Mental Health Care Neglect: State and Federal Attention Needed*. (GGD-81-5) Washington, DC: 1980
67. Giordano MA: 10% of City Inmates Mentally Ill, Study Finds. *Daily News*, January 30, 1983
68. *People v. Spagna. New York Law Journal*, March 18, 1981
69. Wallach RW: *Klostermann v. Carey*. Decision No. 112760/82, New York State Supreme Court, August 20, 1982

Marvin I. Herz

5

Course, Relapse, and Prevention of Relapse

In recent years, a number of important studies have been published regarding both the course of schizophrenia and data about relapse in schizophrenia. Before reviewing that literature, however, one must first deal with the question of diagnosis. What is schizophrenia?

As Fenton et al[1] state, unlike many other medical conditions there are at present no independent, non-interview-derived measures that can provide construct validity for the term schizophrenia. For example, there is no measure of biochemical or physiologic abnormality that is invariably present as a trait marker of schizophrenia. Schizophrenia has been traditionally defined as an illness characterized by the apparent clustering of specific signs and symptoms, which sometimes include a typical course. Kraepelin[2] emphasized a longitudinal deterioration in defining dementia praecox, while Bleuler[3] stressed the importance of cross-sectional symptoms. The new operational definition in DSM-III requires both cross-sectional features of symptomatology, as well as evidence of a six-month duration of illness. Because construct validation is not possible, predictive validity is often used instead. The clinical course of similarly diagnosed patients is followed over time to determine whether they have similar outcomes or respond to the same type of treatments. It is known, however, that patients who have manifested established chronicity will most likely continue to be chronic in the future (chronicity predicts chronicity). The inclusion of course in the diagnosis has been questioned by some experts who believe it is tautologi-

THE CHRONIC MENTAL PATIENT
ISBN 0-8089-1649-1

Copyright © 1984 by Grune & Stratton.
All rights of reproduction in any form reserved.

cal to state that only chronic patients can be considered schizophrenic and then to prove the diagnosis valid because such patients continue to be chronic in the future.

According to Fenton et al,[1] while reliability of diagnosis has increased with the DSM-III definition (if one interviewer rates the patient to be schizophrenic, another is more likely to do so), the validity may not be any better than DSM-II clinical diagnosis in predicting treatment response or a higher prevalence of schizophrenia in the family. The European studies that will be reviewed in this chapter all used a cross-sectional diagnostic schema based on Manfred Bleuler's criteria for establishing a diagnosis of schizophrenia.[3] It is important to keep this in mind since the populations studied may have outcomes different from populations defined by DSM-III criteria.

STUDIES ON THE COURSE OF SCHIZOPHRENIA

Manfred Bleuler[3] reported on a study of 208 schizophrenic patients that he had personally treated and whose cases he had followed until their death or for at least 22 years. He also studied detailed case reports of other groups of schizophrenic patients who had been hospitalized. All patients included in his statistics had gone through at least one severe psychotic phase in their lives and all had been hospitalized. All were diagnosed by several psychiatrists as schizophrenic; borderline psychotic patients were not included. He emphasized that course should not be considered as a diagnostic criterion.

Bleuler found that after a duration of five years the psychosis did not progress any further. Rather, it tended to get better. Improvements after five years are frequent in patients who have had acute psychotic episodes in the past, while they are rare in those whose psychosis has steadily and progressively worsened. Many improved schizophrenic patients remain underactive after a psychotic episode; they lack personal initiative and have somewhat apathetic, colorless personalities: the so-called "deficit symptoms" of schizophrenia. The German psychiatrist Huber[4] agrees with this observation, claiming that the most common outcome after an acute episode is a nonpsychotic deficit state, which occurs in 40 percent of the patients. Bleuler further stated that at least 25 percent of all schizophrenic patients recover entirely after the initial episode and remain recovered permanently. Qualifications for full recovery include a lack of psychotic symptoms, a normal social integration, and the ability to work. About 10 percent of schizophrenic patients, on the other hand, remain permanently hospitalized as severe psychotics, while a middle group of 50 percent to 75 percent of the patients alternate for decades between acute psychotic phases and phases of improvement or recovery. The acute relapses become rarer for this middle group only at an advanced age. While 25 percent of patients have a lasting recovery, the number of recovered patients at any given moment after the onset of the disease is much higher, reaching almost 50 percent. Examining hospitalization alone (after the fifth year of psychosis), 25 percent of all schizophrenic patients are hospitalized at a given moment; 75 percent are not. Bleuler believes that the average course of schizophrenic psychosis has changed in this century: chronicity has become less frequent, while the number of patients characterized by a phasic course with hospital discharge and readmission has increased.

Ciompi[5] conducted a follow-up study of former patients of the Psychiatric University Hospital of Lausanne, born between 1873 and 1897, and hospitalized from the beginning of this century until 1972, who lived in a catchment area of about 500,000 inhabitants today. Twenty-nine percent of all admissions (1,642 patients) were diagnosed as schizophrenic at first admission according to strict Bleulerian criteria. High mortality during the follow-up period and other factors probably introduced a slightly favorable statistical bias in the course of the illness. The follow-up sample was of 289 patients who were examined in their homes by an experienced psychiatrist, using a semi-structured interview of about two hours' duration. Additional information was systematically collected from hospital files, family members, and other sources. Average duration between first admission and follow-up examination was 36.9 years with 50 percent of cases having had over 40 years elapse. Four outcome measures were described: admission to the hospital, type of course, global outcome of schizophrenia, and social outcome.

Admission to hospital

The total duration of hospitalization was less than one year for about half of the probands. About 25 percent, on the other hand, spent more than 20 years in hospital. Most patients spent less than 10 percent of the whole follow-up period in hospital.

Course of illness

An acute onset combined with a phasic course and a favorable outcome was exhibited by 25 percent of the sample and was the most frequent type. Compared to Bleuler's reported 25 percent, only 10 percent of this sample had had only one psychotic episode and one hospitalization. Six percent of the sample followed the most unfavorable course, beginning with an acute onset and leading directly to a severe end-state.

Global outcome of schizophrenia

This was measured by symptomatology at the end-states and was favorable in 49 percent of cases; of these, 27 percent achieved complete remission and 22 percent had minor residual symptomatology; 42 percent had unfavorable outcomes of intermediate or severe degree, nine percent had uncertain outcomes.

Social outcome

Forty percent of the patients lived with their families or by themselves, 20 percent were in community institutions, and the rest were in hospitals. Although the mean age at follow-up was 74 years, more than half were still working. About two-thirds were employed part-time, and one-third full-time. On a global score of social adaptation only one-third were rated good or fair whereas two-thirds were rated as having an intermediate or bad social adaptation. Thus the main residual of the illness was not persistent schizophrenic psychopathology: it was, rather, impaired social functioning.

Ciompi found three factors related to outcome. The first was a personality factor: the better-adapted and more harmonious the premorbid personality, the statistically more probable outcome was a favorable course of the illness. The second was illness Gestalt factor: the more florid and transient and the more acute the onset, the statistically more probable outcome was a favorable course of the illness. Third was an age factor: the further the person had advanced into old age, the statistically more probable outcome was a favorable course of the illness. Ciompi stated that aging seems to have a calming influence on the course of schizophrenia.

The German psychiatrist Huber[4] studied a sample of schizophrenic patients who had never been previously hospitalized and who were admitted to the University Psychiatric Clinic in Bonn between 1945 and 1959. They were systematically followed up between 1967 and 1973. Well-defined Bleulerian and Schneiderian criteria were used in diagnosis. Of the original group of patients that were to be studied, 142 were deceased, 48 refused an interview, and 34 could not be found; for 26, only the relatives were interviewed. Thus out of a total of 758 original residents, 502 were reported on. At the time of the last follow-up, the average duration of illness was 22.4 years. Patients were usually interviewed in their home environments: 85 percent of them lived at home. Among the 435 probands who were not permanently hospitalized, two-thirds had not been under a doctor's care for an extended period of time at the last follow-up. Twenty-two percent of the patients were in a state of complete remission, and 40 percent of patients had no schizophrenic symptoms but were considered to be in a residual deficit state. They suffered from such symptoms as cognitive disturbances, physical and mental exhaustion, disturbance of general well-being and efficiency, loss of drive, energy, and endurance, exaggerated impressionability, reduced threshold tolerance to non-specific stress, sleep disturbance, hypersensitivity to noise and weather, decrease of initiative, tendency to subdepressive moods, loss of liveliness and directness, increased need for sleep, and reduced capacity for adaptation. The remaining 35 percent were categorized as characteristic outcome types of schizophrenia with residual psychotic symptoms. Huber states that the overall pattern of findings is similar to previous long-term studies from Zurich and Heidelberg. Based on his results and those of the other studies he mentions, Huber concluded that schizophrenia does not seem to be a disease of slow, progressive deterioration. Even in the second and third decades of illness, there is still potential for full or partial recovery. Approximately 56 percent of probands were fully employed and therefore considered socially recovered. Of these, about one-third were employed below and two-thirds employed at their previous occupational level. Sixty percent of the women and 51 percent of the men were socially recovered. Patients seemed to maintain better stability after the age of 50.

With regard to prognosis, the presence or absence of secondary cases of schizophrenia or manic depressive psychosis among relatives was not found to be related to the long-term prognosis. Patients with relatively nonpathologic basic personality types had a better prognosis than those with markedly abnormal primary personalities. Elementary school failure was unfavorable prognostically; advanced education was usually favorable. The findings supported the idea that a clear-cut psychological precipitant for an episode may be regarded as a sign of a favorable prognosis. Age of onset had no significant prognostic value. The long-term prognosis in acute onset psychosis was significantly more favorable whereas the reverse was true in insidiously developing psychosis. An interesting finding was that as a result of social incompetence, schizophrenic patients tended to drift towards socioeconomically lower population groups.

Huber's data regarding treatment showed that the subgroup which was not treated during its initial psychotic episode had a significantly worse remission rate than patients who were initially treated with electroconvulsive therapy or with pharmacotherapy, or with a combination of these. There was a suggestion that there was favorable influence on long-term prognosis if a patient receives therapy, especially pharmacotherapy. This is in contrast to the results reported by Ciompi,[5] who stated that schizophrenic patients first admitted in the 40s or 50s had no better long-term course than those first admitted during the early 1900s, when ECT and antipsychotic medication were not available.

Englehardt[6] in the United States reported on a 15-year follow-up of hospitalization for a sample of 646 schizophrenic outpatients. This sample was originally part of an outpatient clinic study of maintenance pharmacotherapy versus placebo treatment. Among the 646 outpatients, 21 percent had never been hospitalized for psychiatric reasons. This sample, therefore, differs from the usual follow-up study sample which ordinarily begins follow-up after patients are discharged from the hospital. Criteria for inclusion in Englehardt's study were: 18 to 45 years old, a primary diagnosis of schizophrenia based on DSM-II criteria, and a history of mental illness of at least one year's duration. Over half the sample showed signs of mental illness for ten years or more. Sixty-eight percent were white, 28 percent black, and 4 percent hispanic; mean age on admission was 30.4 years; 53.6 percent were males. Seventy-five percent were in the lower two socio-economic classes as measured by Hollingshead's two-factor index of social position. The average duration between the study and the follow-up was 14.5 years. Most of the follow-up data were obtained from records of the New York State Department of Mental Hygiene and the Kings County

Psychiatric Hospital. For those patients who were hospitalized during the follow-up period, the investigators were able to verify the diagnosis of schizophrenia in 97 percent of cases. Data are not included for 24 patients who died during the follow-up period.

Results showed that 58.8 percent of the cohort were hospitalized at least once during the 15-year follow-up period. Hospitalization occurred within two years of admission into the study for approximately two-thirds of these patients. The average number of hospitalizations for the group as a whole was 2.7 with a median of 2.0. The average length of stay was 44.4 months; the median was 28.9 months. About 20 percent spent a total of less than three months in mental institutions while another 20 percent of those hospitalized accumulated over seven years of hospitalization. The 76 patients who had been hospitalized for more than seven years represent 11.8 percent of the entire sample of 646 patients. This is similar to the results of Huber, who found that 13.3 percent of his sample were permanently hospitalized. Similarly, Ciompi found that 14 percent of patients had spent 80 percent or more of the follow-up period in a psychiatric hospital. Englehardt found that beginning with the third year, there was a steady decline in the proportion of patients spending at least one day in a psychiatric hospital, leveling off below 13 percent beginning with year 12. This supports the contention of Bleuler, Huber, and Ciompi that schizophrenia does not seem to be a disease of slow, progressive deterioration. Bleuler and others believe that with modest rehabilitative efforts, a clinical plateau occurs after the fifth year, and there may even be a gradual improvement in many chronic cases. Englehardt found that previous history of hospitalization consistently emerged as a powerful predictor of future hospitalization. Overall results showed that 41.2 percent of the cohort succeeded in maintaining a status free of any psychiatric hospitalization with an additional 44 patients (6.8 percent) experiencing only crisis admissions during the follow-up period. Thus, 48 percent, or almost half the group, successfully escaped major psychiatric hospitalization during the 15-year follow-up period. Comparing this study with others, the major difference is that on entry into the study a substantial portion of patients had never been hospitalized. Furthermore, it should be pointed out that relapse and rehospitalization are not synonymous. There are many reasons for rehospitalization, many of which are not related directly to symptomatology. It should be noted that data for the Englehardt study were obtained from records; patients themselves were not interviewed.

What can be learned from the above studies? Bleuler, Huber, and Ciompi found favorable end-states in 53 percent, 57 percent, and 49 percent of the patients, respectively. Many of their findings are similar concerning the variables related to favorable or unfavorable outcome, such as premorbid personality and social adaptation, the type of onset, the form of development, and to some extent the initial symptomatology. All investigators found that there was no correlation between course and outcome on the one hand and genetic factors on the other.

Examining the influence of treatment, Huber identified some possible but questionable indications of a positive long-term effect of neuroleptics as well as electroconvulsive shock treatment, especially when they were given shortly after the onset of the illness. Ciompi, on the other hand, found no such relationship. It should be remembered that these are naturalistic studies, and particular types of patients may receive particular types of treatment. Neuroleptics, for example, may have been used in more severely symptomatic patients. Ciompi and Bleuler are in agreement about effective factors in treatment: a therapist who relates constantly and actively to the healthy aspects of the psychotic patient, the positive therapeutic effect of sudden and surprising changes in the patient's life which may call for the emergence of hidden resources, and calming actions and influences, which can be introduced in many ways (talking, togetherness, and neuroleptic drugs are among the best approaches). Bleuler, however, is against the regular and prolonged use of such drugs.

The basic conclusion is that there is no such thing as a specific course of schizophrenia unless one links the concept of schizophrenia itself to an obligatory bad outcome. It should be remembered that the above studies used Bleulerian or DSM-II classifications in the diagnosis of schizophrenia, and there may be problems with reliability. Also, it is possible that a higher percentage of "sicker patients" were lost to follow-up because of a higher mortality rate and other undetermined reasons.

PROCESS OF RELAPSE

For most schizophrenic patients, the course of the illness is one of exacerbations and remissions. As has been described above, most schizophrenic patients do not have a progressive, downhill course of illness. In view of the evidence that the occurrence of severe psychotic symptomatology is episodic for most schizophrenic patients, it is surprising that these episodes have not been studied in more detail. It may be that this issue was not viewed as a crucial one in the management of schizophrenia because in the past most patients were housed in custodial institutions and little attention was paid to fluctuations in the course of the illness.

Because my colleagues and I[7] were concerned about early therapeutic intervention to prevent the development of full-blown psychotic episodes, we were interested in looking at the natural history of the development of a psychotic episode. Two groups of patients in different parts of the country were studied. In Atlanta (Group A), 99 outpatients who were being treated at two community mental health centers were interviewed. Eighty family informants were seen in separate interviews. Since these were stable outpatients whose psychotic episodes had occurred more than six months prior to the interview, it was decided to interview a group of patients who had recently been hospitalized in an attempt to obtain data closer to the time of relapse. Group B consisted of 46 hospitalized patients in a county hospital in Buffalo, most of whom had been in the hospital for less than two weeks. Patients in Group A were diagnosed as schizophrenic according to DSM-II, while DSM-III was used for Group B. Most patients had been hospitalized at least two or three times. The Atlanta group was primarily suburban or rural and white, 67 percent women. The average age was 38 years, the average level of education was 9.8 years. Only 15 percent were employed, and only 33 percent were married. Approximately 73 percent had been hospitalized three or more times. The Buffalo group was largely urban, 70 percent were women, 68 percent were white, 28 percent were black, and 4 percent Puerto Rican. The average age was 38 years, the average level of education was 9.2 years. Level of employment was 26 percent, only 24 percent were married. Patients were interviewed using the Early Signs Questionnaire, a structured interview, with a few open-ended questions based on items contained in the Psychiatric Status Schedule,[8] Research Diagnostic Criteria,[9] and on clinical experience. Each patient was interviewed individually by a member of the research staff. The same interview was conducted with available family members in Atlanta.

In response to the question, "Could you tell that there were any changes in your thoughts, feelings, or behaviors that might have led you to believe that you were becoming sick and might have to go to the hospital?" approximately 70 percent of the patients in both groups noticed changes. Family members (93 percent) were much more likely to notice changes in the patients than were the patients themselves. The finding that relatives can usually recognize early symptoms of decompensation is of extreme importance for the therapeutic management of the patient, as will be discussed later.

The time interval between the beginning of symptomatology and the need for hospitalization is of great importance if full relapse is to be prevented. If relapse were sudden and abrupt, then therapeutic interventions could not be introduced in time to prevent the occurrence of a full relapse. Results showed that only 7–8 percent of patients and 11 percent of family members stated that the time period was less than one day. About 15 percent of Group B patients and 8 percent of Group A patients and their families noticed a prodromal period of only one to three days. In fact, most patients and family members said that it takes more than a week, 52 percent of Group B patients, 48 percent of Group A patients and 68 percent of families. There should thus be ample time to intervene with crisis intervention techniques, including pharmacotherapy, after prodromal signs begin and prior to the development of a full relapse.

What were the symptoms reported that either appeared for the first time or worsened during the prodromal period before full relapse and hospitalization? The Atlanta patients were outpatients in a relatively stable condition, while the Buffalo patients had recently experienced an acute psychotic episode and were still in the hospital. In spite of the demographic differences between the two groups and the differences in length of time since the last relapse, the rank–order correlation of symptoms reported that appeared or worsened before hospitalization between the Buffalo and Atlanta patients was $r = .85$, $p < .001$ (see Table 5-1). The symptom reported by most patients in both groups was becoming tense and nervous. Generally, the symptoms most frequently reported by patients and family members were of a nonpsychotic nature, the type of dysphoria that nonpsychotic individuals experience under stress, such as eating less, having trouble concentrating, having trouble sleeping, depression, and seeing friends less. The psychotic symptom most frequently reported by patients in both groups was a feeling of being laughed at or talked about. The rank–order correlation of frequency of symptoms reported by Atlanta patients and their relatives was also very high ($r = .78$, $p < .001$). Relatives ranked talking in a nonsensical way third, while it was rated thirteenth by patients. It is likely that patients are not as aware of evidence of a thought disorder as are individuals who interact with them.

Table 5-1.

Symptoms That Appeared or Worsened Before
Hospitalization in Schizophrenic Patients[a]

| | Buffalo Group (N—46) | | Atlanta Group | | | |
| | | | Patients (N=99) | | Families (N=80) | |
Symptom	Rank	%	Rank	%	Rank	%
Tense and nervous	1	80.4	1	70.7	1	83.3
Eating less	2	71.7	10	49.5	17	52.5
Trouble concentrating	3	69.6	5	56.6	3	76.3
Trouble sleeping	4	67.4	3	61.6	7	68.8
Enjoy things less	5	65.2	8	52.5	8	67.5
Restlessness	6	63.0	4	58.6	2	78.8
Can't remember things	6	63.0	14	46.5	10	60.0
Depression	8	60.9	2	63.6	3	76.3
Preoccupied with one or two things	9	59.6	12	48.5	9	65.0
Seeing friends less	9	59.6	7	54.5	18	50.0
Am being laughed at, talked about	9	59.6	9	51.5	14	53.8
Loss of interest in things	12	56.5	5	56.5	6	73.8
More religious thinking	13	54.3	10	49.5	19	47.5
Feeling bad for no reason	13	54.3	19	40.4	22	37.5
Feeling too excited	15	52.2	25	30.3	14	53.8
Hear voices, see things	16	50.0	17	42.4	10	60.0
Feeling worthless	17	48.8	15	44.5	12	56.3
Talking in nonsensical way	18	45.6	13	47.5	3	76.3

From Herz MI, Melville C: Relapse in schizophrenia. *Am J Psychiatry* 1980;137:804. With permission.

Spearman rank-order correlation for Buffalo patients and Atlanta patients $= .85$ ($p < .001$) and for Atlanta patients and families $= .78$ ($p < .001$).

Relatives ranked hearing voices and seeing things tenth and patients ranked such hallucinations as seventeenth. It may be that some relatives detect signs of the development of a psychotic episode only after the patient has already become psychotic and might therefore miss the nonpsychotic prodromal phase, or this finding could be related to the patient's denial of psychotic symptoms. There was little agreement when patients were asked to name the *first* changes in thoughts, feelings, and behavior that might have led them to believe that they were becoming sick and might have to go to the hospital. The symptoms reported, however, are similar to those previously mentioned, i.e., tension, anxiety, nervousness, insomnia, and depression. An important issue was whether the pattern of development of an episode was similar for each episode. Fifty percent of the patients answered that there was similar development of symptom progression until full relapse. Whether individual patients have or do not have the same sequential pattern of symptoms when they suffer a relapse is of great importance to the psychiatrist who plans treatment strategy. When treating a schizophrenic patient in therapy, the therapist should ask patients and significant others what they know about early signs of relapse, what the early symptoms are, whether there is a similar sequential pattern of development of symptoms, whether relapses occur at specific times during the calendar year, whether they are related to particular events, and of great importance, whether the patient becomes uncooperative and begins to deny illness at the start of an episode. If the latter behavior occurs, patients are more likely to relapse since they will often not appear for sessions at the very time they need therapeutic intervention the most. It is very important in these cases to develop relationships with family or other available informants who have been educated about early signs of relapse and who will report the early development of symptoms to the therapist.

Most previous studies on the decompensation process were carried out by gifted clinicians who reported on individual cases. Their usual approach was a detailed case study in which information was gathered retrospectively from both patients and family members. Docherty et al,[10] reviewing the literature on stages of onset of schizophrenic psychosis, were able to sift out specific phases or stages of decompensation based on case reports. They differentiated five stages, the first two stages being nonpsychotic. The first stage was labelled *Over-Extension*. The person begins to experience a sense of being overwhelmed and increasing mental effort is required. Symptomaticaly, the period is characterized by persisting anxiety, irritability, parapraxes, decreasing performance efficiency, and distractability. In this stage, the individual appears to be experiencing a stress and reacting to it. The second stage of decompensation is called *Restricted Consciousness*. During this phase, boredom, apathy, and listnessless are typically present. There is social withdrawal and decreased movement, obsessional and phobic symptoms appear or worsen and somatization frequently occurs. This appears to be a defensive phase against loss of control, with an attempt to limit external stimulation and a reinforcing of neurotic defenses.

The third stage is the first psychotic stage with a breakdown of neurotic defenses, *Disinhibition.* During this phase, relatively unmodulated impulses are expressed. It may bear a close resemblance to hypomania, with sexual promiscuity, rage attacks, and unrestricted spending. Dissociative phenomena and ideas of reference may appear and previously repressed material begins to appear in consciousness. Stage four is *Psychotic Disorganization,* with three distinct subphases: "destructuring of the external world," with an increasing perceptual and cognitive disorganization; "destructuring of the self," with the person losing his sense of self-identity (severe anxiety and the effects of panic and horror are often present, along with hallucinatory phenomena); "total fragmentation," in which the person experiences complete loss of self-control, and phenomena such as catatonia appear. The fifth stage is *Psychotic Resolution.* This period is marked by decreased anxiety and increased organization, although it is on a psychotic level. The forms this resolution takes typically involve the development of an organizing delusional system (paranoid type) or the massive denial of all unpleasant affects and responsibility (hebephrenic type). In our own study, patients were not able to distinguish two nonpsychotic prodromal stages. They did, however, report symptoms which occur in both the first and second stages of Docherty's formulation.

A conclusion that can be drawn from these studies is that for a great many schizophrenic patients who have been in a stable condition, there is a nonpsychotic prodromal phase prior to the development of severe psychotic symptomatology. It is important for the clinician to understand that this occurs, be able to recognize these symptoms, discuss them with the patient, engage the family or other informants as allies who will report early symptoms to the therapist, and be prepared to initiate prompt therapeutic measures to prevent the development of a full-blown relapse. It should be mentioned that we do not yet know whether each time a patient develops nonpsychotic symptomatology it is an early stage in the development of a psychotic episode. A cautious clinician, however, would observe the patient more closely during these times, probably initiate more therapeutic contacts, and perhaps increase medication if indicated.

PREVENTION OF RELAPSE

The majority of schizophrenic patients living in the community are in homeostatic balance with their environment. Particular patients may be asymptomatic, with or without deficit symptoms of schizophrenia, may manifest symptoms such as anxiety, tension or occasional insomnia, or have positive symptoms of the illness such as delusions, hallucinations, or thought disorder. If patients are symptomatic, symptoms may not be sufficiently disturbing to impair at least minimal functioning. According to the vulnerability model of Zubin and Spring,[11] a schizophrenic individual is more vulnerable to stress than normal individuals. If such patients are to be treated successfully, we must find ways of avoiding or decreasing social stressors which may precipitate relapse and/or find ways of decreasing the vulnerability of the patient to stress, either by therapeutic intervention with the patient or by strengthening his social support system. By decreasing stress or strengthening the patient's ability to cope, the likelihood of psychotic relapse should decrease. Furthermore, if patients and family members are educated about the existence and importance of the prodromal period, then patients and families would be more likely to be in contact with the therapist when these early symptoms appear. The likelihood of a full relapse occurring is greatly diminished with early intervention.

Various types of stress have been identified as being related to relapse. Brown and Birley[12] found that there was a marked increase in the frequency of occurrence of certain events compared with control groups during the few weeks immediately before the first onset of acute relapse in schizophrenic patients. They excluded events which could have been the result rather than the cause of a recrudescence of symptoms, and this did not diminish the extent of the association. Some of the events might have been expected to have been experienced as pleasurable while others were considered unpleasant: becoming engaged to be married or receiving a promotion at work on the one hand, and hearing about the death of a relative or being involved in a traffic accident on the other. These types of events occur to most people during the course of their lives, but it seems that patients with schizophrenia have more difficulty coping with these common stresses. In one study[7] that we conducted, most patients questioned weeks or months after a relapse were not able to identify a particular precipitant. Almost all patients interviewed during a prodromal phase, however, were able to identify a specific event.[13] When patients begin to show signs of early relapse, clinicians should carefully question the patient about possible precipitants in order to provide more effective crisis therapy. If the precipitant is identified, the patient can be helped to cope with the situation and his reaction to it in a realistic manner.

Several studies indicate that factors in the family may be responsible for precipitating psychotic episodes in schizophrenic patients. Vaughn and Leff[14] examined a group of schizophrenic patients and their families shortly after the patient's admission to the hospital, using a standard technique to describe and classify their symptoms and to ensure that the diagnosis was unambiguous. A key relative was interviewed while the patient was in the hospital and ratings were made of hostility, emotional overinvolvement (usually overprotectiveness by a parent), and criticism. Of these factors, the last proved most important and could be measured very reliably in terms of the number of critical comments made about the patient during the interview. All three factors were combined into one index called "Expressed Emotion" (EE), which was found to be significantly related to relapse during the nine months after discharge. Two other factors were important in predicting relapse: the amount of time that a patient and key relative spent in face-to-face contact with each other and whether the patient was taking phenothiazine drugs. However, it should be pointed out that patients were not randomly assigned to drugs and therefore a selective factor could have been present.

A hierarchy was established to determine the risk of relapse. Those at most risk (over 90 percent chance of relapse) were living at home in constant face-to-face contact with high EE-score relatives and were not protected by antipsychotic medication. If these patients were taking medication or if they had little contact with the involved relatives, the risk was much lower (40–50 percent). If both of these protective features were present, the risk of relapse was 15 percent, the same as if they had returned to a low EE family. Approximately half of the families were classified in the high EE and half in the low EE categories. It should be pointed out that most of the relatives' criticisms were directed not at florid psychotic symptoms but at long-standing personality traits displayed by the patients, such as lack of sociability, communication, and affection. Of interest is an American replication of the English studies by Vaughn, Synder and Liberman,[15] which resulted in a remarkable duplication of these studies, with 57 percent of the high but only 17 percent of the low EE cases relapsing within nine months of discharge from the hospital. It is apparent that cultural factors play a great role in expressed emotionality. In London about half of the families were high in expressed emotionality, in Los Angeles almost 70 percent of the families were high in this measure, and in India the majority were low.

In view of the importance of families in the course of the illness, it is extremely unfortunate that families are not routinely involved in the therapy of schizophrenic patients. Creer and Wing[16] in England conducted a survey of 80 relatives of schizophrenic patients, revealing that virtually none of the relatives had received any sensible advice about the nature of the condition, how to supervise medication, the likely outcome of treatment, or how to best respond to disturbed or disturbing behavior. Usually when a family member has a chronic physical disability such as paraplegia or renal failure, management is worked out in detail and patients and relatives are taught to predict and prevent many problems and to know what to do in a time of crisis. Not only can family members be educated regarding early signs of relapse and what steps to take to ensure the initiation of prompt and effective treatment, but education and therapeutic efforts have been shown to be effective in diminishing negative effects of family life on the patient. Goldstein et al[17] demonstrated in a controlled study that six sessions of family education following discharge from the hospital were effective in lowering the relapse rate of schizophrenic patients at six months' follow-up. A study by Leff[18] dealt with the attempt to relieve stress on the patient either by decreasing the amount of hostility or over-involvement in the family or by decreasing the amount of time the patient spent with the family by encouraging the patient to attend various programs in the community or to move out of the household. Results have shown that this approach was successful in decreasing relapse rates for patients in high expressed emotionality families. A recent study of patients from high EE families by Falloon et al[19] compared individual support- ive treatment with family treatment. All patients, regardless of treatment condi- tion, were seen according to the same schedule, weekly visits during the first three months, bi-weekly visits for the next six months, and monthly visits there- after. All patients were maintained on medication. In early sessions the family therapy approach involved education about the nature, course, and treatment of schizophrenia, while later sessions were devoted to reducing existing family tensions and improving the problem-solving skills of the family in coping with the causes of stress. Behavioral rehearsal, modeling, feedback, and social rein- forcement were used to enhance skills in the expression of positive and negative feelings, reflective listening, requests for behavioral change, and reciprocity of conversation. At the nine-month assessment, complete data were analyzed for 36 patients, 18 in each group. The findings showed that there were significant advantages of family management using measures of symptom severity, commu- nity tenure, and rehospitalization rate. It should be pointed out that family treatment seemed to ensure better compliance with the medication regimen than the individual treatment, although Falloon argues that this is not the whole explanation for the difference in outcome.

Taken together, these family therapy studies demonstrate that involvement of families in education and treatment can be effective in the long-term manage- ment of schizophrenic patients. Even in families that are not high in expressed emotionality, a therapeutic collaboration should be established. Families can be helped to function as effective caretakers of the patient and in addition receive support and guidance regarding the burdensome behaviors that some patients exhibit.

Various studies have shown that antipsychotic medication is prophylactic for most schizophrenic patients in helping to prevent relapse. Davis et al[20] reviewed the literature in 23 controlled studies and found that 20 percent of patients on active drugs relapsed over varying periods of time; 52 percent receiving placebo treatment also relapsed. Hogarty and Goldberg[21] found that 48 percent of patients on medication relapsed, while 80 percent receiving placebo treatment also relapsed over the course of their two-year study. In order to deal with the issue of patients who may relapse because of drug noncompliance, Hogarty et al[22] compared oral and intramuscular prolixin decanoate and found that approxi- mately 40 percent of patients receiving the drug relapsed in both groups by the end of one year. It seems that medication decreases the patients vulnerability to stress and thus decreases the likelihood of relapse. The medication is generally effective in treating positive symptoms of schizophrenia, such as delusions, hallucinations, thought disorder, disorganization, or agitation. It is not particu- larly helpful, however, for negative deficit symptoms such as apathy, with- drawal, or flat affect. Thus medication may help to abort the development of an acute episode and/or decrease its length and severity. It has been reported that when stable outpatients are taken off medication, most of them do not show immediate signs of relapse. Rather, they show no difference in symptomatology or role functioning. In fact, some patients show increased energy and drive.[20,22] In this respect the medication is prophylactic as are anti-hypertensive and anti-TB medications; there is no discernible effect when one goes off the medication. If a patient inadvertently stops taking his medication and then feels better, he may therefore believe that the medication is not helpful to him. Patient and family education about the role of medication has been largely neglected; patients and families should be informed that medication is especially helpful when the patient starts to become sick again, and that by taking it the likelihood of relapse is greatly diminished. Patients should know that they might not notice any difference or might even feel better if they stop taking the medication while in a stable state, but that they are more likely to relapse in the future if they stay off the medication.

In an attempt to reduce the likelihood of tardive dyskinesia, my colleagues and I conducted a study[13] in which stable outpatients who had a cooperative significant other were taken off maintenance medication. Patients were seen weekly and, together with their family members, were educated about the role of medication and signs of prodromal episodes. When a patient did show evidence of prodromal symptoms, he was placed back on active medication until he became restabilized. Results obtained using this approach have been promising, and we are now conducting a larger scale, systematic double-blind study. Carpenter et al[23] have reported similar positive results using this approach rather than a regimen of maintenance medication. In our protocol, we used a two-month gradual drug withdrawal phase to determine whether patients were controlled by or maintained on medication. There are some patients who are asymptomatic on medication but when the dosage is reduced they show immediate early signs of psychotic deterioration. For these patients the medication is actively "controlling" symptomatology, and needs to be continued on an indefinite basis. The larger group of patients are "maintained" on medication. As it is withdrawn, they show no ill effects. For these patients the medication is prophylactic in helping prevent relapse. Our study included weekly group therapy for all patients and an optional monthly meeting of a family support group. Various studies have indicated that psychosocial intervention can be extremely helpful for many schizophrenic patients in enhancing their functioning and ability to cope with stress, and that drug therapy alone is not sufficient. Individual treatment, group therapy, day treatment, and community supports have all been shown to enhance social functioning and/or reduce rehospitalization rates. It is beyond the scope of this chapter to discuss these in detail.

In summary, recent longitudinal studies indicate that there are grounds for optimism regarding the long-term outcome of schizophrenia with only a small percentage of patients demonstrating a progressive downhill course. In many patients, the course is phasic with exacerbations and remissions. It appears that these patients have an increased vulnerability to stress and a comprehensive therapeutic approach should aim to decrease stress and/or increase the patient's ability to cope. This approach should involve patients and their families. Finally, if attention is paid to incipient stages of relapse, crisis therapy approaches (including pharmacotherapy) can be effective in diminishing the likelihood of the development of a full-blown psychotic episode.

REFERENCES

1. Fenton WS, Mosher LR, Matthews SM: Diagnosis of schizophrenia: A critical review of current diagnostic systems. *Schizophr Bull* 1981;7:452–476
2. Kraepelin E: Dementia Praecox (Barclay RM trans). Edinburgh, ES Livingston, 1919
3. Bleuler ME: The long term course of schizophrenia, in Wynne L, Cromwell RL, Matthysse S (eds): *The Nature of Schizophrenia*. York, J Wiley Sons, 1978, p 631
4. Huber G, Gross G, Schuttler R, et al: Longitudinal studies of schizophrenic patients. *Schizophr Bull* 1980;6:592–605
5. Ciompi L: The natural history of schizophrenia in the long term. *Br J Psychiatry* 1980;136:413–420
6. Englehardt DM, Rosen B, Feldman J, et al: A 15-year followup of 646 schizophrenic outpatients. *Schizophr Bull* 1982;8:493–503
7. Herz MI, Melville C: Relapse in schizophrenia. *Am J Psychiatry* 1980;137:801–805
8. Spitzer RL, Endicott J, Cohen GM: *Psychiatric Status Schedule (ed 2)*. New York, New York State Psychiatric Institute, 1968
9. Spitzer RL, Endicott J, Robins E: *Research Diagnostic Criteria (ed 2)*. New York, New York State Psychiatric Institute, 1975
10. Docherty JP, Van Kammen DP, Siris SG, et al: Stages of onset of schizophrenic psychosis. *Am J Psychiatry* 1978;135:420–426
11. Zubin J, Spring B: Vulnerability: A new view of schizophrenia. *J Abnorm Psychol* 1977;86:103–126
12. Brown GW, Birley JLT: Crises and life changes and the onset of schizophrenia. *J Health Soc Behav* 1968;9:203–214
13. Herz MI, Szymanski HV, Simon JC: Intermittent medication for stable schizophrenic outpatients. *Am J Psychiatry* 1982;139:918–922
14. Vaughn CE, Leff VP: The influence of family and social factors on the course of psychiatric illness. *Br J Psychiatry* 1976;129:125–137
15. Vaughn CE, Snyder KS, Liberman RP, et al: Family factors in schizophrenic relapse. *Schizophr Bull* 1982;8:425–426
16. Creer C, Wing JK: *Schizophrenia at Home*. National Schizophrenia Fellowship, 1974
17. Goldstein MJ, Rodnick EH, Evans JR, et al: Drug and family therapy in the aftercare of schizophrenics. *Arch Gen Psychiatry* 1978;35:1169–1177
18. Leff J, Kuipers L, Berkowitz R, et al: A controlled trial of social intervention in the families of schizophrenic patients. *Br J Psychiatry* 1982;141:121–134
19. Falloon IRH, Boyd JL, McGill CW, et al: Family management in the prevention of exacerbations of schizophrenia. *N Engl J Med* 1982;306:1437–1440
20. Davis JM, Gosenfeld L, Tsai CC: Maintenance anti-psychotic drugs to prevent relapse: A reply to Tobias and MacDonald. *Psychol Bull* 1976;83:432–447
21. Hogarty GE, Goldberg SC, Collaborative Study Group: Drugs and sociotherapy in the aftercare of schizophrenic patients. II. Two-year relapse rates. *Arch Gen Psychiatry* 1974;31:603–608
22. Hogarty GE, Schooler NR, Ulrich R, et al: Fluphenazine and social therapy in the aftercare of schizophrenic patients. *Arch Gen Psychiatry* 1979;36:1283–1294
23. Carpenter WT, Stephens JH, Rey AC, et al: Early intervention vs. continuous pharmacotherapy of schizophrenia. *Psychopharmacol Bull* 1982;18:21–23

Kenneth Tardiff

6

Research on Violence

Violence and chronic mental patients were not discussed in the first edition of this book, except that in response to a concern that there were increasing numbers of patients in correctional facilities it was stated that "outcome studies of patients reviewed elsewhere in this discussion have found no more than one to three percent (and usually zero percent) of ex-patients in jail at follow-up."[1] Yet one of the major barriers to placement of chronic mental patients in the community is the fear that they may manifest violent or other antisocial behavior. Violence by patients may also pose a danger to the persons who treat them. Two studies have found that approximately 40 percent of psychiatrists have been assaulted at least once in their careers,[2,3] and a third has shown that 48 percent of psychiatric residents in one program were assaulted at least once in the several years of their training.[4] Psychiatrists are not alone in being vulnerable to assault by patients; in another study, 24 percent of mental health professionals in several disciplines reported being assaulted at least once in the past year, although more psychiatrists (34 percent) than other mental health professionals reported assaults.[5]

There have been a number of studies that have attempted to assess whether mental patients are more dangerous than the general population. The studies done prior to 1978 have been extensively reviewed by Rabkin.[6] There are a number of problems with the methodologies used in these studies that could account for their conflicting findings. For example, the use of arrest rates may underreport the actual frequency of violence and other dangerous behavior by mental patients since the patient, if identified as a *mental* patient, may be

THE CHRONIC MENTAL PATIENT
ISBN 0-8089-1649-1

Copyright © 1984 by Grune & Stratton.
All rights of reproduction in any form reserved.

79

referred to the mental health system rather than the judicial and penal system. On the other hand, the use of police contacts may overreport the frequency of violent behavior by mental patients compared to the general population because such an episode may be more likely to come to the attention of the police since the person is known to be a mental patient.

After reviewing the studies of criminal behavior among chronic mental patients Rabkin came to the following conclusions: in each study, arrest and conviction rates for various categories of violent crimes for mental patients were found to exceed those of the general population. The rate of acceleration of arrest rates for violent crimes, however, has been greater than that for the general population. She attributes the increase in the number of patients to a change in hospital policies regarding involuntary admission and retention of patients, resulting in a greater proportion of patients being discharged into the community. Furthermore, with overcrowding in the criminal justice system, mental patients who do manifest violence or other criminal behaviors are removed from the community by being placed again in psychiatric hospitals for usually brief periods of hospitalization and subsequent discharge into the community. It appeared that a prior criminal record was the best predictor in trying to determine which patients are at greater risk of subsequent criminal behavior. In the studies reviewed by Rabkin, patients diagnosed as personality disorders, alcoholics, or drug abusers appeared to be more likely to display antisocial and aggressive behavior than were other patients. It was not clear from these studies whether schizophrenics are at greater risk of violent and criminal behavior that are patients in other diagnostic categories. It also appeared that certain other patient characteristics (such as being young, unmarried, male, and belonging to certain ethnic minorities) were associated with increased likelihood of dangerous behavior among mental patients. Lastly and most disturbing, it was assaultive and other violent behavior directed toward others that appeared to be increasing among mental patients, rather than other criminal offenses such as loitering, vagrancy, or public intoxication. Rather than attribute this increased violence to the nature of the psychiatric disorder or hospitalization experience, she concluded that it was social factors and the placement of the mentally ill in the criminal justice system that account for their increased frequency of assaultive behavior.

Monahan[7] also relied on studies done prior to 1978 when addressing the issue of which mental patients are most likely to be violent. As Rabkin did, he reviewed the earlier literature in a scholarly manner and concluded that history of past violence is a strong predictor of future violence. Although some factors such as age, sex, race, economic status, alcohol and drug abuse have been found to be related to the occurrence of violent behavior, his main criticism of studies aiming to predict violent behavior was that the assessment or prediction of violent behavior was made in only one setting—usually the inpatient setting—and may not have taken into consideration factors in other settings. His monograph so extensively reviewed the literature that it is difficult to select only a few of the

studies for discussion in this chapter. The reader is encouraged to read it in its
entirety not only for the individual studies but also for a clear discussion of
approaches to the prediction of human behavior.

Another line of inquiry has involved surveys to determine the frequency and
patterns of violence among chronic mental patients. The characteristics of
patients who are assaultive and nonassaultive have been compared both for those
patients residing in psychiatric hospital as well as those presenting for admission
to psychiatric hospitals. The first series of studies reviewed in this chapter was
based on the survey of 5,164 patients residing in two large state hospitals on
Long Island. Patients who were hospitalized for less than one month were
excluded since the acute phase of the illnesses was not of as great an interest as
was the chronicity. Only 11 percent of the patients were in hospital for one month
to two years; the rest were in hospital for greater than two years, usually for
decades. The only patients excluded were those in special treatment units for
alcoholism or mental retardation, and those under 17 years of age. The surveyors
were experienced staff, predominately nurses in the hospitals. They did not,
however, assess patients on the wards where they worked. Surveyors participated
in training workshops in order to familiarize themselves with the manual of
operational definitions and items on the survey instrument. In order to complete
an assessment of a patient, the surveyor interviewed the patient and the staff
working with the patient, and reviewed the medical record. The instrument for
this survey was a revised version of the one used in a previous in-patient survey
of the psychological and physical status of mental patients.[8] Assault was defined
as a physical aggression toward other persons within a certain time frame (at
least once in the hospital in the three months preceding the survey).

There were slightly more female than male patients overall, and many of the
patients were in the older age groups. The most common primary psychiatric
diagnosis was schizophrenia, approximately 30 percent being paranoid schizophrenia and 36 percent nonparanoid. The next most common diagnosis was
psychotic organic brain syndrome, comprising 20 percent of the total patient
population. Other categories of diagnosis were mental retardation, depression,
and other nonpsychotic disorders, predominately personality disorders. Most of
the patients were white, and most of the non-white population consisted of
blacks.

ASSAULT AMONG CHRONIC INPATIENTS

The first study assessed the frequency of assaultive behavior and compared
assaultive and nonassaultive patients residing in the hospitals.[9] There were 186
(7.8 percent) male patients and 198 (7.1 percent) female patients who had physically assaulted other persons at least once in the three months preceding the
survey. Assaultive patients were more likely than nonassaultive patients to be in

the younger age groups, and in hospital for shorter periods of time. However, these periods were still in terms of years. Younger patients also were overrepresented in the diagnostic groups of nonparanoid schizophrenia, psychotic organic brain syndrome, mental retardation, and other nonpsychotic disorders. Assaultive patients, were surprisingly, underrepresented in the category of paranoid schizophrenia. Assaultive patients were twice as likely than nonassaultive patients to have seizure disorders as a current problem, and those with seizure disorders were more likely to be diagnosed as psychotic organic brain syndromes, mental retardation, or other nonpsychotic disorders. Using an adapted Nurses' Observation Scale for Inpatient Evaluation (NOSIE) scale[10] it was apparent that assaultive patients were more severely impaired than were nonassaultive patients, with regard to psychotic and depressive symptomatology as well as an increased number of attempts at suicide in the past.

Assault at or before Admission to Hospital

The findings of this survey of inpatients can be compared to the findings in my previous study of assault by patients just before or at the time of admission to hospital.[11] In that study, women were less likely than men to be assaultive, in contrast to the inpatient study where women were just as likely to be assaultive. Both studies found increased histories of assaultive behavior by patients with organic brain syndromes. For both men and women, assault in hospital was increased for the patient categories of nonparanoid schizophrenia and mental retardation, but was less likely to occur in the category of paranoid schizophrenia. Assaults outside of hospital were greater proportionally in paranoid schizophrenics, and (in men only) in the nonparanoid schizophrenia category. Lastly, there was no association between seizures and assault in the admissions study.

Both studies point out the increased likelihood of assaultive behavior by the young, and by patients in those diagnostic groups which are difficult to treat (mainly mental retardation and psychotic organic brain syndromes, particularly those of a chronic nature). The finding that hospitalized paranoid schizophrenics were less likely to be assaultive than were paranoid schizophrenics outside of hospitals invites speculation. Perhaps paranoid schizophrenics may be more amenable to treatment with neuroleptics in the early phase of hospitalization. For those patients continuing to reside in hospital, paranoid schizophrenics may be able to control their actions even though delusions or other psychopathologies continue to exist, in contrast to nonparanoid schizophrenics who are more disorganized. As will be seen later in this chapter, paranoid schizophrenics with a history of assault were more likely than other assaultive patients to be seen as no longer dangerous and to be appropriate for community placement. One wonders whether paranoid schizophrenics, once discharged, are prone to discontinue medication, resulting in a re-emergence of delusional thinking, loss of control, and subsequent assaultive behavior. Should there be a policy, analogous to parole, of compulsory compliance with aftercare, use of deponeuroleptics, and even refusal to discharge paranoid schizophrenics with a history of assault who fail to comply with aftercare treatment?

Most of the patients with assault and seizures in the inpatient surveys had problems with arteriosclerosis, senility, alcoholism, mental retardation, or other organic problems. Thus seizures probably reflected gross brain damage which in turn resulted in loss of control, impulsivity, and violence. Temporal lobe epilepsy accounted for few of the assaultive patients with seizures. Lastly the finding that female patients in hospital were just as likely to be assaultive as male patients invites speculation that one's sex role in hospital is less important than diagnosis, age, and other factors in the occurrence of violence in patients who have been in hospital for long periods of time.

Emergency Management of Assaultive Behavior in Hospitals

Returning to the survey of patients residing in hospitals, an assessment was made of which patients received various emergency control methods in the month preceding the survey for behavior dangerous to self or others. As expected, assaultive patients were more likely than nonassaultive patients to have received at least once in the preceding month emergency administration of medication, to have been placed in seclusion, straightjacket, or other physical restraints, and to have received one-to-one or constant observations in the ward in order to control dangerous behavior.

Assaultive patients in the youngest age groups were more likely, almost twice so, to have received all types of control measures. Assaultive patients in the diagnostic categories of mental retardation and other nonpsychotic disorders had a greater likelihood of receiving all three controls, while nonparanoid schizophrenics were more likely to have received only emergency medication and one-to-one supervision. Although the other diagnostic groups were not increased proportionally, these measures (particularly emergency medication and one-to-one supervision) were substantial and no doubt represent considerable staff effort and time in managing dangerous behavior in the wards.

Once again we see the difficulty in managing assaultive patients with mental retardation and other nonpsychotic disorders. Use of seclusion and restraints is a very complex and controversial topic especially where the patient does not pose an imminent danger to others. It is unclear what the legal basis is for seclusion and restraint if used to decrease stimulation received by the patient, to maintain the ward milieu, or as a behavior modification technique. There are, in addition, questions as to how long these measures should last until a physician sees a patient, about the physical and medical aspects of the seclusion room and apparatus for restraint, and how should staff be trained to handle the resistive assaultive patient. The task force established by the American Psychiatric Association will hopefully provide model guidelines that will benefit patients and reassure staff who are involved in the use of seclusion and restraint.

Medications Used for Assaultive Patients

A third study by the author analyzed the types and doses of medications used for the 384 patients with a history of assault in hospital.[12] Approximately three-fourths of the patients were being given neuroleptics routinely, usually alone or in combination with anticonvulsants. Other drug combinations were infrequent. There were two characteristics of the assaultive patients which were related at a statistically significant level to the type of medication they received routinely. Younger patients were more likely to be on neuroleptic drugs while those patients 65 years and older were more likely to be receiving no psychiatric medication on a daily basis. As expected, schizophrenics were more likely than not to be treated with neuroleptics; patients with mental retardation and other nonpsychiatric disorders, however, were also more likely than other patients to be on neuroleptics on a daily basis. Neuroleptic medication for nonschizophrenic patients should be questioned. In general, however, neuroleptics used for assaultive patients seemed to be appropriate and few patients received multiple neuroleptic medications.

Of the assaultive patients on medication, 64 percent were on daily doses in the ranges suggested by the AMA Drug Evaluations,[13] while 20 percent were on doses higher and 16 percent were on doses lower than the suggested ranges. Younger patients were on higher doses and those 65 years old and older were on lower doses. Men were on higher doses than women. Nonparanoid schizophrenics were on high doses while patients with psychotic organic brain syndrome or depression were on low daily doses. As was reported earlier, approximately one fourth of the assaultive patients had seizure disorders. Daily doses of neuroleptics, however, were not related to the presence of a seizure disorder, indicating that the dose of neuroleptics given with anticonvulsants was not lowered despite evidence that neuroleptics can lower the seizure threshold.

Level of Treatment in Hospital Versus Community Placement

The surveyors placed each patient at one of four levels in terms of mental status and treatment needed. For analysis of these data, only patients who had been in hospital for longer than three months were included since one would be more certain that they had stabilized to a large degree and would not be in the acute phase of illness.[14] The levels of care ranged from Level 1 which was the most restrictive and intense to Level 4 which indicated that the patient was stable and appropriate for community placement. As expected, 7 percent of male and 4 percent of female patients with a history of at least one assaultive episode were still dangerous to others at the time of the survey and required a highly secure psychiatric environment. At Level 2, patients with a history of assault were three times more likely than nonassaultive patients to show severe psychotic symptomatology at the time of the survey and to require intensive psychiatric services in the inpatient unit. Most patients, although the proportion was greater for nonassaultive patients, were placed at Level 3, indicating that psychiatric symptoms had stabilized, but there was a continued need for inpatient treatment. Lastly, only 13 percent of male and 12 percent of female patients with a history of assault were deemed appropriate for community placement. Patients without a history of assault were twice as likely to be appropriate for community placement.

The rest of the analysis focused on the 359 assaultive patients in hospitals for longer than three months and determined which assaultive patients were deemed appropriate for community placement and which needed various levels of inpatient supervision. The placement of assaultive patients in the four levels of supervision was analyzed with regard to age, diagnosis, sex, and race. Only age and diagnosis were related to the assignment of patients to levels of supervision. Those assaultive patients assigned to Level 1 (requiring a secure environment for current behavior dangerous to others) were more likely to be under 34 years of age and to have a primary psychiatric diagnosis of mental retardation. Assaultive patients assigned to Level 2 (needing intensive supervision for severe psychotic symptoms but not currently dangerous to others) were more likely to be under 34 years of age and diagnosed as being nonparanoid schizophrenic. Assaultive patients assigned to Level 3, who had stabilized in terms of symptoms but who were not appropriate for community placement, were over 65 years of age and overrepresented in the psychotic organic brain syndrome and other nonpsychotic disorder diagnostic categories. Assaultive patients assigned to Level 4 (appropriate for community placement) were more likely in the 34–64 year age group and in the diagnostic categories of paranoid schizophrenia and depression.

Again, these findings reflect the difficulty in treating assaultive patients with a diagnosis of mental retardation, nonparanoid schizophrenia, and psychotic organic brain syndromes. Speculation about a cycle of stabilization of paranoid schizophrenics in hospital, discharge, subsequent noncompliance with treatment, and increased assaultive behavior in the community has been discussed earlier in this chapter.

OTHER SURVEYS OF ASSAULTIVE BEHAVIOR

Craig analyzed admission data for 876 patients admitted to state hospitals in a single county in New York in a recent retrospective study, using data collected from August 1975 to July 1976.[15] Overall, 31 percent of the patients had a diagnosis of schizophrenia, 35 percent of alcohol abuse, 12 percent of depression, 7 percent of organic brain syndrome, and the rest were in other diagnostic categories. He found that 11 percent of patients hospitalized during the study period demonstrated assaultive behavior just before admission. Assaultive behavior was defined as physical violence toward other persons. He found that schizophrenic male patients, patients with "other" diagnoses, and patients with organic brain syndromes showed significantly more assaultive behavior than patients in the other diagnostic categories. The rates and diagnostic differences between assaultive and nonassaultive patients are basically similar to those found in my admissions study.[11] In Craig's study, the only significant difference in relation to the sex of the patient occurred in the "other" category, where male patients were more likely than female patients to be assaultive. Aside from that finding, once there was stratification by diagnosis there was a lack of statistically significant associations between the age, sex, and race of the patient and the presence of assaultive behavior. He concluded that the nature of the underlying psychopathology is the prime link with assaultive behavior and other characteristics of patients are related to diagnosis.

Kermani studied 53 cases of assaultive patients in an inpatient psychiatric unit of a general hospital.[16] Assaultive acts were defined as any physically abusive behavior of a serious nature which would result in injury or potential injury if not deterred. It could be directed at the patients, staff, or hospital property. This was thus a broader definition than previous studies by Tardiff and Craig cited above. He found that there were two distinct types of violent patients. One involved patients with a long history of antisocial behaviors, and who were often chronically homicidal and suicidal; the other type have neither histories of destructive behavior nor homicidal or suicidal tendencies. The latter type of patient becomes acutely assaultive only during the course of psychiatric illness, which was usually psychotic in nature. Assaults were often the product of delusional thoughts and were preceded by no warning signals. This type of patient responded to neuroleptics with a fair to good prognosis. The first type of assaultive patient with a chronic course, on the other hand, often has a history of drug abuse and depression with suicide attempts. Assault is often in response to uncontrollable impulses and is often preceded by warning signals. The prognosis for this patient in terms of assault, however, is poorer than that of the psychotic acutely assaultive patient.

There were two surveys done outside the United States. Fottrell examined incident reports at two large psychiatric hospitals and one small psychiatric unit in general hospital in England.[17] His use of incident reports could have been problematic since incident reports often underreport assaults, as was demonstrated in a study by Lion and colleagues[18] where the actual occurrence of assault in a state hospital was five times that reported in routine incident reports.

Although he used incident reports, Fottrell felt certain that there was not underreporting of assault since senior nursing and administrative personnel assured him that all assaults had been reported and in fact spot checks on the wards were done. Rates of assault in his survey cannot be calculated since it is not clear how many patients were at risk; he states, however, that there were very few serious assaultive incidents in the hospitals. Furthermore, for all assaultive incidents regardless of severity, there was a preponderance of young patients and female patients who manifested assaultive behavior. Schizophrenia was the most common diagnosis among the offending patients, and the most common victims were staff. The proportion of patients in the nonassaultive patient population with these demographic and clinical characteristics was, unfortunately, not determined. Thus it could not be said that the young, female, or schizophrenic patients were actually overrepresented in the group of patients manifesting assaultive behavior in hospital.

Addad and his group interviewed 116 schizophrenic patients in three French psychiatric hospitals and compared those without a criminal record to those with past criminal behavior, which usually involved assault or homicide.[19] Within the criminal groups several differences were found between the criminal behavior of chronic undifferentiated schizophrenics and paranoid schizophrenics. Although patients of both diagnoses often acted with premeditation, paranoid schizophrenics were more likely to commit crimes against persons, to be under the influence of their illness during the crime, to be secretive about plans, to admit their guilt, and to cite vengeance as a motive than did chronic undifferentiated schizophrenic patients.

Although they were done prior to 1978 there are other studies that have found increased verbal or physical aggression in paranoid schizophrenics, and only one study which found no statistically significant increase in physical aggression in paranoid schizophrenics. Blackburn examined 48 schizophrenic men, hospitalized in England, and found that 63 percent of the paranoid schizophrenics and 24 percent of nonparanoid schizophrenics had a history of previous aggressive behavior.[20] Plansansky and Johnston found that overall 58 (29 percent) out of 205 schizophrenic men hospitalized at Veterans Administration hospital made explicit verbal threats to kill or had actually attacked people sometime in the past.[21] Again, there was increased likelihood of a history of homicidal threats or assaultive behavior in the paranoid schizophrenic group and most of the aggressive threats or behavior occurred during acute psychotic episodes. Shader and his colleagues examined 45 schizophrenic patients, in the inpatient units or in the day hospital of a state hospital, patients who had any recorded episode in which physical aggression was directed toward others.[22] They found that patients diagnosed as the schizoaffective subtype were more likely to have a history of physical aggression while paranoid schizophrenics had no increase; other schizophrenics had a decreased likelihood of aggression. They also noted that schizophrenics who had been hospitalized for longer than 100 days had greater likelihood of aggressive behavior than did those schizophrenics hospitalized for less than that length of time. In a study by Bach-Y-Rita and Veno, 13 out of 62 habitually violent patients from a prison population merited a diagnosis of paranoid schizophrenia in spite of the fact that psychotic inmates, or those perceived as being such by the correctional authorities, were excluded from the unit they studied.[23] They also found another subgroup of habitually violent patients who had a high incidence of self-destructive behavior and self-mutilation.

Fareta assessed 438 psychiatric patients from the ages of 5 to 15 who were admitted to a state psychiatric hospital.[24] She found that 66 (15 percent) patients, all 12 years or older, had a history of serious violence which included homicide, sexual attack, attacks or threats with deadly weapons, arson or serious suicide attempts or threats. Those patients with a history of one or more of these behaviors were more likely to be boys from minority groups, diagnosed as schizophrenic, and having a low average intelligence quotients. She was able to follow only 18 subjects for a period of 18 years; they did, however, have a high degree of continued antisocial and criminal behavior with decreased psychiatric involvement as the subjects matured.

It is appropriate to close this chapter with a study of children who grow up to manifest continued violent behavior since it would be incorrect to think that the violent chronic patient is a problem of the past. Although we tend not to institutionalize patients as much as we have in the past, there are indications that new young chronic patients will pose problems for us in the management of assaultive behavior. We should not, in other words, expect the large population of chronic patients hospitalized in the past to disappear as they succumb to old age. Two groups of researchers, one in California[25] and the other in New York[26] have alerted us to the emergence of young, violent, chronically mentally ill patients. The advances presented in this book and in those to come will, hopefully, help us meet the challenge of this life-threatening aspect of chronic mental disorders.

REFERENCES

1. Minkoff K: A map of chronic mental patients, in Talbott, J (ed): *The Chronic Mental Patient.* Washington, DC, American Psychiatric Association, 1978, pp 11–37
2. Madden DJ, Lion JR, Penna MW: Assault on psychiatrists by patients. *Am J Psychiatry* 1976; 133:422–425
3. Tardiff K, Maurice W: The care of violent patients by psychiatrists: A tale of two cities. *Can Psychiat Assoc J* 1977;22:83–86
4. Ruben I, Wolkon G, Yamamoto J: Physical attacks on psychiatric residents of patients. *J Nerv Ment Dis* 1980;168:243–245
5. Whitman RM, Armao BB, Dent OB: Assault on the therapist. *Am J Psychiatry* 1976;133:426–431
6. Rabkin JG: Criminal behavior of discharged mental patients: A critical appraisal of research. *Psychol Bull* 1979;86:1–27
7. Monahan J: *The Clinical Prediction of Violent Behavior.* US Government Printing Office, Washington, DC, 1981
8. Tardiff K, Deane K: The psychological and physical status of chronic psychiatric inpatients. *Comp Psychiatry* 1980;21:91–97
9. Tardiff K, Sweillam A: The occurrence of assaultive behavior among chronic psychiatric inpatients. *Am J Psychiatry* 1982;139:212–215
10. Honigfeld G, Gillis RD, Klett JC: NOSIE-30: A treatment-sensitive ward behavior scale. *Psychol Rep* 1966;19:180–182
11. Tardiff K, Sweillam A: Assault, suicide and mental illness, *Arch Gen Psychiatry* 1980; 37:164–169
12. Tardiff K: The use of medication for assaultive patient. *Hosp Community Psychiatry* 1982; 13:307–308
13. American Medical Association Department of Drugs, AMA Drug Evaluations, 4th Edition. Chicago, American Medical Association, 1980

14. Tardiff K: Assault in hospitals and placement in the community. *Bull Am Acad Psychiatry Law*, 1981;9:33–39

15. Craig TJ: An epidemiologic study of problems associated with violence among psychiatric inpatients. *Am J Psychiatry* 1982;139:1262–1266

16. Kermani EJ: Violent psychiatric patients: A Study. *Am J Psychother* 1981;35:215–225

17. Fottrell E: A study of violent behavior among patients in psychiatric hospitals. *Br J Psychiatry* 1980;136:216–221

18. Lion JR, Snyder W, Merrill GL: Underreporting of assaults on staff in state hospitals. *Hosp Community Psychiatry* 1981;32:497–498

19. Addad M, Benezech M, Bourgeois M, et al: Criminal acts among schizophrenics in French mental hospitals. *J Nerv Ment Dis* 1981;169:289–293

20. Blackburn R: Emotionality, extraversion and aggression of paranoid and non-paranoid schizophrenic offenders. *Br J Psychiatry* 1968;115:1301–1302

21. Planansky K, Johnston R: Homicidal aggression in schizophrenic men. *Acta Psychiatr Scand* 1977;55:65–73

22. Shader RI, Jackson AH, Harmatz JS, et al: Patterns of violent behavior among schizophrenic inpatients. *Dis Nerv System* 1977;38:13–16

23. Bach-Y-Rita G, Veno A: Habitual violence: A profile of 62 men. *Am J Psychiatry* 1974; 131:1015–1017

24. Fareta G: A profile of aggression from adolescence to adulthood. An 18 year follow-up of psychiatrically disturbed and violent adolescents. *Am J Orthopsychiatry* 1981;51:439–453

25. Sheets JL, Prevost JA, Reihman J: Young adult chronic patients: Three hypothesized subgroups. *Hosp Community Psychiatry* 1982;33:197–203

26. Lamb HR: Young adult chronic patients: The new drifters. *Hosp Community Psychiatry* 1982; 33:465–468

John A. Talbott

7

Education and Training for Treatment and Care

Given the striking interest in the public policy and service delivery issues relating to the care and treatment of the chronically mentally ill, it is surprising that there has been so little interest in education and training issues over the past five years. This is probably the combination of a number of factors, including the traditional neglect of the public mental health sector by academia, the stigma and low status attached to those working in and training people to work in programs serving the chronically mentally ill, and the fact that little training money has been directed toward this population (e.g., compared with consultation-liaison training funds).

It is, in addition, interesting that it seems that more attention in the literature has been paid to training physicians to deal with the chronically mentally ill than to other mental health professionals. This is probably also multidetermined, in part due to the fact that physicians may have the most to learn about treatment and care of this population, because physicians have been in the forefront of the recent surge of interest in the chronically mentally ill, or perhaps that other professional academic groups have fewer resources to expend in pursuit of altering training programs to meet the needs of this population.

In any event, this chapter will summarize the recent thinking and writing regarding training and educational programs to care for the chronically mentally ill. It will review what we know about who now takes care of this population; the curriculum content, experiential exposure and attitudinal factors comprising ideal educational programs; the hows of actually training persons to work with

THE CHRONIC MENTAL PATIENT
ISBN 0-8089-1649-1

Copyright © 1984 by Grune & Stratton.
All rights of reproduction in any form reserved.

the chronically mentally ill; and problem areas in training, such as burnout and countertransference.

EXPERIENCE OF THOSE CARING
FOR THE CHRONICALLY ILL

Schwartz, Kreiger, and Sorenson conducted a survey of 75 psychiatrists in the San Francisco area. 39 percent responded, 82 percent of whom worked part-time or full-time in public settings.[1] Despite the methodological limitations in this pilot study, several findings are of interest.

These individuals had been exposed to long-term experiences caring for severely disturbed patients in their residency training programs. They also had realistic goals about and familiarity with the long-term course of chronic mental illness, were familiar with a comprehensive approach incorporating community supports, supportive psychotherapy, and medication; and they saw these patients as individuals. The research team found that the respondents were most satisfied by small improvements in their patients' conditions, maintaining patients in the community, the positive aspects of the physician–patient relationship, and working with members of a community support service team. They were least satisfied by the frequent relapses that their patients suffered, bureaucratic obstacles, patients' negative attitudes, devaluation of their work by society, and the lack of continuity of care.

The survey, albeit tentative and small in scope, does provide some interesting and logical information that is of help in devising educational programs to train practitioners to care for the chronically mentally ill. It is important to note that since over 50 percent of the *psychiatric* care of the mentally ill is provided by nonpsychiatric physicians, it is critical to include all physician training programs when considering medical education. So much of the care of the chronically mentally ill in rural areas is carried out by family physicians or general practitioners, and in urban areas by general hospital emergency room physicians, that the entire medical community must become aware of the treatment and care needs and services for this population.

In most medical school curricula little attention is currently paid to chronic mental illness and students are rarely or only briefly exposed to clinical work with this population—a striking contrast to their exposure to seriously and chronically medically ill patients. In addition, physicians in nonpsychiatric residencies are woefully lacking in such knowledge and few continuing medical education programs concentrate on the chronically mentally ill.

The next sections will address the levels of education: medical school, residency, and continuing medication education. Within each three areas are stressed—curriculum content, experience, and attitudes, which I believe from the current literature[3-6] are of equal importance, and while overlapping, must be dealt with simultaneously.

EDUCATIONAL PROGRAMS

There are several themes common to all levels of education that must be considered when implementing teaching programs directed to the care and treatment of the chronically mentally ill. Foremost are the special features of this patient population. It is critical that a correct clinical diagnosis be made, in order that treatment planning can be realistic, effective, and rational. A complete and accurate functional assessment must also be made, so that a similarly appropriate rehabilitation plan can be devised. Most clinicians are primarily oriented toward the patient's history and past medical records as they relate to the medical condition. There is frequently little or no emphasis on the patient's level of functioning (interpersonally, socially, and vocationally), and in performing the activities of everyday living. Such a history and current status will often have much more bearing on the treatment and care plan than the traditional medical components of a past history and current status. Another critical element involves the appropriate and effective use of psychoactive medication. Recent research has underlined the importance of determining at what phase in the illness a patient is, so that patients are provided correct medication when relief of acute interfering symptoms is necessary, but not treated with excessive dosages of medication when certain psychosocial tasks demanding coping skills are required.[7] Likewise, the psychopharmacologic treatment of schizophrenia is so dramatically different from the major affective disorders that such differences must be thoroughly understood, even by those who are used to dealing with the problem on a daily basis.

The second major theme relates to the role of the physician in the care of the chronic mentally ill. To date, most physicians have either dealt with such patients by isolating their medical condition from their broader psychosocial condition or have attempted to become all things to all these patients. Neither approach achieves the maximum benefit. Physicians must appreciate the patients' medical and psychiatric problems in their larger social context. They must also realize that a range of disciplines and agencies is required to meet the many disparate needs of this group. Their role, then, must not be one of a medical specialist in isolation or a jack of all trades, but a medical specialist integrated with the larger human services network capable of meeting the needs of the mentally disabled person. Communication, referral, monitoring, and alertness to other problem areas is therefore, critical.

The third major theme relates to the need for a wide variety of professionals and paraprofessionals other than physicians to be involved in caring for the chronically mentally ill. The host of services required by chronic patients living in the community is provided by a number of persons from a variety of disciplines—physicians, nurses, social workers, psychologists, activities therapists (e.g., occupational, recreational, and dance therapists, etc.), rehabilitation counsellors and workers, educators, housing experts, and so on. A new role assumed by some of these, and at times a new profession or paraprofession generally unknown to others in medical practice, is that of the case manager. The case management approach provides the cohesion that links the patient with the services needed (e.g., medical and psychiatric care, housing, income maintenance, vocational and social rehabilitation, etc.).

The fourth theme needing emphasis at all levels of education is that of programs for the chronically mentally ill. Clinicians do not generally realize the wide range of programs required by chronic mental patients. Such persons must be concerned with the patient's daily life. It is not necessary that they be familiar with the specifics of how all the patient's needs are met, nor need they necessarily know all about the programs in a given community that form a network, but they should know how to put the patient and themselves in contact with that network. They should also recognize that they are part of the network, and of a bigger treatment team. Most programs in the network also function as teams, with all the members specified above actively working together, each in his or her own way, using his or her own particular skills to meet the patient's needs.

The final common element is that of the concept of a community support system. While inherent in the above comments on personnel and programs, it is necessary to emphasize that chronic patients require the provision of care by the array of services comprised by a community support system. Just as the patient might or might not have received care in a total institution (such as a state facility) from a variety of personnel and programs—from cooks to radiologists, from psychotherapy to vocational training programs—the same must be available to and accessible by him in the community, and thereby, form his out-of-hospital support system. It is important that educational programs directed toward persons who will be dealing with chronic patients should specify how the elements in this system work and relate to one another.

In addition to these features which are common to all education at whatever level, there are features that should be stressed at each particular level. Their details are given in the following sections, which focus on three areas: curriculum content, experiential training, and attitudinal issues.

Medical School

Attitudes regarding chronic mental illness and the chronic mental patient undoubtedly are the most critical in the education of medical students. The current emphasis on acute treatment, acute medical facilities, and the surgical ("excision") model must be modified. The population with which we are concerned must be seen as being in need of long-term support and care, with exacerbations constituting only a small portion of their "patienthood." Emphasis must shift from acute to chronic, from time-limited to prolonged, from cure to care. Another attitude that must be imparted involves the breadth of the team involved in the optimum care of chronic patients. Most medical students are aware of a nurse, perhaps a secretary or receptionist, and if involved in electives in some areas, a specialty team. The psychiatric and psychosocial team is a much larger entity and requires special attention, especially regarding information exchange, decisions about treatment plans, etc.

Teaching must reflect the multidimensional aspect of the patient's care. Didactic material should encompass not only the medical and psychiatric aspects in the treatment and care of the chronic patient, but the psychosocial and rehabilitation elements as well. Teaching should also involve persons from disciplines other than medicine, preferably not only in the classroom, but in chronic care or community settings.

This last component, experience in chronic care and community settings, is most important. We recognize the great value of experiences outside the hospital in the education of young physicians. Exposure to chronic patients, especially those involved in high-quality programs rather than those who are simply living in board and care homes or welfare hotels, would do much to set medical students thinking in an appropriate frame.

Nonpsychiatric Residency Programs

Nonpsychiatric residency programs represent another level of potential change in orientation in order to facilitate better care of chronic mental patients. Certainly those programs whose graduates deal with large numbers of chronic patients, such as internal medicine, general practice, family practice, and emergency medicine, should offer more teaching in and exposure to chronic mental illness. Even in other specialities, some additional instruction would be useful.

There is a special need to impart our current understanding concerning psychoactive drugs to nonpsychiatric residents. Their use, side-effects, contraindications, cross-over effects, etc., should be identified. The problems of compliance and noncompliance should also be imparted. The dilemma of the detrimental effects of long-term medication (e.g., renal damage or tardive dyskinesia) versus the detrimental effects of its cessation (e.g., recurrence of psychosis, regression, or other disabling symptoms) must be discussed.

It would be experientially useful for all medical specialists to have some actual contact with a mental health or community support team. This is critical in conveying the necessity of team operations, and the wide variety of services needed by chronic patients, as well as helping to educate the physician about how to tap into supportive networks when he is in practice.

With regard to attitudes, the specialist must appreciate that he need not function alone or in isolation, and that the other elements in the helping system are available. Where they are not, the physician needs to know what gaps exist and (in his role as community leader) be cognizant of their existence. The physician also needs to understand the necessity of communicating with the team of persons and network of agencies dealing with the patient.

Psychiatric Residency Programs

There is an equal need for psychiatric training programs to attend to the problems of the care and treatment of the chronically mentally ill. Psychiatric training programs have for years concentrated predominantly on in-patient care of the acutely ill, previously moderately well-functioning person, emphasizing insight-oriented psychologic therapies. With the chronic mental patient population, the education needs are the reverse: the ambulatory care of the chronically ill, never-functioning person, emphasizing rehabilitative and support system elements.

Woefully absent from most university residency programs is any exposure to the truly chronic patient in either an in-patient or high-quality, community-based, team-run program. If there is such, it occurs in the in-patient service of the university hospital, without follow-up exposure to a community support system; or as a grudging duty in a medication clinic in an OPD with little rehabilitative or community support connections, or for a token period in an overwhelmed and poorly-run state hospital or community mental health center. Prestige, quality, and investment do not seem connected with many chronic patient programs to which our residents are exposed. There is also a need for the resident to be involved in an important rather than a token role on an outpatient community team; with a low-intensity, low-contact setting; with emergency crisis exposure to chronic patients; and in consultation with community services. The resident must understand the variety, breadth, and scope of the skills of persons working in a variety of settings in the community care of chronic patients. He must also have the opportunity to work intensively and continuously with chronic patients throughout his residency program, and be assisted in the period of "transition of practice" from residency training, the most critical recruitment period.

Regarding curriculum content, pharmacology is usually emphasized, but too little time is devoted to the problems of the care and treatment of chronic patients, their special needs, the elements of a community support system, and the activities and responsibilities of all members of a community team. It is likewise necessary to improve the teaching of administration and systems approaches, legal issues, supportive psychotherapy, activities therapies, collaboration with patients and families, and knowledge of community-care settings and agencies. Seminars and courses which concentrate on psychopathology, disease entities, and treatment modalities all need alteration to include the elements of disability, functional assessment, and care of the chronically mentally ill over a long period of time. Such a focus should deal with the medical needs of such patients, the necessity for continuity of care and case monitoring, and the importance of a comprehensive spectrum of services. In all these endeavors the resident must receive high-quality teaching and supervision, not second-class treatment. Finally, a critical need is for attitudinal change, both on the part of training directors as well as the general faculty. There are too few professional role models of clinicians dedicated to high quality community care of the chronically mentally ill for interested residents to emulate. Teaching about chronic illness tends to get shunted off to the side or end of courses, and exposure to such patients is perceived as drudgery, as unimportant, or as unsexy. One mechanism for change is the involvement of training programs in the service programs that deal with chronic patients. Salary incentives may also help alleviate the paucity of high-quality persons entering this area. Emphasis also needs to be placed on an exploration of the issues of passiveness and dependency and the psychiatrist's ability to tolerate these, as well as on the necessity to perceive that the chronically mentally ill person can react "neurotically" to the stress of chronic mental illness, as we all would react to other stresses.

Continuing Medical Education (CME) Programs

While changes in the curricula of medical schools and residency training programs can be mandated by their respective faculties, changes in CME practices are less easily influenced, since physicians attend CME courses according to their perceived needs and current interests. Too little CME material is directed toward this patient population. With the increasing interest in the chronic patient, however, it will be interesting to see if the "market" follows the need. Certainly in terms of content there is a pressing need to update practicing physicians on the problems and treatment of the chronic mentally ill. Information about modern drug treatment, community support systems, rehabilitative techniques, and research relating to the prevention of chronicity all have their place in CME programs.

In addition, while many nonpsychiatric physicians have considerable contact with chronic patients in their offices or traditional medical settings (e.g., hospital wards, emergency rooms, etc), they have little exposure to the newer, highly successful psychosocial rehabilitation programs in the community or to comprehensive community mental health programs that serve the chronic patient. Exposure to such programs and services, either in an educational or consultative capacity, should greatly enhance practitioners' effectiveness in dealing with the chronically mentally ill.

A considerable amount of attention should also be given to the attitudes of the practicing physician toward the chronic mental patient. Physicians need to be helped to see persons with chronic mental illness in their total social context, to view their illness as but one part of a complicated skein of problems in life, and to assess the current symptomatology as part of the "whole patient."

There is also a need to retrain and update the training of psychiatrists practicing in chronic care settings (e.g., state hospital, nursing homes, etc.). While such efforts are not the primary responsibility of CME activities, they would not only upgrade the physician's skills in his currently bounded job, but permit the physician to become more involved in providing continuity of care for discharged patients and in developing community supportive care.

Generic Training Programs

An elaborate training scheme for all mental health professions working with the chronically mental ill has been developed by the Western Interstate Commission for Higher Education (WICHE).[8] In a manner somewhat different from that given above, knowledge, skills/abilities, and attitude/personality characteristics have been specified in several key areas: psychiatric/mental health services, including medication, psychotherapy, crisis intervention, hospitalization, and case management; practical/rehabilitative services, including residential services, training in independant living skills, and vocational services; and community services, which include natural support network services, advocacy services, and community development services.

Together, their curriculum contains all the essential ingredients for all training programs dealing with those who will care for the chronically mentally ill, and is an invaluable reference.

The Hows of Training Programs

To implement the principles of education summarized above, several training programs have published descriptions of their programs. One of the most detailed is that from the University of Oregon,[9] where residents spend part of their first year in state hospitals, their third year working in community mental health centers, and their fourth year in a community support program. They thus have exposure to patients in hospital, CMHC, and community programs. The didactic content imparted includes community psychiatry, case management, planning linkages, social network theory, deinstitutionalization, psychosocial rehabilitation, and interdisciplinary collaboration.

Another program, at the Massachusetts Mental Health Center, used a more "traditional" residency, which was then adapted to the need to train residents better regarding chronic care.[10] This program tries to prepare the resident to assume multiple roles after graduation: primary clinician, consultant to a multidisciplinary team, medical backup, and administrator. To do this, the program fosters the residents' involvement with psychosocial rehabilitation programs, nursing homes, vocational rehabilitation programs, families, etc. In addition, didactic content is presented dealing with the natural history of chronic conditions, maintanence medication, work with a multidisciplinary team, therapy with chronic patients, psychiatric rehabilitation, and alternatives to hospitalization.

A final example is that from St. Vincent's Hospital in New York.[11] Here the resident has an experience with chronically mentally ill individuals as part of a Preventive Treatment Program whose purpose is rehabilitation and maintenance of this population. The unifying concept of the program is case management, and the resident functions in a consultative/supervisory relationship with the case manager. There is also a strong research component to the rotation.

In addition to these examples of how it *is* done, Talbott[12] has spelled out how *not* to train residents. He suggests that unsuccessful programs have no linkage with university departments (or a relationship that involves no clinical responsibility), rotations that are token experiences, courses that are unrelated to the chronic mental patient, and separate tracks; they ensure that the role of the resident is either unclear, devalued, overburdened, or narrow in scope (e.g., prescription writing). There are teachers and supervisors who are only psychodynamically/psychoanalytically-oriented or will only supervise "good" therapy patients, or are second class, or burned out, or private practicioners with no public sector experience; courses which are only psychodynamically/psychoanalytically oriented, involve no systems or administrative content, or functional assessment and rehabilitation; role models who are absent, weak, noncharismatic, second class, or burned out. Research is sometimes only nonclinically oriented, or unrelated to the clinical program, or absent altogether in any public affiliation; teams place residents under the supervision of a paraprofessional or have no team leader; services expose the resident only to institutional services, do not use community support programs or community agencies, and offer no family contact, OPD experience, or home visiting–home care. There is also overinvolvement of residents early in their training (e.g., PGY 1 or 2 year) rather than after their identity as psychiatrists has begun to solidify.

NEGATIVE ATTITUDES

A valuable adjunct to all training programs is a series of videotaped "trigger films" made by Robinowitz and associates[13] as part of an American Psychiatric Association–National Institute of Mental Health Project on the Chronic Mentally Ill. In these films, a variety of negative attitudes about work with the chronically ill is presented. The intention is that each trigger film will be followed by a discussion of the filmed incident. These include presentation of material about therapeutic pessimism regarding chronic mental illness (e.g., relapse in schizophrenia), use of only one mode of treatment (e.g., psychodynamically-oriented psychotherapy), dealing with families of the chronically ill, patient compliance with medication, advising a mentally ill spouse about divorce, physician-refusal to do family therapy, make home-visits, or accept chronic patients in a group, accepting jobs in the public sector, supervisors discouraging residents who want to work with the chronically ill (e.g., in a psychodynamic way), teachers denigrating aftercare work with the chronically mentally ill, and negative attitudes about community care of the chronically mentally ill.

Countertransference attitudes have also received special attention in the Massachusetts Mental Health Center Program.[10] Here, the faculty attempts to deal with such issues as hope versus poor prognosis, rehabilitation versus treatment, fear of precipitating psychoses, maintaining limited goals, and finding chronic patients "less interesting."

In addition, Stern and Minkoff[14] have written about the attitudes of those working in community clinic that must be dealt with to care effectively for the chronically ill. These include the notion that the clinic is not appropriate for chronic patients, that it must be all things to all people, and that it should "cure" people. The authors suggest shifting the emphasis of clinicians' attitudes from primary to tertiary prevention; from treating everyone to only treating the sickest patients; from gaining esteem out of seeing "good" patients to gaining it from seeing "difficult" patients; from valuing the ability to treat patients who can benefit from their treatment to use of new techniques; from valuing cure to providing care; and from avoiding the attitude of returning those patients doing badly to state hospitals to finding new resources for them.

Burnout among staff has also been an issue of concern for many years but which in the past five years has continued to challenge experts. Mendel[15] suggests that burnout can be diagnosed when staff begin to blame and label the patients, become bored, complain, increase their frequency of meetings, and show signs of disorganization. It is agreed that burnout is caused by low staff/patient ratios, high numbers of schizophrenic patients, long hours, poor staff/patient interactions, high frequency of staff meetings, few "time-outs," less sharing of work, higher education and rank, longevity in the field, a decreased sense of success and control, a decreased sense of closeness to patients, less humanistic views, and more time with patients, others, and administration. The solutions to burnout among staff flow directly from these causes. They include decreasing unrealistic expectations, not expecting personal needs to be met by patients, recognizing and discussing the problem of burnout openly, altering the case mix, allowing for more "down time," participating in outside education, increasing the staff/patient ratio, decreasing the sequential number of hours of work, sharing patient care responsibility and improving work relations in as many ways as possible.[15-18]

THE FUTURE

As with so many areas involving the chronically mentally ill, an analysis of the literature over the last five years reveals that the trick is no longer isolating what needs to be done but doing it. It is now clear that we know the principles underlying good training programs, what works and doesn't work in translating these principles into actual training situations, and what attitudes need to be overcome to deliver both good training and good service programs. We must now use this knowledge to realize our intentions.

REFERENCES

1. Schwartz S, Krieger M, Sorensen J: Preliminary survey of therapists who work with chronic patients: Implication for training. *Hosp Community Psychiatry* 1981;32:9–800
2. Goldberg ID, Babigian HM, Locke BZ, et al: Role of non-psychiatrist physicians in the delivery of mental health services: Implications from 3 studies. Public Health Reports 1978; 93:240–245
3. Nielsen AC, Stein LI, Talbott JA, et al: Encouraging psychiatrists to work with chronic patients: Opportunities and limitations of resident education. *Hosp Community Psychiatry* 1981;32:767–775
4. Talbott JA: Medical education and the chronic mentally ill. Journal of the National Association of Private Psychiatric Hospitals 1980;11:58–63
5. Wilford BB (ed): Physicians and Chronic Patients: Potentials for Community Based Care. Chicago, American Medical Association, 1981
6. The Chronic Patient: New Approaches to Treatment and Training. Washington, DC, American Psychiatric Association, 1981
7. Segal SP: Attitudes toward the mentally ill: A review. *Social Work* 1978;34:211–217
8. Davis M: From Dependence to Independence: Staffing Community Program for the Chronically Mentally Ill. Boulder, CO, Western Interstate Commission on Higher Education, 1981
9. Cutler, DL, Bloom JD, Shore JH: Training psychiatrists to work with community support systems for chronically mentally ill persons. *Am J Psychiatry* 1981;138:98–202
10. White HS, Bennett, MD: Training psychiatric residents in chronic care. *Hosp Community Psychiatry* 1981;32:339–343
11. Mayo J, Babel R, Carvello, R: Planning for the future in psychiatric training: The place of the chronic care program. *Compr Psychiatry* 1982;23:1–8
12. Talbott, JA: How not to train residents to care for the chronically mentally ill, unpublished paper
13. Robinowitz C, Lurie HJ, Quick SK: Improving psychiatric supervision. Videotape. Washington, DC, American Psychiatric Association, 1982
14. Stern R, Minkoff K: Paradoxes in programming for chronic patients in a community clinic. *Hosp Community Psychiatry* 1979;30:613–617
    Health Services 1979;2:75–83
16. Pines A, Maslach C: Characteristics of staff burnout in mental health settings. *Hosp Community Psychiatry* 1978;29:233–237
17. Lamb HR: Roots of neglect of the long term mentally ill. Psychiatry 1979, 201–207
18. Lamb HR: Staff burnout in work with long-term patients. *Hosp Community Psychiatry* 1979;30:96–98

PART II

Treatment and Rehabilitation

John M. Kane

8

Psychopharmacology

Recent efforts to improve the psychopharmacologic treatment of the chronic mental patient have focused on two major areas: attempts to explain the heterogeneity of drug response in schizophrenia, and attempts to improve the benefit/risk ratio of long-term ("maintenance" or "prophylactic") pharmacologic treatment.

HETEROGENEITY OF DRUG RESPONSE

Despite the proven efficacy of antipsychotic or neuroleptic drugs in alleviating the signs and symptoms of schizophrenia, a substantial minority of patients derive little or no benefit from these drugs. Understanding the basis for these variations in treatment response could lead to more effective treatment strategies and ultimately reduce the numbers of chronic patients and/or improve the outcome of their treatment.

Diagnostic Variables and Patient Characteristics:
The Search for New Biologic Subtypes

The introduction of the DSM-III criteria have been helpful in improving the validity and reliability of psychiatric diagnosis in general. It remains clear, however, that considerable phenomenologic heterogeneity exists among patients receiving the diagnosis of schizophrenia and that more refined criteria for subtypes would also help in improving drug-treatment response. There are few

THE CHRONIC MENTAL PATIENT
ISBN 0-8089-1649-1

Copyright © 1984 by Grune & Stratton.
All rights of reproduction in any form reserved.

studies which provide solid data on differential treatment response between diagnostic subtypes.

Clearly there are different subtypes of schizophrenia based on course and treatment response (e.g., process-reactive, poor prognosis–good prognosis, type I–type II) which may cut across diagnostic subtypes (i.e., paranoid, undifferentiated, schizoaffective, etc.). It makes intuitive sense that response to specific pharmacologic agents should be a useful first step in delineating subtypes. Careful prospective data collection, however, is necessary under controlled circumstances to begin to document accurately patterns of treatment response over time.

One example of a subgroup which might be meaningful is that of childhood asocial schizophrenia.[1] It has been suggested that these individuals who have a history of asocial behavior as children, as well as ineptness and disorganization frequently leading to rejection and scapegoating, are less likely to benefit from neuroleptics than patients without such a premorbid history.[2] In addition, preliminary studies have suggested that these individuals may be more likely to be categorized in the "abnormal" range in CT scan studies[3] and may represent a genetically distinct type of illness from more typical schizophrenia.[4] Though this particular entity requires further validation, it serves as an example of bringing together different perspectives to help establish diagnostic subgroups.

The availability of more sophisticated neuroradiologic techniques has also led to renewed interest in neuroanatomical differences between schizophrenics and normal persons and between subgroups of schizophrenic patients. A considerable literature has evolved on computer-assisted tomography (CAT) scan findings,[5-11] though this area remains controversial in its implications. The positron emission tomography (PET) scan has been utilized to study metabolic activity in specific brain areas,[12] and the development of the nuclear magnetic resonance (NMR) technique holds further promise as well. Although it will take time to clarify fully and specify the "true" abnormalities which might exist, these techniques do point the way to new diagnostic categories and improved specificity of psychopharmacologic treatment approaches.

Genetic approaches, particularly those involving putative biological markers (e.g., platelet monoamine oxidase, dopamine beta hydroxylase, etc.) should be helpful ultimately in establishing more refined diagnoses and treatment strategies. More sophisticated neurochemical and neuropathological postmortem studies in schizophrenia will hopefully provide useful knowledge.

The extent to which these measures correlate with carefully assessed and documented psychopharmacologic treatment response should prove to be valuable.

Drug Treatment Variables

Neuroleptic drugs remain the mainstay of somatic treatment in schizophrenia. No new neuroleptics have been marketed in recent years, although several novel compounds are in various stages of development. It has not been established at present that any specific drug or drug class has any real advantage over any other in terms of therapeutic effect in schizophrenia, or in specific subtypes of schizophrenia. It is clear, however, that the side effects profiles do differ in that high potency drugs cause more Parkinsonian side effects than do low potency drugs. Whether or not any particular drug or drug class has less propensity to produce tardive dyskinesia, however, remains to be established.[13] Tardive dyskinesia has been a major impetus for the development of drugs which have less effect on nigrostriatal dopamine systems (effects hypothesized to be responsible for tardive dyskinesia, but not therapeutic activity[14]) than they do on areas thought to be more relevant to the antipsychotic properties of these drugs. Some investigators have cited animal model studies as suggesting that molindone[15] and thioridazine[16] may be less likely to produce tardive dyskinesia. This, however, has not been well-studied clinically, and it is not clear that currently available animal models are valid with regard to tardive dyskinesia.[17] (This subject will be discussed in more detail below.) Limited experience with "novel" experimental drugs such as clozapine has encouraged attempts to develop drugs which may differ from currently available neuroleptics and thereby possibly avoid producing Parkinsonian side effects or tardive dyskinesia.[18,19]

Blood Levels

Technological advances have allowed for easier measurement of blood levels of neuroleptic medications, holding out the hope that interindividual differences in absorption and metabolism might help to explain variation in treatment response. One hypothesis is that patients who fail to respond to an adequate course of neuroleptics may have very low blood levels and if the blood level could be raised sufficiently a therapeutic response would occur. Another possibility (drawing particularly from data on a specific tricyclic antidepressant, i.e., nortriptyline[20]) is that some patients have a blood level which is too high and this impedes therapeutic response. Unfortunately, this latter possibility has infrequently been supported in those studies investigating blood levels of neuroleptic drugs and clinical response.

Surprisingly, clinical methodological issues have frequently played more of a role in limiting the meaningfulness of results in this area than the chemical methods. We will briefly review some of the most important concerns.

Diagnostic and prognostic heterogeneity have been problems in many studies. Inclusion of patients who do not meet carefully defined and applied criteria for schizophrenia, or patients who have proven refractory to neuroleptics will alter the practitioner's ability to find or to generalize from clinical–chemical correlations. The development of steady state levels following a fixed dose treatment schedule is essential in attempting to establish such correlations. If dosage adjustment is based upon clinical response, for example, then those patients who are poor responders for reasons other than drug blood levels might end up having extremely high blood levels. This could then be interpreted as negating the value of blood levels or suggesting that high levels are counterthera-peutic.

Sufficient length of treatment is also a concern. It is clear that many schizo-phrenic patients require several weeks to benefit fully from a course of neurolep-tics. Level of dosage is important; an attempt should be made to choose dosages within the sensitivity range of a putative dose response curve. Choosing unusu-ally low or high doses might obscure any clinical chemical correlation which does exist.

A variety of psychotropic and nonpsychotropic drugs may affect the phar-macokinetics of neuroleptics, and might also have a direct effect on some meas-ures of clinical response. This is an important concern with antiparkinsonian drugs. Though their effect on neuroleptic blood levels is probably not sufficient to affect treatment response,[21] their effect on extrapyramidal side effects can alter the clinical picture.

Most studies in this area have suffered from small sample sizes, which reduce the ability to find meaningful correlations even if they do exist. Studies made between 1970 and 1975 have been reviewed previously.[22] The data during that period were not adequate to allow any firm conclusions. We will focus for the purposes of this review on studies published between 1976 and 1982.

It is beyond the scope of this chapter to review in detail all studies which have been published in recent years; we will, however, provide a summary of their results.

Chlorpromazine

Chlorpromazine has proven to be a particularly difficult drug to study, due to its complex metabolism. Several investigators have attempted to measure chlorpromazine and a limited number of metabolites.

Curry[23] had originally proposed a "therapeutic window" for chlorpromazine based on 30 chronic patients (no diagnoses given). All patients had been consid-ered severely ill prior to the study and were then rated for global improvement. Those patients with levels between 35 and 350 ng/ml were rated as showing significantly more improvement than other patients. This population was hetero-geneous and the study was not carefully controlled. These results have not been replicated, and the existence of a therapeutic window for chlorpromazine has not been established. Some investigators[24,25] have suggested the importance of the proportion of specific chlorpromazine metabolites to the parent compound. Other investigators,[26] however, have been unable to replicate these findings.

Wode-Helgodt[27] studied cerebrospinal fluid (CSF) and plasma levels of chlorpromazine in 44 in-patient schizophrenics. They found CSF chlorproma-zine levels to be higher in those patients who showed more improvement in psychopathology at 2 weeks after treatment. This relationship was no longer apparent after 4 weeks of treatment. They found no relationship between plasma chlorpromazine levels and clinical response. This might highlight the importance of realizing the difference between neuroleptic blood levels and those levels assumed to be present in the central nervous system. A variety of complex factors will affect the amount of "active" drug which reaches the target site in the central nervous system.

May et al.[28] studied chlorpromazine levels in plasma and saliva in 48 patients treated with fixed dosage for 4 weeks. They reported significant correlations between plasma (and saliva) levels at 24 hours and some measures of clinical outcome, but they found no correlation between steady state chlorpromazine levels and clinical outcome. This highlights the problem of identifying that point in time for measuring drug blood levels which would be most relevant for attempts at correlation with antipsychotic drug effects. Those studies which find significant correlations between blood levels and clinical response during the first few days of treatment may be examining a drug effect which is different from that occurring after several weeks of neuroleptic treatment. It is possible that the alleviation of an activation-dysregulation disturbance occurs more rapidly than the alleviation of such symptoms as delusions, hallucinations, and thought disorder. This possibility, however, has not been systematically studied in the present context.

Butaperazine

Several investigators have studied butaperazine due to its relatively simple metabolism. Two reports have suggested a curvilinear relationship in studies involving this medication. Garver et al.[29] measured red blood cell (RBC) butaperazine levels and found them to be significantly correlated with clinical response after 12 days of treatment. Plasma levels were not found to be related. Casper et al.,[30] in a study involving 24 inpatient schizophrenics, also reported a significant correlation between RBC butaperazine (but not plasma levels) and clinical response, again with a curvilinear relationship suggesting either that blood levels which were too low or those which were too high were not associated with good therapeutic response. It has been suggested that RBC levels may be a better indicator of brain drug levels. The issue of a therapeutic window with this drug (as with other drugs) remains complicated. As the authors of these investigations acknowledge, they do not use doses high enough or a sample size large enough to define the upper limit of a putative therapeutic window. In addition, more attention must be given to characterizing the clinical state of the nonresponders and systematically excluding the possibility that extrapyramidal side effects play some role. These two studies involving butaperazine are among the very few in the literature on neuroleptics which give any support at all to the concept of a therapeutic window.

Several studies have specifically involved schizophrenic patients who were considered to be "nonresponders" to standard courses of neuroleptic treatment. This group has been studied specifically with the hope that blood levels may be related to the lack of response and that substantial increases in dosage would bring about a better therapeutic response. Smith et al.[31] studied 87 inpatients, 42 of whom were considered nonresponders. Those patients in the latter category had significantly lower plasma and RBC butaperazine levels following an acute dose and following fixed dose treatment with butaperazine for 1 to 3 weeks. These investigators did not carry out the next logical step—treating these patients with substantially higher doses of medication in order to increase their blood levels, which might bring about a therapeutic response.

Haloperidol

Morselli et al.[32] studied 9 refractory patients who had been treated with haloperidol 20 mg/day for 6 months. Patients were treated with haloperidol 150 to 200 mg/day for 7 weeks. No clinical improvement was observed despite significant increase in haloperidol blood levels.

Bjorndal et al.[33] treated 23 refractory schizophrenics with haloperidol either 12 to 36 mg or 10 to 240 mg. No difference was found in clinical response between the two groups despite significantly higher plasma haloperidol levels in the group receiving higher doses.

Rimon et al.[34] treated 12 refractory schizophrenics with haloperidol 60 mg/day for 4 weeks and then 120 mg/day for 4 weeks. No correlation was found between blood levels and clinical response and no significant clinical improvement occurred despite a significant increase in plasma and CSF levels at 8 weeks of treatment.

Flupenthixol

McCreadie at al.[35] studied 23 refractory schizophrenics randomly assigned to flupenthixol decanoate 200 mg biweekly versus 40 mg biweekly. No blood level correlations were reported, but the investigators found no differences in outcome between the groups despite significantly higher plasma levels in the high dose group.

In general, these results suggest that the majority of neuroleptic refractory patients are not refractory simply because of low blood levels (though this may be true of a small subgroup of patients). The ideal study would require identifying those patients with low blood levels who had failed to respond to an adequate course of treatment and then randomly assigning them to substantially higher doses (presumably resulting in higher blood levels) or to continue on the same dose for an equal period of time. The studies to date generally use a sample of nonresponders, which in all likelihood include a variety of patients with low, intermediate, and high blood levels. More selective strategies would be necessary to identify that subgroup in whom low blood levels account for poor therapeutic response.

A problem to consider in the relationship between neuroleptic blood levels and clinical response is that many neuroleptics have several potentially active (or toxic) metabolites which may not be measured. The development of the radioreceptor assay[36] which would theoretically measure active metabolites as well as the parent compound, appears to be a major advance in this area. Problems nevertheless remain with this technique, and its applicability across the spectrum of available neuroleptics is far from clear. Despite this, several investigations are encouraging as to the usefulness of this technique. The majority of studies[37-41] reported in recent years involving the radioreceptor assay have been positive; it is also likely, however, that some investigations with negative results have not been published.

The overall value of measuring antipsychotic drug blood levels remains far from clear, and further work must clarify the indications for this procedure. Studies to date have increased our understanding of the pharmacokinetic properties of these drugs, improving our ability to use them in a thoughtful manner. The value of blood levels in long-term maintenance treatment of remitted or partially remitted schizophrenics has not been well studied; since the establishment of minimum effective dosage requirements is an important goal, such investigations should be made. (Long-term maintenance treatment will be discussed below.)

Apart from studies involving measures of neuroleptic blood levels, work has been carried out to determine whether schizophrenic patients might improve more rapidly or more completely on higher than normal doses of neuroleptics. There is evidence that massive doses of high potency antipsychotic drugs such as haloperidol, trifluoperazine, or fluphenazine can be administered in daily doses as high as 500 to 1000 mg.

Eriksen et al.[42] compared treatment response between patients given a five day loading dose of haloperidol 60 mg intramuscularly and patients given haloperidol 15 mg orally once per day. Those patients receiving the high dose treatment for five days had their dosage lowered to a normal dose of 15 mg per day, and were continued on this dosage for the remainder of the three-week study. The therapeutic outcomes for both groups were not different at either 5 days or 3 weeks. The main difference was that the high loading dose group had more side effects, particularly dystonias.

Donlon et al.[43] compared the effects of a loading dose of fluphenazine 80 mg/day with a standard dose of 20 mg/day in a group of acutely exacerbated schizophrenics recently admitted to hospital. Both dose regimes produced similar clinical results. Goldberg et al.[44] compared the efficacy of trifluoperazine 60 mg/day versus 600 mg/day in a double-blind study of newly admitted schizophrenic patients. Both treatments proved to be equally effective in this study as well.

Another popular strategy, despite lack of systematic evidence supporting its superiority, is the so-called *rapid neuroleptization*.[45] This has been particularly popular with haloperidol where patients have received initial doses in the range of 1 to 30 mg IM and total daily dosages up to 100 mg IM. Unfortunately, these studies have frequently lacked appropriate controls. Several studies, for example, compared the effects of rapid neuroleptization of haloperidol to the effects of intramuscular injections of chlorpromazine but the dosages were clearly not equivalent.[45]

Though high dose treatment and rapid neuroleptization seem to be generally well tolerated, it has not been conclusively established that these strategies offer any advantage over more traditional approaches. In addition, long-term consequences of exposure to very high dose treatment has not been studied.

ATTEMPTS TO IMPROVE THE BENEFIT/RISK RATIO OF LONG-TERM PHARMACOLOGIC TREATMENT

Results of Maintenance Medication Studies

Numerous studies employing different methodology, different treatment regimes, assessment and outcome measures, as well as different patient populations, are remarkably consistent in demonstrating the value of maintenance antipsychotic drug treatment in preventing psychotic relapse.[45] There are some misconceptions in the interpretation of these data, however, since a proportion of placebo-treated patients in many trials did not relapse. Unfortunately, the majority of trials reported in the literature were of relatively short duration; it is thus unjustified to assume that those patients who have not relapsed by 6 months or 1 year will never relapse. Survival curves can be helpful in suggesting a more accurate reflection of relapse rates over time.[46] Despite numerous attempts we are at present unable to identify those patients who are not at risk for psychotic relapse when withdrawn from medication. One cannot assume that because a patient has been stable for 2 or 3 years on medication that continuation of drug treatment is no longer necessary to prevent relapse. Hogarty et al.[47] carried out a discontinuation study among patients who had completed at least 2 years of maintenance treatment without evidence of psychotic relapse. The relapse rate among the 43 patients withdrawn from neuroleptics was 65 percent during the following year. This relapse rate was comparable to that occurring among those patients recently discharged from hospital and assigned to a placebo treatment in the earlier phase of the study.

Even those patients presumed to have the best prognosis, the so-called first episode acute schizophrenic, are at risk of relapse within a year following recovery. Kane et al.[48] identified 28 patients with acute onset, first episode schizophrenia, or schizophreniform illness, who had fully recovered and been discharged from hospital. These patients were randomly assigned to fluphenazine or a placebo for a one year period. Forty percent of the patients assigned to placebo treatment relapsed; none of the patients assigned to an active drug ($p < .05$)

relapsed. Though the placebo relapse rate may be less than one would expect with multi-episode schizophrenics, a statistically significant drug effect was still apparent, and further follow-up of this cohort revealed a high relapse rate during the ensuing 2 to 3 years (over 70 percent of the patients experienced a second episode).

These results suggest that under the circumstances in which these trials have been carried out it is difficult to identify patients for whom antipsychotic medication might be unnecessary. This does not eliminate the possibility that more intensive psychosocial treatment strategies might help to reduce the need for medication. This hypothesis, however, requires testing before it should be implemented in clinical practice.

There may be some promise in tactics developed to identify patients at *high* risk for relapse using pharmacologic probes. Angrist et al.[49] and Lieberman et al.[50] have employed dexedrine and methylphenidate respectively in an attempt to ascertain schizophrenic patients' vulnerability to brief psychotic exacerbation following administration of these agents; this was in order to determine their subsequent vulnerability to psychotic relapse following discontinuation of neuroleptic medication. Though relatively few patients have been studied in this paradigm, preliminary results suggest that those patients who do respond with an increase of psychotic symptoms following administration of dopamine agonists (i.e., dexedrine and methylphenidate) are likely to relapse more rapidly than those patients who do not show this response. Further work is necessary to evaluate fully the usefulness of this strategy. The possibility exists that patients could be identified for whom a lengthy period of drug withdrawal might be feasible.

Despite the established efficacy of maintenance drug treatment in schizophrenia, it is surprising how little information is available on optimal maintenance dosage. The potential for reducing a variety of untoward effects such as tardive dyskinesia, akathesia, and akinesia by utilizing lower maintenance doses should be considered. Though there are few data which could be utilized to identify a dose response curve for tardive dyskinesia, the hypothesis that substantial reductions in dosage could reduce risk is compelling.

In addition, dosage may interact with other treatment variables, such as family therapy[51] and environmental factors (e.g., family expressed emotion)[52-54] in ways which could allow substantial dosage reduction in some situations but not in others.

Baldessarini and Davis[55] reviewed those controlled studies which permitted estimates of the equivalent dose of chlorpromazine to be plotted against reduction of relapse. They found no significant dose effect between 100 and over 2000 mg/day and no mean difference in outcome at doses above versus doses below 310 mg. This might suggest that patients can generally be maintained on dosages lower than 300 mg/day chlorpromazine equivalent.

Few studies have attempted to assess prospectively the efficacy of different

fixed dosages or dosage ranges in preventing relapse. Goldstein et al.[51] studied
the efficacy of two dose levels of fluphenazine enanthate (25 mg or 6.25 mg
biweekly), with and without crisis-oriented family therapy for a six week period
in 104 recently discharged schizophrenic patients. Relapse was defined as the
need to alter medication substantially or rehospitalize the patient. Only 10 percent of the entire sample relapsed within the six weeks following discharge. Of
those on the low dose/no therapy condition, 24 percent relapsed; none of the high
dose/therapy group relapsed. The low dose/therapy versus the high dose/no
therapy group had relapse rates of 9 and 10 percent respectively. The study
involved a relatively brief period of controlled treatment. The results were
important, however, in suggesting the potential interaction between dosage and
such psychotherapeutic interventions as crisis-oriented family therapy.

We have carried out a series of studies designed to identify the minimum
effective dosage for maintenance treatment. In a pilot study[56] we openly treated
57 stable, remitted, or partially remitted schizophrenic patients meeting research
diagnostic criteria (RDC) with dosages of fluphenazine decanoate (FD), ranging
from 1.25 to 5.0 mg IM every two weeks for six months. We found the relapse
rate to be higher than we would have expected with standard doses. The majority
of patients, however, were able to maintain good remission during the six month
trial. In a subsequent six month double-blind discontinuation study of 16 of these
patients who had completed six months of low dose treatment, 7 of 8 patients
randomly assigned to placebo relapsed as compared with 1 of 8 patients continuing on active low dose FD (p < .05).

We subsequently reported preliminary results from a double-blind prospective comparison of "low dose" (1.25–5.0 mg/2 weeks) versus "standard dose"
(12.5–50.0 mg/2 weeks) fluphenazine decanoate in outpatient schizophrenics.[57]

Patients participated in the study for one year. Those who experienced a
relapse (as defined by Brief Psychiatric Rating Scale psychotic item scores) were
treated openly with standard doses of fluphenazine decanoate, as needed, in
addition to the (blind) study medication, until restabilized at baseline levels of
psychopathology. At that point the open medication was gradually discontinued
and the patient was continued on the blind medication. Patients were removed
from the study if they experienced two psychotic relapses, an affective episode,
suicide attempt, or if they missed two consecutive appointments. Patients who
developed severe extrapyramidal side effects or tardive dyskinesia were also
removed from the study. Of the 62 patients assigned to low dose treatment, 26
relapsed a total of 31 times (5 relapsed twice); 7of these required hospitalization.
Among the 64 patients receiving a standard dose, 3 patients relapsed a total of 4
times, none requiring rehospitalization. The results of a life table analysis indicate that the cumulative proportion remaining stable after 1 year on low dose
treatment is 44 percent for those receiving a standard dose, the cumulative
proportion remaining stable is 93 percent (p < .001). Though the 45 percent
cumulative relapse rate at 6 months in this study is higher than the 30 percent

relapse rate in the *six* month pilot study, this difference is not statistically significant. In addition, since the initial pilot study was not double-blind, it is difficult to make any meaningful comparisons.

It is clear that when using relapse rate as the sole outcome measure, the low dose preparation is not as effective as standard doses of fluphenazine decanoate. There are other findings, however, which suggest the importance of pursuing this approach. In a subgroup of 51 patients who completed at least 24 weeks in the study analysis, Simpson Dyskinesia Scale scores revealed a significant advantage for low dose treatment. Though these rating scale scores are very low and could not be considered evidence of tardive dyskinesia, the fact that any statistically significant differences were evident after a relatively brief period of time suggests the potential importance of this technique in reducing the incidence of tardive dyskinesia.

In order to assess social adjustment and family burden, interviews with the patient and separately with the family were conducted by a trained research assistant. In preliminary analyses, our findings suggest that low dose patients were rated significantly better than standard dose patients on several measures of psyhosocial adjustment, despite the higher relapse rates. The results of this study encourage further attempts to lower maintenance doses of neuroleptic treatment. It is possible that an intermediate dose (i.e., 1/5th rather than the 1/10th of the standard) might be more effective than the dosage we employed.

Other strategies intended to reduce cumulative drug exposure such as "intermittent" or "targeted" drug treatment are reviewed in another chapter.

Tardive Dyskinesia

Tardive dyskinesia remains the major concern in the long-term use of antipsychotic medication. Many reviews[13, 17, 59] have appeared in recent years discussing clinical description, prevalence, assessment, pathophysiology, treatment, and prevention of TD. Reviews of prevalence and risk factors have often summarized findings from a variety of reports without critiquing the methods and conclusions of specific studies. Kane and Smith[13] reviewed 56 studies presenting TD prevalence among neuroleptic-treated patients and 14 reports involving 19 untreated samples (psychiatric and nonpsychiatric). This mean prevalence uncorrected for rates of spontaneous dyskinesias in the neuroleptic-treated patients was 20 percent. Among those patients with no history of neuroleptic exposure, the mean prevalence of abnormal involuntary movements was 5 percent. The statistical significance of this difference is enormous.

One problem in reviewing epidemiologic data on tardive dyskinesia is the lack of established or universally accepted criteria for the diagnosis of TD. Many other neuromedical disorders produce a similar clinical picture. Particularly difficult is the diagnosis of the mild or questionable case. Prevalence varies markedly with the symptom severity required to identify a "case." Diagnostic criteria for tardive dyskinesia have been recently proposed[60] and should be helpful in generalizing findings and in achieving better communication between investigators. It does appear that the prevalence of tardive dyskinesia has increased during the past 20 years. Explanations for this increase remain speculative.

A number of reports suggest a high prevalence of spontaneous dyskinesias in untreated populations. The overwhelming majority of studies which included both treated and untreated samples found a statistically significant difference when comparing TD prevalence rates between the two groups. Two studies[58,61] that reported a 19 percent and 37 percent prevalence respectively among untreated samples, included elderly patients with a high proportion of senile dementia. In these cases the involuntary movements may have been secondary to a diagnosable organic brain dysfunction other than schizophrenia. It is important to recognize that some schizophrenic patients probably do have movement disorders which are not attributable to neuroleptics; neuroleptics, however, do appear to increase their incidence significantly.

It is unsatisfactory to contrast prevalence rates between populations which may differ on a variety of variables other than exposure to neuroleptics. Ideally, patients would have to be randomly assigned to a drug or to no drug treatment, in large numbers, for long periods to assess the role of neuroleptic treatment in the development of TD. Despite some degree of debate and confusion in this area, the epidemiologic data implicating neuroleptic treatment as the single most significant etiologic factor in producing abnormal involuntary movements in psychiatric patients are quite compelling.

A variety of risk factors have been suggested for the development of tardive dyskinesia. It is widely assumed that the risk of TD development increases with increasing drug exposure. As Kane and Smith[13] have suggested, though this assumed relationship between exposure and prevalence has some intuitive appeal, dose response curves usually have a plateau; increasing the dose beyond a certain point no longer increases the likelihood of a given effect. In the case of tardive dyskinesia, increasing doses may even mask an existing dyskinesia, further complicating the interpretation of available data. Attempts at identifying this response curve for tardive dyskinesia are made difficult by the relative infrequency of the condition and the retrospective nature of the available data. It is quite difficult, in addition, to determine accurately the amount of medication which was actually ingested, not to mention interindividual differences in absorption and metabolism. In fact, few controlled investigations have suggested a relationship between cumulative dose (or length of drug exposure) and TD.[13] That those studies which did report such a relationship generally focused on patients with relatively brief exposure (or low total cumulative dose) may provide important clues in terms of identifying a dose response relationship for TD.[62,63] It may be that there is a period of maximum risk for the development of tardive dyskinesia and vulnerable patients will develop the condition within that period. For those patients without an underlying vulnerability, increasing doses beyond this range may not lead to a substantial increase in the risk of tardive dyskinesia.

Age appears to be an important risk factor in the development of this condition, even though dating the onset of tardive dyskinesia is often problematic (making overestimation of age at onset likely). In addition, the risk in prevalence with age which has been observed in numerous studies might reflect the relative persistence of TD among older individuals. A review by Smith and Baldessarini[64] reported a strong correlation between age and severity of TD and a strong inverse relationship between rates of spontaneous remission of TD and age. Both of these factors might contribute to higher prevalence rates in older age groups even if incidence were not affected by age. Some reviews have suggested that the increased prevalence of TD observed in elderly drug-treated populations may in fact reflect a very high proportion of "spontaneous dyskinesias" seen in the elderly. Several studies[14,65,66] involving normal elderly individuals, however, suggest that the rates of spontaneous dyskinesias among older age groups are not higher than 4 to 8 percent, and these cases are generally mild. It is unlikely, therefore, that the age effect in tardive dyskinesia could be explained solely by the occurrence of false-positive diagnoses.

With regard to sex, it does appear that women have a somewhat higher overall prevalence of TD than men; many of the samples in which the sex relationship was studied, however, were not matched for age and medication exposure. It does appear that more severe forms of the disorder are more likely to develop in women, but whether the sex differences in tardive dyskinesia are artifacts of different drug treatment histories or reflect underlying biologic differences between the sexes remains to be ascertained.

The possibility needs to be explored that some drugs are less likely to produce TD than other drugs. Despite the importance of this possibility, currently available information does not allow any conclusion as to the relative risk of one neuroleptic compared with another. Though several studies[13] have suggested fluphenazine decanoate as producing increased risk, there are major problems in interpreting these findings, since long-acting injectable preparations overcome the noncompliance in pill-taking which has been frequently reported among schizophrenic patients. Any suggested association of tardive dyskinesia with a depot preparation of neuroleptics may at least be partially related to compliance. In addition, given large individual differences in drug metabolism,[22] it is particularly important to consider the role of parenteral routes of administration in increasing actual "neuroleptic exposure" in the brain.

Given these concerns about tardive dyskinesia, recommendations have been made regarding so-called drug holidays or more lengthy drug-free intervals as a way of reducing the likelihood of this problem. The data supporting this idea are minimal at best. Drug-free intervals may be useful in identifying patients with masked or covert dyskinesias, but their role in increasing or decreasing the risk of TD development remains to be established.

Attempts to reduce cumulative drug exposure are clearly justified; the best strategy to employ, however, has yet to be established, and the full impact of dosage reduction in preventing side effects has yet to be determined.

CONCLUSION

We conclude that there have been no major breakthroughs in the pharmacologic treatment of schizophrenia in the past decade. The improvements in treatment have been, by and large, refinements made on earlier observations or more adequate tests of specific hypotheses. During the past ten years, for example, better designed and more sophisticated maintenance medication studies have been carried out which have provided broader, more comprehensive assessments of benefits and risks. Tardive dyskinesia has emerged as a major concern though it had been clearly recognized much earlier. It has taken time to develop a data base sufficient to put this problem in better perspective; it appears reasonable, however, to conclude that despite the occurrence of tardive dyskinesia the potential benefits outweigh the potential risks when long-term treatment is thoughtfully prescribed to carefully diagnosed schizophrenic patients.

It is hoped that new, safer, and more effective drugs will be developed and that our ability to treat patients will benefit from advances in genetics, neurochemistry, neuroradiology, and other disciplines.

REFERENCES

1. Gittelman-Klein R, Klein DF: Premorbid asocial adjustment and prognosis in schizophrenia. *J Psychiatric Res* 1969;7:35–53
2. Klein DF, Rosen B: Premorbid asocial adjustment in response to phenothiazine treatment among schizophrenic inpatients. *Arch Gen Psychiatry* 1973;29:480–485
3. Weinberger DR, Cannon-Spooler E, Potkin SG, et al: Poor premorbid adjustment and CT scan abnormalities in chronic schizophrenia. *Am J Psychiatry* 1980;137:1410–1413
4. Quitkin F, Rifkin A, Tsuang MT, et al: Can schizophrenia with premorbid asociality be genetically distinguished from the other forms of schizophrenia? *Psychiatry Res* 1980;2:99–105
5. Andreasen NC, Smith MR, Jacoby CG, et al: Ventricular enlargement in schizophrenia: Definition and prevalence. *Am J Psychiatry* 1982;139:292–296
6. Golden CJ, Moses JA Jr, Zelazowski R, et al: Cerebral ventricular size and neuropsychological impairment in young chronic schizophrenics. *Arch Gen Psychiatry* 1980;37:619–623
7. Johnstone EC, Frith CD, Crowe TJ, et al: Cerebral ventricular size and cognitive impairment in chronic schizophrenia. Lancet 1976;2:924–926
8. Luchins DJ: Computed tomography in schizophrenia. *Arch Gen Psychiatry* 1982;39:859–860
9. Nasrallah HA, Jacoby CG, McCalley-Whitters M, et al: Cerebral ventricular enlargement in subtypes of chronic schizophrenia. *Arch Gen Psychiatry* 1982;39:774–777
10. Rieder RO, Donnelly EF, Herdt JR, et al: Sulcal prominence in young chronic schizophrenic patients: CT scan findings associated with impairment on neuropsychological tests. *Psychiatry Res* 1979;1:1–8

11. Weinberger DR, Torrey EF, Neophytides AN, et al: Structural abnormalities in the cerebral cortex of chronic schizophrenic patients. *Arch Gen Psychiatry* 1979;36:924–926
12. Brownell GL, Budinger TF, Lauterbur PC, et al: Positron tomography and nuclear magnetic resonance imaging. *Science* 1982;215:619–626
13. Kane JM, Smith J: Tardive dyskinesia: Prevalence and risk factors 1959–1979. *Arch Gen Psychiatry* 1982;39:473–481
14. Klawans HL Jr, Barr A: Prevalence of spontaneous lingual-facial-buccal dyskinesia in the elderly. *Neurology (NY)* 1982;32:558–559
15. Meller E: Chronic molindone treatment: Relative inability to elicit dopamine receptor supersensitivity in rats. *Psychopharmacol (Berlin)* (in press)
16. Borison RL, Fields JZ, Diamond BI: Site-specific blockade of dopamine receptors by neuroleptic agents in human brain. *Neuropharmacology* 1981;20:1321–1322
17. Jeste DV, Wyatt RJ: *Understanding and Treating Tardive Dyskinesia*. New York, Guilford Press, 1982, pp 195–214
18. Kane JM, Cooper TB, Sacher EJ, et al: Clozapine: Plasma levels and prolactin response. *Psychopharmacology (Berlin)* 1981;73:184–187
19. Matz R, Rick W, Oh D, et al: Clozapine, a potential antipsychotic agent without extrapyramidal manifestations. *Curr Ther Res* 1974;16:687–695
20. Kane JM, Rifkin A, Quitkin F, et al: Antidepressant drug blood levels, pharmacokinetics and clinical outcome, in Klein DF, Gittelman-Klein R (eds): *Progress in Psychiatric Drug Treatment*. New York, Brunner Mazel, 1976, pp 136–158
21. Simpson GM, Cooper TB, Bark N, et al: Effect of antiparkinsonian medication on plasma levels of chlorpromazine. *Arch Gen Psychiatry* 1980;37:205–208
22. Kane JM, Rifkin A, Quitkin F, et al: Antipsychotic drug blood levels and clinical outcome. In Klein DF, Gittelman-Klein R (eds): *Progress in Psychiatric Drug Treatment*. New York, Brunner Mazel, 1976, pp 399–408
23. Curry SH: Chromatographic methods for the study of chlorpromazine and some of its metabolites in human plasma. *Psychopharm Comm* 1976;2:1–15
24. Philipsen OT, McKeown JM, Baker J, et al: Correlation between plasma chlorpromazine and its metabolites and clinical ratings in patients with acute relapse of schizophrenic and paranoid psychosis. *Br J Psychiatry* 1977;131:172–184
25. Wiles DH, Kolakowska T, McNeilly AS, et al: Clinical significance of plasma chlorpromazine levels: I. Plasma levels of the drug, some of its metabolites and prolactin during acute treatment. *Psychol Med* 1976;6:407–415
26. Kolakowska T, Wiles DH, Gelder MG, et al: Clinical significance of plasma chlorpromazine levels: II. Plasma levels of the drug, some of its metabolites and prolactin in patients receiving long-term phenothiazine treatment. *Psychopharmacol (Berlin)* 1976;49:101–107
27. Wode-Helgodt B, Borg S, Fyro B, et al: Clinical effects and drug concentrations in plasma and cerebrospinal fluid in psychotic patients treated with fixed doses of chlorpromazine. *Acta Psychiatr Scan* 1978;58:149–173
28. May PRA, VanPutten T, Jenden DJ, et al: Chlorpromazine levels and the outcome of treatment in schizophrenic patients. *Arch Gen Psychiatry* 1981;38:202–207
29. Garver DL, Dekirmenjian N, Davis JM, et al: Neuroleptic drug levels and therapeutic response: Preliminary observations with red blood cell bound butaperazine. *Am J Psychiatry* 1977;134:304–307
30. Casper R, Garver DL, Dekirmenjian H, et al: Phenothiazine levels in plasma and red blood cells: Their relationship to clinical improvement in schizophrenia. *Arch Gen Psychiatry* 1980;37:301–305
31. Smith RC, Crayton J, Dekirmenjian H, et al: Blood levels of neuroleptic drugs in non-responding chronic schizophrenic patients. *Arch Gen Psychiatry* 1979;36:579–584
32. Morselli PL, Zarifian E, Cuchi H, et al: Haloperidol plasma level monitoring in psychiatric

patients, in Cattabeni F, et al (eds): Long Term Effects of Neuroleptics. (Adv Biochem Psychopharmacol. Vol. 24) New York, Raven Press, 1980, pp 529–536

33. Bjorndal N, Bjerre M, Gerlach J, et al: High dosage haloperidol therapy in chronic schizophrenic patients: A double-blind study of clinical response, side effects, serum haloperidol, and serum prolactin. Psychopharmacology (Berlin) 1980;67:17–23

34. Rimon R, Averbuch I, Rozick P, et al: Serum and CSF levels of haloperidol by radioimmunoassay and radioreceptor assay during high-dose therapy of resistant schizophrenic patients. Psychopharmacology (Berlin) 1981;73:197–199

35. McCreadie RG, Flanagan WL, McKnight J, et al: High dose flupenthixol decanoate in chronic schizophrenia. Br J Psychiatry 1979;135:175–179

36. Creese I, Snyder S: A simple and sensitive radioreceptor assay for antischizophrenic drugs in blood. Nature 1977;270:180–182

37. Calil HM, Avery DH, Holister LB, et al: Serum levels of neuroleptics measured by dopamine radioreceptor assay and some clinical observations. Psychiatry Res 1979;1:39–44

38. Cohen BM, Lipinski JF, Pope HG, et al: Neuroleptic blood levels and therapeutic effect. Psychopharmacology (Berlin) 1980;70:191–193

39. Cohen BM, Lipinski JF, Pope HG, Jr, et al: Clinical use of the radioreceptor assay for neuroleptics. Psychiatry Res 1980;1:173–178

40. Rosenblatt JE, Pary RJ, Bigelow LB, et al: Measurement of serum neuroleptic concentration by radioreceptor assay: Concurrent assessment of clinical response and toxicity. Psychopharmocol Bull (3) 1980;16:78–80

41. Tune LE, Creese I, DePaulo R, et al: Clinical state and serum neuroleptic levels measured by radioreceptor assay in schizophrenia. Am J Psychiatry 1980;137:187–190

42. Eriksen S, Hurt SW, Chang S, et al: Haloperidol dose, plasma levels and clinical response: A double-blind study. Psychopharmacol Bull 1978;14:15–16

43. Donlon P, Meadow A, Tuppen J, et al: High vs standard dosage fluphenazine HCL in acute schizophrenia. J Clin Psychiatry 1978;39;800–804

44. Goldberg SC, Frosch WA, Drossman AK, et al: Prediction of response to phenothiazine in schizophrenia: A cross validation study. Arch Gen Psychiatry 1972;26:367–373

45. Donlon PT, Hopkin J, Tupin J: Overview: Efficacy and safety of rapid neuroleptization method with injectable haloperidol. Am J Psychiatry 1979;136:273–278

46. Davis JM, Schaffer CV, Killian GA, et al: Important issues in the drug treatment of schizophrenia. Schizophr Bull 1980;6:70–87

47. Hogarty GE, Ulrich RF, Mussare F, et al: Drug discontinuation among long-term, successfully maintained schizophrenic outpatients. Dis Nerv System 1977;38:494–500

48. Kane JM, Quitkin F, Rifkin A, et al: Fluphenazine vs placebo in patients with remitted acute first episode schizophrenia. Arch Gen Psychiatry 1982;39:70–73

49. Angrist B, Peselow E, Rotrosen J, et al: Relationship between response to dopamine agonists, psychopathology, and neuroleptic maintenance in schizophrenic subjects, in Angrist B, Burrows G, et al (eds): Recent Advances in Neuropsychopharmacology, Vol. 31. New York, Pergamon Press, 1981, pp 49–54

50. Lieberman J, Kane J, Gadaletta D, et al: Methylphenidate challenge and course of schizophrenia. Am J Psychiatry (in press)

51. Goldstein M, Rodnik E, Evans J, et al: Drug and family therapy in the aftercare treatment of acute schizophrenics. Arch Gen Psychiatry 1978;35:1169–1177

52. Brown GW, Wing JK: Influence of family life on the course of schizophrenic disorders: replication. Br J Psychiatry 1972;121:241–258

53. Leff JP, Kuipers L, Berkowitz R, et al: A controlled trial of social intervention in the families of schizophrenic patients. Br J Psychiatry 1982;141:121–134

54. Leff JP, Vaughn C: The role of maintenance therapy and relatives expressed emotion in relapse of schizophrenia: A two year follow-up. Br J Psychiatry 1981;139:102–104

55. Baldessarini RJ, Davis JM: What *is* the best maintenance dose of neuroleptics in schizophrenia? *Psychiatry Res* 1980;3:115-122

56. Kane JM, Rifkin A, Quitkin F, et al: Low dose fluphenazine decanoate in maintenance treatment of schizophenia. *Psychiatry Res* 1979;1:341-348

57. Kane JM, Rifkin A, Woerner M, et al: Low dose neuroleptic treatment of outpatient schizophrenics. I. Preliminary results of relapse rates. *Arch Gen Psychiatry* 1983;40:893-896

58. Delwaide PJ, Desseilles M: Spontaneous buccal linguo facial dyskinesia in the elderly. *Acta Neurol Scand* 1977;56:256-262

59. Fann WE, Smith RC, Davis JM, et al (eds): *Tardive Dyskinesia: Research and Treatment.* New York, Spectrum, 1980

60. Schooler N, Kane JM: Research diagnoses for tardive dyskinesia (RD-TD). *Arch Gen Psychiatry* 1982;39:486-487

61. Brandon S, McClelland HA, Protheroe C: A study of facial dyskinesia in a mental hospital population. *Br J Psychiatry* 1971;118:171-184

62. Crane GE, Smeets RA: Tardive dyskinesia and drug therapy in geriatric patients. *Arch Gen Psychiatry* 1974;30:341-343

63. Pryce IG, Edwards H: Persistent oral dyskinesia in female mental hospital patients. *Br J Psychiatry* 1966;112:983-987

64. Smith JM, Baldessarini RJ: Changes in prevalence, severity and recovery in tardive dyskinesia with age. *Arch Gen Psychiatry* 1980;37:1368-1373

65. Kane JM, Weinhold P, Kinon B, et al: Prevalence of abnormal involuntary movements (spontaneous dyskinesias) in the normal elderly. *Psychopharmacol (Berlin)* 1982;77:105-108

66. Varga E, Sugarman AA, Varga V, et al: Prevalence of spontaneous oral dyskinesia in the elderly. *Am J Psychiatry* 1982;139:329-331

Douglas W. Heinrichs

9

Recent Developments in the Psychosocial Treatment of Chronic Psychotic Illnesses

It is impossible to understand the recent evolution of psychosocial treatments of chronic psychotic illnesses without regarding the dual impact of psychotropic medication and deinstitutionalization. Neuroleptics were originally perceived as a direct competition and threat to psychotherapy, and early investigators posed the question of efficacy in terms of psychotherapy versus neuroleptics. Studies such as the classic investigations of May et al.[1] that showed marked benefits only for medication led many pharmacotherapists to devalue the role of traditional psychotherapy. Many psychotherapists began to work in increasingly defensive isolation from the mainstream of psychiatry.[2,3] As it became increasingly clear that neuroleptics did not "cure" schizophrenia or other major psychotic illnesses, and as the limitations of drug treatment became more appreciated, a different perspective emerged. The question became how to optimally combine pharmacologic and psychosocial strategies into a comprehensive approach for treating these patients. Many of the questions shaping psychosocial developments have thus been determined by the task of interdigitating these developments with pharmacotherapy, including efforts to respond to the following challenges.

Can psychosocial strategies facilitate compliance with medication? It is generally recognized that a major limitation to neuroleptic effectiveness is the high rate of patient rejection. At times this reflects passive noncompliance (e.g., forgetfulness, disinterest). More often the patient consciously rejects medication because of fear of side effects or the implications that medication-taking carries

THE CHRONIC MENTAL PATIENT
ISBN 0-8089-1649-1

Copyright © 1984 by Grune & Stratton.
All rights of reproduction in any form reserved.

for patients' views of themselves and their illnesses. The latter touches on critical aspects of patients' self-esteem, self-image, and grasp of their own psychopathology. The need for psychotherapeutic approaches to address these concerns regarding medication dispels simple-minded notions that prescribing medication stands alone as an optimal treatment for schizophrenia and other psychoses.

Can psychosocial strategies ameliorate those dimensions of pathology and dysfunction for which neuroleptics are relatively ineffective? While for most patients neuroleptics are remarkably helpful in treating hallucinations, delusions, and thought disorder, they have shown little benefit to the deficit state and related negative symptoms. There is a growing awareness that the high level of ongoing dysfunction and impairment in productivity related to chronic psychotic illness derive from the enduring impoverishment of the personality manifested in anergy, amotivational states, social withdrawal, reduced curiosity, constriction of the ideational field, blunted affect, and anhedonia. There is little to suggest that current medications have much to offer in the treatment of these symptoms. Although this syndrome may be neuroleptic-responsive in an occasional patient, many clinicians suspect that for a large number of patients neuroleptics may in fact make these features of the illness worse.[4] Given that the deficit syndrome is so intimately related to the interpersonal functioning and subjective vitality that have traditionally been the realms of psychotherapeutic treatments, there is growing interest in developing psychosocial interventions specifically targeted to these features of the illness.

Can psychosocial strategies be developed for patients who are unresponsive to pharmacotherapy? For an unfortunate minority of patients, neuroleptic medication has little or no effect on chronic, unremitting psychoses and severe functional impairment. These individuals usually constitute long-term custodial burdens on public hospital facilities. In recent years some workers have attempted to construct psychosocial strategies to treat psychotic symptoms in these patients or at least to facilitate increased functioning in spite of them.

In addition to neuroleptic medication the move toward deinstitutionalization has dramatically changed the context in which the psychosocial treatments are provided. Much of the classic, psychoanalytically derived work with psychotic patients presumed a long-term hospitalization, during which patients could be intensively treated on a daily basis and continued in treatment even during periods of considerable negativity and resistance. As a result, such treatment models developed many strategies and raised some questions that are simply inapplicable in the usual context of outpatient community-based care. Two examples suffice to illustrate this. Considerable debate has occurred over the years as to whether fostering severe regression in the early phases of psychotherapy would prove ultimately more conducive to personality maturation and a healthy resolution of the illness. Whatever the correct assessment of that issue, the option is simply precluded in most cases in an age when the norm is brief hospitalization with rapid return to the community, where weekly (let alone daily) therapy sessions are unlikely to be available. Such regression is even more untenable for the patient who is struggling precariously to maintain some basic effectiveness in the community, such as holding a simple job and assuming responsibility for many of his own basic needs. Traditional psychotherapy has similarly placed considerable importance on processing both positive and negative aspects of the transference in treatment. Such effective "working through" can commonly take many months. Such a time frame for dealing with negative attitudes in the patient may not be realistic in a setting where patients have considerable control over whether they continue participating in treatment at all. The common failure of patients to engage or maintain their involvement in aftercare reflects the need for quick, if perhaps dirty, strategies to engage the patient in a productive treatment alliance. For many outpatients, furthermore, practical concerns such as living arrangements, self-care, and financial security dominate the clinical task.

Thus modern developments in psychosocial treatment, in addition to being responsive to questions raised by the use of neuroleptic medication, are also an attempt to deal with challenges posed by changes in the setting and delivery of health care, such as the following.

What sorts of psychosocial intervention are most efficacious for patients who spend the majority of their time as outpatients and are hospitalized only briefly (at times of most acute psychotic exacerbation)? The outpatient setting influences both the form and content of therapy. Frequency of sessions, for instance, is likely to be more limited and less flexible in the outpatient setting. Furthermore, as noted above, participation in treatment requires the active choice and cooperation of the patient who has the final decision about attending or not attending treatment. Beyond this, the issues of the treatment vary dramatically, with a premium on reality-oriented issues very early in the treatment experience.

What psychosocial strategies can be adapted in a cost-effective manner for serving large populations? One consequence of the emergence of deinstitutionalization has been a growing awareness of the breadth as well as depth of treatment (i.e., the proportion of the chronic psychotic population served by an intervention). At times when these individuals were relegated to chronic hospitalization with a virtually hopeless prognosis, ameliorating the suffering and increasing the functioning of even a few patients seemed clearly worthwhile, regardless of the cost. Part of the justification, of course, was the hope that useful strategies derived in such settings could later be adapted to larger groups of patients. Such intensive individual work is still being conducted and has an important function in adding to the depth of our understanding of these illnesses. With the advent of deinstitutionalization, however, there is growing pressure to provide useful psychosocial strategies for the large number of patients who are now struggling in the community. Thus a high premium is placed on interventions that are more discrete and less labor-intensive, as well as those that permit the use of less highly trained professionals.

In light of the new challenges to psychosocial treatment derived from the use of neuroleptic drugs and the deinstitutionalization movement, the following four trends can be seen as characterizing developments in psychosocial treatment for chronically psychotic individuals in recent years. Each can be understood as an attempt to respond to these new demands.

Psychoeducation and the Medical Model

Conceptions of the illness and its origin frequently form our view of the therapeutic task, even though such reasoning is not always sound.[2]

The increased role of medication and growing evidence for a biologic basis for at least the diathesis to chronic psychosis has led to the increased application of a traditional medical model—such a model, although often criticized for being narrow, need not be so.[5] One tenet of such a model is that the illness can be named, described, and basic knowledge about it communicated to patients—and that such communication is useful to elicit the patient's acceptance of the treatment and increase patients' capacity to manage their own illnesses. Such a stance is so fundamental to the practice of most aspects of medicine that it is seldom explicitly cited as a distinct ingredient of treatment. More formalized strategies to educate patients about specific illnesses have at times been developed (for myocardial infarction and for diabetes, for instance). Such efforts date at least to Pratt's classes for instructing tuberculosis patients early in this century.[6]

The very attempt to talk to psychiatric patients about their illnesses in a matter-of-fact, informative manner conveys an attitude of respect and hopefulness. It implies that the patient is capable of understanding basic facts about his illness and deserves to have such knowledge. A shared grasp of the problem can serve as the foundation for collaborative treatment-planning that helps combat the hopelessness and passivity that so often characterize chronic psychosis. Among the most tangible benefits of educational strategies is the increase in patient compliance and cooperation with treatment. An informed patient with an appreciation of the rationale for treatment is more inclined to accept it. It even broadens the range of possible strategies that may be employed. Carpenter et al. [7,8] for instance, are investigating a strategy of intermittent targeted neuroleptic use as an alternative to continuous maintenance drugs that places heavy emphasis on teaching patients to recognize early signs of impending relapse so that medication can be reinstituted and the psychotic episode aborted.

As soon as one begins to talk directly to patients about their illnesses, it becomes clear that patients have many myths and misconceptions that undermine their views of themselves and their futures. Guilt, shame, and hopelessness predominate. The experience of being psychotic (and societal reaction to it) can seriously damage self-esteem. In an interesting discussion of patient reaction to psychosis, Jeffries[9] argues that some of the residual symptoms of schizophrenia may reflect a traumatic neurosis in response to the experience of psychosis. An important function of psychoeducational work is to identify hitherto unspoken fears and to correct myths and prejudices by providing basic information in a context of respect and hope. Strategies of psychoeducation have been incorporated into numerous treatment programs.[10-18]

Work with Families

A major development of psychoeducation has been its extension to the families of psychotic patients. This has been a more dramatic transformation in therapeutic philosophy, perhaps, than the psychoeducation of patients. Therapeutic work with families has traditionally been built on assumptions of an etiologic role of the family environment in the development of the illness—schizophrenogenic mothers, schisms and skews, double binds, gender and generational role reversals, distorted dominance patterns, and so on. Such approaches to family treatment have been dominant despite a lack of consistent evidence for their efficacy or the validity of the etiologic theories on which they are based.[19-21] What is clear is that families have frequently felt frustrated by and disenfranchised from the treatment process and that their legitimate needs have been ignored.[22] Recent rethinkings stress the powerful influence—both positive and negative—of the family on the course and outcome of the psychotic illness without implying an etiologic role. The most empirically substantiated family variable to date—expressed emotion—fits this model.[23-25] Given that an individual is schizophrenic, the presence of high levels of criticism or overinvolvement by relatives adversely affects the course of the illness. There is no implication that high expressed emotion causes schizophrenia—indeed, it has predictive power in depressive illness as well—or even that it would be a harmful attitude for normal children not vulnerable to mental illness. If unhelpful behavior and attitudes of the family can be identified without implicit condemnation of the family itself, a rather straightforward intervention suggests itself. The family can be taught the special needs of psychotic patients and the skills required to meet them, without placing undue burden on the rest of the family. The family can then function as a positive resource for the patient. Presumably this requires that the family would have an understanding of the nature of the psychotic illness, how it alters patients' perceptual, cognitive, and affective capacities, and the problems that the illness creates for the patient in effectively coping with his environment.

Several recent studies have demonstrated impressive results from such family approaches. Goldstein et al.[18] developed a six-session program of education and crisis-oriented problem solving focused on the high-risk transition from hospital to the community, for first and second admission schizophrenics. The family intervention provided benefits in terms of relapse rate and symptomatology, both during the six-session period and over a six-month follow-up. Differences between the groups were present even at a five-year followup. The positive effects on symptomatology applied to both psychotic and negative symptoms. Falloon et al.[11] extended work with families over a nine-month period with decreasing frequency of sessions. They used a didactic presentation of information combined with a behavioral-social skills program to develop increased adaptive skills in both patients and families. A marked advantage for the family therapy cases was demonstrated in terms of reduced hospitalization, relapse, and symptomatology. Leff et al.[12] developed a series of brief didactic lectures combined with practical problem-solving support. This program was specifically designed to reduce high expressed emotion. Results indicate success in this regard, as well as benefits for patient outcome. A number of workers have found benefits from conducting some of the family work in multi-family groups. In addition to being time-efficient for professionals, the multi-family experience reduces the sense of isolation frequently seen in the relatives of chronic psychotics. In addition to mutual emotional support, relatives can often draw on their own experience to suggest practical strategies to one another for dealing with difficult management problems. Anderson, Hogarty, and Reiss[16] have designed an ambitious application of the multi-family model in the form of a "survival skills workshop." This program provides extensive didactic material about the pathogenesis, course, outcome, and treatment of schizophrenia, combined with discussions centered on managing practical problems. Extensive attention is devoted to adjusting family expectations of the patient's recovery from psychotic episodes, with emphasis on accepting an initial period of minimal functioning followed by very gradually progressive steps in patient activity and performance. Shenoy, Shires, and White[13] incorporated an ongoing multi-family group for relatives of schizophrenic patients into the standard program of a mental hygiene clinic for a Veterans Administration hospital. The focus and direction of the group were intended to parallel those of Al-Anon groups for alcoholics. Named the "Schiz-Anon" group, it stressed teaching families the biologic model of schizophrenia, providing an understanding of medication and its rationale, helping families with realistic goal-setting for patients, and working to overcome the alienation and isolation that families experience. They found success in terms of significant reduction in hospital rates, family reports of improvement in patients' social lives, and improved attendance by patients for clinic visits. Heinrichs and Carpenter[17] have incorporated a six-session psychoeducational program for families into the early phases of a "targeted" neuroleptic treatment program, in which patients are kept drug free and medicated only when prodromal symptoms suggesting an impending decompensation appear. Although having many similarities to the model used by Goldstein et al.,[18] there is a special emphasis on teaching the families to recognize subtle changes in the patient's attitude and behavior that typically precede psychotic episodes. It has been demonstrated that although patients are reasonably effective in recognizing prodromal symptomatology, families are even more so.[26]

What all of these programs share is that the family intervention is relatively labor-efficient (in terms of a limited number of sessions and/or a multi-family group model) and that they are based on the assumption that the family can become a valuable ally in the patient's treatment if they are provided direct objective information about the illness and its manifestations. In many ways, the consequence of deinstitutionalization and the limited resources available for community treatment is that the family has been required to take on much of the treatment burden that was previously carried by mental health professionals. Under such circumstances, psychoeducational strategies make particular sense.

If we expect families to share in treatment and management responsibilities, they also have a right to share in the body of knowledge that professionals use as a basis for the development and implementation of therapeutic strategies. The professional becomes the expert consultant to the family, in a sense, while much of the actual day-to-day care is conducted by the latter.

Group Therapy

Given the interest in providing cost-effective treatment to large numbers of patients, it is not surprising that there has been an interest in group therapy for chronic psychotic patients. Enthusiasm has grown with the realization that group intervention is not only usually as good but in many settings is perhaps superior to more labor-intensive forms of treatment. There have been a number of studies in recent years that have found group therapy with these patients to be as good as individual therapy,[27,28] or have found group therapy to be superior.[29-33] These group interventions provided for chronic psychotics have generally differed markedly from the more traditional group psychotherapies offered to neurotic patients that stress introspective self-reflection. With chronic psychotic patients, however, a more concrete and outer-directed stance appears to be more beneficial.[34,35] The group setting may afford an especially effective context for providing psychoeducation for psychotic patients. This is not an altogether novel idea, with scattered experimentation in such strategies dating at least back to the early 1900s.[36] Fenn and Dinaburg[37] have recently described a psychoeducational group program for psychotic patients. There are several suggestions from the literature that understanding and accepting medication, as well as dealing with side effects, is more effectively accomplished for psychotic patients in a group setting.[38,39] Beneficial effects have been demonstrated with ongoing group formats that stress discussions of medication and practical demands of living and community adjustment. Alden, Weddington, Jacobson, and Gianturco[32] have reported a significant reduction in rehospitalization over a two-year period for patients treated with such a group format, compared to those same patients prior to the initiation of group treatment. This study also reports an impressive 97 percent attendance rate for patients during the group therapy. Musnik, Olarte, and Rosen[33] have reported nine-year followup data for patients attending once- or twice-monthly "coffee groups" with a focus on medication issues and practical problems in living. The results suggest a significant reduction in time spent in hospital and some improvement in social and vocational functioning. The bulk of the latter improvement, however, was in the first two years of the group experience, after which time a leveling off tended to occur. It was also found that attendance, but not measures of active participation, influenced patients' outcome. A more ambitious extension of the group format has been used in an attempt to deal with the difficulties many psychotic patients experience with the transition from hospital to the community. Melzer[40] and Gomez[41] have described programs in which group therapy sessions during hospitalization were used to develop a sense of cohesion and mutual support among a group of psychotic patients with subsequent discharge of the patients as a group to a common community placement. Once in that setting, the group continued to meet and provide mutual support. Melzer reports experience with 12 patients discharged to the same home. None had been rehospitalized at three-year followup, although the mean length of time each patient spent in the community between admissions was previously five months. Gomez reports a reduction in the number of readmissions, total days of hospitalization, motivation to find jobs, and responsibility for self-care in a group of patients treated with a similar group format compared to a control group.

In many ways the group format appears to be particularly well suited to chronic psychotic patients, although somewhat different strategies may be required for different types of patients (e.g., withdrawn versus activated).[42] There seem to be several reasons for this. Groups do provide an opportunity for patients who characteristically suffer from social isolation, withdrawal, and awkwardness to establish ongoing contact with others. Patients in a group setting can provide mutual support, acceptance, and understanding. Most programs involving group treatment encourage patients to establish relationships with one another outside of the group sessions. This contrasts dramatically with more traditional group therapies designed for neurotic patients. The group setting, in addition, provides an opportunity for consensual validation of patients' perceptions of themselves, their illnesses, and their environments. This is particularly important for those patients who suffer from considerable impairment in reality-testing. Often patients who have a limited ability to appreciate objectively their own interactions with others can be remarkably insightful in reflecting on the experience of another patient in the group. In addition, many patients find it easier to accept these corrections in their perception of reality from other patients, as opposed to mental health professionals. Finally, the group format allows patients to modulate their activity and the intensity of their interactions in the treatment setting, while still maintaining consistent attendance. Patients can participate in group experiences, even during periods when they are relatively passive, withdrawn, and noncommunicative, without feeling the intense demand to communicate that is difficult to avoid in the individual treatment setting.

Social Skills—Social Learning Theory

Although exploratory investigations with behaviorally-based strategies for chronic psychotic patients have been conducted for many years, there has been a recent surge of interest in using behaviorally-derived techniques for improving patients' social skills and interpersonal problem-solving capacities. Such strategies are intended to focus on precisely those practical skills in daily living that quickly become prominent therapeutic issues in patients discharged to the community after hospitalizations. Strategies that provide some hope for modifying deficiencies in these areas are thus especially appealing. Furthermore, inadequacies in these areas appear to play a particularly prominent role in determining rehospitalization for patients placed in the community.[43] In addition, the deficiencies that social skills strategies stress are, generally, strikingly resistant to improvement with neuroleptic drugs.

In spite of the theoretical appeal and timeliness of these strategies, however, their empirical efficacy is far from clear. In an extensive critical review of the literature, Wallace et al.[44] note that while there is good evidence for the effectiveness of these strategies in altering "topographical" features such as eye contact, voice modulation, etc., it has yet to be strongly demonstrated that social skills training can alter more complex, clinically relevant behavior in the patient. In addition, there is still an unsettled problem: to what extent are gains made in carefully contrived training situations generalizable to the patient's life? Wallace argues that part of the limitation of the existing work results from an excessively narrow conceptual definition of social skills, and argues that a broader perspective could result in more meaningful clinical change. In spite of the limitations in the literature, two studies have been particularly important in bolstering the enthusiasm for these approaches as important elements in the treatment of chronic psychotic patients. Paul and Lentz[45] reported on a carefully controlled three-legged study in which a social learning program was dramatically superior to milieu therapy or a control condition in treating chronic psychotic patients. In light of the extremely severe and chronic impairment of these patients, it is remarkable that over 92 percent of the patients in the social learning program were released from the hospital with continuing community stay without rehospitalization for the minimum followup period of 18 months, contrasting with 71 percent for the milieu therapy program and 48 percent for the traditional hospital program.

Another source of great promise for social skills strategies is their extension from the treatment of the patient to treatment of the entire family. It is reasonable to hypothesize that improving problem solving and problem coping strategies in the entire family unit should be markedly more effective in reducing stress for the schizophrenic patient than strategies designed for the patient alone. In spite of its relatively small sample size, a strikingly robust confirmation of this hypothesis has recently been reported.[11] Comparing 18 schizophrenic patients treated with individual supportive care with 18 patients treated together with their families in a home-based family therapy combining psychoeducation with behavioral problem solving strategies, Falloon et al. found the latter to have a significantly better outcome in proportion of patients experiencing clinical relapse (44 percent versus 6 percent), proportion of patients rehospitalized (50 percent versus 11 percent), mean number of days in hospital (8.39 versus 0.83), total number of admissions (14 versus 2), proportion of patients judged to be in remission at nine-month followup (22 percent versus 56 percent), and maximum symptom severity over the nine-month followup period. This is a particularly promising study in that patients selected for participation had families judged to be particularly problematic for the patients' subsequent adjustment (usually by being high expressed emotion households).

CHALLENGES OF INTEGRATION

Looking at the various factors in the recent evolution of psychosocial treatment for chronic psychotic patients is encouraging from a number of perspectives. These treatment developments have taken into account and are generally well suited to the new setting in which most psychotics are now treated, namely brief hospitalizations at times of crisis, followed by a rapid return to the community and ongoing aftercare in the outpatient setting. They also represent attempts to take into account both the values and the limitations of existing pharmacologic strategies. The treatments tend to be understood in terms of rather straightforward pragmatic goals that stress the development of those capacities necessary to sustain productive functioning in the community. In addition, and to a much greater extent than is seen with previous psychosocial interventions, there is an eye to assessing the empirical efficacy of these interventions. They lend themselves to rather discrete research designs in a way that the older, more comprehensive notions of psychosocial treatment did not. All of this is most realistic and largely for the good. However, it raises two major challenges to integration.

At the theoretical level there is a marked difference between these interventions and earlier strategies. For the most part the latter were derived from a psychological model with a comprehensive view of the origins, development, course, and outcome of psychotic illness. Whether primarily intrapsychic or interpersonal in nature, these comprehensive theories of illness provided a coherence to the total treatment that was not only intellectually satisfying, but encouraged an important continuity and consistency in the therapeutic endeavor. In contrast, recent psychosocial strategies are more inclined to focus on a particular aspect of the patient's psychopathology or problems in living. In many cases these strategies are atheoretical with regard to the origin and nature of the illness, and often provide no overall framework for grasping the comprehensive treatment requirements of the patient. And yet no one of these interventions is offered as the total treatment for psychotic illnesses. Thus the clinician charged with the comprehensive treatment of these patients has relatively little theoretical guidance as to how optimally to combine therapeutic elements from the wide range of available treatment strategies to best meet the patient's total needs. While it is easy to argue that the comprehensive notions behind the older treatment strategies gave a false sense of understanding, they nonetheless provided a heuristic paradigm for the clinician. In the current state of affairs it is all too easy for the clinician to embrace a thoughtless eclecticism in which various treatment techniques are offered to the patient without an integrated strategy. Elsewhere[3] the author has argued that comprehensive models can be developed based upon intervening variables that are less distanced, in terms of fewer orders of abstraction removed, from the clinical data. One such model can be based on behavioral activation, stimulation, and arousal.[17] In such a model, schizophrenic functioning is seen as having an "inverted U" relationship to these intervening variables. On the one hand, excessive stimulation, overarousal, activation, and stress are disruptive to the patient, lead to a deterioration in his or her functioning, and exacerbate symptomatology primarily in the form of cognitive and behavioral disorganization and psychotic symptoms. Inadequate stimulation, challenge, and demands of the patient can, conversely, result in insufficient activation, again leading to a deterioration in the patient's functioning and an increase in psychopathology characterized primarily by negative or deficit symptoms such as social withdrawal, anergy, impaired initiative, loss of motivation, blunted affect, and anhedonia. Within such a framework various elements of the patient's experience and environment can be seen as either increasing or decreasing activation, stimulation, and arousal. At the same time, the range of potential treatment strategies, whether they be pharmacologic or psychosocial in nature, can be thought of as moving the patient to either higher or lower levels of these intervening variables. Thus at any given point patients could be assessed as to whether they are high or low in the activation arousal continuum. Those factors in the patients' environment that contribute to their current level can be identified and addressed, and the range of potential therapeutic interventions that move the patient in the desired direction can be considered singly and in combination. Thus for the overactivated patient interventions such as neuroleptic drugs, reduction of environmental demands and stress, reduced interpersonal contact, and imposing structure on the day-to-day environment of the patient can be considered singly or in combination as possible strategies for reducing activation arousal. Conversely, for the underactivated, underaroused patient with marked deficit symptomatology, numerous treatments suggest themselves as possible candidates for moving the patient to higher levels. They include a reduction or discontinuation of neuroleptic drugs, a graded increase in the demands of the environment, and psychosocial strategies that increase the patient's interpersonal contact and productive activity. Within this framework the integration of treatment for the chronic patient can be seen as an ever-changing titration of elements, designed to keep the patients at the optimum level of arousal and activation. At times treatments that operate in opposing directions can be used in combination to alter the patient's mental, social, and occupational functioning. Thus at a time of increased stress, when the patient is being pushed to be more socially active or to start a job, the introduction or increase in drug dose can be used to offset the increase in activation and arousal that the patient will experience. While this is only one possible model, it illustrates the use of relatively atheoretical intervening variables in constructing a heuristic model which clinicians can use to integrate a wide range of treatment interventions with a given patient and to adjust that package of strategies over time in a sensible way.

Equally difficult are the problems of practical integration of the therapeutic team. Older models of psychosocial treatment are more likely to be administered *in toto* by one highly trained professional who is responsible for the comprehensive treatment of the patient. This professional was also highly informed about the comprehensive, theoretical model on which the treatment was based. In the case of the more recent treatment developments, however, it is quite possible for major elements of the various strategies to be effectively administered by considerably less trained individuals. In these cases it is likely that while the individual may be quite adequately trained in providing the specific intervention in question, they may frequently lack the more comprehensive grasp of the psychopathology and its role in the patient's total life. This can be remedied if the individuals providing the various components of the treatment plan work together as a highly integrated team in which the unique contributions of each member can be understood in the context of the total treatment experience. Someone on the treatment team must be responsible for ensuring that there is a clear understanding of the contribution of each treatment to the comprehensive needs of the patient. Such a team leader must have a wide grasp of biologic, psychologic, and social dimensions of the illness and how they interact. The broad background of the psychodynamically trained psychiatrist is especially well suited for this role.[3]

REFERENCES

1. May PRA: *Treatment of Schizophrenia*. New York, Science House, 1968
2. Heinrichs DW, Carpenter WT: The psychotherapy of schizophrenia, in *Psychiatry 1982: The American Psychiatric Annual Review*. Washington, DC, American Psychiatric Press, 1982, 154–166
3. Carpenter WT, Heinrichs DW: The role of psychodynamic psychiatry in the treatment of schizophrenic patients, in Strauss JS, Bowers M, Downey TW (eds): *The Psychotherapy of Schizophrenia*. New York, Plenum, 1980,239–256
4. Bleuler M: *The Schizophrenic Disorders: Long-term Patients and Family Studies*. New Haven, Yale University Press, 1978
5. Engel GL: The need for a new medical model: A challenge for biomedicine. *Science* 1977;196:129–136
6. Pratt JH: Results obtained in the treatment of pulmonary tuberculosis by the class method. *Br Med* 1908;10:1070–1071
7. Carpenter WT, Heinrichs DW: Early intervention, time-limited, targeted pharmacotherapy of schizophrenia. *Schizophr Bull* 1983;9(4):533-542
8. Carpenter WTC, Stephens JH, Rey AC, et al: Early intervention versus continuous pharmacotherapy of schizophrenia. *Psychopharmacol Bull* 1982;18(1):21–23
9. Jeffries JJ: The trauma of being psychotic: A neglected element in the management of chronic schizophrenia. *Canadian Psychiatric Assoc Journal* 1977;22(5):199–206
10. Mendel WM, Allen RE: Treating the chronic patient. *Curr Psychiatr Ther* 1977;17:115–126
11. Falloon IRH, Boyd JL, McGill CW, et al: Family management in the prevention of exacerbations of schizophrenia: A controlled study. *New Engl J Med* 1982;306(24):1437–1440
12. Leff J, Kuipers L, Berkowtiz R, et al: A controlled trial of social intervention in the families of schizophrenic patients. *Br J Psychiatry* 1982;141:121–134
13. Shenoy RS, Shires BW, White MS: Using a Schiz-anon group in the treatment of chronic ambulatory schizophrenics. *Hosp Community Psychiatry* 1981;32(6):421–422
14. Scher M, Wilson L, Mason J: The management of chronic schizophrenia. *J Fam Pract* 1980;11(3):407–413

15. Fink P: The relatives group: Treatment for parents of adult chronic schizophrenics. *Int J Group Psychother* 1981;31(4):453–468
16. Anderson, CM, Hogarty GE, Reiss DJ: Family treatment of adult schizophrenic patients: A psycho-educational approach. *Schizophr Bull* 1980;6(3)490–505
17. Heinrichs DW, Carpenter WT: The coordination of family therapy with other treatment modalities for schizophrenia, in McFarlane WR, Beels CC (eds): *Family Therapy in Schizophrenia.* New York, Guilford Press, 1983,267–287
18. Goldstein MJ, Rodnick EH, Evans JR, et al: Drug and family therapy in the aftercare treatment of acute schizophrenia. *Arch Gen Psychiatry* 1978;35(10):1169–1177
19. Goldstein MJ, Rodnick EH: The family's contribution to the etiology of schizophrenia: Current status. *Schizophr Bull* 1975;1(14):48–63
20. Liem JH: Family studies of schizophrenia: An update and commentary. *Schizophr Bull* 1980;6(3):429–455
21. Jacob T: Family interaction in disturbed and normal families: A methodological and substantive review. *Psychol Bull* 1975;82:33–65
22. Appleton WS: Mistreatment of patients' families by psychiatrists. *Am J Psychiatry* 1974;131(6):655–657
23. Brown GW, Monck EM, Carstairs GM, et al: The influence of family life and the course of schizophrenic illness. *Br J Preventative Social Med* 1962;16:55–68
24. Brown GW, Birley JLT, Wing JK: Influence of family life on the course of schizophrenic disorders: A replication. *Br J Psychiatry* 1972;121:241–258
25. Vaughn CE, Leff JP: The influence of family and social factors on the course of psychiatric patients. *Br J Psychiatry* 1976;129:125–137
26. Herz MI, Melville C: Relapse in schizophrenia. *Am J Psychiatry* 1980;137:801–805
27. Herz MI, Spitzer RL, Gibbon M: Individual versus group aftercare treatment. *Am J Psychiatry* 1974;131:802–812
28. Levene HL, Patterson V, Murphy BG: The aftercare of schizophrenics: An evaluation of group and individual approaches. *Psychiatr Q* 1970;44:296–305
29. O'Brien CP, Hamen KB, Ray BA, et al: Group versus individual psychotherapy with schizophrenics: A controlled outcome study. *Arch Gen Psychiatry* 1972;27:474–475
30. Shattan SP, Decamp L, Fujii E: Group treatment of conditionally discharged patients in a mental health clinic. *Am J Psychiatry* 1966;122:798–804
31. Prince RM, Ackerman RE, Carter NC, et al: Group aftercare—impact on a statewide program. *Dis Nervous System* 1977;38:793–796
32. Alden AR, Weddington WW, Jacobson C, et al: Group aftercare for chronic schizophrenics. *J Clin Psychiatry* 1979;40:249–252
33. Musnik R, Olarte SW, Rosen A: "Coffee groups": A nine-year follow-up study. *Am J Psychiatry* 1980;137(1):91–93
34. Otteson JP: Curative caring: The use of buddy groups with chronic schizophrenics. *J Consult Clin Psychol* 1979;47(3):649–651
35. Beal D, Duckro P, Elias J, et al: Graded group procedures for long-term regressed schizophrenics. *J Nerv Ment Dis* 1977;164(2):102–106
36. Lazell EW: The group treatment of dementia praecox. *Psychoanal Rev* 1921;8:168–179
37. Fenn HH, Dinaburg D: Didactic group psychotherapy with chronic schizophrenics. *Int J Group Psychother* 1981;31(4):443–452
38. Malhotra HK, Olgiati SG: Fluphenazine therapy in groups. *Comprehensive Psychiatry* 1977;18:89–92
39. Hansell N, Willis GL: Outpatient treatment of schizophrenia. *Am J Psychiatry* 1977;134:1082–1085
40. Melzer M: Group treatment to combat loneliness and mistrust in chronic schizophrenics. *Hosp Community Psychiatry* 1979;30(1):18–20
41. Gomez EA: Small supportive treatment units and the problem of recidivism in indigent chronic schizophrenic patients. *Psychiatr Q* 1981;53(3):178–183

42. O'Brien CP: Group therapy of schizophrenia. *Curr Psychiatr Ther* 1972;17:115–126, 149–154
43. Paul GL: Chronic mental patient: Current status—future direction. *Psychol Bull* 1969;71:81–94
44. Wallace CJ, Nelson CJ, Liberman RP, et al: A review and critique of social skills training with schizophrenic patients. *Schizophr Bull* 1980;6(1):42–63
45. Paul GL, Lentz RJ: *Psychosocial Treatment of Chronic Mental Patients: Milieu Versus Social Learning Programs.* Cambridge, Harvard University Press, 1977

William A. Anthony
Mikal R. Cohen
Barry F. Cohen

10

Psychiatric Rehabilitation

Significant developments in the field of psychiatric rehabilitation have occurred during the last five years. Some indicators of this growth are the development of international psychiatric rehabilitation organizations (e.g., International Association of Psychosocial Rehabilitation Services, World Rehabilitation Association for the Psycho-Socially Disabled), new publications specifically devoted to the topic of rehabilitating the psychiatrically disabled (e.g., Psychosocial Rehabilitation Journal, International Psychiatric Rehabilitation Newsletter), and a renewed focus of certain agencies on research, training, and services relevant to psychiatric rehabilitation (e.g., NIMH's Community Support and Rehabilitation Branch, the National Institute of Handicapped Research).

These developments are the more noticeable advances in the field of psychiatric rehabilitation. The focus of this chapter is on whether or not there have been concomitant advances in the knowledge about psychiatric rehabilitation over the last five years.

THE ROOTS OF PSYCHIATRIC REHABILITATION

The current growth in psychiatric rehabilitation knowledge over the last five years is made possible by three historical developments: the articulation of a rehabilitation philosophy by treatment specialists in physical disability, the fed-

THE CHRONIC MENTAL PATIENT
ISBN 0-8089-1649-1

Copyright © 1984 by Grune & Stratton.
All rights of reproduction in any form reserved.

eral funding of vocational rehabilitation programs for the psychiatrically disabled, and the birth of the psychosocial rehabilitation center movement.

The philosophy of psychiatric rehabilitation has its conceptual base in the practice of physical medicine and rehabilitation. Practitioners who work with the severely physically disabled have had a long-standing concern for the psychosocial rehabilitation of persons with chronic physical disability. A rehabilitation philosophy was articulated decades ago in the field of physical medicine and rehabilitation, and can be found in the writings of the field's leaders.[1-4]

While the last five years have seen a significant increase in activity and knowledge development, financial support at the federal level for psychiatric rehabilitation first appeared in the 1943 Amendments to the Vocational Rehabilitation Act. Prior to that time, the public supported program of rehabilitation concentrated only on the provision of vocational services to the physically disabled. As funding for rehabilitation grew, the philosophy of rehabilitation developed by the leaders in physical rehabilitation was incorporated into the federal legislation of recent years. As a result, rehabilitation was no longer considered to be only vocationally focused; rather it became concerned with a disabled person's functioning in all environments. More recently, when NIMH defined the components comprised by a Community Support System, comprehensive rehabilitation services were identified as an essential component. A history and precedent for federal funding of psychiatric rehabilitation services, research, and training has been established by both the National Institute of Mental Health and the Rehabilitation Services Administration.

Specifically, it was the psychosocial center movement which built on the legislative funding and implemented the physical rehabilitation philosophy in settings which serve the psychiatrically disabled. Grob's history of the psychosocial center movement[5] traces its origins and current status. The early centers such as Fountain House and Horizon House were founded by groups of ex-patients and were designed to meet their needs for mutual aid and support. These early social clubs gave impetus to the comprehensive, multi-service psychosocial rehabilitation centers which are now found throughout the country. Some examples are Thresholds in Chicago, the Social Center in Fairfax, Virginia, Center Club in Boston, Hill House in Cleveland, Portals House in Los Angeles, Fellowship House in Miami, and Boley Manor in St. Petersburg.

Anchored in a rehabilitation philosophy, supported in part by federal and state dollars, these centers have become a major resource to the future growth of psychiatric rehabilitation. It is in these Centers that the philosophy and principles common to all of rehabilitation are put into practice. It is the leaders of these Centers who have continued to articulate and promote a philosophy of psychiatric rehabilitation. Within the last five years, service delivery programs based on the psychiatric rehabilitation philosophy have become a more accepted way of intervening in the lives of the severely psychiatrically disabled.

THE ESSENTIAL PRINCIPLES OF PSYCHIATRIC REHABILITATION

The increasing number of community-based psychiatric settings has led to the rather routine use of the word "rehabilitation" to describe the treatment programs often conducted in these community settings.[6,7] Even 24-hour inpatient settings have been seen as "rehabilitative" psychiatric environments.[8,9] The phrase "rehabilitation programming" is used increasingly in both the treatment professional's vocabulary and the administrator's program description.[6]

Descriptions of model psychiatric rehabilitation programs appear with increasing regularity in the literature.[10] Based on the current wealth of articles about psychiatric rehabilitation, it is now possible to articulate a set of principles basic to most rehabilitation settings. The specification of basic psychiatric rehabilitation principles has heretofore been a difficult task because psychiatric rehabilitation is practiced in many different service delivery settings by practitioners from many different professional disciplines.

The identification of a set of principles basic to psychiatric rehabilitation can serve to highlight the commonalities among diverse psychiatric rehabilitation settings and the different disciplines that practice within them. Anthony[11] lamented the absence of a set of rehabilitation principles in the mental health field when he facetiously characterized psychiatric rehabilitation as "the development of non-traditional settings for the purpose of using traditional techniques by traditionally trained professionals" (p 660). Now, however, the essential principles underlying the practice of psychiatric rehabilitation as well as the training of psychiatric rehabilitation practitioners can be more easily specified. The recent writings of Beard,[12] Lamb,[13] Dincin,[14] Grob,[5] and Anthony,[15] among others, indicate a growing consensus about what constitute the essential principles of psychiatric rehabilitation.

The following principles seem to be basic to the practice of psychiatric rehabilitation, and operate independently both of the setting in which they are practiced and the professional discipline of the practitioner, Table 10-1 lists the following eight principles.

1. *The primary focus of psychiatric rehabilitation is on improving the psychiatrically disabled person's capabilities and competence.* Rehabilitation is directed primarily at maximizing health rather than minimizing sickness, i.e., health induction, not simply symptom reduction. The historical emphasis on physical rehabilitation has always been on increasing competencies rather than on simply alleviating symptoms and pathology. It is a well known axiom of rehabilitation that minimizing or suppressing sickness will not automatically lead toward improvement in functional capacity. Put another way, the emphasis is on *coping* rather than *succumbing,* on the challenge for

Table 10-1.
Basic principles of psychiatric rehabilitation

1. The primary focus of psychiatric rehabilitation is on improving the psychiatrically disabled person's capabilities and competencies.

2. The benefit of psychiatric rehabilitation for the clients is behavioral improvement in their environments of need.

3. Psychiatric rehabilitation is atheoretical and eclectic in the use of a variety of therapeutic constructs.

4. A central focus of psychiatric rehabilitation is on improving vocational outcome for the psychiatrically disabled.

5. Hope is an essential ingredient of the rehabilitation process.

6. The deliberate increase in client dependency can lead to an eventual increase in the client's independent functioning.

7. Active participation and involvement of clients in their rehabilitation process is sought.

8. The two fundamental interventions of psychiatric rehabilitation are client skill development and environment resource development.

meaningful adaptation or change rather than on the difficulties and heartbreak of the disability.[16] As Beard[12] has indicated, a fundamental message of rehabilitation is the "belief in the potential productivity of the most severely psychiatrically disabled client" (p 47).

Dincin[14] speaks of psychiatric rehabilitation as providing opportunities which are "growth inducing." While the specific words used to convey the message of this principle are numerous (i.e., growth, productivity, health, coping, skills, competencies, capabilities), the meaning of the principle remains clear.

2. *The benefit of psychiatric rehabilitation for the clients is behavioral improvement in their environments of need.* The development of therapeutic insight is not a primary goal.[14,15] The emphasis is on reality factors rather than intrapsychic factors,[13] on improving the person's ability to do something in a specific environment. Despite the presence of residual disability, rehabilitation attempts to help the person adjust and adapt to the requirements of specific environments.[5] Psychiatric rehabilitation focuses on the disabled person's ability to perform certain behaviors within certain environments, a focus similar to the emphasis in physical rehabilitation. For example, treatment outcome for a blind person is not just the learning of mobility skills; it is also the application of these mobility skills in certain environments of need (e.g., home, work). The client outcome is thus tied to an environment. Similarly, the psychiatric rehabilitation specialist must not just work toward improving skills (e.g., conversational skills), but must do so with a regard to

the demands of the specific environment in which the client is presently or will be functioning (e.g., community residence, transitional employment placement).

3. *Psychiatric rehabilitation is atheoretical and eclectic in the use of a variety of therapeutic constructs.* The philosophy and principles of rehabilitation guide the practice of psychiatric rehabilitation; no allegiance exists to any personality or psychotherapeutic theory. Consistent with the second and third principles, Grob[5] has characterized psychiatric rehabilitation as "eclectic in theory and pragmatic in adaptation" (p 278). Dincin[14] indicates that the practice of psychiatric rehabilitation is not dependent on the acceptance of a particular theory as to the cause of mental illness. The growth of psychiatric rehabilitation practice has not been dependent on its embrace of any currently popular psychotherapeutic theory.

4. *A central focus of psychiatric rehabilitation is on improving vocational outcome for the psychiatrically disabled.* As Brooks[17] indicated, work is the very essence of rehabilitation. The centrality of vocational issues in psychiatric rehabilitation is most strongly apparent in the Fountain House model of psychiatric rehabilitation. Work is a central ingredient of the Fountain House model and underlies all aspects of this approach. The developers of the Fountain House model believe "that work, especially the opportunity to aspire to and achieve gainful employment, is a deeply generative and integrative force in the life of every human being" (p 47).[12] Grob[5] holds that the appropriate placement of the employable ex-patient is an essential part of the recovery process. Lamb[13] states that "work therapy geared to the capabilities of the individual patient should be a cornerstone of community treatment of long term patients" (p 7). The field of psychiatric rehabilitation is clearly rooted in a belief in the critical importance of work or work-like activities in the rehabilitation of the psychiatrically disabled. Not only is the value of work reflected in the principles, but vocational programming is an integral part of the history and development of the field of psychiatric rehabilitation.

5. *Hope is an essential ingredient of psychiatric rehabilitation.* Rehabilitation is present- and future-oriented, and the tasks of the present are guided by a renewed and revived sense of hope for the future. Dincin[14] suggests that the atmosphere of a psychiatric rehabilitation setting must be pervaded by a sense of hopefulness and an orientation toward the "future." Fountain House attempts to instill a "helpful view of the future."[12] The practitioners of both physical rehabilitation[4] and psychotherapy[18] have recognized the importance of "hope" or positive expectations for improvement as a critical factor in the treatment and rehabilitation process. Anthony, Cohen, and Cohen[6] maintain that the hope for client improvement, no matter what the statistical probabilities of improvement are, is an important component of any rehabilitation intervention. In contrast, the absence of hope for improvement makes the practice of psychiatric rehabilitation problematic. When hopelessness per-

meates a setting and contaminates the practitioners, the interminable and difficult demands of psychiatric rehabilitation practice seem overwhelming, and the potential for client gain is diminished.

6. *The deliberate increase in client dependency can lead to an eventual increase in the client's independent functioning.* Sheltered living, learning, and working settings, which allow for greater levels of client dependency, are the traditional settings in which rehabilitation interventions occur.[13] While a healthy concern exists about the danger of overdependency, the psychiatric rehabilitation philosophy has distinguished between types of dependencies.[19] Dependency on a limited number of people and settings is a natural first step in rehabilitation, and in itself is not inherently destructive.[14]

    The technology of psychiatric rehabilitation is limited in its ability to achieve total client independence. Furthermore, dependence on people, places, or things is a normal state of affairs. Interventions which allow for a certain degree of dependency at certain times, such as (for example) the use of "enablers" or aides, may in fact be maximizing the client's functioning in other environments at other times.[20]

7. *Active participation and involvement of clients in their rehabilitation is sought.* Client involvement in psychiatric rehabilitation is the active participation by the client (e.g., communication of values, experiences, feelings, ideas, and goals) throughout all the phases of rehabilitation. The research literature suggests that the rehabilitation goals of clients and practitioners frequently differ.[21] The literature also confirms that helping[22] and teaching[23] is difficult without client involvement. Psychiatric rehabilitation incorporates the client's perspective in the assessment and intervention phases as well as the practitioner's perspective.[24]

    Client participation can also include involvement of clients in the delivery of services to other clients. Fountain House is presently undertaking a member (client) training program designed to increase and enrich the various roles which members assume in the Fountain House psychiatric rehabilitation model.[12] Examples of activities in which members can become involved include outreach services to other members, member education, and tutoring, advocacy, and conduction of evaluation studies.

    Client involvement requires rehabilitation procedures that can be explained to and understood by the client. The rehabilitation intervention cannot seem mysterious to the client. The practitioner is constantly trying to demystify rehabilitation. Most critical to client involvement is the practitioner's commitment to the goal of client involvement and the practitioner's belief that rehabilitation is done *with* clients and not *to* them.

8. *The two fundamental interventions of psychiatric rehabilitation are client skill development and environmental resource development.* Interventions which attempt to change either the disabled person or the disabled person's environment are the time-tested double foci of rehabilitation.[16] The focus on

person change typically involves clients learning the specific skills which they need in order to function more effectively in their environments. The focus on environmental change typically involves modifying the environment to accommodate or maximize the client's present skill functioning.

Practitioners of physical rehabilitation have traditionally used both types of interventions with their clients. The physical therapist, for example, teaches the paraplegic client new skills (e.g., how to make a wheelchair-to-bed transfer) or changes the client's environment to better accommodate the client's present skill level (e.g., ramps, wheelchair accessible bathrooms).

Similar to the approach used in physical rehabilitation, the rehabilitation approach with the psychiatrically disabled client also focuses on building client skills and modifying environments. The psychiatric rehabilitation approach is based on the research literature which has indicated that it is the psychiatrically disabled client's skills, not symptoms, that relate most strongly to rehabilitation outcome.[15,25] In addition, rehabilitation research has shown repeatedly that psychiatric clients can learn a variety of physical, emotional, and intellectual skills regardless of their present symptomatology. Furthermore, these skills, when properly integrated into a comprehensive rehabilitation program that provides environmental reinforcement and support for their use in the community, can have significant impact on the client's rehabilitation outcome.[15] Psychiatric rehabilitation settings vary in how systematically they approach skill building or environmental resource development. Skill teaching and resource development may be informal and experiential,[12,14] or planned and systematic.[26-28]

Similarly, some settings strongly emphasize resource development interventions,[12] while other settings focus on development of client skills.[29]

These two types of psychiatric rehabilitation interventions have been researched extensively, although often not in the context of a comprehensive rehabilitation setting. The next section of the chapter surveys the research foundation of these fundamental rehabilitation interventions.

THE MAJOR INTERVENTIONS OF PSYCHIATRIC REHABILITATION

The psychiatric rehabilitation intervention should ideally occur after a rehabilitation diagnosis and plan have been developed. Similar to the diagnostic and planning phase, the intervention phase varies between settings with respect to how systematically and formally it is done. A rehabilitation diagnosis gathers information about the client's current level of skills relevant to the demands of the environment in which the client wants to function. The rehabilitation diagnosis also collects information about those aspects of the client's environment which may have an impact on the attainment of the client's rehabilitation goals. The rehabilitation diagnosis is the basis for the development of the rehabilitation plan, which is designed to increase the client's skills and/or to develop an environment more helpful to the client's functioning.[6]

The two major types of psychiatric rehabilitation interventions, client skill development and environmental resource development, are built on information collected and organized in the rehabilitation diagnostic and planning phases. Various aspects of these two major interventions have been investigated by a wide range of researchers, and have been reported on in journals of psychology, rehabilitation counseling, psychiatry, occupational therapy, nursing, and social work. Sufficient research has accumulated that it is now possible to summarize the research carried out over the last decade on each of these interventions.

The Origins of Client Skill Development Research

Carkhuff suggested in 1972 that training clients directly in the skills which they need to function in society is the preferred method of treatment.[30] Research by Carkhuff et al. on client skill training[22,30-34] led to a redefinition of the "training as treatment" approach into a "teaching as treatment" therapeutic approach.[35] This redefinition reflected the fact that as the therapist moves from training individual clients to teaching groups of clients, he or she must become more knowledgeable about the learning-management processes and those teaching skills needed by the therapist to facilitate the skill learning of groups of clients.

Parallel to the development of the "teaching as treatment" approach of Carkhuff were the client skill training developments of the "behavioristic" approaches,[36,37] which have culminated in the concept of "social skills training."[38] Skills training programs were developed for many different clients with a variety of skill deficits. For example, the literature has reported on such programs as diverse as public speaking for anxious clients,[39] study deficits for students,[40] and education for migraine headache sufferers.[41]

Also occurring at much the same time were client skill development studies conducted in rehabilitation settings and/or reported in rehabilitation journals. These skill training studies focused on teaching all types of disabled clients various job-related skills.[29,42,43]

Research into the Effects of Client Skill Development

Over 70 percent of the client skill development research has been based on nonpsychiatric populations.[44] The earliest skill development studies appeared in the late 1960s. Table 10-2 lists only those studies which have been undertaken with the severely psychiatrically disabled population. Because the research has not previously been combined and presented in this way, Table 10-2 lists the major studies which have been conducted over the last decade.

Given the number of behavioral deficits and the range of symptomatology of the psychiatrically disabled population, an initial research question was whether severely psychiatrically disabled clients would be amenable to a skills training approach. The shaping of appropriate behaviors in chronic patients as opposed to direct teaching methods had been the previous treatment of choice.[45] This type of token economy approach, unfortunately, relies on strict reinforcement procedures which do not normally exist beyond the controlled treatment setting.[46] Token economies appear, consequently, to have limited value for those clients being discharged to less restrictive settings, and are rather inefficient at teaching clients responses that are not in their repertoire. There have been suggestions, furthermore, that token learning is really just that (i.e., the learning itself is rarely valued by the client).

More recent skill training studies have investigated the ability of the chronic population to learn skills through a variety of systematic skill training programs,

Table 10-2.
Studies of client skill development approaches with
the severely psychiatrically disabled

Skills Trained	Authors
Social behaviors	Bellack, Hersen, & Turner[54]; Eisler, Blanchard, Fitts, & Williams[55]; Jaffe & Carlson[48]; Malm[56]; Marzillier & Winter[52]; Williams, Turner, Watts, Bellack, & Hersen[50]; Wood, Lenhard, Maggiani, & Campbell.[57]
Social behaviors and activities of daily living	Becker & Bayer[58]; Bell[59]; Lillie & Armstrong[60]; Retchless[61]; Scoles & Fine[62]; Weinman, Sander, Kleiner, & Wilson[63]; Wood, Lenhard, Maggiani, & Campbell.[57]
Interpersonal behaviors	Cole, Klarreich, & Fryatt[64]; Goldsmith & McFall[65]; Hinterkopf & Brunswick[66]; Pierce & Drasgow[33]; Vitalo.[34]
Conversation and assertiveness	Finch & Wallace[51]; Hersen, Eisler, & Miller.[67]
Controlling aggression	Cheek & Mendelson[68]; Matson & Stephens[69]; Rutner & Bugle.[70]
Vocational skills	Azrin & Philip[29]; Kline & Hoisington[71]; McClure[72]; Prazak[73]; Rubin & Roessler[74]; Shean[75]; Stude & Pauls[42]; Ugland.[43]
Problem-solving skills	Bedell, Archer, & Marlowe[76]; Coche & Flick[77]; Siegel & Spivack.[78]

using didactic techniques, modeling, role-playing, feedback, and reinforcement. The general outcome of these studies reiterated the principle advanced by Anthony and Margules[47]: skill training with specific objectives and specific techniques can improve skill levels, regardless of symptomatology.

Of those studies specifically undertaken with the severely psychiatrically disabled, variability existed in the target skill behaviors generalized, the target behaviors maintained at the point of follow-up, and the teaching techniques used by the practitioners.[38,48-50]

Finch and Wallace,[51] for example, found that patients trained in role-playing improved in role playing but not in staff communication and social contact. Marzillier and Winter,[52] using a single-subject design, indicated that in individual patients some generalization did occur, but that the effects of the new skills did not generalize to measures of increased confidence or self-esteem. Vitalo and Ross[53] directly applied the rehabilitation skills training approach suggested by Anthony[15] with moderately chronic outpatients and found that it resulted in a significantly greater number of skills (e.g., as measured by the number of new friends, new activities developed) at the end of training. Vitalo and Ross[53] also reported that the clients in the skill training group experienced symptomatic relief similar to a "medications-only" comparison group. Many of these skill training studies are reviewed in this book in Chapter 13.

Research conducted on Carkhuff's "teaching as treatment" approach and the psychoeducational or social skills training approach is extremely relevant to the field of psychiatric rehabilitation. More directly identified with psychiatric rehabilitation, however, are those studies which have trained psychiatrically disabled clients in various vocational skills, such as job seeking, career decision-making, and work adjustment (Table 10-2).

Most of the vocational skill development research has focused on career placement or job seeking skills. The technology of career placement training, first developed over 14 years ago by the Minnesota Rehabilitation Center,[79] has become a credible rehabilitation intervention. Research conducted throughout the 1970s indicates that training clients in career placement skills does have a significant impact on vocational outcome.[29,42,43,72] Evidence of the intense interest in career placement training is provided in a comparative review of six current career placement packages.[80]

An occupational skills/work adjustment skills training program conducted at a state hospital was reviewed by Rubin and Roessler.[74] Thirty-seven of the 40 patients who entered the program completed it, 22 obtained jobs, and six enrolled in further training. Client outcome research into the effects of skills training in career decision-making is rarely reported in the literature. In a small, quasi-experimental study, however, Kline and Hoisington[71] did investigate the impact of a work values group which met for 1.5 hours per week for 12 weeks. Over 50 percent of the participants in the work values group obtained employment; in the comparison group only 10 percent obtained employment. These data suggest the potential impact of career counseling interventions on vocational outcome. Client skill development is considered to be a basic rehabilitation intervention.

In summary, researchers from a number of different perspectives have investigated the impact of skill development approaches with the severely psychiatrically disabled. At present, the research suggests that psychiatrically disabled clients can be taught a wide range of physical, emotional, and intellectual skills. Furthermore, when these skill development interventions are combined with a facilitative environment which reinforces and supports the use of these skills, this type of intervention can have a positive impact on the clients' ability to live more independently, learn more efficiently, and work more productively.

One of the major problems confronting skill development approaches in rehabilitation is that the effects of skill training are situation specific. Practitioners of psychiatric rehabilitation who attempt to teach their clients the skills they need to function in specific environments have often failed to get the client to accurately use those skills in the environment of need. For example, occupational skills learned in a hospital-based setting are not readily used in the community.[15] Newly learned skill behaviors are very much situation specific.

Psychiatric rehabilitation skill teaching programs must become less contrived and simulated. Efforts need to be made to arrange for teaching to take place in the environment of need, in more natural-like environments. Psychiatric rehabilitation must operate on the principle that generalization does not just occur—generalization must be programmed. Cohen, Ridley, and Cohen[81] reviewed the issue of skill generalization in psychiatric rehabilitation and suggested the following principles:

1. Use the natural reinforcers present in the environment of need to reward appropriate responses in the training environment;
2. Provide support services to follow along the client in the environment of need;
3. Teach support persons the skill of selective reward to be applied in the environment of need;
4. Teach the client to identify intrinsic motivation as a replacement for extrinsic reward;
5. Increase the delay of reward gradually;
6. Teach in a variety of situations;
7. Teach variations of response in the same situations;
8. Teach self-evaluation and self-reward;
9. Teach the rules or principles which underlie the skill;
10. Use gradually more difficult homework assignments;
11. Involve the client in setting goals and selecting intervention strategies.

Research into the Effects of Environmental Resource Development

Environmental resource development interventions attempt to alter the people, places, and/or things in the client's environment in order to help the client attain his or her goal. If successful, environmental resource development interventions make the client's environment more supportive of the client's rehabilitation goal and more appropriate in its demands relevant to the client's rehabilitation goal. Environmental resource development interventions attempt to help the clients make use of existing environments, modify existing environments to make them more supportive or appropriate, and/or create new environments where none exist.

The Community Support Program is an environmental resource development intervention on a systems level. Research relevant to the Community Support Program is presented in Chapter 18. The use of "networking" as a means of organizing environmental support is also presented in this book.

Specific examples of environmental resource development approaches for clients might be the placement of the client in activities (e.g., sheltered workshop activities) which closely match the client's current skill level; helping a family member to model, reward, and prompt the client to facilitate the client's performance of needed tasks; and the assignment of the client to a practitioner who shows understanding and acceptance of the client.

In essence, there have been two types of client outcome studies which have manipulated the environmental resource dimension. The first type of study has used both client skill development and environmental resource development approaches in concert; it is thus impossible to identify the unique contributions of either to client outcome. The second type of study has researched intervention strategies that are more exclusively focused on modifying the environment in which the client functions. These studies which focus more exclusively on environmental interventions will be examined first.

Environmental interventions attempt to provide the client with supportive persons, supportive settings, or both. A "support person" might offer support through a number of different roles (i.e., as an advocate, companion, counselor and/or advisor). Attempts at making the setting more supportive focus more on the programs or resources within the environment than on support persons per se. The purpose of distinguishing between supportive persons and supportive settings is simply to highlight the different ways in which environmental modifications occur. In practice, these modifications often occur simultaneously.

The main identifying feature of both types of supportive interventions, as distinguished from skill development interventions, is that they do not attempt to change the client's behavior. The attempt, rather, is simply to support and accommodate the client's present level of functioning. The early studies by Katkin[82,83] and a more recent study by Cannady[84] have clearly demonstrated the positive impact on client outcome of a support person. Cannady[84] employs citizens from the discharged patients' rural neighborhood to function as "supportive case workers." Results indicate that over a 12-month period in-patient days can be decreased by as much as 92 percent.

Witheridge et al.[85] have reported on the use of a support team with individuals at high risk for readmission. Working out of the clients' homes and neighborhoods, this team had as its goal to develop individualized support systems. Of the original 50 participants, 41 remained in the program. One year follow-up data indicated that days hospitalized decreased from 87.1 to 36.6.

A study by Stickney et al.[86] investigated the effects of introducing a support person and a more supportive environment, separately and in combination. Stickney studied the impact of four predischarge formats, which differed in level of person and environmental support. The goal of the discharge plans was to increase use of the community mental health center and decrease recidivism for 400 patients discharged from a state mental hospital. Four different discharge referral systems using four different levels of support were used.

1. Minimal support: The patient was given the phone number of the community mental health center.
2. Increased person support: The patient was given the phone number of the community mental health center and an aftercare nurse visited the patient in the hospital and explained the services of the community mental health center to the patient.
3. Increased environmental support: The patient was given the phone number of the community mental health center; the patient was also given a specific appointment at the center.
4. Increased person and environmental support: The patient was given the phone number of the community mental health center; the patient was also seen by the aftercare nurse and a specific appointment was scheduled.

The results of the study demonstrated the impact of increasing person and environmental support on both client compliance with referral and one year hospital recidivism rates. With minimal support, the referral compliance and recidivism percentages were 22 and 68; with increased person support, 36 and 39; with increased environmental support, 68 and 31; and with both increased person and environmental support, 75 and 28. Thus, whenever an added element of support was introduced, the referral compliance percentage increased and the recidivism rate decreased.

Other studies[20,87] have investigated the relationship between support persons and rehabilitation outcome. In each of these studies, however, the effect of the support person could not be differentiated from the impact of skill training. Valle[87] investigated the relationship between levels of interpersonal skills of the supportive counselor and rehabilitation outcome. He reported that the relapse rate of alcoholic clients was significantly related to the level of interpersonal skills of their counselors. In other words, the best predictor of client drinking behavior at 6, 12, 18, and 24 month follow-up was the interpersonal skill level of his or her counselor.

Weinman and Kleiner[20] did not measure the interpersonal skills of their support persons. Their study compared the effectiveness of community-based "enablers" with two hospital-based conditions: socioenvironmental therapy and traditional hospital treatment. The enablers' major roles were to teach their patients skills and escort them to various community resources. Results of the project concluded that this combination of person support plus skill training was superior to one or the other of the hospital-based treatment approaches in terms of recidivism, client self esteem, and client instrumental and role performance.

In summary, various studies exist which show that environmental resource development (i.e., variations in the level of support offered by persons or settings with whom the client interacts) do have an impact on client rehabilitation outcome. These studies, in combination with the client skill development studies, lend support to the continued development of a comprehensive rehabilitation approach as a primary approach with the severely psychiatrically disabled. Furthermore, the history of the client skill development and environmental resource development approaches, as practiced in physical medicine and rehabilitation, provide the conceptual underpinnings to the psychiatric rehabilitation approach.

TRAINING PSYCHIATRIC REHABILITATION PRACTITIONERS

As the field of psychiatric rehabilitation attempts to become better defined and empirically grounded, it becomes increasingly possible to specify the skills and knowledge relevant to the practice of psychiatric rehabilitation. Psychiatric rehabilitation is not the exclusive province of any one discipline.[88]

While the field is not discipline-specific, it is possible to identify some of the basic psychiatric rehabilitation practitioner skills, independent of discipline. Once these skills are identified, it is possible to teach these skills and evaluate the impact of this training on the practitioners and ultimately on their clients. Within the last five years, several psychiatric rehabilitation practitioner training projects have been funded by the National Institute of Mental Health and the Rehabilitation Services Administration. The particular skills which a practitioner needs in order to implement a psychiatric rehabilitation approach have been developed into training packages.[89] Six training manuals and an Instructor's Guide were developed for the purpose of teaching the skills of psychiatric rehabilitation practice to student interns and practicing professionals. Results of the project indicated that the skills of psychiatric rehabilitation practice can be successfully learned, observed, and measured, and that trainees consider these skills to be important in the performance of their jobs. Furthermore, the results suggest that clients of counselors who scored high on paper-and-pencil assessments of these skills are more apt to report feeling involved, understood, and having learned new skills.

A current NIMH-funded knowledge utilization study is assessing the capacity of these same psychiatric rehabilitation practitioner skills to be disseminated and utilized by mental health and rehabilitation agencies using a "train the trainer" dissemination approach.[90] Representatives of selected agencies from around the country are presently being trained in these psychiatric rehabilitation skills and how to teach these skills to others. These newly trained trainers will then train their agency staff in these skills, and the agency staff will use these skills with their clients. This project will assess the viability of this training-the-trainer-approach in facilitating knowledge dissemination and utilization of the psychiatric rehabilitation skills.

In 1976 the largest psychiatric rehabilitation training program in the country was initiated by Fountain House, under a grant from NIMH.[91] The purpose of this grant was to make it possible to develop and conduct a staff training program designed to assist community mental health centers and other public and voluntary mental health agencies to establish rehabilitation services, based on the clubhouse model, which would enable the chronically mentally ill to move more successfully and productively into the community. Between January 1977, and December 1982, individuals from agencies located in 38 states, the District of Columbia, Canada, and Sweden, completed the three week training program at Fountain House. The significant outcomes since the training period include: an increase in the number of clubhouses from 18 to 148; the number of transitional employment programs from 21 to 102; the number of participating employers from 122 to 507; the number of job placements from 360 to 1154; and the amount of wages earned by members working on transitional employment placements from $1,033,152 to $4,436,048 per year.

Fountain House has recently embarked on a Member Training Project. The purpose of this project is to enrich and enlarge the ways in which members are encouraged to take active leadership roles in the clubhouse program. Seven member leadership roles have been identified:

1. The role of *reaching out* to other members.
2. The role of *tutor* for other members.
3. The role of assisting other members in the *development of rehabilitation plans*.
4. The role of developing educational materials, including the creation of a *member literature*.
5. The role of active participation in *intake and orientation* of new members.
6. The role of *advocacy* for other members, for the clubhouse itself, for the clubhouse movement across the country, and for a wider understanding by the community at large of the significance and importance of member involvement in their own rehabilitation.

7. The role of active member participation in the *systematic gathering and recording of information* concerning the contribution of the clubhouse model in the rehabilitation or community adjustment of the chronically mentally ill.

Between January 1980, and December 1982, 81 members and 23 staff from 41 clubhouses in 17 different states, the District of Columbia, and Sweden have participated in the Member Training Project. Follow-up data indicate that clubhouses are quickly implementing the various member leader roles. Additionally, beginning in January 1981, all clubhouse staff who participate in the staff training program will also gain experience at Fountain House in the seven member leadership roles. Follow-up information indicates that these member roles are being implemented by the staff training program. Fountain House currently envisions the staff training program and the member training program being combined into a single training program.

In a different type of training approach, a Rehabilitation Services Administration grant is currently funding the development of a psychiatric rehabilitation training program for state vocational rehabilitation counselors. A model program for training state vocational rehabilitation professionals has been developed, implemented, and described in detail.[92]

FUTURE DIRECTIONS IN PSYCHIATRIC REHABILITATION

Acceptance of the concept of rehabilitation and the creation of psychosocial rehabilitation settings has laid the foundation for an emerging consensus about the principles underlying the psychiatric rehabilitation field. The identification of these principles and the accumulating body of research evidence relevant to the major psychiatric rehabilitation interventions has paved the way for developments in the next decade (i.e., client outcome research and the use of the psychiatric rehabilitation knowledge base in formulating mental health policy).

The various components of what has come to be known as the psychiatric rehabilitation approach have been researched extensively. In almost all studies, client skill development and environmental resource development interventions have been found to be related to various types of client rehabilitation outcome (i.e., more frequent and higher levels of client independent living and vocational functioning). Dozens of research studies reviewed elsewhere[25,90,93] have reported a positive correlation between client skills and rehabilitation outcome. The time-tested philosophy and principles of rehabilitation tie these various research studies together into a cohesive, empirically based field of psychiatric rehabilitation. The groundwork has been laid and the need is apparent for outcome research to be conducted in comprehensive rehabilitation settings.

The practicality and value of future client outcome research has been increased because the expertise of the rehabilitation practitioner, the essential ingredients of the rehabilitation setting, and the main types of rehabilitation interventions can now be specified in observable and measurable ways. The information from future research will be more replicable and generalizable to other settings.

In addition, the psychiatric rehabilitation knowledge base has progressed to the extent that it has implications for national policy development. For example, Anthony[15] has shown how research pertaining to the prediction of vocational functioning has direct relevance to the procedures and regulations used in Social Security disability determinations. In this instance the research data suggest that estimates of future employment should be based more on measures of clients' work adjustment skills than on measures of client symptomatology.

The present knowledge base of psychiatric rehabilitation also suggests directions for state and local policy. State institutions and community-based settings should be assessed on their capacity to implement a psychiatric rehabilitation approach. Numerous studies have demonstrated that time-limited community-based treatment is not superior to time-limited hospital-based treatment in improving client functioning.[94] State policy makers must pay increasing attention to *what* is being done rather than to *where* it is being done.

In summary, there is an increasing consensus as to psychiatric rehabilitation philosophy and principles, necessary practitioner expertise, and the basic types of rehabilitation interventions. Progress in psychiatric rehabilitation over the next five years will be a function of trying to further develop and test this emerging consensus through empirical research.

REFERENCES

1. Dembo T, Leviton GL, Wright BA: Adjustment to misfortune—a problem of social psychological rehabilitation. *Artificial Limbs* 1956;3:4–62
2. Kessler HH: *The crippled and the disabled: Rehabilitation of the physically handicapped in the United States.* New York, Columbia University Press, 1953
3. Rusk HA, Taylor EJ: *New hope for the handicapped: The rehabilitation of the disabled from bed to job.* New York, Harper, 1949
4. Wright BA: *Physical disability: A psychological approach.* New York, Harper, 1960
5. Grob S: Psychosocial rehabilitation centers: Old wine in a new bottle, in Barofsky I, Budson R (eds): *The Chronic Psychiatric Patient In The Community.* Jamaica, NY, SP Medical and Scientific Books, 1983, pp 265–280
6. Anthony WA, Cohen MR, Cohen BF: The philosophy, treatment process and principles of the psychiatric rehabilitation approach. *New Directions In Mental Health* 1983;17:67–74
7. Fairweather G: The development, evaluation and diffusion of rehabilitative programs: A social change process, in Stein L, Test M (eds): *Alternatives to mental hospital treatment.* New York, Plenum Press, 1978, pp 295–308
8. Allen RE, Velasco FE: An inpatient setting: The contributions of a rehabilitation approach. *Rehabilitation Counseling Bulletin* 1980;23:108–117
9. Furman WM, Lund DA: The assessment of patient needs: Description of the level of care survey. *Journal of Psychiatric Treatment and Evaluation* 1979;1:29–37
10. Bachrach LL: Overview: Model programs for chronic mental patients. *Am J Psychiatry* 1980;137:1023–1031

11. Anthony WA: Psychological rehabilitation: A concept in need of a method. *Am Psychol* 1977;32:658-662

12. Beard JH, Propst RN, Malamud TJ: The Fountain House model of psychiatric rehabilitation. *Psychosocial Rehabilitation Journal* 1982;5:47-59

13. Lamb HR: *Treating the Long Term Mentally Ill.* San Francisco, Jossey-Bass, 1982

14. Dincin J: A community agency model, in Talbott JA (ed): *The Chronic Mentally Ill.* New York, Human Sciences Press, 1981, pp 212-226

15. Anthony WA: *Principles of Psychiatric Rehabilitation.* Baltimore, University Park Press, 1979

16. Wright G: *Total Rehabilitation.* Boston, Little, Brown, 1980

17. Brooks, GW: Vocational rehabilitation, in Talbott JA (ed): *The Chronic Mentally Ill.* New York, Human Sciences Press, 1981, pp 96-100

18. Frank JD: Reply to Telch. *J Consult Clin Psychol* 1981;49:476-477

19. Havens LL: Dependence: Definitions and strategies. *Rehabilitation Record* 1967; March-April, 23-28

20. Weinman B, Kleiner RJ: The impact of community living and community member intervention of the adjustment of the chronic psychotic patient, in Stein L, Test M (eds): *Alternatives to Mental Hospital Treatment.* New York, Plenum Press, 1978, pp 139-159

21. Makas E: Increasing counselor-client communication. *Rehabil Lit* 1980; September-October, 235-238

22. Carkhuff R: *Helping and Human Relations, Vol. I & II.* New York, Holt Rinehart & Winston, 1969

23. Aspy DN, Roebuck FN: *KIDS Don't Learn From People They Don't Like.* Amherst, MA, Human Resource Development Press, 1977

24. Anthony WA, Cohen M, Farkas M: A psychiatric rehabilitation treatment program. Can I recognize one if I see one? *Community Ment Health J* 1982;18:83-96

25. Anthony WA, Cohen MR, Vitalo R: The measurement of rehabilitation outcome. *Schizophr Bull* 1978;4:365-383

26. Cohen MR, Vitalo R, Anthony WA, et al: *Psychiatric Rehabilitation Practice Series: The Skills of Community Service Coordination (Book 6).* Baltimore, University Park Press, 1980

27. Cohen MR, Farkas M: *The Skills of Psychiatric Rehabilitation Videotape Series.* Boston, Boston University Center for Rehabilitation Research & Training in Mental Health, 1981

28. Unger, KV, Cohen MR, Cohen BF: *Users' Guide to the Psychiatric Rehabilitation Videotape Series.* Boston, Boston University Center for Rehabilitation Research & Training in Mental Health, 1982

29. Azrin NH, Philip RA: The job club method for the job handicapped: A comparative outcome study. *Rehabilitation Counseling Bulletin* 1979;23:144-155

30. Carkhuff R: New directions in training for helping professionals: Towards a technology for human and community resource development. *The Counseling Psychologist* 1972;3:12-20

31. Berenson D, Berenson S, Carkhuff R: *The Skills of Teaching.* Amherst, MA, Human Resource Development Press, 1978

32. Collingwood T, Douds A, Williams H, et al: *Developing Youth Resources.* Amherst, MA, Carkhuff Institute of Human Technology, 1978

33. Pierce R, Drasgow J: Teaching facilitative interpersonal function to psychiatric inpatients. *Journal of Counseling Psychology* 1969;16:295-298

34. Vitalo RL: Teaching improved interpersonal functioning as a preferred mode of treatment. *J Clin Psychology* 1971;27:166-171

35. Carkhuff RR, Berenson BC: *Teaching As Treatment.* Amherst, MA, Human Resource Development Press, 1976

36. Lazarus A: *Behavior Therapy and Beyond.* New York, McGraw Hill, 1971

37. Paul G, Lentz R: *Psychosocial Treatment of Chronic Mental Patients.* Cambridge, MA, Harvard University Press, 1977

38. Hersen M, Bellack A: Social skills training for chronic psychiatric patients: Rationale, research findings and future directions. *Compr Psychiatry* 1976;17(4):559–572

39. Fremouw W, Zitter RA: A comparison of skills training and cognitive restructuring relaxation for the treatment of speech anxiety. *Behavior Therapy* 1978; 9(2):248–260

40. Lent R, Russell R: Treatment of text anxiety by use of controlled dissemination and study skills training. *Journal of Counseling psychology* 1978;25:217–224

41. Mitchell K, White R: Self-management of tension headaches: A case study. *J Behav Ther Exp Psychiatry* 1976;7:246–254

42. Stude EW, Pauls T: The use of a job seeking skills group in developing placement readiness. *Journal of Applied Rehabilitation Counseling* 1977;8:115–120

43. Ugland RP: Job seekers' aids: A systematic approach for organizing employer contacts. *Rehabilitation Counseling Bulletin* 1977;22:107–115

44. Hersen M: Limitations and problems in the clinical applications of behavioral techniques in psychiatric settings. *Behavioral Therapy* 1979;10:65–80

45. Comes-Schwartz B: Modification of schizophrenic behavior. *Behavior Modification* 1979;3:439–468

46. Maxmen J, Tucker G, LeBow M: *Rational Hospital Psychiatry.* New York, Brunner-Maxel, 1974

47. Anthony WA, Margules A, Collingwood TR: Rehabilitation counseling: A decisive approach. *J Rehabil* 1974;40(3):18–20

48. Jaffe P, Carlson P: Relative efficacy of modeling and instruction in eliciting social behavior from chronic psychiatric patients. *J Consult Clin Psychol* 1976;44:200–209

49. Waldeck J, Emerson S, Edelstein B: Cope: A systematic approach to moving chronic patients into the community. *Hosp Community Psychiatry* 1979;30(8):551–554

50. Williams M, Turner S, Watts J, et al: Group social skills for chronic psychiatric patients. *European Journal of Behavior Analysis and Modification* 1977;1:223–229

51. Finch B, Wallace D: Successful interpersonal skills training with schizophrenic inpatients. *J Consult Clin Psychol* 1977;45:885–890

52. Marzillier J, Winter K: Success and failure in social skills training. *Behavior Research and Therapy* 1978;2(1):61–75

53. Vitalo R, Ross C: Applications of the principles of psychiatric rehabilitation programming, in Anthony WA (ed): *Principles of Psychiatric Rehabilitation.* Baltimore, University Park Press, 1979, pp 193–202

54. Bellack A, Hersen M, Turner S: Generalization effects of social skills training and chronic schizophrenics: An experimental analysis. *Behavior Research & Therapy* 1976;14:391–398

55. Eisler R, Blanchard E, Fitts H, et al: Social skills training with and without modeling for schizophrenics and non-psychotic hospitalized psychiatric patients. *Behavior Modification* 1978;2:147–172

56. Malm U: The influence of group therapy on schizophrenia. *Acta Psychiatr Scand* 1982;65(Suppl 297):1–65

57. Wood P, Lenhard S, Maggiani M, et al: Assertiveness training of the chronic mental patient. *J Psychiatr Nurs* 1975;13:42–46

58. Becker P, Bayer C: Preparing chronic patients for community placement: A four-stage treatment program. *Hosp Community Psychiatry* 1975;26(7):448–450

59. Bell RL: Practical applications of psychodrama: Systematic role-playing teaches social skills. *Hosp Community Psychiatry* 1970;21:189–191

60. Lillie M, Armstrong HE: Contributions to the development of psychoeducational approaches to mental health service. *Am J Occup Ther* 1982;36:438–443

61. Retchless M: Rehabilitation programs for chronic patients: Stepping stones to the community. *Hosp Community Psychiatry* 1967;18:377–378

62. Scoles P, Fine E: Aftercare and rehabilitation in a community mental health center. *Social Work* 1971;16(5):447–456

63. Weinman B, Sander R, Kleiner R, et al: Community-based treatment of chronic psychotics. *Community Ment Health J* 1970;6:12-21
64. Cole JR, Klarreich SH, Fryatt J: Teaching interpersonal coping skills to adult psychiatric patients. *Cognitive Therapy & Research* 1982;6:105-112
65. Goldsmity, J, McFall R: Development and evaluation of an interpersonal skill training program for psychiatric inpatients. *J Abnorm Psychol* 1975;84:51-58
66. Hinterkopf E, Brunswick LK: Teaching therapeutic skills to mental patients. *Psychotherapy: Theory, Research and Practice* 1975;12:8-12
67. Hersen M, Eisler R, Miller P: An experimental analysis of generalization in assertive training. *Behavior Research and Therapy* 1974;12:295-310
68. Cheek RE, Mendelson M: Developing behavior modification programs with an emphasis on self-control. *Hosp Community Psychiatry* 1973;24:410-416
69. Matson J, Stephens R: Increasing appropriate behavior of explosive chronic psychiatric patients with a social skills training package. *Behavior Modification* 1978;2(1):61-75
70. Rutner IT, Bugle G: An experimental procedure for the modification of psychotic behavior. *J Consult Clin Psychol* 1969;33:651-653
71. Kline A, Hoisington B: Placing the psychiatrically disabled: A look at work values. *Rehabilitation Counseling Bulletin* 1981;25:365-369
72. McClure DP: Placement through improvement of client's job-seeking skills. *Journal of Applied Rehabilitation Counseling* 1972;3:188-196
73. Prazak JA: Learning job seeking interview skills. In Krumboltz J, Thoreson C (eds): *Behavioral Counseling*. New York, Rinehart & Winston, 1969, pp 414-428
74. Rubin SE, Roessler RT: Guidelines for successful vocational rehabilitation of the psychiatrically disabled. *Rehabil Lit* 1978;39:70-74
75. Shean G: An effective and self-supporting program of community living for chronic patients. *Hosp Community Psychiatry* 1973;24:97-99
76. Bedell JR, Archer RP, Marlowe HA: A description and evaluation of a problem solving skills training program. In Upper D, Ross S (eds): *Behavioral Group Therapy: An Annual Review*. Champaign, IL, Research Press, 1980, pp 3-35
77. Coche E, Flick A: Problem solving training groups for hospitalized psychiatric patients. *Psychol* 1975;91:19-29
78. Siegel JM, Spivak G: Problem-solving therapy: The description of a new program for chronic psychiatric patients. *Psychotherapy: Theory, Research and Practice* 1976;4:368-373
79. Anderson JA: The disadvantaged seek work—through their efforts or ours? *Rehabilitation Record* 1968;9:5-10
80. Wesolowski MD: Self directed job placement in rehabilitation: A comparative review. *Rehabilitation Counseling Bulletin* 1981;25:80-89
81. Cohen BF, Ridley D, Cohen MR: Teaching skills to severely psychiatrically disabled persons. In Marlowe H, Weinberg R (eds): *Proceedings of the 1982 CSP Region 4 Conference*. University of South Florida, Tampa, FL, 1983
82. Katkin S, Ginsburg M, Riftkin M, et al: Effectiveness of female volunteers in the treatment of outpatients. *Journal of Counseling Psychology* 1971;18:97-100
83. Katkin S, Zimmerman V, Rosenthal T, et al: Using volunteer-therapists to reduce hospital readmissions. *Hosp Community Psychiatry* 1975;26:151-153
84. Cannady D: Chronics and cleaning ladies. *Psychosocial Rehabilitation Journal* 1982;5:13-16
85. Witheridge TF, Dincin J, Appleby L: Working with the most frequent recidivists: A total team approach to assertive resource management. *Psychosocial Rehabilitation Journal* 1982;5:9-11
86. Stickney SK, Hall RW, Gardner ER: The effect of referral procedures on aftercare compliance. *Hosp Community Psychiatry* 1980;31:567-569
87. Valle S: Interpersonal functioning of alcoholism counselors and treatment outcome. *J Stud Alcohol* 1981;42(9):783-790
88. Farkas M, Anthony WA: training rehabilitation counselors to work in state agencies, rehabilitation and mental health facilities. *Rehabilitation Counseling Bulletin* 1980;24:128-144

89. Anthony WA: *A Skills Training Approach In Psychiatric Rehabilitation.* Grant # MH14502 Final Report, National Institute of Mental Health, 1980

90. Anthony WA: *A Psychiatric Rehabilitation Training Technology.* Grant # 2T24-MH14502, National Institute of Mental Health, 1982

91. Fountain House. Rehabilitation of the Mental Patient in the Community. Grant # 5T24-MH14471, National Institute of Mental Health, 1976

92. Creasey DE, McCarthy TP: Training vocational rehabilitation counselors who work with chronic mental patients. *Am J Psychiatry* 1981;138:1102–1106

93. Anthony WA: Explaining psychiatric rehabilitation by an analogy to physical rehabilitation. *Psychosocial Rehabilitation Journal* 1982;5:61–65

94. Dellario D, Anthony WA: The relative effectiveness of institutional and alternative placements for the severely mentally disabled. *Journal of Social Issues* 1981;37(3):21–33

Carol L.M. Caton

11

Length of Hospitalization

Innovations in the clinical care and treatment of chronic mental illness over the past decade have facilitated greater control over its positive and negative symptoms. To effect the most desirable clinical outcome, however, the chronic mental patient requires long-term care from the mental health delivery system, which includes the following:

1. Drug therapy, carefully monitored both for efficacy and side effects.
2. Crisis intervention to stabilize episodes of psychosis, carried out on an inpatient basis if the patient is violent, suicidal, or otherwise unmanageable in a community setting.
3. An extended duration of full or partial hospitalization or outpatient care in order to implement specific psychosocial therapies.
4. Housing alternatives if the patient is unable to live independently or with family.

Still at issue is the length of time specific interventions should be in effect to produce the optimum outcome.[1,2] Although treatment responses vary among individuals, responses to psychotropic medication usually occur within hours or days, while psychosocial therapies require weeks, months, or years.[3,4] Despite this generally recognized fact, there has been little study and evaluation done on the effect of duration of psychiatric treatments, in order to guide policy and program planning. A notable exception, however, is the work on length of hospitalization.

THE CHRONIC MENTAL PATIENT
ISBN 0-8089-1649-1

Copyright © 1984 by Grune & Stratton.
All rights of reproduction in any form reserved.

STUDIES ON LENGTH OF HOSPITALIZATION

Concern about the effect on patients of days spent in hospital stems from a steady shortening of hospitalization episodes following the widespread use of psychotropic medications in the 1960s. One of the first studies of brief hospitalization and aftercare in the deinstitutionalization era was reported by Caffey et al.[5] In this study, 201 schizophrenic men recently admitted to 14 Veteran's Administration hospitals were randomly assigned to three groups: the treatment received by the first consisted of twenty days of intensive hospital care followed by outpatient treatment by the same staff for a one-year period; the second received standard hospital care (mean length of stay was 75 days) with the usual follow-up treatment; the third received standard hospital treatment (mean length of stay was 88 days) plus the special aftercare program given to the brief-hospitalization group.

Between 77 percent and 83 percent of subjects in all groups received individually tailored doses of antipsychotic medication. Brief-treatment patients did not receive a drug treatment substantially different from standard treatment groups. Individual therapy of a supportive nature alone or in conjunction with group therapy was the form of psychotherapy offered to all treatment groups. Frequency of aftercare visits was at least once per month for about half of the study subjects in the special follow-up care program, while those who received the usual aftercare visited less frequently. Symptom rating scales, used within three days after admission and then again at three weeks, six months, and one year after admission, were used to assess the efficacy of treatment programs.

Outcome evaluation revealed that the brief-hospitalization group did as well as those who stayed in the hospital for a longer period of time. The short-stay group did not experience more readmissions to hospital or a greater tendency to have a shorter stay in the community before the first readmission. The longer-stay group was more symptomatic than the brief group at three weeks (the point of discharge for brief-stay patients), but showed fewer symptoms when they were finally discharged. There were no differences, however, between the brief and standard hospital treatment groups in adequacy of community adjustment. Both groups treated with the special aftercare program showed less psychopathology at the end of 12 months, demonstrating the value of intensive aftercare therapy.

Another well-controlled study conducted by Glick et al.[6,7] and Hargreaves[8] compared the clinical effectiveness of short-term hospitalization (defined as 21 to 28 days) to that of long-term hospitalization (90 to 120 days). Patients were randomly assigned to brief or long-term inpatient care and were treated intensively. All subjects were placed on partially fixed drug dosage schedules so that there were no major differences in amount of phenothiazine medication given during the first three weeks of hospitalization. In contrast to the work of Caffey et al., this study did not include an aftercare component, although patients were referred for follow-up care. Both treatment groups were assessed with symptom and adjustment rating scales at admission and at their respective discharge times, and were followed-up for a two-year period.

Treatment results for 141 schizophrenic patients showed that at four weeks the short-term group was functioning better than the long-term group. At their discharge after 90 to 120 days of hospitalization, however, the long-term group showed significantly better functioning. Two year follow-up data on 119 of the 141 patients indicated that those with relatively good prehospital functioning did better with long-term than with short-term hospitalization. In contrast, those with relatively poor prehospital functioning did as well, or perhaps even better, two years after a short-term than after a long-term hospitalization. All trends noted above were more apparent in women than in men.

A problem in interpreting the two year outcome findings in this study is that they may have been influenced more by the nature of the postdischarge treatment than by the length of hospital care. Long-term patients in the Glick et al. study inadvertently received more treatment than did the short-term patients. Long-term patients with poor prehospital functioning received more antipsychotic drugs, although there were no differences in the amount of psychotherapy received by poorly functioning patients in both treatment groups. Long-term patients with good prehospital functioning, however, received more follow-up psychotherapy than did their short-term counterparts. Despite the fact that patients hospitalized in the long-term unit received more medication and psychotherapy during the two-year follow-up period than did the patients discharged from the short-term unit, two year outcome data show that short-term patients did as well, if not slightly better, than those treated with a longer hospital stay.[6,8]

Further evidence in favor of brief hospitalization has emerged from the studies of Herz[9] and Endicott.[10,11] In their studies, 175 patients with families suffering from functional disorders (63 percent of whom carried a diagnosis of schizophrenia) were randomly assigned to one of three groups: intermediate-term (60 days) inpatient care with discharge to an aftercare clinic, "short-day": in which an average 11-day inpatient stay was followed by day care on the same ward and then referral to an aftercare program, and a "short-out" group in which after an average 11-day inpatient stay, patients were followed-up on an outpatient basis. If patients were readmitted during the two year follow-up period, they returned to their initial inpatient assignments.

Follow-up data showed that the average number of days spent in inpatient care throughout the two-year study was 115 in the intermediate-term group, 27 days in the short-day group, and 47 in the short-out group. Unlike Glick's study, there was no statistical difference among the three groups in terms of prognostic parameters, except that fewer married patients were in the short-out group.

Assessment of psychopathology and social functioning at two years revealed that the short-day group showed the least psychopathology and impaired social and occupational functioning, while the intermediate-term group showed the most disturbance. Moreover, short-term patients were less of a psychological and financial burden to their families,[9] challenging the view that brief inpatient stays merely shift the burden of caring for the patient away from the hospital staff and onto the family. It is of interest that at the outset of Herz's study, the staff favored long-term treatment, believing that short-term inpatient care would eventually result in more psychopathology and a greater number of rehospitalizations.

Uncontrolled studies comparing patients treated with short-term inpatient care to those receiving longer term hospitalization lend support to findings from rigorously designed experiments.[1,12] Caton reported a study of 119 chronic schizophrenics who were treated on brief stay (mean length of stay was 21 days) and long-stay (mean length of stay was 70 days) units in New York City.[1] Modalities used during the in-patient phase were antipsychotic drugs and discharge planning. All patients were referred for aftercare treatment, but because therapy was not controlled, treatment noncompliance was high. Findings revealed that length of in-patient stay bore no relationship to number of rehospitalizations, aftercare treatment compliance, or clinical and social functioning in the community. Rather, a patient's post-discharge experiences with treatment and the effect of relationships with significant others in the community were critical factors in determining subsequent use of in-patient services. Findings from the Caton study suggest that for already chronic schizophrenic patients a brief hospital stay poses no additional clinical risk, especially if it is followed by an aftercare program in which there is an aggressive effort to hold patients in treatment.

THE NEED FOR FURTHER STUDY OF LENGTH OF HOSPITALIZATION

Despite convincing findings from well-designed studies, there continues to be considerable variation in the length of in-patient stay for chronic schizophrenic patients treated in facilities under the auspices of different administrations. Brief hospitalization has become part of routine psychiatric care in general hospitals with high per diem costs, a trend reinforced by the policies of insurance carriers and third-party payers. Length of stay in state mental institutions, however, has continued to be greater. It is unclear whether a longer stay is either necessary or of benefit to some chronically ill patients. The issue of length of stay is particularly relevant in a time when mental health program planners are eager to shift resources from institutional settings to community programs.

Although the deinstitutionalization movement has altered patterns of treatment for schizophrenia,[13] the need for the psychiatric in-patient setting has not been eliminated.[14] Treatment of new as well as former patients now usually consists of brief in-patient care (days or weeks) followed by outpatient aftercare, in contrast to the long-term in-patient treatment characteristic of the asylum. A high rate of readmission to hospital has accompanied greater reliance on community-based care.[15] Experimental studies of brief hospitalization[5-11] conducted during the post-deinstitutionalization era have reported rehospitalization rates of about 60 percent over two years, even when community treatment has been well controlled. Moreover, well-designed investigations of the drug treatment of schizophrenia[16] have revealed that episodes of relapse requiring hospitalization occur despite continuous use of antipsychotic medication. An important innovation in the management of chronic mental illness has been the community-based 24-hour crisis team. Stein and Test[17] have demonstrated that such an approach can markedly reduce use of the inpatient setting when the patient's clinical picture is not clouded by substance abuse or dangerous or destructive behavior. While their model program was highly successful in a medium-sized midwestern university town, it has not been generalized to large public systems of care in urban metropolitan areas mandated to serve patients with different ethnic, social class, and clinical characteristics.[18] Episodes of rehospitalization are thus a fact of life for the chronic schizophrenic patient managed in typical mental health delivery systems across the nation.

While rehospitalizations have characterized the course of chronic schizophrenia, there is no consensus on the optimum duration of inpatient stay for each episode. Definitions of brief and standard lengths of stay have varied from one investigation to another, making comparison of findings difficult. Moreover, patient populations studied have been mixed diagnostically and have been at both acute and chronic stages of illness.

Although important progress has been made in studying the effect of length of hospital stay, more work is needed.[18,19] In a study reporting the limitations of brief hospital treatment, it was found that severe impairment and the inability of the family to support a patient in that condition rule out rapid return of the patient to the community.[20] This underscores the need for treatments to match the patient. Research is required to identify the clinical and social characteristics of patients who might benefit from long-term hospitalization. Future studies in this area should carefully specify the treatment goals of an extended in-patient stay, and the modalities used to achieve such objectives. Indeed, there is a significant trend in treatment research in psychiatry to improve the description and measurement of treatment interventions. Length of hospitalization should be linked to successful implementation of specific drug and psychosocial therapies. In addition, study of duration of hospital stay must be viewed in relation to other elements of care provided by the mental health delivery system. The works of Caffey et al.,[5] Glick et al.,[6-8] Herz et al.,[9] Endicott,[10,11] and Caton[1] have explored the effect of length of in-patient stay in concert with aftercare services. Future studies should also examine the effect of duration of aftercare in the long-term treatment of the chronic mental patient.

REFERENCES

1. Caton CLM: Effect of length of inpatient treatment for chronic schizophrenia. *Am J Psychiatry* 1982;139:856–861
2. Gudeman JE, Shore MF, Dickey B: Day hospitalization and an inn instead of inpatient care for psychiatric patients. *N Eng J Med* 1983;308:749–753
3. Hogarty GE, Goldberg SC, Schooler NR, et al: Drugs and sociotherapy in the aftercare of schizophrenic patients. II. Two year relapse rates. *Arch Gen Psychiatry* 1974;31:603–608
4. Hogarty GE, Ulrich RP: Temporal effects of drug and placebo in delaying relapse in schizophrenic outpatients. *Arch Gen Psychiatry* 1977;34:297–301
5. Caffey EM, Galbrecht CR, Klett CJ: Brief hospitalization and aftercare in the treatment of schizophrenia. *Arch Gen Psychiatry* 1971;24:81–86
6. Glick ID, Hargreaves WA, Drues J, et al: Short vs. long hospitalization. VII. Two-year follow-up results for nonschizophrenics: A prospective controlled study. *Arch Gen Psychiatry* 1977;34:314–317
7. Glick ID, Hargreaves A, Raskin M, et al: Short versus long hospitalization: A prospective controlled study. II. Results for schizophrenic patients. *Am J Psychiatry* 1975;132:385–390
8. Hargreaves WA, Glick ID, Drues J, et al: Short vs. long hospitalization: A prospective controlled study. VI. Two-year follow-up results for schizophrenics. *Arch Gen Psychiatry* 1977;34:305–311
9. Herz MI, Endicott J, Spitzer RL: Brief hospitalization: A two-year follow-up. *Am J Psychiatry* 1977;134:502–507
10. Endicott J, Cohen J, Nee J, et al: Brief vs. standard hospitalization: For whom? *Arch Gen Psychiatry* 1979;36:706–712
11. Endicott J, Herz MI, Gibbon M: Brief versus standard hospitalization: The differential costs. *Am J Psychiatry* 1978;135:707–712
12. McNeill ND, Stevenson J, Longabauch RH: Short term inpatient care and readmission rates: The CMHC approach versus the private approach. *Hosp Community Psychiatry* 1980;11:751–755
13. Bachrach LL: *Deinstitutionalization: An Analytic Review and Sociological Perspective.* Rockville, MD, National Institute of Mental Health, Series D, Number 4, 1976
14. Steering Committee on the Chronically Mentally Ill: Towards a National Plan for the Chronically Mentally Ill. Washington, DC, US Department of Health and Human Services, 1980
15. Goldman HH, Taube CA, Regier DA, et al: The multiple functions of the state mental hospital. *Am J Psychiatry* 1983;140:296–300
16. Goldberg S, Schooler N, Hogarty G, et al: Prediction of relapse in schizophrenic outpatients treated with drug and sociotherapy. *Arch Gen Psychiatry* 1977;34:171–184
17. Stein LI, Test MA: An alternative to mental hospital treatment, in Stein LI, Test MA (eds): Alternatives to Mental Hospital Treatment. New York, Plenum Press, 1978, pp 43–55
18. Bachrach LL: Overview: Model programs for chronic mental patients. *Am J Psychiatry* 1980;137:1023–1031
18.a DeFrancisco D, Anderson D, Pantano R, et al: The relationship between length of hospital stay and rapid readmission rates. *Hosp Community Psychiatry* 1980;31:196–197
19. Group for the Advancement of Psychiatry: The Positive Aspects of Long Term Hospitalization in the Public Sector for Chronic Psychiatric Patients. New York, Mental Health Materials Center, 1982
20. Reibel S, Herz MI: Limitations of brief hospital treatment. *Am J Psychiatry* 1976;133:518–521

Leona L. Bachrach

12

Principles of Planning for Chronic Psychiatric Patients: A Synthesis

In the early 1960s I observed at close hand the planning and execution of a study of ischemic heart disease among Israeli civil servants. That research, a comprehensive epidemiological inquiry, was conducted by the National Institutes of Health with PL 480 funds. In an effort to render its design as multivariate as possible, physiological, sociological, demographic, nutritional, and psychological factors were examined for their potential relationship to heart disease. In those years, Israel provided a natural laboratory for studying relationships among cultural factors and medical events, because almost everyone there had come from some other place, and national heritages were still largely intact.

The Israeli and American scientists who organized the investigation chose a battery of research instruments, one of them a psychological status questionnaire. To the researchers' surprise, when subjects were asked, "Are you happy with your wife?" some answered simply, "Which wife?" The study's designers had forgotten, or had never known, that new immigrants who had contracted polygamous marriages in their countries of origin were permitted to keep those marriages intact, although new polygamous unions were forbidden. What is more, the difficulties with this question did not even surface in carefully conducted pilot runs.

This anecdote illustrates several axioms that are basic to research design. It reminds us that in any scientific investigation it is crucial to know, first, what

THE CHRONIC MENTAL PATIENT
ISBN 0-8089-1649-1

Copyright © 1984 by Grune & Stratton.
All rights of reproduction in any form reserved.

questions to ask and, second, how to ask them. It also contains a third lesson: that it is possible to be culture-bound even within one's own society. Objective detachment requires more than dedication and good will; it also depends on a knowledge of and sensitivity to intervening variables.

These fundamental tenets of research are equally applicable to service planning. Both activities seek to synthesize existing knowledge in an effort to amend existing practices, so that new concepts may emerge. Both activities will exhibit serious failure unless the right questions are asked in the right ways and with a minimum of prejudice and bias. And finally, in both activities the acquisition of knowledge is a cumulative process.

In this chapter some of the problems that affect planning for and delivery of services to chronic psychiatric patients are examined. Nine planning principles that have gained wide acceptance in the past five years are discussed in an attempt to respond to these problems. It must be noted, however, that these planning principles are not the exclusive creation of the past five years. They are, rather, products of an evolutionary process that began in the early days of deinstitutionalization. The years since 1955 (when the nation's resident population in state mental hospitals peaked) have witnessed considerable trial and error in program design. Knowledge gained from these efforts, often painfully and with negative consequences for patients, is continually being synthesized.

Since the late 1970s, service planning for chronic psychiatric patients has intensified efforts to capitalize upon the lessons of the past. It is both more tentative and less dogmatic than earlier planning efforts. This is, of course, a positive sign, for it indicates that service planning, instead of relying on slogans as it did in the past,[1-3] is beginning at last to proceed in a cautious manner by tempering idealism with objective assessment of needs and problems.

EMERGING ISSUES IN SERVICE DELIVERY

Like today's planning concepts, today's problems in delivering services to chronic psychiatric patients are related to the deinstitutionalization movement, whose roots may be traced to the latter part of the last century.[4] For all practical purposes, however, the current history of deinstitutionalization began in post-World War II America, when progressive social reformers and fiscally conservative policymakers united in a rare coalition. Their unity provided them with strength. Based on the belief that community-based care for chronic patients is both more humane and less expensive than institution-based care, these ordinarily antagonistic interest groups were able to promote widespread reductions in the scope of traditional services and rapid development of alternative service sites in the community. They were provided with fuel for their initiatives by dramatic advances in psychopharmacology, which controlled patients' most obvious and distressing symptoms and made them appear to be less ill.

These efforts quickly resulted in changes in the target population that were unique in scope and consequences. Never before in the nation's history had the chronically mentally ill exhibited such an array of treatment histories and service needs.[2,5-7] Some patients were released from institutions after as many as five or six decades in residence, while others who were equally ill were denied admission to institutions in the first place. Of those released, some were shunted to places that could be described as "mini-institutions," facilities where, by most measures, the quality of their lives deteriorated.[8,9] Other patients exhibited a persistent dependency on institutional care and developed patterns of repeated admission and discharge. At the same time, substantial numbers of patients remained in institutions—individuals who, even in an era that idealized the benefits of community-based care, were deemed "poor risks" for discharge.

These changes in the population of chronic psychiatric patients were accompanied by intense territorial feelings among many staff members. There was considerable ego-investment in specific approaches to patient care, and professionals began to attack other professionals openly. In counterdevelopments in many parts of the country, lay people stepped in to fight the warring professionals, and a growing anti-professional emphasis took root. This anti-professionalism has persisted and intensified to this day in selected communities.

It is not surprising that these tensions affected patient care. They certainly did little to ease the transition to a new style of service delivery. The shift to community settings did not, in any general sense, lead to improved circumstances for the chronically mentally ill. In spite of humane goals and noble intentions, the initiatives of deinstitutionalization planners often resulted in patient neglect, as more and more individuals met with severe barriers to treatment. The chronically mentally ill, who were to have been the beneficiaries of Kennedy's[10] "bold new approach" to service delivery, continued to suffer as they had in the past from inadequate attention to their most basic needs.

Certainly there were notable exceptions, and many chronic psychiatric patients benefitted from the new emphases in service delivery.[11,12] It is not the intent of this chapter to minimize those efforts that met with success. Indeed, the ability of such services to transform the lives of the chronically mentally ill has reinforced the basic assumptions underlying the deinstitutionalization movement: that community-based care may represent a highly therapeutic option for these patients; that communities have the potential for providing a full range of necessary services for individuals with severe mental disabilities; and that communities may sometimes be encouraged to assume responsibility for the care of their most severely disabled members.[5] By demonstrating that we can, in fact, attend to the needs of chronic psychiatric patients in noninstitutional settings, these services have encouraged, and continue to provide, great hope for the future.

A major and lasting contribution of the deinstitutionalization movement is that we have learned to think about the needs of chronic psychiatric patients in new ways. As innovative approaches to treatment have evolved,[13] the importance of social support systems,[14] of the great potential in involving families in the care of their disabled members whenever possible,[15,16] and of developing appropriate residential alternatives[17,18] has been documented. Rehabilitation has emerged as a specialty field in the care of these patients,[13,19,20] as we have sharpened our understanding that we must focus on the patient's functional and adaptive skills even as we look for ways to deal with his or her underlying pathology. These are no small accomplishments.

There is mounting evidence, however, that the most severely disabled psychiatric patients have, in general, not been adequately and humanely served by existing service structures and that they are regularly overlooked by the psychiatric service system in this era of deinstitutionalization.[21] Indeed, in most parts of the country, serious problems associated with deinstitutionalization now appear to outweigh positive developments.

More specifically, it may be noted that the very process of service planning is far more complex today than it was in pre-deinstitutionalization days. The once institution-based population of chronic psychiatric patients has been splintered into so many subgroups that there is now a need to plan highly diversified programs—a task for which our imagination, our creativity, and also our pocketbooks, have generally not been adequate. When differences in patients' institutional histories are superimposed on disparities in their levels of functioning, the result is a complicated, multidimensional array of program and service requirements.[1]

A second problem in caring for chronic psychiatric patients today is inherent in the fact that the service needs of these individuals tend to endure, even though in the early years of deinstitutionalization it was predicted that without the negative effects of institutional residence, chronicity would disappear—at least for most patients. In sharp contrast to the persistence of service needs, however, community-based programs tend to ignore the long-term aspects of chronic disability. Hansell[22] has written that community-based psychiatric services tend to be patterned after programs for the "single-episode user of services" and so exhibit "a deficiency of interest in people with lifelong disorders" (p 105). Emergent service structures in deinstitutionalization have thus tended to underemphasize the need for continuity in the care of chronic patients.[23]

There have also been practical difficulties associated with providing comprehensive care to chronic psychiatric patients. These individuals require a combination of psychiatric, medical, social, rehabilitative, and vocational services. In the past, when all of these services could be delivered within a single physical setting, providing comprehensive care was relatively simple. But today's services for this population are divided among many health and human service agencies in the public and private sectors, and successful service delivery depends upon the fine tuning of initiatives that originate with separate (and sometimes competing) authorities.

Fourth, many efforts ostensibly designed as services for chronic psychiatric patients actually resist treating the most severely ill individuals. Community-based programs have often effectively extruded the chronically mentally ill in order to serve a population that is described by Zusman and Lamb[24] as "healthy but unhappy" (p 889). There is in fact a deepening concern among service providers that scarce resources are being deflected toward patients with less severe disabilities at the expense of those who are most disabled and least able to compete successfully.[25]

Fifth, service delivery continues to take place against a backdrop of stigma that is exceedingly difficult to ignore.[26,27] Neither the successes of model programs in serving chronic psychiatric patients[28] nor the active and growing concern of patient advocacy groups has succeeded in bringing about the revolution in public opinion that originally was expected to accompany deinstitutionalization. In very recent years the failure to modify popular opinion about the chronically mentally ill has been reflected in the drying up of federal support, both financial and philosophic, for deinstitutionalization programs. The President's Commission on Mental Health in the Carter administration, by legitimizing concern for the mentally ill, signalled progress in service planning; both the symbolic and substantive contributions of that body have, however, been reversed in the 1980s.[29-31]

Sixth, the development of services for chronic psychiatric patients often occurs in an informational vacuum. Although recent research has included a number of serious attempts to conduct rigorous outcome studies, such efforts are still sparse. Thus, although there is an urgent need for empirical data to inform efforts in service planning, the validity of research in this area is limited. Specific information deficits include difficulties in defining treatment goals, identifying suitable outcomes, developing measures to test those outcomes, securing appropriate baseline premorbid measures of patient status, designing instruments sensitive enough to measure small increments of progress in patient status, and sorting out sources of variance within the large and complex field of factors, including drug treatments, that affect outcomes.[32,33]

PLANNING PRINCIPLES

This summary of problems attending the planning of services for chronic psychiatric patients in the 1980s may lead to pessimism.[21] It does not require a crystal ball to predict that the future holds difficulties that threaten the care of these patients. We no longer possess the luxury of experimentation—of seeking out "models" and testing alternative procedures—that we had when deinstitutionalization was young, when idealism was more prevalent, and when emerging problems were less visible.

From another perspective, however, these difficulties may be regarded as developmental accompaniments of the implementation of public policy.[34,35] It is from the vantage point of cumulative experience that innovative concepts of care and new planning principles are best delineated. Thus, even though our service structures appear to be in serious disarray, and the generous federal support that characterized the early years of deinstitutionalization has all but evaporated, it is possible today to point to a series of tested planning principles. These interrelated principles, which have been derived from a quarter of a century's experience in program design, demonstrate the absolute importance of asking the right questions in the right ways and with a minimum of prejudice and bias.

Precise Goals and Objectives

A most basic principle in designing services for chronic psychiatric patients revolves around the need for precision in stating goals and objectives.[36,37] It is no longer sufficient to equate progress in service delivery with shifts in the locus of care for these patients. Instead, the articulation of specific goals and the enumeration of the programmatic objectives that will ensure their realization are understood to have critical importance.

Having specific and well-defined goals and objectives is closely tied to the need to define target populations with great care. The early years of deinstitutionalization gave birth to a number of mental health programs that sought to eliminate various social ills. In so doing, these service initiatives became "boundaryless" programs capable of "busting the boundaries" of traditional psychiatric service structures.[38] At that time, community mental health adopted a markedly broader view of its mission than (and concerned itself with clientele and problems not previously regarded as the domain of) more traditional psychiatric services. Today, it is increasingly acknowledged that the prevalence of chronic mental illness is not synonymous with the existence of social problems: that the populations subsumed under these two headings, though often overlapping, are not coterminous.[25,39] It is also recognized that an early step in implementing successful services must be the careful and specific description of what individuals will be enrolled in community-based psychiatric services.

Priority Setting

Closely related to the need for defining goals and stating program objectives is a second planning principle, the assignment of top priority to chronic patients in any programs designed for their care. In general, because these patients are not usually effective advocates on their own behalf, they do not fare well when they must compete for scarce resources with patients who are less severely impaired and often more attractive to staff.[24,39] In addition, as expressed in a message from the parent of a chronically ill mental patient,[16] one frequently overlooked barrier to care is that the mentally ill individual is often "unable to realize his great need for help and is resistant to treatment" (p 1). For these reasons, chronic psychiatric patients should not have to fight to be admitted to care programs. Any program purporting to offer services to them should back that intention up by removing barriers that impede access to care, whether those barriers are of a physical, economic, or psychologic nature. This planning principle does not imply that every psychiatric service structure must be directed toward chronic patients; but it does mean that when these patients have been targeted as the recipients of specific services, special efforts must be undertaken to assure that they are not somehow pushed aside.

Reassessment of Institutional Services

A clear definition of goals and objectives also invites reassessment of the place of institutions in the spectrum of services for chronic psychiatric patients,[21,40-43] a third planning principle. In recent years, the exclusive superiority of community-based care has increasingly come under question,[44] and there has been a moderation of the polarized views that characterized the early years of the movement. This change in thinking accompanies the understanding that institutionalism may occur in community-based facilities, as well as in state hospitals, unless individual patients' needs are carefully assessed and met. It acknowledges that *where* care is given is less important than *what* happens within a program and that well-designed institution-based programs are also capable of sensitivity.[45]

The literature is now beginning to feature contributions that view admission to institutional care as something other than systems failure,[46] a real departure from the early years of deinstitutionalization. There is an increasing number of suggestions that chronic psychiatric patients, like patients with other chronic illnesses, may even benefit from periods of hospitalization, either short- or long-term; and that there are sometimes therapeutic advantages in the removal of patients from the community.[47]

Range of Service Interventions

A midpoint of estimates suggests that the number of chronically mentally ill individuals in the United States is in the neighborhood of 2,000,000.[48] Only about 138,000 of them, or seven percent, live in state mental hospitals.[49] The remainder may be found in a variety of residential settings. Many move about frequently from one residence to another, either within a given community, between communities, or between the community and the state hospital or some correctional facility.[13,50-52] Some receive psychiatric and support services, others do not. Individuals in these various subgroups of the chronically mentally ill have different kinds of program needs, depending on their respective symptoms, their functional levels, their institutional histories, and their prognoses.

Thus it is not surprising that the chronically mentally ill require an array of programmatic interventions. A fourth planning principle is that service systems for chronic psychiatric patients must consist of a network of interrelated programs that meet the varied needs of a very diverse patient population. This means in practical terms that the service system must not settle for just one modality or approach, because there are too many different kinds of patients to be served. If we have learned one major lesson from the experiences of the past couple of decades, it is that there is no single right way or place to treat chronic psychiatric patients. A variety of interventions is needed.

Viewed structurally, service systems for chronic psychiatric patients should consist of at least seven different classes of services, including screening and referral services, crisis stabilization services, a network of residential alternatives, a range of treatment settings, a network of treatment services, transportation services, and information and evaluation services.[53] Since each of these structural categories is described at length in the literature, I shall not elaborate upon them here. Certain fundamental concepts that relate to these structural components of service systems, however, may be stressed.

The first concept to note is that of *functional equivalence*. Under each of the seven structural headings noted, a variety of specific interventions may be of potential use in order to meet the same service need. The range of residential alternatives, for example, might include halfway houses, board and care homes, and cooperative apartments. If one of these classes of alternatives is not fully developed, another may be used to fulfill the same service function. Thus, if a given service system lacks the capacity to design and implement cooperative apartments, it may compensate by offering more halfway houses, board and care homes, or other residential alternatives.

A second concept relating to service structures is that *specific elements may vary among communities*. Service planning must not occur in a vacuum; it must relate to real people and real communities. Thus, any specific community's interventions will depend on who its patients are, on what resources those patients have, and on what resources the community has. Community resources extend beyond available finances and personnel to include more subtle offerings, like neighborhood helping networks[54] and the degree to which families of patients may be engaged as active participants in service delivery.[15,16]

A third concept relating to service structures involves the *importance of trade-offs* and is really a corollary of the first two. Where a range of alternative modalities may potentially serve the same function, not every community must provide every possible intervention. A community may thus not need as many hospital beds for chronic psychiatric patients if it has sufficient beds in emergency crisis shelters. It may not, in addition, need to offer as much in the way of in-patient treatment services if there are enough effective outpatient and partial hospitalization programs available. Conversely, serious problems in replacing state hospitals with community facilities arise when efforts to provide functional equivalents for hospital-based services have been inadequate.[55]

Interagency Cooperation

Precise delineation of goals and objectives, assignment of service priorities, designing an array of service interventions—all these are dependent upon cooperative enterprise. The multiplicity of agencies and auspices typically involved in providing services to chronic psychiatric patients thus leads to a fifth principle, the need for cooperation, communication, and linkages among the agencies and personnel involved.[56-59] Cooperation among agencies is essential for integrating service delivery, avoiding duplication, controlling or reducing service delivery costs, and attacking turf-related opposition to specific program interventions.[37]

In some communities it has been possible to unify services for chronic patients on the administrative level, so that all the agencies offering treatment and support come under a single planning and coordinating authority.[60,61] Pepper and Ryglewicz[62] summarize as the major benefit of such a unified service system "the shift from an inherently competitive model of service provision, plagued by inconsistent policies of diverse agencies, to an integrated system that, while it may not achieve continuously smooth operation, at least cherishes integration and consistency as goals" (p 764). Indeed, where such administrative arrangements are possible, the unified service approach appears to hold great potential for enhancing the quality of care delivered to chronic psychiatric patients.

Even in a unified service system, however, the importance of participating agencies' maintaining their unique identities is stressed.[62] It is essential that efforts to establish interagency cooperation not be confused with a quest for regulated coordination and blurring of agencies' identities. There are genuine categorical differences in the needs of chronic mental patients, and the possibility should not be overlooked that separate and highly focused programs may at times be more responsive to those differences.

Individualized Programming

Services for the chronically mentally ill may be delivered with varying degrees of sensitivity to the needs of individual patients. The least sensitive planning—which is not properly described as planning at all even though it purports to be—makes little effort to match patients and programs. It is instead wholesale placement of patients without concern for their special needs, and it may occur either within an institution or in the community. It leads to what is popularly called "dumping."

Effective planning occurs when an effort has been made to match patients and programs. Thus, many recent contributions to the literature stress the importance of a sixth planning principle, the necessity for individually-designed treatment regimens.[13,19,23,63] Individualized programming is an essential part of treatment, whether specific interventions include chemotherapy, psychotherapy, psychosocial rehabilitation, or some combination of these or other treatment modalities.

The simplest kind of matching involves placing the patient in a program that appears to be compatible with his or her current level of functioning. Even greater sensitivity is introduced when the process has been carried a step further to anticipate a higher level of functioning by placing the patient in a program that will provide him or her with resources for skill development. With such an individualized skill training or rehabilitation approach, placement is based on the patient's potential for future development; his or her capabilities, not disabilities, are emphasized.[19]

There are, however, some patients who do not respond to skill training, and it is essential that their care also be assured in service planning.[33] To fail to do this is to be trapped by one of the common pitfalls in existing programs—overlooking patients who do not fulfill special admission criteria.[28] The critical point in service planning is that treatments be individually and realistically prescribed. Without such specificity, services for chronic psychiatric patients may be absurd at best—the equivalent of teaching the hearing impaired to depend on a guide dog[19]—and unequivocally insensitive and destructive at worst.

Cultural Relevance

But it is not enough for services to be oriented toward individual patients; they must also be tailored to conform to the local realities of the community in which they are offered. Abbott[64] points out that because patient care inevitably has "major social components," any successful program will "reflect the character of the community in which the patients are being served" (p 35). Thus, a seventh planning principle is that services for chronic psychiatric patients must be culture-specific and culturally relevant. Although certain broad planning principles such as those discussed here may certainly be identified and generalized, there is ample evidence that successful services for these patients are basically local and idiosyncratic.[32,57]

The principle of cultural relevance points up the dangers inherent in attempting to "clone" demonstration programs. That a treatment intervention works in one time and place by no means ensures its success in another. Indeed, one of the serious problems that has recently surfaced in service planning for chronic psychiatric patients is a prevailing dedication to the search for instant solutions. The functionalist approach in anthropology and sociology[65,66] teaches that because the components of culture always strive for equilibrium, any changes introduced are likely to set off a chain reaction. When a change is basically incompatible with the existing culture base, shock waves of unanticipated direction and intensity may inadvertently be set off. A therapeutic community approach, for example, will probably fail in an authoritarian society, not because the approach necessarily lacks therapeutic merit, but rather because the personnel in the community have no cultural precedent for shared decision-making.

These kinds of problems underscore the absolute necessity, in service planning, for asking the right questions in the right ways and with a minimum of cultural bias. A red flag should thus immediately be raised when a headline announces that new programs for chronic psychiatric patients will be "spawned" from a functioning "model,"[67] or when we are told that agencies have been funded specifically to "develop models that can be used elsewhere."[68] Even though it may at times be possible to make local adaptations of another community's ideas in treating chronic psychiatric patients, it is basically poor planning to adopt a tested approach without first seriously studying the sociologic differences between the two communities, and second, attempting to introduce appropriate modifications in service design. It may well be that the required modifications will be so basic and extensive that the whole notion of reproducing the approach will be rendered meaningless.

Flexible Format

Closely related to the principle of individualized treatment discussed above, an eighth critical principle in planning services for chronic psychiatric patients is that program formats be flexible enough to be responsive to the ever-changing needs of individual patients. Flexibility relieves the patient of pressures that may be placed upon him or her always to exhibit "progress" or to move "forward" along some "continuum."[23] It acknowledges that, as with members of other populations of chronically disabled individuals, it is generally inappropriate to think in terms of linear progress with chronic psychiatric patients.[64] A flexible format in programs for these patients permits the flow in services to correspond to changes in their circumstances, whether they progress or decompensate.

Flexible program formats not only respond to the changing needs of individual patients, they also make it easier to modify the service system in accord with changes in aggregate service demands. It may be anticipated that the population of chronic psychiatric patients will become even more heterogeneous in years to come. It will be necessary to provide for an ever-increasing population of noninstitutionalized patients, many of them never hospitalized. That population will age slowly, and their service needs will change accordingly.

Service systems are already experiencing an inability to meet the unprecedented demands of a population of service "misfits," who are often young adults with very serious disorders.[50,69,70] Even though today's modal chronic psychiatric patient is a younger individual who does not exhibit the effects of prolonged institutionalism, we continue to plan programs for veteran state hospital residents. In short, an inflexibility in concept has fostered preoccupation with designing "aftercare" programs for institutional dischargees. The resulting stereotyped services, geared toward helping passive individuals adapt quietly to life in the community, do not answer the needs of many younger patients who make active and vocal demands on the psychiatric service system.

Caution and Restraint

A ninth planning principle involves the need to guard against being seduced by the "quick fix," an understandable tendency when public policy is an outgrowth of strongly held ideals. Service planning for chronic psychiatric patients is far too complex a phenomenon to be amenable to quick-and-easy solutions, and new initiatives should be adopted cautiously. This is not always easy to do. In these times of scarce resources, there is often special pressure to produce programmatic solutions that will quickly eliminate the serious disjunctions between our intentions and our practices.

In recent years, case management has been proposed as a viable strategy to combat fragmentation in services for chronic psychiatric patients. Case management is itself frequently regarded as a basic planning principle in service design.[71] I shall approach case management somewhat differently in this discussion, however, and use it to illustrate the importance of the principle of exercising caution and restraint.

There is a fundamental difference between the role of the case manager and the function of case management that is, unfortunately, more often than not overlooked. Case management refers to the integration of services on the patient level and includes such important activities as arranging appointments and referrals, arranging and monitoring actual service delivery, coordinating personnel from multiple agencies, and providing active patient advocacy.[72] It is specifically directed toward assuring implementation of the patient's individualized treatment plan and thus facilitates continuity in his or her psychiatric care. The function of case management is implicit in all of the planning principles discussed here.

Although there is a rapidly growing body of thoughtful literature on case management in services for chronic psychiatric patients, it remains a troublesome concept. There is considerable argument, for instance, over who should "do" case management—the patient's therapist, a specially trained individual with few, if any, clinical responsibilities, or a "natural helper."[13,73,74] Some service systems have adopted a team case management approach in order to enhance the patient's access to services and to reduce the likelihood of staff burnout.[75]

There is also little unanimity on the subject of whether providing case management requires establishing a separate bureaucratic stratum with unique case manager job descriptions. This argument reflects to some extent a confusion of independent and dependent variables. I submit that if a system of care is truly responsive to the needs of chronic psychiatric patients, that is *prima facie* evidence that *de facto* case management exists, whether or not there are people called case managers.

Despite this conceptual confusion, the integrative function implied in the concept of case management is absolutely essential to adequate care for chronic psychiatric patients.[76] Rigid beliefs about the "correct" way to perform this function notwithstanding, the literature indicates that, in practice, case management may be, and is, performed in a variety of ways and by a variety of personnel. In many small communities and even in some larger ones, the function may be provided by a family member. In other instances, a nonprofessional staff member (a secretary or receptionist, for example) may perform, or certainly assist in, this function. I have visited a community mental health center where some very effective case management is performed informally by a retired investment broker who drives the center's van. Although this individual has taken on none of the professional facets of patient care, he is exquisitely sensitive to patients' needs for professional intervention and sees to it that they receive timely help. The importance of this kind of "natural helping" must not be minimized.

On the other hand, failure to designate case management as a formalized service system element with specifically named and trained case managers may in some communities reduce the quality of patient care, particularly in those places where the community is slow to initiate efforts on behalf of the chronically mentally ill. There are effective arguments on both sides of the controversy as to whether case management as a separate bureaucratic entity makes sense, or whether it simply adds an unnecessary level of bureaucracy to the service system. Similarly, there are cogent arguments on both sides of the debate over whether case managers should be distinct from therapists. Because different systems of care implement the case management function in different ways, it is counterproductive to set the concept in concrete. Case management should instead be approached cautiously and should be viewed with due appreciation of a community's special needs, strengths, and weaknesses.

Service planning for chronic psychiatric patients is often an expression of humane concern and idealism. These qualities, which are essential for the development of sensitive programs,[19,56,77] may inadvertently promote the acceptance of seductive solutions that promise dramatic, if not extravagant, results. I believe that the recent preoccupation with the notion of case management illustrates this tendency and risks introducing a false sense of security. It generates a complacency that may ultimately prove counterproductive. By interchanging the presence of a bureaucratically defined case manager with the responsible execution of the complex function of case management, the planning process may easily fall victim to metonymy—confusing the label with the thing labelled. The risk in such confusion is the tendency to mask basic planning problems and divert concern from real issues by adopting "quick fixes."

DISCUSSION AND CONCLUSIONS

Nine principles of service planning for chronic psychiatric patients which have evolved in this era of deinstitutionalization have been identified and discussed. These include formulating precise goals and objectives, assigning priorities in service delivery, reassessing institutional services, arranging a range of service interventions, fostering interagency cooperation, designing individualized programs, designing culturally relevant programs, using flexible program formats, and exercising caution and restraint. The last of these principles perhaps has a narrower base of support than the others. It is in some ways the most difficult to implement, because it may interfere with the momentum that has developed in deinstitutionalization planning. In fact, some planners fear that conservative anti-community forces may gain a foothold if too much caution and restraint are introduced. They feel that a community forced to deal with its chronically mentally ill members will rally to some extent; given an opportunity to rationalize institutional care, however, it will regress.

It is not easy, of course, to test such an assumption; too many uncontrolled variables intervene. Yet there is a growing sense today, evident in both the professional and popular literature, that some slowing down of the deinstitutionalization movement in its early years might have led to better outcomes at this time. My own studies of the problems in planning and delivering services for chronic psychiatric patients lead me to concur with this view. I would urge, accordingly, that care be taken not to continue in the trap of using slogans, catchwords, and stereotyped service interventions like "aftercare" and "case management" in such a way as to obliterate basic service issues. I would advocate candor and objectivity in dealing with these issues. The right questions must be asked in the right ways and with a minimum of bias.

The planning principles discussed here do not constitute a definitive listing. Although space considerations make it necessary to limit this discussion, it would be misleading not to mention some additional points that have very legitimately been stressed in service planning for chronic psychiatric patients. I have written elsewhere of the need for accessible and timely information on patients, programs, and service systems as a basic planning principle.[2,56] Principles stressed by other authors include dedicated leadership, specialized training of staff, and a positive organizational and administrative climate.[28,57,77-81]

As it was five years ago, the struggle to plan appropriate and responsive services for chronic psychiatric patients is uphill. Despite substantial progress on some fronts, our difficulties in caring for these individuals are more complex than they were several decades ago. As problems have increased, however, so has our knowledge of how to deal with them. Program planning for these patients continues to require the formulation of complex policy decisions and planning strategies. But today's planners, unlike those of the past, have at their disposal considerable experience on which to base new planning decisions.

REFERENCES

1. Bachrach LL: Is the least restrictive environment always the best? Sociological and semantic implications. *Hosp Community Psychiatry* 1980;31:97-103
2. Bachrach LL: An overview of deinstitutionalization, in Bachrach LL (ed): *New Directions for Mental Health Services: Deinstitutionalization, No. 18*. San Francisco, Jossey-Bass, 1983, pp 5-14
3. Talbott JA: Current cliches and platitudes in vogue in psychiatric vocabularies. *Hosp Community Psychiatry* 1975;26:530
4. Grob GN: Historical origins of deinstitutionalization, in Bachrach LL (ed): *New Directions for Mental Health Services: Deinstitutionalization, No. 18*. San Francisco, Jossey-Bass, 1983, pp 15-29
5. Bachrach LL: A conceptual approach to deinstitutionalization. *Hosp Community Psychiatry* 1978;29:573-578
6. Dorwart RA: Deinstitutionalization: Who is left behind? *Hosp Community Psychiatry* 1980;31:336-338
7. Kinard EM, Klerman LV: Changes in life style following mental hospitalization. *J Nerv Ment Dis* 1980;168:666-672
8. Kinard EM: Discharged patients who desire to return to the hospital. *Hosp Community Psychiatry* 1981;32:194-197
9. Lehman AF, Ward NC, Linn LS: Chronic mental patients: The quality of life issue. *Am J Psychiatry* 1982;139:1271-1276
10. Kennedy JF: Message from the President of the United States to the 88th Congress. Document No. 58. Washington, February 6, 1963
11. Stein LI, Test MA (eds): *Alternatives to Mental Hospital Treatment.* New York, Plenum, 1978
12. Talbott JA (ed):*Chronic Mental Patients: Treatment, Programs, Systems.* New York, Human Sciences Press, 1981
13. Lamb HR: *Treating the Long-Term Mentally Ill: Beyond Deinstitutionalization.* San Francisco, Jossey-Bass, 1982
14. Stein LI (ed): *New Directions for Mental Health Services: Community Support Systems for the Long-Term Patient, No. 2.* San Francisco, Jossey-Bass, 1979
15. Goldstein MJ (ed): *New Directions for Mental Health Services: New Developments in Interventions with Families of Schizophrenics, No. 12.* San Francisco, Jossey-Bass, 1981
16. Hoyer P: President's message. AMI Update (Alliance for the Mentally Ill of Greater Milwaukee), July 1982, pp 1-3
17. Budson RD: Sheltered housing for the mentally ill: An overview. *McLean Hosp J* 1979;4:140-157
18. Budson RD (ed): *New Directions for Mental Health Services: Issues in Community Residential Care, No. 11.* San Francisco, Jossey-Bass, 1981
19. Anthony WA, Cohen MR, Cohen BF: Philosophy, treatment, process, and principles of the psychiatric rehabilitation approach, in Bachrach LL (ed): *New Directions for Mental Health Services: Deinstitutionalization, No. 18.* San Francisco, Jossey-Bass, 1983, pp 67-79
20. Creasey DE, McCarthy TP: Training vocational rehabilitation counselors who work with chronic mental patients. *Am J Psychiatry* 1981;138:1102-1106

21. Estroff SE: Psychiatric deinstitutionalization: A sociocultural analysis. *J Social Issues* 1981;37:116–132
22. Hansell N: Services for schizophrenics: A lifelong approach to treatment. *Hosp Community Psychiatry* 1978;29:105–109
23. Bachrach LL: Continuity of care for chronic mental patients: A conceptual analysis. *Am J Psychiatry* 1981;138:1449–1456
24. Zusman J, Lamb HR: In defense of community mental health. *Am J Psychiatry* 1977;134:887–890
25. Langsley DG: The community mental health center: Does it treat patients? *Hosp Community Psychiatry* 1980;31:815–819
26. Baron RC: Changing public attitudes about the mentally ill in the community. *Hosp Community Psychiatry* 1981;32:173–178
27. Nuehring EM: Stigma and state hospital patients. *Am J Orthopsychiatry* 1979;49:626–633
28. Bachrach LL: Overview: Model programs for chronic mental patients. *Am J Psychiatry* 1980;137:1023–1031
29. Hunter M: Concern on aid for mental health is raised in light of law's repeal. *New York Times*, October 15, 1981, p B12
30. Mott AH: Block grants. *New York Times*, 20 March, 1981, p A27
31. Scallet LJ: View from Washington. Newsletter of the National Alliance for the Mentally Ill, March/April 1981, pp 4–5
32. Bachrach LL: Assessment of outcomes in community support systems: Results, problems, and limitations. *Schizophr Bull* 1982;8:39–61
33. Bachrach LL, Lamb HR: Conceptual issues in the evaluation of the deinstitutionalization movement, in Stahler GJ, Tash WR (eds): *Innovative Approaches to Mental Health Evaluation.* New York, Academic Press, 1982, pp 139–161
34. Scherl DJ, Macht LB: Deinstitutionalization in the absence of consensus. *Hosp Community Psychiatry* 1979;30:599–604
35. Talbott JA: Deinstitutionalization: Avoiding the disasters of the past. *Hosp Community Psychiatry* 1979;30:621–624
36. Bachrach LL: Developing objectives in community mental health planning. *Am J Public Health* 1974;64:1162–1163
37. Hagedorn H: *A Manual on State Mental Health Planning.* Rockville, MD, National Institute of Mental Health, 1977
38. Dinitz S, Beran N: Community mental health as a boundaryless and boundary-busting system. *J Health Soc Behav* 1971;12:99–108
39. Stern R, Minkoff K: Paradoxes in programming for chronic patients in a community clinic. *Hosp Community Psychiatry* 1979;30:613–617
40. Peele R, Luisada PV, Lucas MJ, et al: *Asylums* revisited. *Am J Psychiatry* 1977;134:1077–1081
41. Spiro HR: Reforming the state hospital in a unified care system. *Hosp Community Psychiatry* 1982;33:722–728
42. Talbott JA: *The Death of the Asylum: A Critical Study of State Hospital Management, Services and Care.* New York, Grune & Stratton, 1978
43. Treffert DA: Sane asylum: An alternative to the mental hospital, in Masserman JH (ed): *Current Psychiatric Therapies, Vol. 17.* New York, Grune & Stratton, 1977, pp 309–314
44. Zaleski J, Gale MS, Winget C: Extended hospital care as treatment of choice. *Hosp Community Psychiatry* 1979;30:399–401
45. Massachusetts Association for Mental Health: Statement on the Fiscal Year 1982 Budget for the Massachusetts Department of Mental Health, Boston, 28 May 1981
46. Group for the Advancement of Psychiatry Committee on Psychopathology: *The Positive Aspects of Long Term Hospitalization in the Public Sector for Chronic Psychiatric Patients.* New York, Mental Health Materials Center, 1982

47. Strange RE: The rise, fall, and rebirth of hospital psychiatry. Advance (Virginia Department of Mental Health and Mental Retardation) 1981;31:16-18

48. Goldman HH, Gattozzi AA, Taube CA: Defining and counting the chronically mentally ill. Hosp Community Psychiatry 1981;32:21-27

49. Witkin M: Number of Resident Patients, Total Admissions, Net Released, and Deaths, State and County Mental Hospitals:United States, 1950-1980. Rockville MD, National Institute of Mental Health Division of Biometry and Epidemiology, September 1981

50. Bachrach LL: Young adult chronic patients: An analytical review of the literature. Hosp Community Psychiatry 1982;33:189-197

51. Stelovich S: From the hospital to the prison: A step forward in deinstitutionalization? Hosp Community Psychiatry 1979;30:618-620

52. White RD: Mentally ill, retarded suffer in crowded jails. Washington Post, November 19, 1981, pp Md-1, Md-7

53. Bachrach LL: Planning services for the chronically mentally ill patients. Bull Menninger Clin 1983;47:163-188

54. Garrison V: Support systems of schizophrenic and nonschizophrenic Puerto Rican migrant women in New York City. Schizophr Bull 1978;4:561-596

55. Bachrach LL: Deinstitutionalization: An Analytical Review and Sociological Perspective. Rockville, MD, National Institute of Mental Health, 1976

56. Bachrach LL: Planning mental health services for chronic patients. Hosp Community Psychiatry 1979;30:387-393

57. Gaylin S, Rosenfeld P: Establishing community services for the mentally ill: A summary of lessons learned. Psychiatr Q 1978;50:295-298

58. Maryland Mental Hygiene Administration: Guidelines for Psychosocial Rehabilitation Programs in Maryland. Baltimore, September 1982

59. New York State Department of Mental Hygiene: Appropriate Community Placement and Support: Phase One: Five Year Mental Health Plan Albany, NY, January 1978

60. Beigel A, Bower WH, Levenson AI: A unified system of care: Blueprint for the future. Am J Psychiatry 1973;130:554-558

61. Muzekari LH, Knudsen H, Meyer E: The interlocking treatment system: A model for the delivery of state hospital-CMHC services. Hosp Community Psychiatry 1981;32:273-276

62. Pepper B, Ryglewicz H: Unified services: Concept and practice. Hosp Community Psychiatry 1982;33:762-765

63. Cotton PG: Psychiatric care of the deinstitutionalized patient, in Bachrach LL (ed): New Directions for Mental Health Services: Deinstitutionalization, No. 18. San Francisco, Jossey-Bass, 1983, pp 55-66

64. Abbott B: Tailoring the service system to the community. Hosp Community Psychiatry 1978;29:35-36

65. Malinowski B: The Dynamics of Culture Change. New Haven, Yale University Press, 1945

66. Merton RK: Social Theory and Social Structure Rev. ed. Glencoe, IL, Free Press, 1957

67. Sirovatka P: Grant helps spawn 91 programs on NYC model. ADAMHA News, September 5, 1980, p 3

68. Roberts SV: Former mental patients find fellowship at Miami center, New York Times, January 13, 1978, pp B1, B5

69. Minkoff K: Deinstitutionalization: Problems and Prospects. Paper presented at the Institute on Hospital and Community Psychiatry, Louisville, KY, October 1982

70. Pepper B, Ryglewicz H (eds): New Directions for Mental Health Services: The Young Adult Chronic Patient, No. 14. San Francisco, Jossey-Bass, 1982

71. Intagliata J: Improving the quality of community care for the chronically mentally disabled: The role of case management. Schizophr Bull 1982;8:655-674

72. Buckingham RW, Lupu D: A comparative study of hospice services in the United States. Am J Public Health 1982;72:455-463

73. Granet RB, Talbott JA: The continuity agent: Creating a new role to bridge the gaps in the mental health system. *Hosp Community Psychiatry* 1978;29:132–133

74. Johnson PJ, Rubin A: Case management in mental health: A social work domain? *Social Work*, 1983;28:49–55

75. Test MA: Continuity of care in community treatment, in Stein LI (ed): *New Directions for Mental Health Services: Community Support Systems for the Long-Term Patient No. 2*. San Francisco: Jossey-Bass, 1979, pp 15–23

76. Schwartz SR, Goldman HH, Churgin S: Case management for the chronic mentally ill: Models and dimensions. *Hosp Community Psychiatry* 1982;33:1006–1009

77. Marlowe HA, Spector P, Bedell J: Implementing a psychosocial rehabilitation program in a state mental hospital: A case study of organizational change. *Psychosocial Rehabilitation J* 1983;6:1–11

78. Cutler DL, Bloom JD, Shore JH: Training psychiatrists to work with community support systems for chronically mentally ill persons. *Am J Psychiatry* 1981;138:98–101

79. Nielsen AC, Stein LI, Talbott JA, et al: Encouraging psychiatrists to work with chronic patients: Opportunities and limitations of residency education. *Hosp Community Psychiatry* 1981;32:767–775

80. Polak PR, Kirby MW: A model to replace psychiatric hospitals. *J Nerv Ment Dis* 1976;162:13–22

81. White HS, Bennett MB: Training psychiatric residents in chronic care. *Hosp Community Psychiatry* 1981;32:339–343

James T. Barter

13

Psychoeducation

In the past two decades there has been an increased interest and importance placed on approaches to mental illness which deal with other than the usual biomedical or psychologic treatments. The emergence of a new industry of social rehabilitation centers and programs, the rise of significant numbers of self-help groups, renewed interest in social support systems and network theory, turning back to the family as a collaborator in the treatment of the mentally ill member, an interest in educational approaches—these are significant to understanding modern treatment of the chronic patient.

All these social approaches depend, in varying degrees, on a formalized, traditional educational approach—books, lectures, seminars, and a teacher/pupil relationship. Psychoeducation refers to the use of educational techniques, methods, and approaches to aid in the recovery from the disabling effects of mental illness or as an adjunct to the treatment of the mentally ill, usually within the framework of another ongoing treatment approach or as part of a research program. It is the purpose of this paper to provide an overview of psychoeducation as it has been developed within the different contexts of family therapy, self-help groups, and social rehabilitation programs.

PSYCHOEDUCATION IN FAMILY THERAPY

The historic thesis of family therapy in western culture has been that family psychodynamics are responsible for the mental illness of a member of that family, or actively collaborate in its perpetuation.[1-6] There have been detractors

THE CHRONIC MENTAL PATIENT
ISBN 0-8089-1649-1

Copyright © 1984 by Grune & Stratton.
All rights of reproduction in any form reserved.

from this general thesis. Hirsch and Leff,[7] in a comprehensive review of the literature on abnormalities in the parents of schizophrenics, assert that there is no scientific evidence for this proposition. From the publications and statements of many self-help and parents' groups, there is an absolute rejection of the idea that families cause schizophrenia or other psychoses, and anger over these "blaming" theories.[8-11] Increased knowledge about genetic and biologic theories of causation of major mental illness support the contention that families deserve support and not scapegoating.

A major development in family therapy has been the research into expressed emotion (EE), and its effect on the course of schizophrenia. Expressed emotion refers to a standardized measure of overinvolvement, hostility, and critical comment made by the patient's relatives, directed toward the patient. Brown, Birley, and Wing,[12] following up on their earlier research, showed that schizophrenics returning to a high EE family environment were at greater risk for relapse and return to hospital. Numerous replications of this work have been carried out and show that the rate of relapse in high EE families is generally five to seven times higher than in low EE families.[13-16]

These results suggest that the outcome for patients living with high EE families might be altered by teaching the families better methods of coping with the disturbed member. The goal of such an educational effort is to change the attitudes of these high EE family members in the direction of increased support, less emotional involvement, and decreased criticism. Several centers have become involved in this research and use psychoeducational techniques as one of several approaches to treatment and improved outcome.

Psychoeducational approaches to the family are a recent development. Most of the studies are less than ten years old. They represent a major shift in therapy away from treating the family as the causative factor or the sustaining force in the patient's illness. The family is enlisted instead, as an active collaborator in the treatment of the mentally ill family member through participation in educational seminars rather than "family therapy."

Change in patterns of care for the severely mentally ill increase the importance of the family as caretakers. Generally speaking, most psychotic individuals receive a brief course of in-patient treatment and then are referred for some form of community aftercare. A majority of these individuals return to live with their families. Families differ in their ability to care for disturbed and disturbing relatives. This has led to requests for specific help in learning how to cope, and to an increased interest among professionals in and sensitivity to the problems that families have in dealing with mentally ill members.

Family intervention programs almost all rely on the use of adequate doses of psychotropic medication in both control and experimental groups and only alter other variables. Some form of psychoeducational approach to the families, usually at the beginning of therapy and often excluding the identified patient, is almost universally included.

The common content of the psychoeducational approaches used in these family programs includes factual information about the etiology of schizophrenia, with careful attention to genetic and biochemical theories and conscious downplaying of implications that the staff believe that the family is in any way responsible for the illness or its subsequent course. Current information about the nature of schizophrenia including its usual mode of onset, symptoms, expected course, and outcome is also a part of this kind of approach. The individual is defined as suffering from a illness, and not as simply being stubborn or misbehaving. Treatment approaches are presented including family, group, and individual treatment, and the role of psychotropic medications. The emphasis on medication includes a discussion of the major drugs used in the treatment of psychoses, their effectiveness in reducing symptoms, the importance of continuing on the drugs, their side effects, and how to manage problems around medication. General advice is also given about how to reduce stress in the household and how to deal with crises.

These family educational sessions have several functions. There is the obvious benefit of peer support from others who have had similar experiences dealing with a psychotic family member. Much sharing goes on between group members, and individuals seem to be less reluctant to ask questions or share experiences in such a setting. The family is also aided in seeing that they need to set long-term goals for the patient and give up the expectation of a rapid recovery or return to a pre-illness level of good functioning in the immediate post-hospital phase.

Psychoeducation in Self-help Groups

Many health and mental health professionals do not give proper attention to the social context in which chronically ill patients and their families exist. With the concentration on the disease process there is often an inadequate response to the needs of those whose emotional lives are affected by contact with the chronically ill or disabled. Family members receive little professional attention. Self-help groups seem to arise as a response.

There has been a virtual explosion in the number of self-help groups. Particularly in health and mental health fields, self-help groups have been formed which touch on every diagnosis and treatment modality. Groups can be and are devoted to single issues, or broadly to "mental health." Self-help groups are alleged to be among the most rapidly growing human services.[17] A recently published directory lists over 400 such groups, serving 15,000,000 people.[18]

One can define a self-help group as an organization of persons that meets regularly on a face-to-face basis and assist one another in changing behaviors or attitudes. They often define themselves as dealing with problem areas which lie outside the traditional medical or mental health care system. Usually they have lay leadership and are non-profit enterprises.

Gottlieb[19] devised a typology of such groups, with three major categories. *Loss-transition groups* are those in which members deal with a major event involving the loss of or disruption of a relationship with a loved one. *Mothers Against Drunk Drivers, (MADD)* is an example of such a recent group, started by a parent of a teenage girl who was killed by a drunk driver. *MADD* offers support to others who have suffered such a loss, as well as helping the survivors through the legal processes involved in punishing the perpetrator.

There are also *one-step removed groups,* in which the relatives or friends of an affected person band together for mutual support. Many mental health self-help groups are of this kind. Examples include Al-anon, which involves the teenagers of alcoholic parents, and the American Schizophrenia Association for Families of Schizophrenics.

Stress-coping and *stress-support* groups are the third category. In these groups the members have a clinically diagnosed or diagnosable medical or mental condition or disorder, such as diabetes or bipolar depressive illness.

Several functions of self-help groups have been identified.[17,19-20] One primary function is to provide a context within which meaningful interactions can occur. This facilitates sharing of factual information about the disease process and how to deal with it, suggestions for altering attitudes of professionals seen as detrimental to the aims of the group, and providing emotional peer support in a safe arena. Most of the groups subscribe to the idea that "only someone who has been there can truly know how it feels." They also serve as reference groups and role models for positive redefinition of feelings of stigma, guilt, or inadequacy. An attitude of helping others as a means of increasing one's own self-esteem is another useful function. Finally, they lead to increased consciousness of consumer control of treatment services and the way in which they are delivered.

Formal psychoeducation is a major vehicle in achieving the goals of many of these self-help groups. Some groups publish newsletters, pamphlets, and books, dealing with the specific affliction with which the group is identified. While professionals may be asked to speak at meetings or give advice, most educational materials are developed within the group. Two examples of such groups are presented below.

The Schizophrenia Association of Greater Washington[8,11] provides a spectrum of educational services for its members. Surveys of the membership indicated a need for specific knowledge of the disease and practical information on management of its afflicted members. Seminars were offered in response on the nature of schizophrenia, coping with disturbed behavior, and the problems likely to be encountered in moving the chronic mental patient into the community. Books likely to be of interest to members are evaluated and recommended. Especially popular are those with a particular emphasis on first-hand accounts of successful coping such as Park's account of mothering an autistic child.[21]

The National Schizophrenia Foundation (NSF) of Great Britain (founded in 1974) has had a similar experience with education for its members. The NSF was established for political lobbying, policy formulation, research, and education.

Since its inception, the NSF has used publications to educate people about schizophrenia. Some of the early pamphlets were devoted to "horror stories" detailing neglect and maltreatment of schizophrenics and their relatives. The effect of these was to put pressure on the Department of Health and Social Security to evaluate the care of patients in the community and to improve facilities for care of the schizophrenic. A secondary effect was the creation of a sense of shared purpose among members of the NSF and new recruit members.[22]

The NSF published a pamphlet ("Schizophrenia") giving information about the disease. It received national media attention and has been a steady best-seller since its publication.

The NSF has voluntary coordinators who are called on to provide advice and information about mental illness resources and treatment. Coordinators are themselves trained with residential study weekends, and receive a three-months' refresher course. The voluntary coordinators meet with families, and lay and professional groups, to provide information about schizophrenia.

There has been little scientific evaluation of the results of these educational efforts by self-help groups, although there are many testimonials and reports of general satisfaction. Since the members define what they want to know and often participate in the delivery of the seminars, it is not surprising that these self-reports are generally positive.

There has been extensive use of educational methods by some groups to espouse a particular theory of causation or treatment of schizophrenia. The American Schizophrenia Association and the Huxley Institute for Biosocial Research, for example, believe in the value of orthomolecular treatment for schizophrenia. They have been responsive to the needs of parents and relatives for information about the illness and its causes, and have, in addition, published many books and pamphlets. They also provide speakers for seminars about orthomolecular treatment.

Professionals need to be aware of self-help groups and their psychoeducational materials. These groups represent a critical secondary prevention resource. They provide support to people going through a crisis or coping with a stressful event. They are also beginning to have a profound effect on health and mental health practice.

PSYCHOEDUCATION AND SOCIAL REHABILITATION

Social rehabilitation programs have arisen in response to the need of many deinstitutionalized patients for psychosocial community programs. Many chronic patients do not live with their families, and they are alienated and lack the supportive structure that the family provides. They are not apt to be tied into self-help groups because they lack even rudimentary social networks. The success of early models such as Fountain House in New York, Horizon House in Philadelphia, and Thresholds in Chicago, spawned a whole new national industry. In California, special legislation was passed mandating a priority for social rehabilitation approaches. The federal social support system published guidelines and encouraged state efforts to create social rehabilitation efforts. The result has been a standardization of approaches and systematization of knowledge and skills needed to operate such programs. Educational approaches have been the mainstay of many social rehabilitation programs.

Social rehabilitation programs do not come out of a psychologic or biomedical tradition. Their roots are more firmly grounded in rehabilitation theory and social work approaches. Often the patients who are referred for services are on medications or involved in some form of psychological treatment. Programs focus on helping participants acquire practical living skills. These include learning appropriate social and interpersonal behaviors in a normalizing environment, and reducing those specific behaviors which lead to regression and rehospitalization.

Psychoeducational approaches permeate all levels of social rehabilitation programs. This is, in part, a recognition of the important value that our society places on education and educational methodologies as a means of helping the individual achieve personal goals. On the other hand, it is a response to the specific deficits which many of the patients suffer. Some come from backgrounds of poverty, and have little or no formal education. Others have been educated, but their psychoses have interrupted or interfered with the learning processes. Finally, the educational approach has practical value in increasing the patients' self-esteem by imparting the message that the staff believes them to be capable of understanding and learning complex information.

Examples of the ways in which educational approaches are integrated into social rehabilitation programs include the teaching of community survival skills, health education, work readiness, and basic remedial education.

"Community survival skills" refers to the acquisition of practical knowledge that will increase the ability of the chronic mental patient to live in community settings. The formerly institutionalized person whose basic necessities of food, clothing, and shelter were provided by the institution may be helpless when faced with providing for himself or herself in the community. Thus programs focus on teaching a person how to plan a meal, go shopping, cook and serve it; how to get to the program site, using public transportation, how to deal with public agencies such as social services, hospitals, or the conservator. For those living in satellite housing, how to budget money, pay the rent, keep the apartment clean, and avoid trouble with the landlord become essential skills.[23]

Health education is a frequent element in social rehabilitation programs. It has its parallel in general medical practice, where patients suffering from chronic medical conditions are often provided with copious information about their own disease and how to cooperate in its treatment. Enlisting the patient as a collaborator in treatment is a new approach in mental health. Social rehabilitation programs are in the forefront of these efforts.

Medication education is an example of one approach to having the patients help to manage their own treatment. It has been recognized that the failure to take medication is a frequent precursor to recurrence of symptoms and rehospitalization. Patients are often confused about why they are on medications, are ill-informed about side effects and how to manage them, and discontinue them without the doctor's knowledge.

Medication education assumes that the patient should have a more responsible role in the treatment relationship. Through an educational experience, the patient is able to understand the basis of drug therapy and becomes less dependent on rumor or peer group experience as the primary source of drug information. Such projects are able to produce well-informed patients able to assist the physician in determining a dose of medication which is minimal, clinically effective, and avoids disabling side effects.

Other health-related issues such as nutrition, herpes, effects of street drugs on mental illness, contraception, vitamins, hypertension, smoking, and cancer are often covered. Lectures, pre- and post-lecture tests, brochures, workbooks, case history materials, films, and film strips have all been used with success in these educational programs.

Patients who do well in the early phases of social rehabilitation become candidates for the work readiness program. Such training has the goal of helping the client secure worthwhile employment. The content typically deals with barriers to the employment of the mentally ill. These include the lack of positive attitudes toward work, improvement of basic work habits, development of saleable skills, and increasing motivation.

Work readiness seminars explore the impact of full time work (and wages) on SSI payments, supervisor–employee relationships, how work changes lifestyle, and prejudices against employing the formerly mentally ill, especially those on medication. The programs also provide practical work experiences in addition to seminars and discussion groups. These can range from volunteer work placements where the individual's readiness to work can be assessed with regard to placement in real, wage-paying jobs.

This employment continuum is a supportive one. Constant feedback is provided, and clients are encouraged to ventilate feelings while learning coping skills.

Basic remedial education is designed to help patients overcome their educational deficits. The lack of basic skills in reading, writing, and arithmetic often interferes with community adjustment or acts as a barrier to employment. Many clients hide these basic skill deficits, employing many strategies to keep them hidden from others to avoid lowered self-esteem. Sophisticated assessments of educational skill levels are therefore offered, and programs are tailored to meet goals such as passing the GED exam or preparing for community college enrollment. Integrating adult education through the regular school district extends the resources available without increased expense to the program, and provides a normalizing experience.

SUMMARY

Psychoeducation is a promising and helpful adjunct to the treatment of the chronic mental patient. Family therapy, social rehabilitation, and self-help groups are in the forefront in using this methodology. There are many common factors of the approach. Information is disseminated and shared, patients and families feel supported, advice about difficult problems is shared, and standard educational methods are employed in a variety of formats. Wider use of the psychoeducational approach to more traditional psychiatric settings is both feasible and desirable.

Educational programs are so imbedded in the matrix of social rehabilitation programs and self-help group efforts that their value as a unique tool has not been recognized by psychiatrists. This is because they are not generally involved with these entities. Traditional mental health programs have also been slow to develop psychoeducational approaches, perhaps because the tradition of psychiatry has focused on individual psychodynamics and biomedical approaches. Behavior modification is the most closely-allied treatment, and some psychoeducational approaches use behavioral techniques in their applications.

It is important that psychiatrists take an interest in psychoeducation because of its value in the rehabilitation of the chronic mental patient. Such an interest is also prudent considering the concern expressed in recent years about the declining image of psychiatry and the success of other professionals in expanding their roles in the treatment of the chronic mental patient. The success of the orthomolecular movement is as much a result of the extensive use of psychoeducational methods to inform patients and their families as it is to dissatisfaction with traditional psychiatric practice.

The most visible use of psychoeducation in psychiatry is found in certain family therapy research projects. There, psychoeducation opens up the possibility of a wide range of socially acceptable interventions, constrained only by the limitations of current educational technology and theory. Widespread use is not yet apparent. This is ironic considering how pervasive these techniques are among self-help groups and social rehabilitation programs.

The value of the psychoeducational approach to families is that it substitutes education and collaboration for blaming the family for causing or perpetuating the illness. There is some suggestion of family fault still contained in the EE theory, but the emphasis on education appears to overcome family resistance. It is reasonable to expect further refinement and wider acceptance of this approach in the future, considering the current interest and number of ongoing projects.

Educational methods are important to building and sustaining the social support system of the chronic patient, and contribute to the possibility of a successful community adjustment. From the participant's point of view, acceptability is enhanced because information is provided, techniques are familiar, and it is seen as neither medical or origin nor controlled by psychiatric professionals.

Psychoeducation should be more widely incorporated into traditional psychiatric settings, such as outpatient clinics, partial hospitals, and in-patient settings. Topics which could be covered are extensive, including stress management, medications, general health and nutrition, and the nature of mental illness. The acceptability of this approach to families and patients makes it a powerful tool.

REFERENCES

1. Bateson G, Jackson D, Haley J, et al: Toward a theory of schizophrenia. *Behav Sci* 1956;1:241-264
2. Bowen M: A family concept of schizophrenia, in Jackson D (ed): *The Etiology of Schizophrenia.* New York, Basic Books, 1960, pp 346-372
3. Henry J: *Pathways to Madness.* New York, Random House, 1971, p 477
4. Laing R: *The Politics of the Family and Other Essays.* New York, Pantheon, 1971, p 131
5. Lidz T, Fleck S, Cornelison A: *Schizophrenia and the Family.* New York, International Universities Press, 1965, p 477
6. Wynne L, Ryckoff I, Day J, et al: Pseudomutuality in the family relations of schizophrenics. *Psychiatry* 1958;21:205-220
7. Hirsch SR, Leff JP: *Abnormalities in Parents of Schizophrenics.* London, Oxford University Press, 1965, p 200
8. Kint MG: Schizophrenia is a family affair: Problems of families in coping with schizophrenia. *Orthomolecular Psychiatry* 1978;7:236-246
9. Lamb HR, Oliphant E: Schizophrenia through the eyes of families. *Hosp Community Psychiatry* 1978;29:803-806
10. Appleton WS: Mistreatment of patients' families by psychiatrists. *Am J Psychiatry* 1974;131:655-657
11. Hatfield AB: Help seeking behavior in families of schizophrenics. *Am J Community Psychol* 1979;7:563-569
12. Brown GW, Birley JLT, Wing JK: Influence of family life on the course of schizophrenic disorders: A replication. *Br J Psychiatry* 1972;121:241-258
13. Leff JP: Schizophrenia and sensitivity to the family environment. *Schizophr Bull* 1976;2:566-574
14. Leff JP, Vaughn C: The role of maintenance therapy and relatives' expressed emotion in relapse of schizophrenia: A two-year follow-up. *Br J Psychiatry* 1981;139:102-104
15. Vaughn CE, Leff JP: Patterns of emotional response in the relatives of schizophrenic patients. *Schizophr Bull* 1981;7:43-44
16. Falloon IRH, Liberman RP, Lillie FJ, Vaughan CE: Family therapy of schizophrenics with high risk of relapse. *Fam Process* 1981;20:211-222
17. Borman LD: Introduction, in Borman LD, et al (eds): *Helping People to Help Themselves.* New York, Hayworth Press, 1982, pp 3-15
18. Evans G: *The Family Circle Guide to Self-help.* New York, Ballantine, 1979, p 240
19. Gottlieb BH: Mutual-help groups: Members' views of their benefits and of roles for professionals, in Borman LD, et al (eds): *Helping People to Help Themselves.* New York, Hayworth Press, 1982, pp 55-68

PART I I I

Community Treatment

Robert E. Love

14

The Community Support Program:
Strategy for Reform?

In 1977, the National Institute of Mental Health (NIMH) launched the Community Support Program (CSP)[1]: "a modest but potentially significant pilot program . . . . designed to improve services for . . . adult psychiatric patients whose disabilities are severe and persistent but for whom long-term skilled or semi-skilled nursing care is inappropriate" (p 319). According to Judith Clark Turner, director of CSP from 1977–83, this federal-level initiative was undertaken because there was no coherent federal policy toward the chronically mentally ill (CMI), responsibility for the care of discharged CMI was fragmented and confused, there was no systematic approach to financing community-based services, mainstream mental health agencies lacked commitment to serve the CMI, and advocacy efforts on behalf of the CMI were disorganized and ineffective.

NIMH proposed to address the needs of the estimated 800,000 to 1.5 million CMI who resided in community settings[2] by awarding federal contracts to state mental health authorities to stimulate the development of Community Support Systems (CSSs). These CSSs were to provide comprehensive mental health, rehabilitation, and support services to help the CMI "develop their potentials without being unnecessarily isolated or excluded from the community"[1] (p 329).

In each local CSS service area, a "core service agency" was responsible for mobilizing staff and resources to:

THE CHRONIC MENTAL PATIENT
ISBN 0-8089-1649-1

Copyright © 1984 by Grune & Stratton.
All rights of reproduction in any form reserved.

1. Locate potential clients and assure them access to services;
2. Help clients meet basic human needs (food, shelter, clothing, medical care) and apply for entitlements;
3. Provide mental health care;
4. Provide 24-hour quick response crisis assistance;
5. Provide comprehensive psychosocial services, including needs evaluation, training in living, employment, and social skills, and opportunities for employment and social activity;
6. Provide a range of rehabilitative or supportive housing arrangements for an indefinite period;
7. Offer backup support and education to families, friends, and community members;
8. Encourage community involvement in the planning and delivery of services;
9. Establish grievance procedures and mechanisms to protect the rights of clients;
10. Provide case management to assure continuous access to services.

These local CSSs were to operate as integrated service delivery *systems,* with clearly defined responsibilities for program planning, development, monitoring, and evaluation.[3]

Between 1978 and 1984, NIMH committed over $42 million to the promotion of CSP. This paper will examine the impact of this effort at the federal, state, local, and client levels. With the exception of one recent book,[4] much of the relevant material has not been published; it exists as reports issued by or through NIMH.

Today CSP faces an uncertain future. Judith Clark Turner, who nurtured the program from its inception seven years ago, resigned as director in 1983. For each of the past three years, Congressional intervention has been necessary to rescue CSP from the $0.0 budget proposed by the Reagan administration. Whatever its ultimate fate, however, CSP has not inspired major reforms in the mental health service system, and the unmet needs of the CMI residing in our communities remain a significant social and mental health problem.

CSP AT THE FEDERAL LEVEL

The main responsibility of CSP at the federal level was to award and monitor state CSS development contracts. In addition, CSP was to assume federal leadership in developing and implementing a national CSP research and evaluation plan, providing technical assistance and disseminating "state of the art" information to the states, collaborating with other federal health, rehabilitation, housing, and human service agencies to develop or improve the delivery of services to the CMI, and encouraging nationwide advocacy efforts on behalf of the CMI.

Funding and Monitoring State CSS Operations

In its first full year of operation (fiscal year 1978), CSP distributed $4.4 million to 20 states. Eight states received strategy development contracts to design and execute three-year CSS implementation plans. Twelve states were given demonstration and replication contracts to select and evaluate local CSS demonstration projects which would then serve as operating models for statewide expansion.[5]

Over the next three years, 17 of these first-round states continued to receive funds, totalling $4.5 million in 1979, $6.2 million in 1980, and $7.2 million in 1981. Contracts averaged approximately $290,000 a year, with a range of $65,000–$555,000. As states reached the end of their funding cycles, however, these amounts were significantly reduced. Consequently, about half the first-round states reported that they would no longer be able to employ a full-time project director to coordinate state CSP efforts.[6]

Over the continued objections of the Reagan administration, which wanted to incorporate CSP into federal block grants, Congress appropriated approximately $4.8 million to the program in 1982, $5 million in 1983, and $5.5 million in 1984. These funds were largely used to extend the CSS strategy development grants to previously unfunded states. The new grants were issued on a year-to-year basis and were limited to $125,000 per state.[3]

During the first two years of CSP operation, NIMH was unable to monitor state program performance consistently because of the lack of central office staff and high project officer turnover.[7] Staffing improved somewhat in 1979, when CSP became a formal branch of NIMH, but the CSP implementation section never had more than 3–5 full-time members. CSP also faced continual problems documenting state and local CSS development activities. One report concluded that it was not feasible for most states to collect data related to resource mobilization, local CSS development, or statewide service improvement.[8] Yet this information was essential to assess accurately the impact of CSP at the state and local levels.

The state CSPs, on their part, indicated in 1981 that they were making progress in meeting the needs of the CMI, and 7 of 9 rated the influence of NIMH as "moderately" or "very positive." Their major complaints included excessive federal reporting requirements, inadequate technical assistance, and the uneven quality of project officers.[8]

CSP Research and Evaluation

Early CSP research and evaluation efforts were hampered by staffing and funding limitations, bureaucratic delays, and a lack of appropriate research instruments. In 1979, the NIMH Division of Biometry and Epidemiology assumed responsibility for CSP research, freeing CSP staff and providing additional research expertise and resources. Based on recommendations by Schulberg[9,10] and other researchers,[11-14] NIMH adopted a multi-level research and evaluation strategy to assess the numbers and needs of the target population, the system changes necessary to implement CSP, the costs of CSS operations, and the benefits of CSP to clients and the community.

Needs Assessment

Existing estimates of the size of the noninstitutionalized CMI population in the US[2,15] did not account for local demographic and socioeconomic variations, and were often of little assistance to local-level planners.[16] NIMH therefore funded a needs assessment program to generate more accurate figures for local-level use.[11,12] As part of this program, three "synthetic estimation" techniques were developed and pretested.[17]

Strategy Evaluation

The 1980 Exploratory Evaluation[18] or "evaluability assessment" examined CSP from a systems analysis perspective. Inconsistencies in the logic of CSP strategies and objectives were identified and possible solutions or management options were proposed. Several of the suggestions were incorporated into the 1980 CSP grant announcement.[3] The evaluation also revealed differences between federal program objectives and actual state and local operations. A set of performance indicators was designed to measure improvements in state and local service delivery. The resulting performance measurement system was first tested in the 1981 Short Term Evaluation,[8] and is currently being refined to provide states with a self-assessment tool.[19]

In a 1981 overview of CSP, Katz made several program strategy recommendations to NIMH based on his interviews with state and local project directors.[7] In 1982, Stroul reviewed state CSP activities in order to identify both successful and unsuccessful CSS implementation strategies.[6]

Cost Outcome Analyses

Although the debate over the costs of institutional care versus community placement remains unresolved, several researchers have suggested that community-based care costs no more than in-patient treatment.[20,21] For example, the average estimated costs for 18 New York State CSP clients totalled $10,460 in 1980.[22] In comparison, the costs of care in US mental hospitals averaged over $20,000 a year in 1977.[23] Recognizing the importance of this issue, NIMH sponsored an examination of three Colorado CSS demonstration sites in 1981 in order to establish the feasibility of estimating CSS cost effectiveness and outcomes.[13] Encouraged by the results, NIMH launched a full-scale investigation of CSS cost outcomes in 1983.[19]

Client Survey

The 1980 Client Survey gathered comprehensive information on 1471 clients at 18 local CSS sites using the Uniform Client Data Instrument.[24] In 1983, NIMH sponsored a longitudinal follow-up study using this instrument to assess the long-term effects of CSS participation on clients.[19] This project is also examining the quality of life of a subsample of clients employing measures suggested by a 1980 New York State CSP report.[25]

State-Sponsored Research

Several states, including Colorado, Massachusetts, Michigan, and New York, have conducted their own research and evaluation programs. New York, for example, had completed 68 CSP-related projects by 1981.[26] Spaniol reviewed state-sponsored research in 1981.[27]

Future Research

In 1982, Congress appropriated $960,000 specifically for CSP research. Because of time constraints, this money was directed toward ongoing or unfunded projects examining state-level CSS implementation, service delivery and financing strategies, development and staffing of local CSSs, and client drop-out and quality of life.[19] With an additional 1983 appropriation of $700,000, NIMH proposed to explore unexamined research issues such as the effectiveness of different types of CSS delivery systems and the service needs of additional subgroups of the CMI (e.g., the young, the elderly, and the homeless).[28]

Technical Assistance and Information Dissemination

Regional and national Learning Community Conferences provided consumer and advocacy groups, mental health personnel, and regional CSP staff with a valuable opportunity to exchange information and receive technical assistance. Organized to develop a common conceptual understanding of CSP goals and promote periodic reassessment of CSP assumptions and policies, these conferences emerged as a highly successful element in federal CSP strategy. Summaries of the proceedings of the first five learning conferences are available.[29,30] The sixth conference was held in June 1983, and attracted over 300 participants.

NIMH offered additional technical assistance and information during CSS site visits and meetings of project directors. It also published reports in periodicals such as the *Community Support Service Journal*,[31] which it helped sponsor. The 1980 Exploratory Evaluation, however, concluded that technical assistance and information on the current "state of the art" had not been distributed on a systematic basis because of personnel and resource limitations.[18] In 1982, NIMH responded to this need by implementing portions of a comprehensive technical assistance plan developed in cooperation with the Boston University Center for opened a Technical Assistance Resource Center to collect and disseminate CSP information, make referrals, and offer technical assistance. It published an extensive annotated bibliography of CSP-related research[32] and a technical assistance resource directory[33] in 1983, and began issuing a quarterly newsletter, *Community Support Network News,* in 1984.

Collaboration with Other Federal Agencies

NIMH directed much of its early collaborative effort toward developing the National Plan for the Chronically Mentally Ill[15] and the 1980 Mental Health Systems Act, both of which were abandoned before they had any substantial policy impact. CSP was able to negotiate a cooperative agreement with the Rehabilitation Services Administration for joint planning and program implementation of services, research, and training. CSP also participated in the Department of Housing and Urban Development (HUD) Demonstration Program for Deinstitutionalization of the Mentally Ill. Inaugurated in 1978, the program never lived up to expectations.[34]

Katz observed in 1981 that additional federal-level interagency collaboration was necessary to modify federal laws and regulations that the states had identified as impeding the delivery of services to the CMI (e.g., HUD Section 202 and SSI regulations). He noted that NIMH had "not been able to invest sufficient staff time on federal interdepartmental and interagency activities," describing efforts as "fragmented and intermittent"[7] (p 23).

Organizing Advocacy Networks for the CMI

Recognizing the importance of interest groups in generating political and social support for the CMI, CSP encouraged their involvement in national and local activities, invited them to learning conferences, and kept them informed of CSP initiatives.

One of the most active grass-roots movements has been the National Alliance for the Mentally Ill, which represents local organizations of families, relatives, and friends of the CMI. Professional associations have also worked on behalf of the CMI, including the National Mental Health Association, the National Council of Community Mental Health Centers, the American Psychiatric Association, and the American Psychological Association.

These organizations recently joined together to form the National Community Support Advocacy Network. This coalition has concentrated on expanding the delivery of community support services to the CMI. It has sought formal legislative authority for CSP and has lobbied to increase the CSP budget. For the last three years these groups successfully helped stop the Reagan administration from dismantling CSP—the last identifiable symbol of direct NIMH involvement in delivering services to the mentally ill.

CSP AT THE STATE LEVEL

A major objective of CSP was to convince state and local governments to reassume their traditional responsibility for the CMI, many of whom had been discharged into local communities without adequate planning or provision for support services. To achieve this end, NIMH sponsored a unit of CSP advocates within each of the participating state mental health authorities. These units seldom numbered more than six full-time staff members. After defining the target population, estimating its size, and assessing its needs, each state CSP office was to improve the responsiveness of the state mental health system to the CMI through modification of state mental health policies to promote CSS objectives, mobilization or redirection of necessary state resources, introduction of appropriate legislative or regulatory initiatives, fostering of interagency collaboration and agreements, provision of technical assistance and training, and organization of advocacy groups for the CMI.

These state-level activities will be briefly examined using information drawn from the third and fourth year reports of the 17 first-round states as well as from intramural[7] and extramural[6,8,18,27] NIMH studies. Progress reports from the second-round states were not available.

Defining the Target Population

In order to assure a homogeneous target population, NIMH proposed that all CSP clients meet the same strict standards of disability and functional impairment. Most states, however, adopted definitions that differed somewhat from the NIMH version.[8] Consequently, only about 60 percent of the clients included in the 1980 Client Survey met all of the NIMH criteria, although the majority of clients did appear to be mentally disabled.[24]

Estimating the Size of the Target Population

Using "synthetic estimation" techniques, a recent NIMH-sponsored pilot study suggested that the number of noninstitutionalized CMI ranged from 4.3 to 4.8 per thousand.[17] Earlier, less sophisticated estimates by the first-round CSP states averaged about 4 per thousand.[11] A separate study using a definition similar to that of NIMH reported figures of 0.7 to 2.5 per thousand.[16] The National Plan for the Chronically Mentally Ill cited incidences of between 4 and

7.5 per thousand.[15] Given these disparities, NIMH has continued to fund research to develop accurate techniques for calculating the numbers of CMI at the sub-state level.[19]

Assessing the Needs of the Target Population

Rather than undertake formal needs assessments, most states "have taken an ad hoc approach to needs determination and . . . have accepted as valid conventional and/or expert wisdom."[8] (p IV–7) When asked in the 1981 Short Term Evaluation to rank the 10 CSS components on the basis of client need, only 3 of 9 states supported their rankings with empirical data. This may explain the absence of agreement on the priority of any one component except the provision of rehabilitative and supportive housing, which was ranked first or second by 5 of 9 states.[8]

Most states acknowledged the importance of needs assessment—a complex and not altogether scientific enterprise.[35] Several states used such statistics to allocate scarce resources, provide baselines for program evaluation, and convince decision-makers of the necessity for CSSs.[6,27] Many states deplored the lack of accurate statewide information regarding the mentally ill,[8] but only about half mentioned formal needs assessment activities in their fourth year reports.

Modifying State Policies

A few states (e.g., Colorado, Maine, New York, Oregon) incorporated the CSS model into their state mental health plans. In addition, about one-third of the states designated the CMI as a priority population. This classification has been accompanied by a substantial allocation of resources in some states (New Jersey, for instance) but not in others (such as Alabama).

Mobilizing Resources

In 1982, NIMH estimated that $18 were spent at the state level for every $1 invested in CSP at the federal level. The 1981 Short Term Evaluation took a more cautious view: "States have been able indeed to mobilize resources on behalf of the target population. However, the extent to which such mobilization has occurred, how it occurred, the specific resources mobilized, and what the resources are being used for remain largely unknown."[8] (p IV–17)

About two-thirds of the states mentioned increased state expenditures for the CMI in their fourth year reports. A few tabulated the figures: from 1978–1982, New York State spent $121.7 million for CSS-related programs (four times total federal CSP expenditures), Florida spent $29.3 million, and New Jersey, $26.4 million. Other states recorded smaller amounts, ranging from tens to hundreds of thousands of dollars.

States were only moderately successful in tapping new sources of federal funds. About half the states participated in the 1978 HUD Demonstration Program for Deinstitutionalization of the Chronically Mentally Ill. The program was unfortunately plagued with problems and seldom produced more than 50 additional housing units in any one state.[34] A few states also received Section 1115 Medicaid Waivers to pay for services to clients housed in these units.

After reviewing activities in this area, Katz concluded that states had been more successful "in obtaining or diverting additional mental health resources for the CSP target population than in increasing resources from other mainstream federal and state agencies"[7] (p 23).

Introducing Legislative and Regulatory Initiatives

Several state CSP units consulted with legislators, drafted or introduced legislation, and testified or lobbied on issues such as protection of client rights, discharge planning, continuity of care, and case management.[6] Almost half the states introduced housing or zoning legislation affecting the CMI.[8] A few, including Arizona and Florida, enacted mental health legislation based on CSS principles.

Other states succeeded in implementing CSS programs through administrative and budget modifications (e.g., New York and New Jersey). They developed standards for a range of residential and rehabilitative options, incorporated CSS components into departmental program regulations, and provided for the funding and delivery of aftercare services.[6]

Fostering Interagency Collaboration and Agreements

The CSP initiative emphasized interagency collaboration as a means of coordinating service delivery and offering the CMI support services from agencies traditionally outside the mental health system. Most state CSPs participated on state and local advisory committees and task forces. According to Stroul, the most successful of these groups had a clearly defined assignment and some degree of power.[6]

At least half the states reported negotiating interagency agreements to expand services to the CMI. These agreements occurred most frequently with state vocational rehabilitation, social service, and housing agencies.[6] The Short Term Evaluation termed these activities and agreements "numerous and generally productive."[8] (p IV–8)

Providing Technical Assistance and Training

State CSP offices organized "innumerable statewide and regional conferences, workshops, and seminars" to provide technical assistance and training, according to Stroul.[6] (p 55) These meetings focused on CSS components and philosophy, case management, accessing services, preparing grant applications, and client rights. Several states produced written or videotaped educational materials. States also received Mental Health Manpower Development Grants from NIMH to train case managers and other CSS staff. Successful local CSS demonstration sites were sometimes used to provide on-site instruction to staff from other regions.

Organizing Advocacy Groups for the CMI

About two-thirds of the states described efforts to generate public awareness of and support for the CMI in their fourth year reports, although only four states cited constituency/coalition building as a major part of their CSS strategy.[6] State CSPs helped arrange meetings or conferences which offered technical assistance and information to advocacy and family support groups. About one-quarter of the states published some form of newsletter to disseminate information about CSP. Other states produced television programs and commercials, issued press releases, and even sponsored plays about the CMI.

CSP AT THE LOCAL LEVEL

The development of local CSSs was a major focus of CSP in 1977. In each local CSS area a "core service agency" was to coordinate delivery of the 10 CSS components, and "case managers" were to assure client access to services. An examination of these three program elements—local CSS development, the core service agency, and case management—suggests that they have undergone considerable transformation since their introduction.

Developing Local CSSs

All first-round states were required to produce three-year statewide strategy plans for organizing local CSSs.[5] Twelve of these states received contracts to broaden the operation of an existing community mental health center (CMHC), social service agency, or psychosocial rehabilitation program into a local CSS. These demonstration CSSs were to function as examples for statewide expansion. By 1980 there were over 15 CSS sites operating in 12 states, servicing more than 4200 clients.[24] NIMH concluded that the success of these model sites confirmed the soundness of the CSS approach. Direct financial support for the sites was gradually withdrawn, and the development of local demonstration CSSs was made an optional grant activity.[3] A few of the states, including Florida and Texas, continued to pursue the CSS demonstration strategy; New York State, whose own efforts predated CSP, recorded the operation of over 100 CSS-type programs in 1983.

As Bachrach pointed out, however, model programs do not necessarily become "prototypes for diffusion."[36] The 1981 Short Term Evaluation thus found that: "Although the notion of a 'CSS' appears to guide some of the projects' efforts conceptually and states rely on the CSS rhetoric in describing their overall efforts, states generally did not find the term applicable to their unique circumstances"[8] (p IV–18). Some states made no effort to develop local CSSs. Others met with resistance from established agencies, the state mental health administration, or state and local governments. Katz found "little evidence that a significant number of CSSs have been established"[7] (p 25). This represents a major failure of the original CSP implementation strategy.

Core Service Agencies

Each local core service agency was "to assume the leadership for improving services for the client group"[1] (p 335). In states with CSS demonstration sites, these agencies generally delivered services directly to clients. In the remaining strategy development states, however, core service agencies emphasized area-wide planning, coordination, and program development. This confusion of roles led CSP to eliminate the core service agency concept from grant announcements after 1980.[3] Turner instead proposed to separate these tasks, assigning service delivery to "community support agencies" and area-wide planning to "area mental health authorities."[37]

Case Management

To gain insight into the background and activities of CSP case managers, 211 were asked to complete a two-page questionnaire as part of the 1980 Client Survey.[24] The questionnaire results indicated that the median age of case managers was 33 years, 62 percent were women, and 87 percent were white. Case managers were highly qualified; most had a college education (88 percent), nearly half had advanced degrees, and they had worked with the mentally disabled for an average of 7 years. Case managers with professional training tended to be more effective than paraprofessionals, according to Intagliata, but they also experienced "burn out" more quickly.[8]

Two-thirds of the CSP case managers worked as part of a team rather than as individuals. Intagliata reported that the team approach generally reduced "burn out" and client dependency, provided more continuous coverage and coordination, and involved more personnel in decision-making.[38] Lamb[39] and Deitchman[40] stressed how important it was for case managers to maintain a personal relationship with their CMI clients. Although this may have been more difficult in a team setting, case managers reported knowing 75 percent of their clients either moderately or very well, and had met with 52 percent of them during the 30-day survey period.[24] Caseloads averaged 34 clients, 28 of whom were enrolled in CSP.

Three fifths of the case managers listed job titles which implied a direct service orientation: therapist, psychologist, counselor, or social worker. Only 5 of the 211 interviewees gave "case manager" as their job title. Case managers devoted 32 percent of their work time to providing direct services, allocating the remainder of their time to assessment (10 percent), service coordination (9 percent), planning (8 percent), monitoring (8 percent), client advocacy (7 percent), follow-up (6 percent), service evaluation (6 percent), information/referral (6 percent), and other (8 percent).

There has been considerable debate over the role of case managers as direct service providers/therapists versus independent service coordinators. Lamb supported "therapists-case managers" because of their high level of client trust and understanding.[39] Intagliata, however, noted that therapy-oriented case managers emphasized direct services while neglecting management functions,[38] and Deitchman indicated that the poverty work associated with the CMI was not "popular with office-bound therapists."[40] (p 788)

For most states, this debate was resolved by budgetary constraints; few state mental health agencies could afford an independent case management system. Instead, states generally assigned case management activities, such as planning, linking, monitoring, and advocacy, to existing staff. Several states proceeded to make these services reimbursable. By 1980, CSP was emphasizing the need for "resource management services" rather than case managers per se.[3]

CSP AT THE CLIENT LEVEL

The 1980 Client Survey [24] did not directly consider whether CSP was achieving its ultimate goal—to enrich the quality of life of the CMI by improving service delivery. The survey did, however, provide valuable information about CSP clients, including client background, income, employment, housing, social activity, family relationships, clinical history, medical problems, community living skills, behavioral problems, and service utilization. The following discussion is limited because portions of these data are reported elsewhere.[4,24,41]

Client Demographics

The median age of clients was 41.8 years; 53 percent were female, and 89 percent were white. More than half had a high school education, and only 11 percent were currently married.

Income

The median annual income of clients was reported to total $3900. Only 19 percent of the clients actively earned a salary. With an income totalling half the national median and very little earning power, poverty was a serious problem for this population. As Deitchman argued: "Chronically disabled psychiatric clients don't need community support services because they are schizophrenic; they need them because they are poor"[40] (p 788).

Entitlements contributed significantly to client survival. Almost half (47.7 percent) of the clients received Supplemental Security Income (SSI), 34.9 percent received Social Security or Disability Insurance (SSDI), and 22.1 percent received other social service benefits. These funds have become even more critical as mental health agencies have turned to third party reimbursements to pay for direct services.[42]

Employment

Only 25.9 percent of the clients were employed, a finding consistent with previous surveys.[43,44] Of this group, 41.8 percent were employed in competitive jobs, and only 35 percent worked full-time. Most were placed in unskilled, semi-skilled, or clerical positions. Two-fifths of the clients were clearly unemployable, but one-third may have had some potential for employment. Many states encouraged a vocational role for clients, even if this role was quite limited.[27]

Housing

Two thirds of the clients lived in cities. Over half (55.2 percent) of the clients lived in situations with little or no supervision; 42.8 percent lived with other CSP room/housemates. A large proportion (40.4 percent) resided in private homes or apartments. Living arrangements for the remaining clients varied considerably: board and care homes (12.6 percent); cooperative apartments (11.5 percent); family or foster care (10.3 percent); supervised or transitional group homes (9.6 percent); hospitals or nursing facilities (8.7 percent); and boarding or rooming houses or hotels (7 percent). These overall percentages masked significant site differences, suggesting that clients were sometimes being placed in whatever housing was available and not necessarily in housing that was appropriate.

Social Activity

CSP clients appeared to engage in more social activity than was previously reported in other studies of the CMI.[43] The most common form of such activity was socializing with friends, and clients were most likely to socialize at home. Unfortunately, 16.9 percent of the clients never engaged in any scheduled daytime activity, and 23.5 percent did so only once a week or less. Again there were significant site differences. Lodges and psychosocial clubs which operated on the Fairweather or Fountain House models were able to offer clients scheduled activities 5–7 days a week.

Family Involvement

Contrary to the stereotype of the CMI as a population cut off from family contact, 80 percent of the CSP clients were reported to socialize with family members, and 67 percent had involved family members living within a one-hour drive. Moreover, 31.8 percent of the clients actually lived with parents, spouses, or other family members. This last figure was lower than previous estimates,[45] supporting the observation of Minkoff that the percentage of clients living at home was declining as deinstitutionalization progressed.[43] Nevertheless, families were "an important resource in providing services to the CMI"[27] (p 28), a finding that confirmed the value of offering families backup support and education as part of the CSS approach.

Outreach and Referral

Only 0.2 percent of the clients (9 out of 4200 cases) entered a CSS program through outreach efforts, although outreach was listed as the first of the 10 CSS components. Similarly, only one client in ten was referred through a nontraditional channel such as a school counselor, relative, roommate, or member of the clergy. Yet many Americans still turn to such sources for mental health advice; one study found that 39 percent of those seeking help first consulted with a member of the clergy.[46]

Clinical History

Almost all clients had been hospitalized for psychiatric care (92.3 percent). The most prevalent diagnoses were schizophrenia (69 percent) and depressive disorders (12 percent). Clients had been hospitalized for a median total of 3.1 times, beginning at the median age of 24.8 years. The median time spent in institutions for psychiatric care was 22.5 months; however, 27.5 percent of the clients had spent a total of 11 or more years in such institutions. About one third of the clients had been hospitalized in the previous year for a median of 5.9 weeks. Similarly, 29.2 percent of the clients received partial hospitalization or day care during the previous year for a median of 25.3 weeks. These latter findings support previous short-term readmission data[43,44] suggesting that a substantial proportion of clients may require admission to in-patient or outpatient facilities on a repeated basis.

Medical Problems

Almost half (44.7 percent) of the clients had at least one chronic medical problem severe enough to interfere with daily functioning. Many of these conditions were associated with diet, medication, or personal hygiene: obesity/undernourishment (27.4 percent); medication side effects (21.8 percent); impaired motor control (20.4 percent); circulatory and heart disorders (18.9 percent); hypertension (18.8 percent); and dental disorders (18.1 percent). An essential CSS component, medical care and supervision should be offered in a broad context and include "teaching the basic tenets of diet, nutrition, and self-care"[47] (p 7).

Most clients (84.4 percent) received psychotropic medication. There were no significant site differences, and iatrogenic disorders were common. Although CSP symbolized the movement of the mental health system from a medical to a social service model, it apparently did not offer alternatives to the widespread use of psychotropic drugs.

Community Living Skills

An assessment of the ability of CSP clients to perform various skills necessary for successful community tenure revealed that few clients required assistance in the elementary areas of personal hygiene, dressing, or moving about. But a significant number of clients either needed considerable assistance with or could or would not perform some of the more complex activities. For example, 30.8 percent could not secure the necessary support services, 27.6 percent could not manage funds, and 25.1 percent had difficulty verbalizing needs. Additional training or long-term support should be available to help clients accomplish some of these more complex tasks.

Behavioral Problems

Case managers were asked to report the degree to which clients had problems with 15 behaviors often associated with the CMI. Relatively few clients engaged in activities which were of serious concern to the community. Instead, clients tended to have the most problems with actions that were highly visible but comparatively benign: causing complaints from household, having trouble at work or school, engaging in bizarre behavior, and exhibiting temper tantrums. A small percentage of clients had moderate (2.6) or serious (1.5) problems with the law in a one-month period, and 3 percent had been crime victims; these are higher crime rates than would be found in the general population.

Service Utilization

Clients used an average of 4.4 of the 10 CSS service components over a one-month period. The most commonly provided components were case management, medical and mental health care, and psychosocial rehabilitation; every service was used by at least 5 percent of the clients. Case managers were involved in the delivery of 83 percent of these services.

Relationships Between Client Variables

A number of preliminary analyses were conducted[4,24] using intercorrelations and analyses of variance to explore the relationships among several client variables. Because of sampling and statistical limitations, the results should be viewed primarily as directions for future research.

These analyses revealed that older clients tended to be better adjusted socially, to have fewer behavioral problems, and to receive fewer services than younger clients; they had fewer basic living skills, however, and were less socially active. Higher-income clients were better adjusted socially, had more basic living skills, and received fewer services. Males were more disabled, more poorly adjusted socially, had more behavioral problems, and received more services. Educated clients had more basic living skills, fewer behavioral problems, engaged in more social activities, and received fewer services. Employed clients had more basic living skills, fewer behavioral problems, were better adjusted socially, and received more services. Clients with chronic medical problems had fewer basic living skills and were likely to be unemployed. Clients living in situations with moderate supervision generally did as well as or better than clients living in either highly supervised or unsupervised situations. Clients with recent or prolonged hospitalizations tended to be poorly adjusted, with fewer basic living skills and more behavioral problems. Clients with fewer basic living skills, more behavioral problems, and higher disability ratings used more services.

CONCLUSION

In the mid-1970s, the federal government acknowledged, somewhat belatedly, that community care for the deinstitutionalized CMI was inadequate; there was, however, little interest in committing significant categorical funds to address the problem. Instead, in 1977 NIMH suggested CSP: a model program "embracing a philosophical stance [and] a broad range of strategies . . . directed at raising consciousness of a problem and system change"[18] (p II–44). Seven years and over $42 million later, the influence of CSP is apparent. It brought visibility to the plight of the CMI and articulated their need for community support. By proposing that local CSSs offer housing, employment, and other rehabilitative and support options to the CMI, it furnished states and localities with a framework for planning and delivering services traditionally unavailable through the mental health care system. It unquestionably generated a substantial amount of activity on behalf of the target population, particularly at the state level.

Nevertheless, documenting the direct accomplishments of CSP has proven difficult, partly because of the systems-level intervention strategy adopted by NIMH and partly because CSP has not gathered comparable data on specific state and local accomplishments. It is clear that CSP did not achieve—and may never achieve—its ultimate goal of improving the quality of life of the CMI, for reasons related as much to federal and state fiscal and social policies as to CSP itself.

The federal government approached the problem of community care for the CMI with the assumption that a small-scale investment of seed money could be leveraged into a large-scale solution. Specifically, NIMH reasoned that additional resources for helping the CMI could be procured by collaborating with other federal agencies (housing, employment, etc.) and gaining access to mainstream federal programs (SSI, Medicaid, etc.). Neither assumption proved accurate. As a result, NIMH was unable to develop the programmatic or financial resources necessary at the federal level to support community services.

Although some states successfully modified mental health care policies to meet the needs of the noninstitutionalized CMI, it became "increasingly difficult to continue developing or expanding CSS services in an atmosphere of fiscal austerity"[6] (p 88). State institutions still commanded a major share of the mental health budgets, federal block grants were largely directed toward CMHCs, and federal mainstream programs such as SSDI and Medicaid suffered severe cutbacks. As many as half of the state CSP offices may close when their federal funding ends. Unless CSS concepts have become an integral part of state mental health care systems, they too may disappear.

Much of the state-level activity focused on interagency collaboration and coordination. Service integration has not worked in the past (Model Cities, OEO) and as Lamb warned: "This solution of 'fixing the bureaucracy' also holds out the hope that we can improve conditions for the severely mentally ill at very little added cost and thereby provides a rationalization for appropriating minimal funds"[47] (p 107).

Not long after CSP was launched, it became apparent that NIMH did not have sufficient resources to induce local service areas to develop CSSs. Although the operation of CSS demonstration projects provided valuable information about CSS clients and functions, these models have not been widely replicated. CSP implementation strategy remains unrealized at the local level.

CSP is no longer a pilot program. Many of the individual CSS components—as well as the concept of a system of mental health care—have become widely accepted as essential elements in community-based treatment of the CMI. Without such a system at the local level, the CMI will remain condemned to inappropriate institutionalization or to repeated journeys in and out of hospitals. Some will drop out of the system altogether. If the states can not or will not reassume responsibility for the CMI, and the federal government ceases its efforts to develop alternatives, then the momentum generated on behalf of this population during the last seven years will be lost.

ACKNOWLEDGMENT

The author would like to thank Ardith Bausenbach for her help in preparing this manuscript.

REFERENCES

1. Turner JC, TenHoor WJ: The NIMH Community Support Program: Pilot approach to a needed social reform. *Schizophr Bull* 1978;4:319-348
2. Goldman HH, Gattozzi AA, Taube CA: Defining and counting the chronically mentally ill. *Hosp Community Psychiatry* 1981;32:21-27
3. NIMH announcement—Community Support Systems Strategy Development and Implementation Grants. Rockville, MD, NIMH Community Support Program, Sept 1980
4. Tessler RC, Goldman HH (eds): *The Chronically Mentally Ill: Assessing Community Support Programs.* Cambridge, MA, Ballinger, 1982
5. NIMH Community Support Section Requests for Proposals No. NIMH-MH-77-0080-0081. Rockville, MD, NIMH, July 1977
6. Stroul BS: Community Support Program: Analysis of State Strategies. Boston, Center for Rehabilitation Research and Training in Mental Health, Boston University, Sept 1982
7. Katz J: Report on NIMH Community Support Program. Rockville, MD, ADAMHA, Division of Treatment, OPPC, Dec 1981
8. Ben-Dashan T, Morrison L, Kotler M: Community Support Program performance measurement, system development, and short-term evaluation, Final Report. Silver Spring, MD, Macro Systems, May 1981
9. Schulberg HC: Community Support Programs: Program evaluation and public policy. *Am J Psychiatry* 1979;136:1433-1437
10. Schulberg HC, Bromet E: Strategies for evaluating the outcome of community services for the chronically mentally ill. *Am J Psychiatry* 1981;138:930-935
11. Ashbaugh JW, Hoff M, Bradley V, et al: Assessing the needs of the community support system target population: Selected methods for national and state application. NIMH Contract No. 278-79-0036 (OP). Washington DC, Human Services Research Institute, 1980
12. Ashbaugh JW: Assessing the need for community supports, in Tessler RC, Goldman HH (eds): *The Chronically Mentally Ill: Assessing Community Support Programs.* Cambridge, MA, Ballinger, 1982, p 141-158
13. Sorenson JE, Kucic AR: Assessing the cost outcomes and cost effectiveness of community support programs: A feasibility study. Denver, CO, University of Denver, School of Accounting, July 1981
14. Bachrach LL: Assessment of outcomes in community support systems: Results, problems and limitations. *Schizophr Bull* 1982;8:39-61
15. National Plan for the Chronically Mentally Ill, Final Draft Report to the Secretary of Health and Human Services. Washington, DC, DHHS, 1980
16. Szymanski HV, Schulberg HC, Salter V, et al: Evaluating the local prevalence of persons needing community support programs. *Hosp Community Psychiatry* 1982;33:370-373
17. Ashbaugh JW: Estimating the size of the non-institutionalized adult chronically mentally ill population in state and sub-state areas: Some preliminary estimates and estimation methods. NIMH Contract No. 278-0036 (OP). Washington, DC, Human Services Research Institute, 1983
18. Stroul BS, Morrison L, Kotler M, et al: Final report of the exploratory evaluation of the NIMH Community Support System. Silver Spring, MD, Macro Systems, June 1980
19. NIMH 1982 CSP research initiative: Description of research and evaluation projects. Rockville, MD, NIMH Community Support Program, Jan 1983
20. Kiesler, CA: Mental hospitals and alternative care: Noninstitutionalization as potential public policy for mental patients. *Am Psychol* 1982;37:349-360
21. Sharfstein SS, Clark HW: Economics and the chronic mental patient. *Schizophr Bull* 1978;4:399-414

22. Bisongno J, Braren M, Ingalls R, et al: The public cost of treating the chronically mentally ill in the community. *Community Support Services Journal* 1980;4:3-6

23. Rubin J: Cost measurement and cost data in mental health settings. *Hosp Community Psychiatry* 1982;33:750-754

24. Bernstein AG, Love RE, Davis GE: Collaborative data collection and analysis for Community Support Program demonstration projects. NIMH Contract No. 79-0031 (OP). Washington, DC, Market Facts, 1981

25. Quality of life: Evaluating the Community Support Program. Albany, NY, New York State Office of Mental Health, Bureau of Community Support Systems, June 1980

26. Lannon PB: Evaluation of the New York NIMH Community Support Program: A position paper and status report. Albany, NY, New York Community Support Program, Bureau of Demonstration Projects, Mar 1981

27. Spaniol L: Evaluating local CSS programs serving the chronically mentally ill: Findings, issues and conclusions. Boston, Center for Rehabilitation Research and Training in Mental Health, Boston University, June 1981

28. NIMH announcement—State Service System Research on the Chronically Mentally Ill. Rockville, MD, Jan 1983

29. A Network For Caring: Summary proceedings of four learning community conferences and one conference on manpower and development training. Rockville, MD, DHHS Publication No. (ADM) 81-1063, 1982

30. A Network for Caring: Proceedings of the fifth national conference, 1981. Boston, Center for Rehabilitation Research and Training in Mental Health, Boston University, 1983

31. *Community Support Service Journal*, CSP Grant No. 278-78-007. Wingdale, NY, Harlem Valley Psychiatric Center, 1979-1983

32. Chapados JT, Pack M, Marsh L, et al: Annotated bibliography for community support services and programs. Boston, Center for Rehabilitation Research and Training in Mental Health, Boston University, 1983

33. Community Support Program technical assistance resource directory. Boston, Center for Rehabilitation Research and Training in Mental Health, Boston University, 1983

34. Ben-Dashan T, Morrison L, Kotler M, et al: Exploratory Evaluation of the HUD/HHS Demonstration for Deinstitutionalization of the Chronically Mentally Ill, Final Report. Silver Spring, MD, Macro Systems, Mar 1982

35. Sallis J, Henggeler SW: Needs assessment: A critical review. *Administration in Mental Health* 1980;7:200-209

36. Bachrach LL: The role of model programs in the care of chronic mental patients, in Talbott JA (ed): *The Chronically Mentally Ill: Treatment, Programs, Systems.* New York, Human Sciences Press, 1981, pp 300-314

37. Kennedy C, Turner JC: Core service agency concept: Implications for future planning and legislation. Rockville, MD, NIMH Community Support Services Branch, 1980

38. Intagliata J: Improving the quality of community care for the chronically mentally disabled: The role of case management. *Schizophr Bull* 1982;8:655-674

39. Lamb HR: Therapist-case managers: More than brokers of services. *Hosp Community Psychiatry* 1980;31:762-764

40. Deitchman WS: How many case managers does it take to screw in a light bulb? *Hosp Community Psychiatry* 1980;31:788-789

41. Tessler RC, Bernstein AG, Rosen BM, et al: The chronically mentally ill in community support systems. *Hosp Community Psychiatry* 1982;33:208-211

42. Woy JR, Wasserman DB, Weiner-Pomerantz MS: Community mental health centers: Movement away from the model? *Community Ment Health J* 1981;17:265-276

43. Minkoff K: A map of chronic mental patients, in Talbott JA (ed): *The Chronic Mental Patient.* Washington, DC, American Psychiatric Association, 1978, pp 11-37

44. Engelhardt DM, Rosen B, Feldman J, et al: A 15-year followup of 646 schizophrenic outpatients. *Schizophr Bull* 1982;8:493–503
45. Goldman HH: Mental illness and family burden: A public health perspective. *Hosp Community Psychiatry* 1982;33:557–559
46. Mollica RF: From asylum to community: The threatened disintegration of public psychiatry. *N Engl J Med* 1983;308:367–373
47. Turner JC, Shifren I: Community support systems: How comprehensive?: *New Directions for Mental Health Systems* 1979;2:1–13
48. Lamb HR: What did we really expect from deinstitutionalization? *Hosp Community Psychiatry* 1981;32:105–109

H. Richard Lamb

15

Alternatives to Hospitals

Where are the chronically mentally ill who are not in hospitals? In the past five years we have learned more about where they are and about the circumstances that caused them to be there and the conditions in which they live. This chapter will first discuss some of the community living arrangements that serve as alternatives to long-term hospitalization and then look at what has unfortunately become an alternative to acute hospitalization for many seriously mentally ill in crisis, namely the county jail. Those who are homeless and living on the streets are discussed in Chapter 4, by Ellen Baxter, though some of their problems will be touched on in the section on the mentally ill in jail.

The long-term patient's survival, not to mention his rehabilitation, begins with an appropriately supportive and structured living arrangement. Other treatment and rehabilitation are of little avail until the patient feels secure and is stabilized in his living situation. Deinstitutionalization means granting asylum in the community to a large marginal population, many of whom can cope to only a limited extent with the ordinary demands of life and who have strong dependency needs. Most of the long-term mentally ill need both financial and emotional support, that is, persons or agencies upon which they can be dependent in order to survive in the community.

Probably about half of the chronic population in California lives with relatives[1]; the proportion is probably higher still in states that have experienced less in-migration and where more long-term patients have families in the state. Relatives, with varying degrees of difficulty, thus provide much of the needed support. Although some of the remaining long-term patients are able to live inde-

THE CHRONIC MENTAL PATIENT
ISBN 0-8089-1649-1

Copyright © 1984 by Grune & Stratton.
All rights of reproduction in any form reserved.

pendently, supportive settings appear necessary for a sizable proportion. There is a wide range of out-of-home living arrangements run as governmental, private nonprofit, or proprietary facilities. Some are transitional in their aims, others are designed to be long-term. It is beyond the scope of this chapter to describe all these possibilities. One purpose of this chapter, however, is to discuss in some depth four kinds of long-term living arrangements in widespread use—board-and-care homes, locked skilled nursing facilities with special programs for psychiatric patients, foster care, and satellite housing.

BOARD-AND-CARE HOMES

A recent study in a medium-sized California county showed that approximately one-third of the long-term psychiatric patients in the community younger than sixty-five years of age who were diagnosed as psychotic live in board-and-care (boarding) homes.[1]

To what extent are the lives of these patients limited both by their illnesses and by their environment? What is the proper role of board-and-care homes and what should be done to help them maximize the quality of life for their residents and provide a therapeutic milieu?

Board-and-care homes are not the result of careful planning and well-conceived social policy. On the contrary, they sprang up to fill the vacuum created by the rapid and usually haphazard depopulation of our state hospitals. Suddenly, many thousands of former state hospital patients needed a place to live, and private entrepreneurs, both large and small, rushed in to provide it.

"Board-and-care home" is a term used in California to describe a variety of facilities, many of which house large numbers of psychiatric patients. The number of residents ranges from one to over a hundred, though according to the state licensing agency the majority of patients in Los Angeles are housed in facilities of fifty beds or larger. Board-and-care homes are unlocked and provide a shared room, three meals a day, supervision of medications, and minimal staff supervision.

In my study of a large (110 bed) board-and-care homes in Los Angeles,[2] nine of ten residents had either never tried living alone or had experienced failure the last time they tried. In talking at length with the individuals in this study, there were consistent recountings of an inability to cope with social and vocational demands, an inability to withstand life's pressures, and a paucity of interpersonal relationships. Approximately one tenth of the persons in this study were particularly aware and insightful; they recognized that they became anxious and overwhelmed in social or vocational situations. With varying degrees of reluctance, they had made a conscious decision to limit their exposure to pressure and, in some cases, to avoid pressure of any kind.

The persons in this environment have, therefore, come to what one might call "adaptation by decompression." They have found a place of asylum from life's pressures, but at the same time a place where there is support, structure, and some treatment, especially in the form of psychoactive medications. For a large proportion of long-term psychiatric patients, the board-and-care home has not only replaced but has taken over the functions of the state hospital.

Board-and-care homes provide structure in a variety of ways. Medication management and supervision is one way; psychiatrists come to the facility and prescribe psychoactive drugs for the majority of the residents, and the staff members dispense these medications at regular times. The better members of the staff are reasonably aware of residents who are becoming symptomatic, or more floridly so, and convey this information to the visiting psychiatrists, who may then adjust medications accordingly. Moreover, the staff often sees problems that are causing residents to become symptomatic and may intervene by manipulating the residents' environments to ease the pressure. In many board-and-care homes, the staff supervises the residents' money and disburses it according to their estimate of the residents' abilities to handle it. The residents are frequently overprotected by this additional structure, but there is flexibility and the staff generally tries to give the residents as much responsibility as they can handle. Serving meals at fixed times not only adds structure but ensures that residents will eat properly and regularly. Many residents report that their eating habits were erratic when they lived alone—often to the point of undermining their physical health and certainly their sense of well-being. Although having all their meals prepared may be more than some residents require, most of them have a feeling of being taken care of and of being relieved of a major responsibility.

Despite the protection and structure, board-and-care home residents may have a great deal of freedom. In the facility where my 1979 study was done, for instance, everyone was free to come and go at any hour. Although 5 percent of the residents never leave the building, the other 95 percent use community resources to varying degrees, mostly by visiting local supermarkets and eating places, and by taking walks in the neighborhood. Many, of course, probably could and should do more; these patients might well be better stabilized and involved in vocational and other community programs if treatment and rehabilitation were made available within the facility by persons skilled in working with residents with limited ego strength. But for those who cannot benefit from rehabilitation, an inactive, even reclusive, life-style in a pressureless setting may be the highest level at which they can function for any sustained period of time without decompensation.[3]

It may be correct but misleading to refer to these persons as "regressed" or "institutionalized"; one may be seeing not just the results of their living environment but also the results of their inherent limitations and lack of capabilities.

Although the extensive use of board-and-care homes presents problems, they do serve a need—by housing tens of thousands of patients and providing a return to their operators, both in terms of income and also a sense of purpose and of usefulness. Operators who have no special skills but do possess a home and a desire to feel needed and busy are, in fact, a vast, underutilized resource in our society.

Improving Board and Care Homes

It is especially important to take action to improve and maintain the quality of facilities such as board-and-care homes—including adequate financing of them *and* supervision of the physical environment, food, quantity and quality of staff, and whether there are appropriate treatment and activity programs, both in-house and outside these facilities. Screening out unsuitable board-and-care home administrators so that only the competent and ethical are allowed into this field is a critical factor, as is the subsequent training of these persons. Also essential are strong, well-staffed licensing agencies that are both effective and sensitive to the consequences of their actions. Persons working for a licensing agency need to be comfortable in using their authority when required. First, however, licensing personnel should try to form an alliance with the operators of these facilities so that they work together to improve the patients' living environment and treatment; they should avoid getting into an adversary position with operators unless the operators give them no other choice. If the latter happens, at least some of those operators should be forced out of the field, since if compelled to make changes they do not want to make, some operators may become resentful and take our their resentment on patients in subtle ways.

The issue of funding is critical. Many community living arrangements, including board-and-care homes, are financed by the patients' Supplemental Security Income (SSI) grants, very small amounts when compared with Medicaid per diem rates for skilled nursing facilities, costs of hospitalization, and rates for most community rehabilitation facilities. Even the most conscientious board and care home operator cannot provide the kinds of services that are needed at these rates. Increased stabilization in the community and increased involvement in vocational and other community programs can be obtained by providing more services within the facility. This requires greatly enriching facility staffing by increasing the numbers, expertise and training of staff, or by having local mental health staff in sufficient numbers who come to the facility and provide a variety of services. The need for increased funding for community living arrangements, public or private, is obvious.

I have seen two kinds of arrangements where quality of treatment has been greatly improved in board and care homes. In the first, local community services have sent professionals and paraprofessionals out to work with each patient in board-and-care homes, and to consult with the administrators and staff. Such programs (if carried out properly with adequate staff and sufficient community programs to which to refer patients) are not cheap, but they can transform a simple residential setting into a therapeutic one.

In the second kind of arrangement, a mental health professional has taken over the facility and hired trained or trainable staff in numbers sufficient to work with each patient living there, individually, in groups, and in activity programs. This supplants the minimal staff supervision normally found in board and care homes. The result is often increased stabilization of patients who had previously had a stormy course in the community, and an increased number of patients in vocational and other community programs. But in the instances I have observed, the cost of such facilities has increased by approximately 100 percent even from the previous California SSI rate (in California the state supplement already doubles the federal SSI rate), and these facilities are now available only to private pay patients who can afford this greatly increased rate.

There is no optimum size of community facilities for long-term patients. Some patients do best in a small, family-like setting where there is considerable interaction with other residents and the operator of the facility. Others seem to do poorly with too much closeness and too much contact with nurturing persons and do better in a large facility where they can "get lost" when they need to and avoid interpersonal contact at times when they cannot deal with it.

Access to Treatment and Rehabilitation

There is evidence that a high proportion of long-term severely ill patients—almost half in my study[2]—will not utilize a psychosocial rehabilitation program even when it is across the street from their board and care home. The attendance dropped by half when a ride in the board and care home van was required. When a public bus ride was involved, only 3 percent would attend the program. It is possible that many of the non-users would have participated in a similar program had it been located in the facility. These findings have major implications for mental health planning. Simply enlarging existing clinics and rehabilitation facilities will not reach a large proportion of the board-and-care home population even though it would be a more normalizing experience for them to venture forth and attend a program outside the facility. It may well be that long-term patients who function well in community mental health centers and vocational rehabilitation centers are in the minority of the total chronic population, especially when we include all those tucked away in board-and-care home, living alone, or living with their families.

Goals, Empty Lives, and Contentment

Chronically disabled patients in board-and-care homes have feelings just like anyone else about not having goals, about not being able to reach their goals if they have them, about involutional concerns, about getting old. This holds true not only for those in the involutional group but also for those who are turning thirty and assessing their lives thus far. Many feel that life has no meaning and are distressed by feelings of inadequacy. This may seem self-evident, and yet there is a tendency to forget that long-term patients are affected by the stresses and concerns of each phase of the life cycle. They too have existential concerns just as do we all.

Many are acutely aware of their situations; their lives seem bleak and empty, and they are beset by depression, anxiety, or both. A repeated theme among the residents in my board-and-care home study,[2] was "I'm just living day by day, waiting for the end." One man referred to being here as "being at the bottom of the dumps." Perhaps some would benefit from better medication management. And surely this group should be the object of a concentrated effort at outreach from community agencies to provide individual and group psychotherapy and social and vocational rehabilitation. But there are those in board-and-care homes, just as there are those in society generally, for whom we do not have the answers with regard to making their lives happy, anxiety-free, and meaningful. Some retreat into fantasy or grandiose delusions to escape from or deny the reality of their lives. This may happen despite medication, or because the patient refuses to take it in order to facilitate his escape from reality.[4] Others are too disorganized to be fully aware of reality.

In my study,[2] more than two fifths of the patients were considered content or reasonably content. Some of these persons probably were not living up to their full potential for social and vocational functioning, and some observers would see their lives as without meaning. For a number of residents, however, the board-and-care home had become an asylum after a lifetime of chaos, instability, and hardship. Their lives had in past years been characterized by many psychotic episodes and hospitalizations, each episode further disrupting their sense of psychological integrity and their interpersonal and family relationship. Many appeared to have become stabilized at the board-and-care home; their predominant feeling was a sense of relief.

Those who have experienced life in board-and-care homes have stressed the importance of helping these long-term patients keep their respect and dignity.[5,6] Many residents appear reluctant to criticize the board-and-care home or the staff. But some speak freely about both the positive and negative aspects of the various board-and-care homes where they have lived. It becomes clear that residents are quite sensitive to the way they are treated, both well and poorly. To quote one alert and verbal patient who had recently come from a board-and-care home now closed by the state licensing agency. "If you are housed in a dilapidated, poorly maintained building, fed poor-quality food, and treated impersonally by the staff, you cannot help but feel that you aren't worth much, for otherwise you would not be treated that way." It does immeasurable damage to the residents' self-esteem to be served their meals an hour late by kitchen staff, to find no one on the staff who seems to appreciate the importance of the "little things" of everyday living, and to be rebuffed when they make what to them is an important request. For some of the chronically mentally disabled, the board-and-care home or similar facility may be a lifetime residence. Our society has an obligation to provide them services, improve the quality of their lives, and help them gain a sense of self-respect.

WHEN MORE STRUCTURE IS NEEDED:
THE LOCKED SKILLED-NURSING FACILITY

That some patients might need to reside in a long-term, locked, intensively supervised facility in the community was a foreign thought to many who advocated return to the community in the early years of emptying the state hospitals. "Those patients who need such a secure environment can remain in the state hospital" was the rationale. But the general feeling in those earlier years seemed to be that such patients were few and that community treatment and modern drugs would take care of most problems. More people are now recognizing that a significant number of severely disabled patients present major problems in management and can survive outside state hospitals only if they have a sufficiently structured facility in the community.[7] It should be emphasized that structure is more than just a locked door; other vital components are high staff–patient ratios and enough high-quality activities to structure most of the patient's day.

There are a number of long-term severely disabled psychiatric patients who lack sufficient impulse control to handle living in an open setting such as a board-and-care home or with relatives. They need a high degree of external structure and control to compensate for the inadequacy of their internal controls. The total number of such patients may not be great when compared to the total population of severely disabled patients. If placed in the community in living arrangements without sufficient structure, however, this group can easily be disruptive to the community and take up a large portion of the time of mental health professionals, not to mention other agencies such as the police. More important, they may be impulsively self-destructive or may present a physical danger to others.

The problems of these patients are not unlike those found in the residual group of patients left behind in state hospitals after deinstitutionalization.[8] These patients are characterized by assaultive behavior, severe overt major psychopathology, lack of internal controls, reluctance to take psychotropic medications, inability to adjust to open settings, problems with drugs and alcohol, and in some cases self-destructive behavior. Some are frightening to others because of their appearance and/or their actions.

Such patients need not be kept in state hospitals, however. An alternative employed in California is the locked skilled-nursing facility with special programs for the mentally ill, which gives patients in need of structure a chance for treatment and rehabilitation in a setting in their home community.[7] An intensive program that schedules most of the patient's day is a key element in providing structure. The size of the facility, usually about 100 beds or smaller, makes it possible for every staff member to know every patient and thus contribute to making the treatment milieu more personal. This is in contrast to putting patients in an isolated, large state hospital, where the treatment may be inadequate or impersonal and foster a life of institutional regression. And it resolves the problem of repeated placements in open settings, such as board and care homes followed by repeated decompensations and hospitalizations.

We need to learn from the history of state hospitals in the United States to keep the size of these facilities small—no more than a hundred beds. The state hospitals began as small, well-run therapeutic facilities and were gradually expanded to the huge institutions we know today. We must therefore resist adding on a wing here and a wing there and keep these facilities small, by statute if need be. Staffing patterns must likewise be maintained at levels conducive to individualized therapy, and sufficient treatment and rehabilitation programs must be mandated.

The treatment milieu emphasizes not only structure but also goals; each patient is encouraged to make effective use of the program even though reaching such goals may take several years. Periodic staff reviews look closely at this issue of goals, and patients who refuse to involve themselves in the program are considered for transfer to a less treatment-oriented facility. One of the primary goals of the program is not only to involve patients in active treatment but to prepare them for living in a less structured setting as well. There is thus an attempt to limit the length of stay to the least time necessary to achieve this goal of needing less structure. The emphasis on reducing the length of stay at the locked skilled-nursing facility can be a factor motivating the patient to make progress and not simply become "institutionalized" in this setting.

Many workers in community mental health deny their patients' need for structure; too often they fail to note the degree of structure required when assessing patients' needs in community placement. And since this degree of structure is not provided in the community, these persons are condemned to repeated decompensations and rehospitalizations (the revolving door syndrome), or long periods in state hospitals. At the same time, many professionals working in both state and local hospitals take the hospital structure and the patient's resulting sense of security for granted. Thus they too fail to take into account in their community planning the fact that most community settings do not have this degree of structure. Failing to recognize the patients who need structure, they send them out to insufficiently structured placements and thus contribute to patients' repeated decompensation and rehospitalization.

FOSTER CARE

A foster home is defined as care in a small family setting. According to Linn,[9] "small" means five or fewer patients in a family home. The prototype of foster care is that of Geel, a town in Belgium where mental patients have been cared for in the homes of its townspeople for over seven hundred years. In Geel, homes are still limited to one or two patients and patients are seen as an integral part of society and especially of the family. Patients have a bedroom of their own, which facilitates privacy. They share their meals and leisure activities with the family, and participate (though less today than in the past) in the family's domestic and income-producing work, thereby supplementing the modest payments for their care made by the state.[10] Cuvelier[11] describes foster care in Geel as a process in which the patient arrives rootless and homeless and then has the experience of living with a family in a normal home. The patient participates in daily home activities, is expected to behave well, and gradually becomes a family member in the sense of forming affective bonds as he or she learns to adapt to the day-to-day demands of the family: the patient thus assumes a family role. In the United States the greatest use of this arrangement has been made by the Veterans Administration, which has about 11,000 psychiatric patients in foster care.[9]

Linn, Klett, and Caffey[12] describe three characteristics of foster homes associated with improvement in social functioning: more children in the home, fewer fellow patients in the home, and size of the home in terms of fewer total occupants. With specific regard to schizophrenics, more activity in the home (higher degree of sponsor-initiated leisure activities) and more intense supervision were associated with deterioration in social adjustment. This finding is consistent with observations of Wing[13] that schizophrenics become symptomatic when they are unable to withdraw from too much social stimulation. It is also consistent with my own observations that many schizophrenics do poorly in small homes where there is much nurturing and closeness and gravitate toward larger facilities where they can withdraw when they need to and limit their interaction and involvement with other people.

Foster care operators tend to be understandably particular about whom they will take into their homes and live with. It is one thing to deal with a hostile paranoid patient or one with distasteful personal habits on an eight-hour shift; it is quite another to live with that person twenty-four hours a day. Thus, despite the appeal of "family living," foster care is not the living arrangement of choice for many long-term patients. Nevertheless, the experience of the Veterans Administration, the lessons of Geel, and my own observations in many small homes indicate that foster care can be an important resource for a large population of long-term psychiatric patients and is greatly under-utilized in the United States.

SATELLITE HOUSING

No therapeutic housing program comes closer to helping long-term patients live normal lives in the community than satellite housing. Satellite housing offers patients, with the aid of the satellite housing staff, a lifestyle they could not otherwise attain or maintain because of their illness—a lifestyle with freedom,

considerable independence, integration into the community, and a sense of dignity. Satellite housing may be in apartments, duplexes, or small, single-family
dwellings. The housing is leased by the residents or the mother agency or co-
leased by both. Here patients live in small groups of 2 to 5 without live-in staff
but with professional supervision. Satellite housing is especially suited for
patients who cannot quite survive in an independent living arrangement but do
not require the support and structure of a board-and-care home or foster home.
Satellite housing is an extremely attractive concept, but it should be emphasized
that it is not for everyone. Whether a patient is ready to handle this degree of
independence must be carefully assessed in each case if we are not to set patients
up for painful failures. The demands on the severely disabled posed by even
semi-independent living should not be underestimated.

In satellite housing, shopping, cooking, and housework are shared, and
residents have the responsibility of paying the rent (either directly to the landlord
or to the agency). Staff members assigned to satellite housing programs are
available as needed for guidance and counseling, both for individuals and
groups, and are also on call around the clock for emergencies. In a typical
satellite housing program, residents of three or four apartments form a stable
group for regular meetings, sometimes with staff and sometimes without. These
group meetings are hosted by the residents within their own housing units on a
rotating basis.

Sometimes a "satellite apartment program" is simply an apartment house in
which most of the apartments are occupied by patients. In my opinion this is not
really satellite housing; satellite housing programs should not involve more than
one or two apartments in any one building and the apartments should be scattered
about the community if we are to achieve our goal of integrating patients into the
community.

Acquisition by a satellite housing program of a large number of community
apartments increases the possibility that roommates can be matched in terms of
age, personality, interests, and level of functioning. Apartments of four persons
generally work out better than those housing only two. With four persons in a
unit, there is more peer support when one of the patients is not doing well or is in
crisis. The larger group also means that patients can withdraw when they need to
limit their interpersonal contacts, a situation that could easily leave a single
roommate feeling alone, unsupported, and rejected.

Satellite housing programs often have a high-expectation philosophy—that
is, residents are expected to have a meaningful daytime activity outside of the
house in addition to helping with the chores at home. This requirement should be
flexible. Many residents comfortably spend their days in short-term day treatment centers, vocational rehabilitation programs, or competitive employment.
But some patients, otherwise entirely suited for satellite housing, will only be
able to deal with a low-key social activity center a few hours a week. Still others
may find the requirement for an outside activity of any kind more than they can
handle, at least at first. One should avoid hasty decisions to shift these patients to

facilities such as board-and-care homes. A satellite unit can be organized on a family model; some residents may have an outside daytime activity while others remain at home, perhaps taking responsibility for cooking the meals and cleaning the house. Simply living in the unstructured setting of a satellite apartment, with only a few responsibilities, is the limit of many patients' capabilities. Asking only this much of such patients is for them high expectations.

Ideally, staff intervention will also be flexible. The fragile, fearful resident with a limited anxiety tolerance needs more staff support than other residents. A period of close contact between staff and resident, apartment mates, and therapist may often head off a crisis that might otherwise have led to rehospitalization. The resident will occasionally have to be removed from the apartment and placed for a brief period in a halfway house, community crisis house, or local hospital.

Who has primary responsibility for the patient in satellite housing? This question is an important one. There is merit in the satellite housing requirement that each patient have a primary therapist who deals with the main issues in the patient's life as well as crises. Otherwise the satellite housing staff can easily find itself in the role of primary therapist for most of the patients and responsible for all aspects of their lives. This responsibility reduces the time and energy the staff can devote to their primary task: the housing program.

There should be a willingness to decrease services as well as to increase them. Some satellite residents can stabilize at a level where staff intervention or supervision is needed only occasionally. At this point, the residents have made a normal adjustment to the community and the goal of integration into the community has been attained.

THE MENTALLY ILL IN COUNTY JAIL

Deinstitutionalization has led to large numbers of mentally ill persons in the community. At the same time, there are a limited amount of community psychiatric resources, including hospital beds. Society has a limited tolerance of mentally disordered behavior and the result is pressure to institutionalize persons needing 24-hour care wherever there is room, even if it means jailing the chronic mental patient.

Indeed, several studies describe a "criminalization" of mentally disordered behavior,[14,15] that is, a shunting of mentally ill persons in need of treatment into the criminal justice system instead of the mental health system. Rather than hospitalization and psychiatric treatment, the mentally ill are said to be subject to inappropriate arrest and incarceration. Legal restrictions placed on hospitalizing persons involuntarily are also said to result in a diversion of some patients to the criminal justice system.

A study of 203 inmates (102 men, 101 women) in a large urban county jail[16,17] revealed that these inmates had been referred for psychiatric evaluation by the jail staff who considered them to have psychiatric problems severe enough to warrant special housing. Eighty-eight percent had a history of psychiatric hospitalization. Ninety-three percent had a prior arrest record, 63 percent with at least one prior felony arrest. Sixty-nine percent exhibited severe, overt major psychopathology. Sixty-seven percent were diagnosed as having schizophrenia and 28 percent as having major affective disorders. Psychiatric hospitalization was recommended for 65 percent, that is, they were judged to meet the criteria for involuntary hospitalization (i.e., dangerous to self or others or gravely disabled). Thirty-nine percent had been living, at the time of arrest, on the streets, on the beach, in missions, or in cheap hotels. Only 12 percent of the men and 7 percent of the women had been supporting themselves through employment at the time of arrest (not including the ten women who supported themselves through prostitution). It is thus clear that this population of male and female inmates has had extensive experience with both the criminal justice and mental health systems, is characterized by severe acute and chronic mental illness, and generally functions at a low level.

Almost half of those men and women charged with misdemeanors had been living on the streets, on the beach, in missions, or in cheap hotels, compared with a fourth of those charged with felonies (p < .01). One can speculate on some possible explanations for this finding. Persons living in such places obviously have a minimum of community supports. It is possible that the less serious misdemeanor offense is frequently a way of asking for help. Still another factor may be that many of this group of uncared-for mentally ill persons are being arrested for minor criminal acts that are really manifestations of their illness, their lack of treatment, and the lack of structure in their lives. These were certainly the clinical impressions of the investigators as they talked to these inmates and their families and read the police reports. It should be added, however, that it appeared that there were some inmates, even though overtly psychotic, whose underlying antisocial character problems appeared to play a major role as causative factors for their alleged criminal behavior.

It was striking that a large proportion (78 percent of the men, 70 percent of the women) of the sample had histories of serious physical violence, ranging from assault to murder. The relationship between history of serious physical violence against persons and severe overt psychopathology (p < .01) suggests that at least some of this violence may represent a psychotic loss of control in these persons. Again, this is consistent with the investigators' clinical impressions.

There is a significant difference in the percentage of those ages 18 to 35 with a history of residence in a board-and-care home and those older than 35 (p < .02). Obviously, the older one is the more opportunity one has had to live in different situations, including board-and-care homes. In talking with these men and women about such facilities, other factors emerged: the tendency of the younger mentally ill person to hold out for autonomy rather than living in a protected supervised setting, and to resist entering the mental health system and being labeled as a psychiatric patient, even to the extent of living in a board-and-care home. A large number of these younger persons had had board-and-care homes recommended to them repeatedly as part of their hospital discharge plans, but had consistently refused to go to them. It appeared that many of these persons eventually gave up the struggle, at least temporarily, and accepted a board-and-care home placement. It should be noted, however, that most of these persons had left their board-and-care homes after relatively brief periods. In some cases this living situation did not appear to be sufficiently structured for them. In other cases, what came across as these men and women spoke was their desire to regain their autonomy, their isolated lifestyle, and their freedom to engage in antisocial activities. Despite the fact that a high proportion of this population had serious psychiatric problems, only eight men and five women were living in board-and-care homes at the time of arrest.

With regard to criminal charges on the current arrest, 39 percent of the men were charged with crimes of violence. Of these, 58 percent were charged with assault and battery or assault with a deadly weapon, which is consistent with the finding of Whitmer[18] who noted that many young male paranoid schizophrenics are arrested for assault.

A large proportion (70 percent) of the female sample had histories of serious physical violence ranging from assault to murder. Moreover, 23 percent were charged with violent crimes on this arrest. Violence is probably a factor resulting in many of these women being in jail rather than hospitals. Fifty-seven percent of persons hospitalized for mental illness in Los Angeles County (county and state hospitals) are men and 43 percent are women. There are, however, far fewer psychotic mentally ill women incarcerated in county jail than psychotic mentally ill men (the estimate from this study is about one woman to every four men). One can only speculate on the reasons for this. Women generally have a far lower arrest rate. Perhaps too, society is more reluctant to send the mentally ill female to jail than to hospitals. It may also be that violence or a reputation for violence counter-balances this reluctance.

Involving Families

The family was reached in 47 percent of the cases. In almost every case the family was not only cooperative, but seemed extremely appreciative that someone would take an interest in their relative and in them when the patient was in jail. These families needed to talk about the problems they had experienced with their mentally ill relatives and were desirous of information about the options available for treatment and management. Working with the family is a crucial part of psychiatric intervention with the mentally ill in jail.

Jail versus Hospital

Determining why an inmate had been arrested rather than taken to a hospital was not a simple matter. In many cases, of course, it was clear why the person had been arrested. For instance, almost all persons who are thought to have committed a felony are arrested and brought to jail regardless of their mental condition. This group comprised 44 percent of the population studied. The criminal justice system, charged by society with the responsibility of removing persons charged with serious crimes from the community, sees no alternative but first to place the person charged with a felony in custody in a secure setting and then arrange for psychiatric treatment, if necessary. If the person is thought to have committed a serious crime, the criminal justice system generally does not want to leave this person in the hands of a psychiatric hospital where security may be lax, where the offense may be seen as less important than the patient's illness, and where the person may be released by the hospital back to the community after a relatively short period of time. Persons with outstanding bench warrants, usually for failure to appear in court for traffic infractions, are also routinely brought to jail regardless of other circumstances. This group constituted 7 percent of the sample.

It is with persons charged with misdemeanors (51 percent of the sample) that the question becomes more complex. A person who appears mentally ill to a mental health professional may not be obviously mentally ill to a policeman, who, despite his practical experience, is a layman in these matters. Some mentally ill persons prefer to see themselves as criminals rather than as "crazy," and present themselves accordingly.[19]

Mental illness may also appear to the police as alcohol or drug intoxication, especially if the person has been using alcohol or drugs at the time of arrest. Still another factor is that in the heat and confusion of an encounter with the police and other citizens, which may include forcibly subduing the person, signs of mental illness may go unnoticed. As one policeman put it after a difficult arrest, "He didn't look any more mentally disturbed than any other criminal."

The demands of citizens are still another factor. Many stores have a policy that *anyone* caught shoplifting should go to jail, and store managers are instructed to make a citizen's arrest and call the police, with no exceptions. Another example is the bus station, located in the midst of what is now "skid row," where management wants to eliminate the presence of persons who try to live there or who harass or beg from passengers. In the brief and sometimes not too friendly interaction with security guards, it is often difficult for the guards to differentiate mental illness from alcoholism and the character problems of many of the denizens of the neighborhood. In still another kind of situation, the person who has just been assaulted by a psychotic patient is frequently not inclined to be sympathetic to the mental status of his assailant even when the mental disturbance is evident. Thus, an angry citizen may insist on signing a citizen's arrest and having the person taken to jail.

A factor that undoubtedly plays an important role is the age-old conflict between the police and emergency room physicians, a problem that is made worse by a shortage of psychiatric beds. The police complain, often with justification, that they are made to wait with their prospective patients for inordinate periods of time in emergency rooms and are thus taken out of service. Even then, they may be told after the person is finally examined that there are no beds available, and that the police thus still have responsibility for the person. Or they may leave in the hospital the person who just a short time before constituted a clear menace to the community, and later find that the emergency room psychiatrist has ignored the judgment of the police and has released the person back to the community.

There is considerable merit to the complaints of the police. The public hospital clinician, faced with the daily realities of crowding, inadequate staffing and physical plants, and an increasing volume of paperwork, will try to avoid admitting the disturbed person to the hospital.[20] Because of this, many policemen do not want to bring persons to hospitals, and they are often not inclined to try to talk a citizen out of a citizen's arrest. Or in the case of a person who has both committed a misdemeanor and is clearly mentally ill, the police may well take the route of booking the person into jail, which is less time-consuming and ensures the person's removal from the community pending further evaluation, rather than bringing him to a hospital. Furthermore, the police do not know whether an uncooperative person will meet the criteria for involuntary hospitalization; if they consider the person a danger to society, jail is a more reliable way to take that person out of circulation, at least temporarily.[14] In still other instances, the mental disturbance is recognized by the police but, as one policeman told us, "He seemed crazy, but he knew right from wrong in regard to this offense and we felt he should go to jail." It should not be forgotten that the police see their responsibility as being primarily to protect society; psychiatrists are often ambivalent about their perception of themselves as being primarily responsible to the individual, as opposed to the social guardianship role thrust upon them by society.

A study in Pennsylvania found that mental illness-related incidents coming to police attention increased 227.6 percent from 1975 to 1979.[21] It should be emphasized that the police have been left with the responsibility of dealing with these aspects of mental illness and crime and violence in an informal "common-sense" way, without any formal mandate to do so or development of a formal policy.

Has There Been Criminalization of the Mentally Ill?

There appears to be a limit to society's tolerance of mentally disordered behavior. This is especially true for those who have direct contact with the mentally ill, namely the courts, professionals, families, and other citizens.[22] Many believe that if the entry of persons exhibiting such behavior into the mental health system of social control is impeded by changes in commitment laws, shortages of hospital beds and deinstitutionalization, some of these persons will be forced into the criminal justice system of social control. We have already seen in the discussion of jail versus hospital how this can happen.

There has been considerable discussion of the "criminalization" of the mentally ill over the past decade. There are those[23,24] who doubt this phenomenon, saying that persons who have committed criminal acts and are mentally ill have always been found in jail in large numbers, that there is now simply an increased recognition and identification of them. Unfortunately, there are no good studies spanning the periods before and after deinstitutionalization that allow us to put our current situation into perspective.

There are, however, data suggestive of a diversion of patients into the criminal justice system. Abramson[14] showed that following the enactment of the Lanterman-Petris-Short Act in California (which eliminated the indefinite commitment and made many far-reaching changes in the procedures for securing involuntary hospitalization), there was an increasing resort to criminal procedures to secure long-term, indefinite commitment by raising the issue of competence to stand trial. This was done regardless of the severity of the "offense" if the patient's behavior was sufficiently disturbed or disturbing.

Studies in recent years have shown that the arrest rates for ex-hospital patients are higher than those for the general population.[25-27] There have been various attempts to account for these increased arrest rates. Steadman et al.[27] concluded from their data that this increase is due almost entirely to the increased number of persons with arrest records who are being admitted to mental hospitals. Sosowksy, however, has shown that ex-hospital patients from a California county with no previous arrests were arrested roughly three times more often than the general county population and five times more often for serious violent crimes.[28] Grunberg and associates[29] have suggested that more liberty for the traditional hospital patient is likely a crucial factor in explaining the observed increase. Sosowsky[26] has stated, "It may be true that the mentally ill, traditionally treated in state hospitals, are more violent than the general public and that more liberty does result in more crime and violence" (p 42). It thus seems possible that mental status as such is causally related to the increased arrest rate, and that those who would have been hospitalized before deinstitutionalization are now in the community and more subject to arrest.

What Can Be Done?

Clearly, the system of voluntary mental health outpatient treatment is inadequate for this population, who is extremely resistant to it. If they do agree to accept treatment, they tend not to keep their appointments, not to take their medications, and to be least welcome at outpatient facilities.[18] This is confirmed by our findings, which showed only 10 percent receiving any form of outpatient treatment (even including those receiving only medications) at the point of arrest, and only 24 percent who had ever received outpatient treatment at any time.

In my opinion, there needs to be much more emphasis on ongoing involuntary treatment such as mandatory aftercare and conservatorship for persons such as those in the this study. Social controls are important not only for society, but also for these patients, who lack the internal controls to manage their own lives; their lives without structure and controls are chaotic and characterized by intense anxiety, depression, fear, and deprivation.

Crisis services and voluntary outpatient treatment are an important beginning. What is needed, however, is an all-out effort with sufficient funding to provide adequate ongoing community treatment services, both outpatient and residential, to this group. Part of this effort needs to be adoption of a treatment philosophy that external controls, such as mandatory aftercare and conservatorship, can be a positive and often crucial therapeutic modality for those who lack the internal controls to deal with their impulses and to organize themselves to cope with life's demands. There must also be pressure on government agencies that serve as public guardians to implement these recommendations in a timely manner. We can then hope to interrupt this continual pattern of jail and hospital and help these persons achieve some measure of order and security in their lives.

REFERENCES

1. Lamb HR, Goertzel V: The long-term patient in the era of community treatment. *Arch Gen Psychiatry* 1977;34:679–682
2. Lamb HR: The new asylums in the community. *Arch Gen Psychiatry* 1979;36:129–134
3. Murphy HBM, Engelsmann F, Tcheng-Laroche F: The influence of foster-home care on psychiatric patients. *Arch Gen Psychiatry* 1976;33:179–183
4. Van Putten T, Crumpton E, Yale C: Drug refusal in schizophrenia and the wish to be crazy. *Arch Gen Psychiatry* 1976;33:1443–1446
5. Allen P: A bill of rights for citizens using outpatient mental health services. In Lamb HR (ed): *Community Survival for Long-Term Patients.* San Francisco, Jossey-Bass, 1976, pp 147–170
6. Reynolds DK, Farberow NL: *Endangered Hope: Experiences in Psychiatric Aftercare Facilities.* Los Angeles: University of California Press, 1977
7. Lamb HR: Structure: The neglected ingredient of community treatment. *Arch Gen Psychiatry* 1980;37:1224–1228
8. Dorwart RA: Deinstitutionalization: Who is left behind? *Hosp Community Psychiatry* 1980;31:336–338
9. Linn MW: Can foster care survive? In Budson RD (ed): *New Directions for Mental Health Services: Issues in Community Residential Care.* No. 11. San Francisco: Jossey-Bass, 1981, pp 35–47
10. Srole L: Geel, Belgium: The natural therapeutic community. In Serbin G, Astrachan B (eds): *New Trends of Psychiatry in the Community.* Cambridge, MA, Ballinger, 1977, pp 111–129
11. Cuvelier F: *Patterns of Interaction Between Mental Patient and Caretaker.* Paper presented at International Symposium on Foster Family Care, Geel, Belgium, May 16, 1975
12. Linn MW, Klett CJ, Caffey EM: Foster home characteristics and psychiatric patient outcome. *Arch Gen Psychiatry* 1980;37:129–132
13. Wing JK: *The Management of Schizophrenia in the Community.* Paper presented at the annual meeting of the American College of Psychiatrists, Atlanta, Feb 1977
14. Abramson MF: The criminalization of mentally disordered behavior. *Hosp Community Psychiatry* 1972;23:101–105
15. Urmer A: A Study of California's New Mental Health Law. Chatsworth, CA, ENKI Research Institute, 1971

16. Lamb HR, Grant RW: The mentally ill in an urban county jail. *Arch Gen Psychiatry* 1982;39:17–22

17. Lamb HR, Grant RW: Mentally ill women in county jail. *Arch Gen Psychiatry* 1983;40:363–368

18. Whitmer GE: From hospitals to jails: The fate of California's deinstitutionalized mentally ill. *Am J Orthopsychiatry* 1980;50:65–75

19. Sadoff RL: Criminal behavior masking mental illness. *Corrective Psychiatry and Journal of Social Therapy.* 1971;17:41–47

20. Bassuk EL, Schoonover SC: The private general hospital's psychiatric emergency service in a decade of transition. *Hosp Community Psychiatry* 1981;32:181–185

21. Bonovitz JC, Bonovitz JS: Diversion of the mentally ill into the criminal justice system: The police intervention perspective. *Am J Psychiatry* 1981;138:973–976

22. Lamb HR, Sorkin AP, Zusman J: Legislating social control of the mentally ill in California. *Am J Psychiatry* 1981;138:334–339

23. Steadman HJ, Ribner SA: Changing perceptions of the mental health needs of inmates in local jails. *Am J Psychiatry* 1980;137:1115–1116

24. Arthur Bolton Associates. A study of the need for and availability of mental health services for mentally disordered jail inmates and juveniles in detention facilities. Report to the California State Legislature, Sacramento, October 1976

25. Zitrin A, Hardesty AS, Burdock ET: Crime and violence among mental patients. *Am J Psychiatry* 1976;133:142–149

26. Sosowsky L: Crime and violence among mental patients reconsidered in view of the new legal relationship between the state and the mentally ill. *Am J Psychiatry* 1978;135:33–42

27. Steadman HJ, Vanderwyst D, Ribner S: Comparing arrest rates of mental patients and criminal offenders. *Am J Psychiatry* 1978;135:1218–1220

28. Sosowsky L: Explaining the increased arrest rate among mental patients: A cautionary note. *Am J Psychiatry* 1980;137:1602–1605

29. Grunberg F, Klinger BI, Grument BR: Homicide and the deinstitutionalization of the mentally ill. *Am J Psychiatry* 1977;134:685–687

Arthur T. Meyerson
Greta S. Herman

16

Aftercare: Current Status

Several years ago Astrachan[1] wrote "a major dilemma that is still only poorly addressed, even in theory, is how best to coordinate multiple service needs for emotionally, financially and educationally disadvantaged patients. The failures of total institutions are well known. They are, however, matched by our inability to assist the severely disabled with medical, rehabilitative, housing, and financial resources" (p 1367). More recently, Goldman, et al. concluded that "outpatient care has not replaced inpatient care" and that "state mental hospitals have not been replaced by community based facilities" (p 129).[2]

The dilemma that Astrachan described in 1978 remains with us today. What works and for whom are the essential questions for those committed to the development of appropriate aftercare systems for the chronically mentally ill. In less than 30 years the deinstitutionalization movement has reduced the population in public mental hospitals to a third of its former size. But as Ozarin and Sharfstein[3] and Bassuk and Gerson[4] have pointed out, that achievement has been offset by high hospital readmission rates, reflecting both a lack of adequate and coordinated rehabilitation and support services, and substandard living conditions for patients in the community. The disparity between aftercare needs and community realities has been documented time and again. One study in Los Angeles County found that 43 percent of in-patients could be served in alternative, ambulatory settings.[5]

Research into the biologic processes that underlie behavior and mental function has proceeded apace and has attracted both public and professional attention as well as research support. Less attention has been paid, however, to the

THE CHRONIC MENTAL PATIENT
ISBN 0-8089-1649-1

Copyright © 1984 by Grune & Stratton.
All rights of reproduction in any form reserved.

psychologic and social factors that interact with these biologic processes, as Kety[6] has observed. This chapter focuses on recent contributions in the realm of psychosocial aspects of aftercare. Somatic treatments have been reviewed elsewhere, and their general efficacy is well established.

In a recent literature review, Braun and his co-authors[7] included studies that met generally accepted scientific standards of research design, conduct of the investigation, and clarity of writing. They cited only 44 papers related to aftercare and published over a 15-year period that met those criteria, and only 22 of the papers were published between 1977 and 1981. Many of the latter were duplicate descriptions of the same research or were review articles.

If one were to limit this chapter to a review of well-designed studies it would thus be thin indeed. All those papers that even suggested the possibility of relevant information bearing on the questions under consideration were therefore included. Obviously, even with such a broad net, there must be studies that have not been covered. Those included here, however, should at least be representative.

PSYCHOSOCIAL REHABILITATION

The field of psychosocial rehabilitation is expanding rapidly, as demonstrated by the establishment of the International Association of Psychosocial Rehabilitative Services and the Community Support Program of the National Institute of Mental Health.[8] The general goal is reintegration of the psychiatrically disabled into the community by maintaining and augmenting whatever level of functional independence a patient may achieve. Rehabilitation has generally focused on programs to develop social skills and independent living capabilities, emphasizing vocational components.[8]

Summers[9] studied the consecutive admissions to a large urban psychiatric aftercare clinic over a nine month period, and found a group of chronically unemployed, socially isolated patients who had been rehospitalized numerous times, and whose problems derived more from their empty lives and inability to function than from their psychopathologic symptoms. He concluded that aftercare clinics are generally unprepared to meet the needs of such patients. Lamb's study[10] of 101 board-and-care residents found that of the 61 persons who had received rehabilitation services, only 12 were still involved. One was employed, three were in training programs or school, and eight were in sheltered workshops. Solomon et al.[11] studied the placements, activity levels, and hospital admissions of 263 chronic patients in an aftercare program over an 18-month period, and found that almost half were doing little or nothing at 18 months. They concluded that essential services were provided for this group, but that their integration into the community was hampered by insufficient recreational and vocational activities.

A study by Wasylenki and others[12] of 319 patients referred for aftercare showed that 85 percent received individual therapy, and 77 percent received some form of drug therapy, but only 30 percent received rehabilitation services. Many of the staff did not appear to understand the need for programs to combat social isolation and social inadequacy; they tended to see withdrawn patients as poorly motivated and failed to refer them to rehabilitation services. The authors suggested that as length of stay decreases, hospital staff become more involved with acutely psychotic patients and lack time for adequate aftercare planning. These findings suggest that practitioners skilled in rehabilitation needs assessment and in the coordination of aftercare services could have a significant impact, a position that Anthony and others[13] have repeatedly taken.

What are accepted measures of outcome of rehabilitation treatment? These studies generally used recidivism, employment, and level of functioning as dependent variables. Anthony and others[13] point out that recidivism data show remarkable consistency despite differences in populations, institutions, and geographic area. In the 46 articles Anthony reviewed, figures of 30 to 40 percent recidivism at five to six months, 35 to 50 percent after one year, 60 to 75 percent after three to five years were typical. Beard[14] recently reported a five year followup study that claimed a significantly lower rehospitalization rate for Fountain House clients than for control subjects at one, two, and five years. Those who were rehospitalized spent 40 percent fewer days in the hospital than controls. The more contact patients had with the program, the less likely they were to be rehospitalized. Unfortunately, little controlled comparative research has been done on the impact of comprehensive psychosocial rehabilitation centers on recidivism and employment.[8] The difficulty with Beard's study is the absence of randomly selected controls; the possibility exists that those patients who select Fountain House are predisposed to less hospitalization than those who dropout. There continues to be a dearth of employment outcome data for rehabilitation programs.

What are predictors of outcome? Psychiatric indicators such as symptom remission and discharge ratings have proven to be very poor predictors of either community tenure or performance,[13] but in some studies social indicators have been useful. A study by Freeman and others[15] found that a high level of performance was associated with living away from the family, and a study by Douzinas and Carpenter supported that finding.[16] Findings on the benefits of workshop programs have been inconsistent. One followup study indicated that only younger, less impaired clients had been able to return to competitive employment after their workshop experience.[11] Others found that age and impairment were not significantly related to successful outcome.[16,17] A recent study by Dincin and Wineridge,[18] one of the rare randomized clinical trials available, compared a "comprehensive rehabilitation program" with "supportive treatment" and found only 14 percent of the patients in the rehabilitation program had been rehospitalized, compared with 44 percent of the controls. Douzinas and Carpenter[16] found that successful completion of the rehabilitation program was the strongest predictor of successful vocational functioning in the community.

Criteria for outcome must be established, and, as Anthony and Farkas[19] suggest, studies must be controlled for diagnosis, drugs, age, previous psychiatric history, and must be utilized in the context of a comprehensive "client outcome planning model." Outcome data obtained at the present time for rehabilitation and resocialization treatments remain of questionable scientific validity in the absence of well-conducted studies. Major difficulties in all studies are lack of randomization, poor diagnostic rigor, poor control of process variables, and confusing outcome measures. The weight of evidence is not sufficient to answer our questions concerning what works, and for whom; we are relying on the state of the art developments, which have not been validated scientifically, when we recommend active rehabilitation efforts. Certainly some patients do benefit, but who are they, and what are the effective process variables? General agreement appears to exist that those patients with loss of social skills and/or whose vocational adaptation is compromised deserve at least a trial in a comprehensive rehabilitation program.

DAY TREATMENT

Partial hospitalization programs now treat a wide range of patients using a variety of treatment orientations and program formats. A number of early controlled studies[20,21] evaluated partial hospitalization as an alternative to in-patient care and, for the most part, answered the question of whether some patients could be treated with less than full-time care. Meltzoff and Blumenthal[22] described several studies that compared day treatment with the usual outpatient mental health care and found day treatment to be more effective. More recent studies, however, were neither controlled for diagnosis nor for drug treatment.[23] May and others[24] pointed out that milieu therapy can have toxic antitherapeutic effects when techniques and methods developed for neurotics and character disorders are indiscriminately applied to psychotic patients, particularly schizophrenics. Goldberg[25] claimed that patients with symptoms of motor retardation, emotional withdrawal, and anxiety were a high risk group for day treatment. There is evidence, however, that day treatment of a supportive and perhaps long-term nature can help to prevent relapse, enhance functioning, and decrease symptomatology.[23] Finding the environmental equilibrium between too much stimulation (which produces relapse), and too little stimulation (which fosters apathy), is the critical issue. A recent study by Schooler and Spohn[26] also found some adverse effects associated with socioenvironmental therapy in in-patients.

In the study by Linn and others[23] at 10 Veterans Administration hospitals, schizophrenic patients being discharged were randomly assigned to receive day treatment plus drugs or drugs alone. Patients' functioning improved in all the day treatment centers, but six of the centers were found to delay relapse significantly, reduce symptomatology, and modify patient attitudes. These centers were characterized by more occupational therapy and a sustained nonthreatening environment. Less successful centers had more professional staff hours, more group therapy, and a high patient turnover treatment philosophy.

The Linn study suggests that the effects of day treatment are most pronounced at 24 months, a finding similar to that of Hogarty and others[27] in a study of major role therapy. Althoff,[28] however, reported a study in which the results achieved with time-limited treatment were as good as those without time limits, in the judgment of the program staff; objective outcome data were lacking. Fifty percent of the patients were described as psychotic, but diagnosis was also poorly defined.

Davis and others[29] studied 1410 patients in another type of time-limited day treatment in 34 VA day hospitals. The day hospitals provided crisis intervention for patients who had not had prolonged hospitalizations and for whom a diversity of therapeutic approaches was indicated. Only 36 percent of the patients were schizophrenic; the rest were either neurotic or had personality disorders. Three months after admission to the day hospital, evaluation of the patients in relation to nine treatment goals showed that treatment was helpful in all areas except promoting economic independence; it was most effective in reducing perceptual-cognitive dysfunctioning, emotional distress, and interpersonal difficulties. Analysis of the patients' functioning at discharge showed that the schizophrenic group improved had less than patients with other diagnoses.

Lieberman and others[30] studied the impact of day treatment in a community residence that housed 230 "regressed" chronic mental patients, of whom 78 percent were schizophrenic. Residents on two floors of the home received an enriched program, while residents on the other four floors received a minimum of therapeutic interventions. A comparison of residents' ratings on assessment scales early in the program and after seven months showed that residents on all floors improved on measures of socialization, but the improvement in the experimental group was not much greater than that in the control group. Blume and others[31] described a day treatment program in Long Beach, New York, where 700 to 1000 former mental patients were housed in a community of 33,000. The effects of the program were assessed by comparing a group of 26 patients continuing in day treatment with a group who dropped out. This is, unfortunately, a biased control because sicker patients may have dropped out. Nineteen percent of active-treatment patients were rehospitalized within 14 months, compared with 35 percent of the dropouts. Both groups manifested an increase in symptomatology; it was, however, four times as great in the nontreatment group.

Day treatment studies do seem to have better definition and description of process variables and patient characteristics than studies of rehabilitation programs. Outcome variables are also relatively well selected. The number of process variables in a day program is so large, however, that specifying why one program is better than another, or what works within a program and for whom, remain challenging questions, for future research. It nevertheless seems reasonable to conclude that day treatment is an effective form of aftercare, and that day treatment, when coupled with appropriate drug treatment, yields reduced recidivism and a better quality of life.

FAMILY TREATMENT

In this era of deinstitutionalization, families have become the primary source of care for many schizophrenics and others released from state hospitals. That fact has generally been ignored by mental health professionals, who until recently have done little to involve families in patients' care or to assist in solving the problems of dealing with chronic mental patients at home. Families need clear, nontechnical explanations, and the most accurate prognosis possible.[32,33] They also need advice about the availability of community resources and appropriate techniques for handling disturbing behavior. Groups such as the National Alliance for the Mentally Ill[33] are attempting to address these issues and to end the exclusion of the family from the mental health system.

Most studies report that patients who live alone, with no family member to take an interest in them and supervise them, comply poorly with treatment plans.[34] Several studies indicate a positive relationship between family support and medication compliance. Blackwell's work,[35] in particular, demonstrated that 82 percent of a sample of schizophrenic patients who were supervised by their families were compliers.

Other aspects of the effects of family relationships on the course of schizophrenia have been reviewed by Vaughn and Leff.[36] Relatives' expressed emotion, especially hostility or overinvolvement, has adverse effects. Leff et al.,[37] in a 1982 study, did a randomized clinical trial of a program of family intervention, in patients with "high contact" with families that embodied high "expressed emotion." All received drugs, and the relapse rate in the control group was 50 percent compared with those receiving family sessions, a group for families and patients, and a program of education, where relapse was only 9 percent. only 9 percent.

Persistent attempts by several family members to express interest in and establish a relationship with the patient seem to reverse the tendency toward withdrawal and affective blunting, according to El-Islam.[38] This study, unfortunately, is based on the Indian division of family structure into "nuclear" versus "extended" models and has limited applicability.

Two recent studies[39,40] add to the credibility of appropriate family intervention as an efficacious approach to the treatment of schizophrenia when combined with other therapies, particularly somatic ones. Shenoy and others[39] found that "Schiz-Anon"-type groups for relatives of schizophrenic patients led to improved compliance by patients with aftercare regimens and significantly reduced recidivism. Boyd and others[40] described a study in which 40 patients were randomly assigned to either home-based family treatment or clinic-based supportive individual psychotherapy. The family treatment program consisted of educating families about schizophrenia, developing communication skills, and problem-solving, along with other behavioral strategies. It was found to reduce rehospitalization and recidivism significantly and was cost-effective.

A re-examination of the technique of multifamily group therapy combined with medication as the principal method of aftercare was undertaken by Lansky and others[41] and indicates some positive trends. Unlike Lansky, many proponents of multifamily therapy were family therapists whose views often differed from what has been called the "medical model" of symptoms and disease. The resulting lack of attention to psychiatric symptoms and diagnoses has led to a failure to distinguish genuine morbid phenomena from the context in which they are precipitated or the use to which they are put by all concerned.

In conclusion, studies have demonstrated the efficacy of family treatment in reducing recidivism and symptomatology, but the findings are by no means definitive. The utilization of family support for a discharged patient and of educating responsible family members about their significant role in the patient's care, however, does not really require scientific proof. One needs to know which families are useful and educable and which are noxious, and that information is emerging.[37] Clearly, we no longer hold the family "guilty" of causing the patient's illness, and this is an important contribution in itself.

GROUP TREATMENT

A number of studies in the past have focused on group versus individual aftercare treatment,[42,43] and have demonstrated at least equal efficacy. A recent study by Alden et al.[44] used 15 chronic schizophrenic patients as their own controls and compared the patients' rehospitalization rates during two years of active group psychotherapy with their rehospitalization rates in the two years before they joined the group. The rehospitalization rates were found to be significantly lower during the group therapy period. Despite the small sample size and the questions raised by making comparisons over two different time periods, the study offers convincing data that group therapy does have significant benefits for chronic schizophrenic patients. The attendance rate for the group—97 percent—was extremely high for any form of psychotherapy.

HOUSING

The December 1980 report to the Secretary by the Department of Health and Human Services, *Toward a National Plan for the Chronically Mentally Ill*,[45] addressed the issue of a proper posthospital environment for mentally disabled persons. The report called the lack of adequate and stable housing opportunities linked with support services perhaps the major unmet need of the chronically mentally ill. It noted that increasingly large numbers of patients are living in board-and-care homes, single-room-occupancy residences, and other settings that are generally run-down and unsafe, and that offer few meaningful activities for residents.

In order to meet the housing needs of chronic patients in the community, the report recommended emergency or short-term crisis facilities (such as hostels or respite care centers), transitional settings oriented toward rehabilitation (such as group homes and shared apartments), and homes offering supportive or sustaining environments for the more disabled and chronically ill. There have been substantial barriers to the development of such housing arrangements, including community opposition, scarcity of suitable affordable facilities and apartments, lack of categorical funding at local and state levels, and lack of involvement of the private sector. For facilities that do exist, there has been no clear authorization of funds and responsibility for supervision, regulation, and upgrading of services.

BOARD-AND-CARE HOMES

"Board-and-care" is a name applied to any of a variety of unlocked facilities for up to several hundred residents. They provide a room (usually shared), meals, supervision of medication, and a minimal amount of staff supervision.[10] The board-and-care home is not a transitional residence and does not encourage acquisition of skills. Residents are often placed there with little planning, no followup and with little expectation of an eventual move to independent status. Van Putten and Spar[46] have described the typical board-and-care resident as a "chronic schizophrenic between the ages of 16 and 70 who has lived in the home for 3.03 years. He spends 8.46 hours per day in bed (time limited primarily due to sponsor's efforts) and the rest of the day in virtual solitude, either watching TV, or wandering aimlessly about the neighborhood, sometimes stopping for a nap on a lawn or park bench. He is virtually free of responsibility. He sees a psychiatrist 1.72 times per month and is maintained on the equivalent of an average dosage of 760 mg of chlorpromazine. He is further characterized as mildly symptomatic, less than 3 on the Brief Psychiatric Rating Scale, but scoring higher on scales which reflect blunted affect and extreme social withdrawal" (pp 461–462).

Descriptions such as these have led some to equate today's board-and-care homes with yesterday's back wards of state mental hospitals. Some see these homes as temporary way stations on a patient's road to recovery; others see them as maintaining patients within the community, with a decent standard of living, and consider that a worthwhile and even admirable final outcome.[47] As can be imagined from these differing objectives, many criteria can be used to judge the success or failure of board-and-care homes. Should recidivism, symptomatology, or maintenance of basic needs be used as outcome measurements? How much weight should be given to the patients' own satisfaction with their living arrangements?

Lamb[48] addressed the latter question in a study of 101 patients in board-and-care homes in Los Angeles. He reported that 40 percent described themselves as content or reasonably content, and 52 percent had no desire to change anything in their lives. These patients were not living up to their full social, vocational, and esthetic potential, and certain observers would see their lives as empty and meaningless. Lamb points out, however, that for a number of patients the board-and-care home has become an asylum after a lifetime of chaos, instability, and hardship.

There has been little definitive research aimed at identifying the elements of a residential facility that affect patient outcome. We could not find even one controlled study that rigorously assesses the contribution of enriched care in a board-and-care population. The early and widely quoted studies by Lamb and Goertzel,[49,50] in which chronically hospitalized schizophrenics who were eligible for placement in a board-and-care home were assigned to board-and-care homes or to a "high expectancy setting" did demonstrate a modest improvement for the experimental group.

Betz and others[47] recently developed a checklist of items, using both tested and untested assumptions, to describe boarding homes as either good or bad. Factors they considered included adequate meals in a clean, safe environment; principles of normalization and community integration; combining the mentally ill with non-mentally ill residents; welcoming friends and relatives; availability of aftercare services, and supervision and reinforcement of medication compliance.

It is clear that only those boarding homes should be chosen that most closely meet the needs of individual residents. Melick and Eysaman[51] surveyed 1999 residents of 26 homes in an attempt to determine if their needs were considered greater than, less than, or consistent with the level of services provided in these homes. The results suggest that a substantial proportion of former patients could benefit from some kind of psychiatric rehabilitative services not available in the homes.

Even long-term homes with lower expectations of patients need not resemble back wards if active social and recreational programs are built into them, as Easton[52] has stated. The challenge seems to be in determining which types of homes are nontherapeutic holding cells, which promote only general maintenance of a patient's functioning, and which promote development of a patient's potential and active integration into the community.[47]

One type of board-and-care facility is the foster home. Linn et al.[53] define a foster home as "a traditional family setting in which a patient lives with at least one responsible adult" (p 129). They conducted a study[54] in which patients were randomly assigned to foster care or to continued hospitalization. Within four months of placement, foster home patients had improved to a greater degree in social functioning than had the institutionalized patients. Factors associated with improved outcome in foster homes were more children in the homes, fewer boarders, and smaller size. Too much stimulation in the environment, more supervision by foster care sponsors, and more intensive follow-up by social work staff, were bad for schizophrenic patients but good for nonschizophrenic patients. Linn et al.[55] have followed-up 210 male foster care patients for 1 year with encouraging results.

It appears reasonable to draw two conclusions without further scientific validation: board-and-care homes should be humane living environments, and they should be integrated into complete care programs for appropriate patients.

TRANSITIONAL RESIDENCES

Transitional residences provide supervision and support for newly discharged patients for a limited period while they adjust to more independent living and reintegration into the community.[56-62] Goals of these residences are often to assist former patients in developing daily living skills and improving interpersonal relationships and perhaps in returning to full time employment or meaningful activity in the community. The sponsoring agency assumes responsibility for helping residents move to longer-term living situations in the community, and for determining when residents are ready to make such moves.

A typical transitional residence, described by Goldmeier et al.,[63] might be a cooperative apartment sponsored by an agency that provides a consultant mental health professional or paraprofessional who visits regularly, meets with residents and residential managers to review the progress of the residents, and is available in crises. The agency acts as the lessee of the apartment, obtains and screens referrals, and selects residents. Rent payments and maintenance charges are shared by the residents. The pooling of resources and emotional support provided by this arrangement exemplify the cooperative nature of the endeavor.

Budson and Jolley[64] described another transitional living program called Berkeley House, which accommodates 23 patients in downtown Boston. This program, affiliated with McLean Hospital, stresses the importance of developing a psychosocial network and requires that residents participate in a program outside the house. Weekly meetings are held for former residents to help them deal with their problems in community living.

Followup of 78 patients who had lived at Berkeley House during the first three years of operation showed that they had remained in the program an average of 7.5 months and had been hospitalized an average of 125 months before their admission. At followup, 91 percent were living independently and

74 percent were working or in school. While the study did not use a control group or random assignment, these figures are quite impressive.

Again, it seems clear that humane environments, linked with complete care and treatment programs, are justified. Which patient requires which environment, however is still a matter of art or general judgment, and not of scientifically validated principles.

OUTCOME OF COMMUNITY AFTERCARE

A number of studies have attempted to view the outcome of community care provided to chronic patients in a more global fashion. These studies often focus on what happens to a pool of deinstitutionalized patients treated in the community or on the effects of specific community programs without defining the process within those programs. Despite the lack of definition of process variables, the results of some of these studies is of interest.

Dickey et al.[65] studied 27 chronic patients 4 years after their discharge from a state hospital. Rehospitalization among the group dropped dramatically once the patients were appropriately placed in the community, and the patients had a higher average mental status score at followup than a group of institutionalized patients. The vast majority of patients preferred life in the community to life at the state hospital. This study purports to demonstrate once again that "organized and systematic aftercare is essential to maintaining chronic patients as residents in the community" (p 329).

A number of studies have used recidivism or rehospitalization as the criterion for evaluation of community programming. Byers et al.[66] followed 129 patients released within a two-year period from a large state hospital, and studied the relationship between ultimate recidivism and the type of community support system available to them. Although no single factor was adequate in predicting hospital readmission, the amount of aftercare received was found to be an important factor. Patients' current situation and environmental influences, however, appeared to be more important predictors of recidivism or rehospitalization than whether they received aftercare services.

Winston et al.[67] also studied the relationship between aftercare and rehospitalization rates for patients of mixed diagnoses admitted to an in-patient unit of a municipal hospital over 2.5 years. They found that those who received aftercare were rehospitalized less often than those who did not. Rehospitalization rates were higher for schizophrenic patients than for those with other diagnoses, and highest for schizophrenics who failed to enter aftercare programs. Almost half the patients receiving treatment during the study period could not be located, however, leading the authors to question whether patients who were contacted were representative of the total group.

In another study of 421 patients who made between one and 65 visits to an aftercare clinic, McCranie and Mizell[68] found a significant relationship between an increased number of aftercare visits and a reduced likelihood of rehospitalization, especially among the more severely disabled psychotic patients. The patients were classified as psychotic and nonpsychotic; no diagnoses were specified. The fact that the patients continuing in aftercare were a self-selected group may have skewed results in a favorable direction. Nevertheless, the findings again tend to support the efficacy of aftercare in preventing rehospitalization.

The difficulty with such studies is that without identification of specific process variables in the aftercare programs it is impossible to replicate findings for the purpose of research or program development. None of these studies was controlled for medication. One possible common link may be that patients who comply with aftercare programs also comply with medication and are therefore the beneficiaries of positive results induced by pharmacology rather than by aftercare. Another possibility is that compliance with aftercare produces compliance with pharmacotherapy; and that while the pharmacotherapy is the active treating agent, the involvement in an active aftercare program is a prerequisite for compliance with pharmacotherapy, at least for some patients.

Hogarty et al.[69] studied relapse rates in a population of 105 schizophrenic patients who, after discharge, received either oral fluphenazine or long-acting fluphenazine decanoate, in the context of high and low degrees of social therapy. Relapse rates for all groups in the first year were nearly identical; over more time, there was a reduced risk of relapse in the group which had guaranteed medication and social therapy. Social therapy had no prophylactic effect on the noncompliant group studied, and guaranteed medication in the absence of social therapy was of limited effectiveness.

In contrast to these three studies which indicated a correlation between aftercare or continuity of care and reduced rehospitalization, the study of Tessler and Mason[70] found no significant difference between 146 patients participating in aftercare and 67 non-participants with regard to rehospitalization. Of interest in their study was that 30.2 percent of their patients used aftercare facilities only as a source of medication and did not use any other available services.

Other studies have examined the relationship between length of stay and readmission rates. De Francisco and others[71] presented data showing that an increase in length of stay from 9 to 26 days was associated with a 55 percent reduction in the rate of rapid readmission (readmission within one month of discharge). The authors acknowledged, however, that further study was needed before one could conclude that the longer stay was responsible for the reduction.

In contrast, McNeill et al.[72] found no significant difference in readmission rates for a group of private patients with a mean length of stay of 19.5 days and a group of CMHC patients with a mean stay of 10.5 days. They suggested that the linkage between brief in-patient treatment and aftercare programs was the reason for the reduced readmission rate.

The difficulty with both these studies lies in the lack of diagnostic specificity for in-patient populations, premorbid predictors of outcome, and medication controls during the aftercare program. Both studies, however, appear to lend credibility to the importance of continuity of care, whether it is produced by effective linkages between in-patient and aftercare programs, or by the development of good relationships during a prolonged in-patient stay that are translated into compliance after hospitalization.

A number of studies have examined the significance of variables that bear on the transition from hospital to aftercare programs. Stickney and others[73] studied referral procedures for patients discharged from a state hospital and found that simple changes in procedures could increase aftercare compliance and reduce recidivism. For example, aftercare compliance increased significantly when specific followup appointments were scheduled at the time of discharge.

Fiester and others[74] found that aftercare no-show rates could be substantially reduced by a brief phone call from the hospital reminding the patient of the appointment. Kovacs,[75] however, found letters to be as effective as telephone calls. Burgoyne et al.[76] suggest that owning a telephone is a socioeconomic indicator and that higher socioeconomic achievement may be the significant factor associated with compliance with a first outpatient visit and not whether the patient is given a prompt by phone.

Prue et al.[77] examined the effect of distance on aftercare compliance and found that the greater the distance between the patient's residence and the aftercare program, the less likely he was to attend. While the patients in this study were alcoholics, the implications for the development of local aftercare services with outreach and transportation seem equally applicable to mental patients.

Bene-Kociemba et al.[78] found early intervention in the areas of housing, finances, and medication to be especially important in prolonging the community tenure of discharged state hospital patients. While the term of study was 6 months after discharge, a limited period, the study serves to underscore the importance of effective treatment planning and active bridging of hospital services with community supports.

Freeman et al.[79] developed a system for monitoring the care of a large number of schizophrenic patients in an urban area. Their purpose was to learn whether such a system was feasible in an urban health district, and they concluded that it was "practical, effective, and relatively economical to operate" (p 416). Such a system would, of course, be of tremendous benefit in large urban areas where continuity of care is often disrupted because of the multiple agencies with which a patient must maintain or develop contact.

Intagliata[80] reviewed the literature on "The Role of Case Management" and points to a "number of important unanswered research questions about the delivery and input of case management" (p 655). Intagliata points to several reports of program evaluation supporting the efficacy of case management in improving the "accessibility, comprehensiveness and volume of services."[81-83]

The weight of the evidence from these studies on the effect of community support programs does justify the following conclusions:

1. Effective programs of aftercare, comprehensive in nature, do increase community tenure and level of community adjustment, and do reduce recidivism and rehospitalization rates.
2. The effectiveness of the programs is enhanced by thorough integration with the original referring inpatient service. A variety of specific interventions to improve disposition and ultimate compliance have been suggested.
3. Which specific process variables are effective and what specific patients benefit from aspects of aftercare programs remain researchable questions. If prolonged community tenure is desirable, however, then intervention in the area of housing, finances, and medication is especially important.

PATIENT VARIABLES

A number of patient variables may affect outcome and responsivity of patients to specific aftercare interventions. Recent work correlating positive CAT scan findings with reduced responsivity to pharmacology and rehabilitative efforts in patients with so-called "negative symptoms" or a "defect symptom" type of schizophrenia[84] is of interest but beyond the scope of this chapter. These studies are extraordinarily promising, although their clinical role remains in question.

Carpenter et al.[85] studied the prognostic significance of individual signs and symptoms relevant to a diagnosis of schizophrenia in 61 schizophrenic patients at five-year followup. Patients with the best and worst outcomes were selected, and the data on the two groups were analyzed to determine which signs and symptoms were associated with outcome. The authors found that only restricted affect predicted poor outcome, whereas depression, anxiety, and nuclear symptoms of schizophrenia were not significant predictors.

More recently Serban and Gidynski[86] examined the relationship between mental status and community adjustment in 100 chronic schizophrenic outpatients. They found that anxiety and depression did appear to be significantly correlated with patient functioning and stress in the community, while primary symptoms were only peripherally correlated with patient adjustment.

The seemingly contradictory findings in these two studies highlight the need for more research aimed at identifying predictors of patient adjustment in the community and the kind of aftercare programs needed to maintain that adjustment.

The new population of young adult chronic patients has been the subject of a number of recent papers.[87-90] These patients, described by Caton[89] as typically young, more likely to be male, and highly transient, tend to seek short-term help from in-patient services and psychiatric emergency units in times of crisis, but are usually unwilling to accept continuing care voluntarily. According to Caton there is a lack of fit between this group's characteristic style of interaction and existing community-based programs. Developing services for this patient group is a major challenge.

Tsuang et al.[91] recently demonstrated the extreme stability of Research Diagnostic Criteria (RDC), and by inference, DSM III, when applied retrospectively to a group of patients with schizophrenic and major affective disorders. Their study showed that diagnostic stability for schizophrenic patients remained at 93.5 percent over a 30-40 year period. That encouraging finding indicates that as we become more adept in diagnostic rigor, we may be able to replicate studies correlating patient characteristics with treatment process variables and outcome, and to put the findings to practical use.

In addition to the research reports briefly summarized here, a number of general or overview articles describe research strategies that have implications for the design of aftercare services.[92-97]

CONCLUSION

The weight of the research evidence seems to justify the following summary statements about aftercare in its many dimensions:

- "Bridging" strategies are needed to maximize continuity of care and minimize geographic, personnel, and temporal gaps between hospitalization and implementation of aftercare. The need is particularly intense in the dimensions of housing, financial support, implementation of medical and pharmacologic treatment. Case management is vital for many patients.
- Day hospital programs have proven their efficacy as alternatives to long-term and even short-term in-patient stays for many patients as well as functioning as important transitional programs. Determining which patients might benefit from the kind of rehabilitative efforts that require day hospitalization and which might not, however, remains a researchable question.
- Earlier studies have shown group psychotherapy to be at least as efficacious as individual therapy in the treatment of chronic schizophrenic patients in the community. More recent evidence supports the efficacy of group psychotherapy for this patient population. Compliance with group therapy, as with aftercare in general, seems to be related to and may be a result of compliance with pharmacotherapy, but the relationship is impossible to evaluate at present.
- Appropriate family approaches are proving efficacious in reducing recidivism and in enhancing compliance.
- The efficacy of specific rehabilitation approaches has not been demonstrated for specific populations of the chronically mentally ill. In addition, identification of active process variables in social and vocational rehabilitation

programs remains a problem. There seems to be no question that such approaches are helpful to patients, but which approaches and which patients remains a key question.

- In the area of housing, including board-and-care homes, halfway houses, and other transitional living facilities, there seems to be no question that on a simple, humane level, patients do benefit from appropriate environments. Several studies support the notion that appropriate housing prolongs residency in the community and decreases recidivism and rehospitalization when coupled with other elements of aftercare. There are few data, however, to specify which patients belong in which environments at which times in the course of their illnesses.

The question of what works and for whom remains of considerable significance since the prognosis for schizophrenia is relatively poor[98] and schizophrenia patients will continue to require community programming that is comprehensive and ongoing.[99] The concept of a delivery system that provides care rather than cure, and does so on a continuing basis, is inherent in the conclusions of the articles reviewed here and of this chapter itself. As Stein and Test have demonstrated,[99] when special programming is discontinued, many of the gains deteriorate, and the use of the hospital rises sharply. The results suggest that "community programming should be comprehensive and ongoing" (p 392).[99] Thus, inherent in the conclusions drawn from the articles we have reviewed is the emerging notion of a care rather than cure delivery system.

REFERENCES

1. Astrachan BM: Mental Health Care Delivery Systems: Discussion. *Am J Psychiatry* 1978;135:1366–1367
2. Goldman HH, Adams NH, Taube CA: Deinstitutionalization: The data demythologized. *Hosp Community Psychiatry* 1983;34:129–134
3. Ozarin LD, Sharfstein SS: The aftermaths of Deinstitutionalization: Problems and solutions. *Psychiatr Q* 1978;50:128–132
4. Bassuk EL, Gerson S: Deinstitutionalization and mental health services. *Scientific American* 1978;238:46–53
5. Fowler G: A needs-assessment method for planning alternatives to hospitalization. *Hosp Community Psychiatry* 1980;31:41–49
6. Kety SS: The syndrome of schizophrenia: Unresolved questions and opportunities for research. *Br J Psychiatry* 1980;136:421–436
7. Braun P, Kochansky G, Shapiro R, et al.: Overview: Deinstitutionalization of psychiatric patients: A critical review of outcome studies. *Am J Psychiatry* 1981;138:736–749
8. Mosher LR, Keith SJ: Research on the psychosocial treatment of schizophrenia: A summary report. *Am J Psychiatry* 1979;136:623–629
9. Summers F: Characteristics of new patient admissions to aftercare. *Hosp Community Psychiatry* 1979;30:199–202
10. Lamb HR: The new asylums in the community. *Arch Gen Psychiatry* 1979;36:129–134
11. Solomon EB, Baird R, Everstine L, et al.: Assessing the community care of chronic psychotic patients. *Hosp Community Psychiatry* 1980;31:113–116

12. Wasylenki DA, Goering P, Lancee W, et al.: Psychiatric aftercare: Identified needs versus referral patterns. *Am J Psychiatry* 1981;138:1228–1231

13. Anthony WA, Cohen MR, Vitalo R: The measurement of rehabilitation outcome. *Schizophr Bull* 1978;4:365–380

14. Beard JH, Malamud TJ, Rossman E: Psychiatric rehabilitation and rehospitalization rates: The findings of 2 research studies. *Schizophr Bull* 1978;4:622–638

15. Freeman SJJ, Fischer L, Sheldon A: An agency model for developing and coordinating psychiatric aftercare. *Hosp Community Psychiatry* 1980;31:768–771

16. Douzinas N, Carpenter MD: Predicting the community performance of vocational rehabilitation clients. *Hosp Community Psychiatry* 1980;32:409–412

17. Gray JA: A followup study of psychiatric patients in a sheltered workshop program. *Hosp Community Psychiatry* 1980;31:563–566

18. Dincin J, Witheridge TF: Psychiatric rehabilitation as a deterrent to recidivism. *Hosp Community Psychiatry* 1982;33:645–650

19. Anthony WA, Farkas M: A client outcome planning model for assessing psychiatric rehabilitation interventions. *Schizophr Bull* 1982;8:13–38

20. Hertz MI, Endicott J, Spitzer R, et al.: Day vs. inpatient hospitalization: A controlled study. *Am J Psychiatry* 1971;127:1371–1382

21. Wilder J, Levin G, Zwerling I: A 2 year followup evaluation of acute psychiatric patients treated in a day hospital. *Am J Psychiatry* 1966;122:1095–1101

22. Meltzoff J, Blumenthal RL: *"The Day Treatment Center,"* Principles, Application, and Evaluation. Springfield, IL, Charles C. Thomas, 1966

23. Linn MW, Caffey EM, Klett CJ, et al.: Day treatment and psychotropic drugs in the aftercare of schizophrenic patients. *Arch Gen Psychiatry* 1979;36:1055–1056

24. May PRA, Tuma AH, Dickson WJ: Schizophrenia—A follow-up study of result of treatment: Design and other problems. *Arch Gen Psychiatry* 1976;33:474–478

25. Goldberg SC, Schooler NR, Hogarty GE, et al.: Prediction of relapse in schizophrenic outpatients treated by drug and sociotherapy. *Arch Gen Psychiatry* 1977;34:171–184

26. Schooler C, Spohn HE: Social dysfunction and treatment failure in schizophrenia (abstr). *Schizophr Bull* 1982;8:85–97

27. Hogarty GE, Goldberg SC, Schooler NR: Drug and sociotherapy in the aftercare of schizophrenic patients: Two-year relapse rates. *Arch Gen Psychiatry* 1974;31:603–608

28. Althoff JG: Time limits in and leaves from a day treatment program. *Hosp Community Psychiatry* 1980;31:841–844

29. Davis JE, Lorei RW, Caffey EM Jr: An evaluation of the VA day hospital program. *Hosp Community Psychiatry* 1978;29:297–302

30. Lieberman HJ, Winston A, Marolla F: A social interaction program for chronic psychiatric patients living in a community residence. *Hosp Community Psychiatry* 1978;29:806–809

31. Blume RM, Calin M, Sacks J: A collaborative day treatment program for chronic patients in adult homes. *Hosp Community Psychiatry* 1979;30:40–42

32. Hatfield AB: The family as partner in the treatment of mental illness. *Hosp Community Psychiatry* 1979;30:338–340

33. Lamb HR, Oliphant E: Schizophrenia through the eyes of families. *Hosp Community Psychiatry* 1978;29:803–805

34. Strickland R, Alston J, Davidson J: The negative influence of families on compliance. *Hosp Community Psychiatry* 1981;32:349–350

35. Blackwell B: Treatment adherence. *Br J Psychiatry* 1976;129:513–531

36. Vaughan CE, Leff JP: The influence of family and social factors on the course of psychiatric illness. *Br J Psychiatry* 1976;129:125–137

37. Leff JP, Kuipers L, Berkowitz R, et al.: A controlled trial of social intervention in the families of schizophrenic patients. *Br J Psychiatry* 1982;141:121–134

38. El-Islam MF: A better outlook for schizophrenics living in extended families. *Br J Psychiatry* 1979;135:343–347

39. Shenoy RS, Shires BW: Using a Schiz-Anon group in the treatment of chronic ambulatory schizophrenics. *Hosp Community Psychiatry* 1981;32:421-422

40. Boyd JH, McGill CW, Falloon I: Family participation in the community rehabilitation of schizophrenics. *Hosp Community Psychiatry* 1981;32:629-632

41. Lansky MR, Bley CR, McVey GG, et al: Multiple family groups as aftercare. *Int J Group Psychother* 1978;28:211-224

42. Herz MI, Spitzer RL, Gibbon M: Individual versus group aftercare treatment. *Am J Psychiatry* 1974;131:808-812

43. O'Brien CP, Hamm KB, Ray BB, et al.: Group vs. individual psychotherapy with schizophrenics: A controlled outcome study. *Arch Gen Psychiatry* 1972;27:474-478

44. Alden AR, Weddington WW Jr, Jacobson C, et al.: Group aftercare for chronic schizophrenia. *J Clin Psychiatry* 1979;40:249-252

45. Report to the Secretary by the Department of Health and Human Services Steering Committee on the Chronically Mentally Ill: Toward a national plan for the chronically mentally ill. 1980, pp 2-34

46. VanPutten T, Spar JE: The board-and-care home: Does it deserve a bad press. *Hosp Community Psychiatry* 1979;30:461-464

47. Betts J, Stan J, Reynolds P: A checklist for selecting board-and-care homes for chronic patients. *Hosp Community Psychiatry* 1981;32:488-501

48. Lamb HR: Board-and-care home wanderers. *Arch Gen Psychiatry* 1980;37:135-137

49. Lamb HR, Goertzel V: High expectations of longterm ex-state hospital patients. *Am J Psychiatry* 1972;129:471-475

50. Lamb HR, Goertzel V: Discharged mental patients. Are they really in the community. *Arch Gen Psychiatry* 1971;24:29-34

51. Melick CR, Eysaman CO: A study of former patients placed in private proprietary homes. *Hosp Community Psychiatry* 1978;29:587-589

52. Easton K: Boerum-Hill: A private long-term residential program for former mental patients. *Hosp Community Psychiatry* 1974;25:513-517

53. Linn MW, Klett CJ, Caffey EM Jr: Foster home characteristics and psychiatric patient outcome. *Arch Gen Psychiatry* 1980;37:129-132

54. Linn MW, Klett CJ, Caffey EM Jr: Relapse of psychiatric patients in foster care. *Am J Psychiatry* 1982;139:778-783

55. Linn MW, Caffey EM Jr, Klett CJ: Hospital vs community (foster) care for psychiatric patients. *Arch Gen Psychiatry* 1977;34:78-83

56. Orndoff CR: Transitional housing. *Psychiatr Q* 1978;50:269-273

57. Carpenter MD: Residential placement for the chronic psychiatric patient: A review and evaluation of the literature. *Schizophr Bull* 1978;4:384-398

58. Zanditon M, Hellman S: The complicated business of setting up residential alternatives. *Hosp Community Psychiatry* 1981;32:335-338

59. Burger AS, Kimelman L, Lurie A: Congregate living for the mentally ill: Patients as tenants. *Hosp Community Psychiatry* 1978;29:590-593

60. Armstrong B: The community lodge: Helping the chronically mentally ill help each other. *Hosp Community Psychiatry* 1979;30:705-708

61. Dubin WR, Ciavarelli B: A positive look at boarding homes. *Hosp Community Psychiatry* 1978;29:593-595

62. Segal SP: Sheltered-care needs of the mentally ill. *Health Soc Work* 1979; 4:42-57

63. Goldmeier J, Shore MF, Mannino FV: Cooperative apartments: New programs in community mental health. *Health Soc Work* 1977;2:120-141

64. Budson RD, Jolley RE: A crucial factor in community program success: The extended psychosocial kinship system. *Schizophr Bull* 1978;4:384-398

65. Dickey B, Gudeman JE, Hellman S, et al.: A followup of deinstitutionalized chronic patients four years after discharge. *Hosp Community Psychiatry* 1981;32:326-332

66. Byers ES, Cohen S, Harshbarger DD: Impact of aftercare services on recidivism of mental hospital patients. *Community Ment Health J* 1978;14:26-34

67. Winston A, Pardes J, Papernik DS, et al.: Aftercare of psychiatric patients and its relation to rehospitalization. *Hosp Community Psychiatry* 1977;28:118-121

68. McCranie EW, Mizell TA: Aftercare for psychiatric patients: Does it prevent rehospitalization? *Hosp Community Psychiatry* 1978;29:584-587

69. Hogarty GE, Schooler NR, Ulrich R, et al.: Fluphenazine and social therapy in the aftercare of schizophrenic patients: Relapse analyses of a two-year controlled study of fluphenazine decanoate and fluphenazine hydrochloride. *Arch Gen Psychiatry* 1979;36:1283-1294

70. Tessler R, Mason JH: Continuity of care in the delivery of mental health services. *Am J Psychiatry* 1979;136:1297-1301

71. DeFrancisco D, Anderson D, Pantano R, et al.: The relationship between length of hospital stay and rapid-readmission rates. *Hosp Community Psychiatry* 1980;31:196-197

72. McNeill DN, Stevenson J, Longabaugh RH: Short-term inpatient care and readmission rates: The CMHC approach versus the private approach. *Hosp Community Psychiatry* 1980;31:751-755

73. Stickney SK, Hall RCW, Gardner ER: The effect of referral procedures on aftercare compliance. *Hosp Community Psychiatry* 1980;31:567-569

74. Feister AR, Cooley ML, Bausinger L: The effects of phone prompts on non-attendance rates at a CMHC aftercare clinic. *Hosp Community Psychiatry* 1979;30:312

75. Kovacs KV: Telephone or letter outreach to outpatients who fail to keep first appointments. *Hosp Community Psychiatry* 1981;32:278-279

76. Burgoyne RW, Acosta FX, Yamamoto J: Telephone prompting to increase attendance at a psychiatric outpatient clinic. *Am J Psychiatry* 1983;140:345-347

77. Prue DM, Keane TM, Cornell JE, et al.: An analysis of distance variables that affect aftercare patients. *Community Ment Health J* 1979;15:149-154

78. Bene-Kociemba A, Cotton PG, Frank A: Predictors of community tenure of discharged state hospital patients. *Am J Psychiatry* 1979;136:1556-1561

79. Freeman H, Cheadle AJ, Korer JR: A method for monitoring the treatment of schizophrenics in the community. *Br J Psychiatry* 1979;134:412-416

80. Intagliata J: Improving the quality of community care for the chronically mentally disabled: The role of case managers. *Schizophr Bull* 1982;8:655-674

81. Baker F, Jodrey D, Morell M: *Evaluation of Case Management Training Program: Final Report.* New York, New York School of Psychiatry, 1979

82. Caragonne P: Implications of case management: A report on research. Paper presented at the Case Management Conference, Buffalo, NY, April 1979

83. Caragonne P: An analysis of the function of the case manager in four mental health social services settings. Report of the Case Management Research Project, Austin, TX, 1980

84. Weinberger DR, Bigelow LB, Kleinman JE, et al.: Cerebral ventricular enlargement in chronic schizophrenia: An association with poor response to treatment. *Arch Gen Psychiatry* 1980;37:11-13

85. Carpenter WT Jr, Bartko JJ, Strauss JS, et al.: Signs and symptoms as predictors of outcome: A report from the International Pilot Study of Schizophrenia. *Am J Psychiatry* 1978;138:940-944

86. Serban G, Gidynski CB: Relationship between cognitive defect, affect response and community adjustment in chronic schizophrenics. *Br J Psychiatry* 1979;134:602-608

87. Pepper B, Kirshner MC, Ryglewicz H: The young adult chronic patient: Overview of a population. *Hosp Community Psychiatry* 1981;32:463-469

88. Schwartz SR, Goldfinger SM: The new chronic patient: Clinical characteristics of an emerging subgroup. *Hosp Community Psychiatry* 1981;32:470-475

89. Caton CLM: The new chronic patient and the system of community care. *Hosp Community Psychiatry* 1981;32:475-478

90. Green RS, Koprowski PF: The chronic patient with a non-psychotic diagnosis. *Hosp Community Psychiatry* 1981;32:479–481

91. Tsuang MT, Woolson RF, Winokur G, et al.: Stability of psychiatric diagnosis. *Arch Gen Psychiatry* 1981;38:535–539

92. Test MA, Stein LI: Community treatment of the chronic patient: Research overview. *Schizophr Bull* 1978;4:350–364

93. Goldberg SC, Schooler NR, Hogarty GE, et al.: Prediction of relapse in schizophrenic outpatients treated by drug and sociotherapy. *Arch Gen Psychiatry* 1977;34:171–184

94. Smith CJ, Smith CA: Evaluating outcome measures for deinstitutionalization programs. *Social Work Research and Abstracts* 1979;15:23–30

95. Schulberg HC: Community support programs: Program evaluation and public policy. *Am J Psychiatry* 1979;136:1433–1437

96. Bachrach LL: Continuity of care for chronic mental patients: A conceptual analysis. *Am J Psychiatry* 1981;138:1449–1456

97. Bachrach LL: General hospital psychiatry. *Am J Psychiatry* 1981;38:879–885

98. Harrow M, Grinker RR, Silverstein ML, et al.: Is modern-day schizophrenic outcome still negative. *Am J Psychiatry* 1978;135:1156–1162

99. Stein LI, Test MA: Alternative to mental hospital treatment. *Arch Gen Psychiatry* 1980;37:392–397

David Cutler

17

Networks

In the search for more cost-effective strategies for the development of services for the chronically mentally ill population, networks are beginning to be regarded as a new panacea. Popular methods made operational under the rubrics of "Community Support Systems" and "Case Management," appear to be based on the belief that somehow reorganizing the social milieu (or network) within which the patient exists will provide a buffer against relapse. Although these are noble aspirations, we may be in serious danger of raising expectations in a manner similar to the deinstitutionalization movement of the 1950s, 1960s, and 1970s, without delivering any measurable decrease in prevalence of chronic mental illness.[1] Nonetheless, tertiary preventative natural networks should be developed, particularly in these times of decreasing public funding without an associated decrease in the incidence of chronic mental illness. Although Greenblatt et al.[2] have suggested that "enough information is now available" for mental health providers to design and use network-based approaches, there is little evidence to indicate that research or clinical methods based on this perspective have had much effect on service delivery systems,[3,4] let alone on the patients themselves. Beels[5] has suggested that (particularly with regard to schizophrenics) we need to understand the normal development of social networks better in order to distinguish what is a product of the disease from what may be more the result of treatment environments. To date, few practitioners are familiar with the theory that informs the rationale for application, the skills necessary to develop network models in a practical form, or even the terminology needed to communicate with other workers. Certainly a broad understanding of these perspectives among the

THE CHRONIC MENTAL PATIENT
ISBN 0-8089-1649-1

Copyright © 1984 by Grune & Stratton.
All rights of reproduction in any form reserved.

mental health disciplines will be necessary before ideas can become programs and methods can be evaluated in the light of what is practical and effective.

The intent of this chapter is to examine the relevant research literature on networks as it pertains to the chronically mentally ill and to identify factors likely to have a bearing on treatment. A summary of characteristics of the support network for a chronic mental patient, based on findings from the literature and on clinical experience, will be followed by a comment on some clinical and programmatic approaches involved in improving the structure and functioning of networks for the chronically mentally ill.

BACKGROUND

Current concepts concerning networks and the chronic patient have developed in recent years, spurred ideologically by the community mental health movement and methodologically by the development of family therapy techniques and innovative developments in social systems research. The seminal work of Jones[6] on therapeutic communities provided us with the first awareness of the power of the milieu and the potential for positive change that can be brought to bear in an open system. Cumming and Cumming[7] later developed the notion of environmental therapy, paving the way for a revolutionary look at the therapeutic and nontherapeutic aspects of hospitals. Caplan's early work[8] had implications for this approach, which in his later work[9] becomes a major impetus calling for "support systems as a sanctuary for persons undergoing stress" (p 6). Yet the social intervention methods necessary to transfer therapeutic environments into the "community" have been much slower to develop. Most of what has continued to prevail in most outpatient mental health service settings seems to be, rather, primarily a one-to-one model with the wistful fantasy that therapy will enable the client-patient to develop his own support system. There is obviously a giant step between the potentially controllable milieu in the hospital and the complex, haphazard, free-for-all which exists in a free society.

It is nonetheless important to begin looking at the relevant literature by examining the most basic of social units through some of the earlier writings on communications theory and family therapy. Beginning with the family therapy movement in the 1950s and 1960s, reflected in the works of Bateson, Jackson, Haley, and Weakland,[10] Minuchin,[11] and Satir,[12] the family approach expanded gradually to sophisticated methodologies in family network therapy, developed first by therapists doing home visits, and later incorporating others who happened to be at home.[13] Other similar forms[14,15] have added variations on the theme, evolving an interesting spectrum of structured methods to work with persons' individual family networks and including significant others who might play a part. Pattison and Pattison[16] showed how network analysis can therapeutically disrupt the cycle of psychotic behavior reinforced by patterned responses found in the networks of schizophrenics.

Another method[17] has the additional feature of focusing on roles and attitudes of agency people, while dividing up within the network sessions the various advocacy, executive, and facilitative functions of the therapist[18] among a team of providers to the family. The intent of this method differs slightly in that it is less interested in therapy per se and more focused on reorganizing relationships between family members and significant community persons and establishing checks and balances to keep them functional (so as to prevent further fragmentation, crisis, and symptomatology). The effort provides a positive experience for all concerned, including family members and agency staff.[19] Following these events, the network appoints a monitor to see that activities and agreements are carried out. This sort of effort resembles and functions like a giant planning–linking conference which one does when developing a treatment plan for a chronic patient.[20]

Other more direct and "therapy-like" innovative methods are developing rapidly and show promise in terms of dispelling the long-term mistrust between families of chronic patients and therapists. Psychoeducational methods described by groups on both sides of the Atlantic[21-25] appear far less mystifying and relatively easy for practitioners to administer. Research by these groups[21-24] seems to confirm the efforts of those methods in reducing the relapse rate in terms of symptomatology, as well as the utilization of hospital. Neither the English nor the American groups emphasize it, but they often conduct their family education meetings and patient interviews in the home, which undoubtedly has a "network effect" of its own. The education of the schizophrenic patient and his family about the nature of his "illness" runs counter (as Berkowitz et al.[25] have pointed out) to the usual assumption among family therapists that labelling a family member as a patient or as sick is taboo. Yet as Beels and McFarlane[26] have pointed out, this viewpoint "necessitates a narrow and mistaken view of the illness." They conclude in their recent review of the literature that the psychoeducation approach should be a major element in future systems-oriented family treatment programs. These new family treatment models usually involve some combination of multiple family support groups, family psychoeducation concerning the nature of the disorder, and training the family to reinforce the patient's taking responsibility to develop basic social and living skills around the house.

Although these new developments in the family therapy field are encouraging, they do not provide us with a scientific base for the application of social network methodology. How are these entities structured? How do they function? The work of Barnes[27] and his analysis of relationships in a Norwegian fishing village, and Bott,[28] who looked at a London neighborhood and the relationship between family and social networks, are usually regarded as the earliest attempts to describe the dimensions of networks. But it was Boissevain[29] who gave us a most interesting visual image of what these things might look like. He thought of social networks in terms of concentric zones. He described six zones, including the "personal cell" (close relatives and intimate friends); "intimate zone *A*"

(other relatives and friends); "intimate zone *B*" (friends and relatives who provide emotional support); the effective zone (neighbors, associates, and others
where there is instrumental support); the nominal zone (other work associates,
distant relatives, and other contacts with little importance); and the extended
zone (persons who may be quite inactive, forgotten, or may be acquainted with
persons in other zones). This schema, likening networks to a solar system sur-
rounded by a group of moving bodies, has given us a basic picture of what these
entities might look like. Todd[30] has further broadened our visual imagery of
networks by identifying three morphologic subtypes prevalent in our culture:
integrated, dispersed, and segmented (Fig. 18-1). Hurd, Llamas, and Pattison[31]
have found similar subtypes but defined them in terms of *extended kin dominant,
nuclear family dominant,* and *balanced* (about half kin and half non-kin). In the
extended family situation, everyone knows everyone else and little can happen
without everyone knowing about it. Here the loyalty and obligation is to the
family group, not the individual or his "personal freedom." A dispersed network, on the other hand, represents to some degree a reaction to an integrated
network in that it is very small and in extreme form no one knows anyone else.
Independence is a major characteristic.

A segmented or balanced network is halfway between. There are groups of
people who know each other but don't know the other groups. Kin and non-kin
both play significant roles and have responsibilities in each segment. Opportunities exist in such a situation to develop different kinds of self-esteem through
instrumental and affective dimensions of these relationships.

In general, there are two perspectives researchers have taken to examine
social networks. One, the "general network approach," looks at all of the connections among individuals who are members of a particular population. It is a
useful method of investigating characteristics of a community which aid program
planners with prevention-oriented efforts. Although mostly used for primary
prevention, it may also be viewed as a means of finding natural helpers who may
be recruited to "provide help to people in trouble before the trouble turns to
mental illness."[32] Obviously, it may be of great value as a perspective for clinical
staff attempting to tap into existing support systems to provide sustenance and
socialization for the chronically mentally ill persons in the community.[33]

The other perspective, which lends itself both to research and to direct
clinical methodologies, is called the "personal network" approach. This method
has been directly used by Pattison,[34] Cohen and Sokolovsky,[35] Mitchell,[36] Cutler,[37] Hammer,[38] and many others to examine the nature and impact of major
network variables on categories of individuals. This perspective is quite useful in
providing information about the personal networks of chronic patients. Unfortunately, there is considerable disagreement as to what measure and what sort of
instrument to use. Lin et al.,[36] McFarland et al.,[40] Cohen and Sokolovsky,[35] and
Pattison et al.[34] have all recently addressed the issue of methodological problems
in the use of network inventories. Each investigator seems to have a slightly

A.

(1) Closed system
(2) Very dense (high feedback)
(3) Highly supportive
(4) Not tolerant of new roles

INTEGRATED

B.

(1) Open system
(2) Low density (low feedback)
(3) Minimal support
(4) Considerable freedom for
       new behaviors

DISPERSED

C.

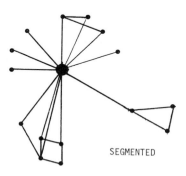

(1) Open system
(2) Medium density (some feedback)
(3) Supportive
(4) Significant opportunity for
       reinforcement of new behaviors

SEGMENTED

Fig. 18-1. Network types.

different approach, leaving even many experts confused when trying to interpret someone else's work. For example, schizophrenic or other chronically mentally ill persons are known to be poor historians and tend to lack absolute understanding of the nature of the relationship in which they are involved. Sokolovsky and Cohen[41] present what would appear to be a highly effective instrument for this population (the network analysis profile), which gathers data not only from the focal person but also from others in the immediate vicinity. Although this method addresses the problem of poor validity (due to the use of a patient as the sole informant), it requires considerably more time to administer than other methods and is not likely to be used in a clinical situation. The Pattison psychosocial Kinship System Inventory gathers data exclusively from the focal person, is quicker and easier to use, yet it would seem less likely to be valid with a severely mentally ill person as the only informant.

STRUCTURAL NETWORK CHARACTERISTICS

Structural characteristics are the morphologic aspects which define the limits and connections in networks. They include: size, kin, density, clustering, dispersion, and durability.

Size

The most obvious and perhaps the most commonly discussed variable in the literature is that of network size. Several researchers have reported a variety of interesting findings with a variety of age groups, diagnostic categories, and cultures. Pattison et al.[39] reported that emotionally healthy individuals live in functional psychosocial kinship systems of between 20 and 25 persons with whom they share interdependence for affective and instrumental support. He noted that psychotics had 4–6 persons in their networks. In a later study, Pattison et al.[31] found that persons with thought disorders had networks averaging about 13 in size. Similarly, in a major study of personal networks of ex-mental patients in single-room-occupancy hotels in New York, Sokolovsky et al.[42] determined that the schizophrenic group had an average of 10.2 persons in their networks. These findings have led to the obvious conclusion that psychotic individuals have smaller networks. Froland et al.[45] used network analysis to compare the characteristics of social networks to factors associated with positive social adjustment in mental health clients of the Marion County, Oregon Mental Health Program. They found smaller networks associated with hospital treatment and larger ones for those patients who were surviving as outpatients.

Kin

Another most interesting dimension is that of kin versus non-kin. Froland's group found greater contact with friends and kin in outpatients than with inpatients. Tolsdorf,[43] in a study of medical patients versus psychiatric patients, noted that although the numbers of kin are no different, the proportion of kin members in the networks of psychiatric patients is twice that of the networks of medical patients. Generally, the smaller the network the larger the proportion of kin present. This fact has a bearing on other dimensions as well, since more kin usually means higher density and overburdened (often high EE) relationships within the family.

Clustering and density

Density is defined as the rate of actual to possible connections among a set of individuals. Clustering is the number of mostly separate groups of three or more individuals in the network. Hirsch,[44] in a study of widows coping with the loss of the spouse, found that those who were involved in multi-clustered normal-size networks tended to overcome their grief more quickly and had less risk of the development of depression than those who were involved in denser networks primarily made up of family. His findings also indicated that multiplex friendships are significantly related to higher self-esteem and more satisfying social interaction in clusters. Increased density (a situation where most members of the network have relationships with one another) was negatively related to mental health in his study. In other words, those persons who did well had a good deal of separation between their family clusters and the other segments of their network, had less interruption of role identities within those segments and were minimally disturbed by the death of a family member. Hammer[38] feels that the measuring of clustering is more relevant than that of density in schizophrenics. She points out that there are typically five or six clusters with six persons each in the average network, whereas schizophrenics may have only one or possibly no definable clusters. High density and lack of clustering leave the schizophrenic patient trapped in a dense, intensive context which contains high EE factors as well and does not allow room for new relationships and roles which may lead to improved self-esteem.

INTERACTIONAL CHARACTERISTICS

Interactional characteristics are measures of the relationship which exist between individual network members. Unlike structural variables, they refer to the dynamic and functional qualities of these relationships. The interactional dimensions which are discussed below include multiplexity, reciprocity, nature/intensity and frequency of contact.

Multiplexity

"Multiplexity" or "multidimensionality" refers to the number of different functional areas, role relationships, or types of exchanges which characterize the ties between the focal person and other network members. Mitchell[36] discusses this concept in terms of the "content" areas, such as economic assistance, kinship obligation, religious involvement, or friendship, which the network link comprises.

Sokolovsky et al.,[42] used observational data to identify content areas (e.g., visiting and conversation, personal assistance, loans, etc.) of relationships of schizophrenics residing in a Manhattan SRO. They discovered that this group had significantly fewer multiplex relationships than other SRO residents, and that increased symptomatology was related to fewer multiplex relationships. These differences were most significant when the residents with no psychotic history were compared to schizophrenics with residual symptoms, the former group having over twice the number of multiplex relationships with kinship members, and three times the number of multiplex non-kin relationships. Multiplexity was also found to be associated with rates of rehospitalization within the schizophrenic group. Those tenants with psychotic histories who had not been readmitted since arriving at the hotel were able to form over two times the number of multiple linkages within the hotel as those who had been hospitalized.

Tolsdorf,[43] utilizing the structural/content/function taxonomy for categorizing network variables, identifies two measures which have relevance to multiplexity. He defines "multiplexity" as a content variable based on twelve "content areas" (primary kin, secondary kin, primary friend, secondary friend, economic, recreational, political, religious, sexual, fraternal, mutual aid, and service). Tolsdorf also delineates three broad "functions" which individuals in a network may serve for one another: support (tangible and intangible), advice, and feedback. From this scheme he develops a number of content variables which express the incidence and distribution of these functions in the network. Comparing a group of general medical in-patients to psychiatric in-patients he found that the former had three times the number of multiplex relationships than the latter. Forty-four percent of the medical patients' linkages were characterized as multiplex, while only 21 percent of psychiatric patients' linkages were multiplex.

Froland et al.[45] measured the multiplexity of network ties by the number of different kinds of exchanges (such as financial, emotional and personal support, entertainment, etc.), that are reported to occur within relationships. Among the mental health clinic patients studied they found more multiplexity within primary kin relationships. However, primary friendship involved only a slightly smaller degree of multiplexity. Greater multiplexity was also found with agency or institutional ties, such as professional helpers, than with secondary ties (relatives and acquaintances).

Reciprocity

The mutuality of affective and instrumental interchanges which characterize network relationships is referred to as reciprocity. Thus, if there is a balance of giving and receiving between the focal person and a network member, the relationship is said to be reciprocal or symmetric. Mitchell[36] describes this flow as "directedness," the inequality of transactions in relation to the focal person determining the directionality of the relationship.

Tolsdorf[43] found the directionality of functional relationships to be the most significant factor distinguishing the difference between the groups of medical and psychiatric patients he studied. Medical patients tended to have much more functional symmetry in their networks than psychiatric patients. That is, there was more reciprocity between the focal persons and network members in the former group; among psychiatric patients the measure of functional reciprocity indicated that they received more functional support from their network ties than they gave in return. Psychiatric patients also had twice the proportion of asymmetric relationships than the medical subjects had in their networks.

Froland's research,[45] however, did not reveal such a dramatic imbalance in the symmetry of relationships of psychiatric clients. Using the categories of spouse/children, other family, and good friends, he found that almost 80 percent of the clients he sampled reported asymmetrical relationships with their spouse and children. Other family members were more often perceived as receiving more help from the client than they provided. The opposite was true of "good friends" who were seen as providing more assistance to the client than he or she gave in return.

Contact Frequency

The frequency with which a person has contact with members of his network regardless of the method of contact (i.e. face-to-face, phone, mail, etc.), is often taken into account in network studies.

Among the mental health clinics in Froland's study, there was more frequent and direct contact (face-to-face, versus phone or mail) with primary friends than with family or relatives.[45] This was true both for those network members living nearby and for those living far away. Contact with network members living far away was least frequent for spouse and children rather than other family, relatives, or good friends.

Nature-intensity

The nature of kin relationships has been most thoroughly studied by the group at the Maudsley in London.[23,24] As mentioned previously, they have shown that these relationships have an unusually high "index of expressed emotion." In essence, there is a tendency in families of schizophrenics to take too seriously the feelings of others, to be critical of a patient, and to show generalized or rejecting types of hostility. The higher the EE the greater the stress on the patient. Schizophrenic patients who come from families with high stress (EE) are associated with high relapse rates.[23] In addition, family members of such patients tend to have a high degree of social isolation and invest much of their personal energy into the relationship with the schizophrenic patient. This work has been replicated by Falloon and his group at USC[19,22] and is becoming the research cornerstone for the new family counselling methods mentioned earlier.[25]

Tolsdorf's study[43] not only noted smaller networks for the group of psychiatric patients, but also what he called a "negative network orientation." Tolsdorf defines this attitude as "a set of expectations or beliefs that it is inadvisable, impossible, useless, or potentially dangerous to draw on network resources" (p 413). In Tolsdorf's study, all 10 of the psychiatric subjects demonstrated a negative network orientation. This finding is certainly consistent with Test's ingenious observation that chronic mental patients are "born with an inborn error of metabolism which prevents them from manufacturing network cement."[46]

In summary, then, the research shows the following with respect to chronic mental patients:

1. They tend to live in smaller networks.
2. They tend to have a greater proportion of their energies involved in kin relations.
3. They often have intensely negative or ambivalent qualities to their kin relationships (high EE).
4. They have fewer segments and higher density networks.
5. They have few long-term relationships except with kin.
6. There is very little multiplexity in their relationships (they do not have multidimensional aspects to their relationships).
7. There is very little reciprocity: chronically mentally ill tend to identify themselves as not doing much for other people.

These conclusions leave much unanswered. To what extent are social adjustment and hospital recidivism correlated with network variables? How do we know that these are the crucial variables or that manipulating them will be helpful? Do more networks always bode better for schizophrenic people? Perhaps additional size, clusters, or reciprocity will be too much stress for them. The answers are not yet entirely clear, but a knowledge of network variables and perhaps basic social network data on each patient would be very valuable in the planning for treatment of the chronically mentally ill.

Certainly an awareness of basic research findings with respect to these variables should at least lead us to make some assumptions about what might be promising interventions with regard to a clinical framework for network-building with chronic mental patients. To begin with, since chronically mentally ill persons apparently have this "negative network orientation"[43] there is little remaining doubt that without a great deal of encouragement from therapists, family members, psychiatrists, and/or case managers, they are not likely to involve themselves in more "normal-looking" social networks. Therefore most practitioners, particularly case managers, are aware that it is usually necessary to convince other network members to make the first move towards the patient. In addition, most clinicians now realize that they not only need to attempt to organize networks for patients, but that they should also organize their own resource networks in the community which can be utilized for new patients as they enter the system.[39] There are, then, a number of strategies one might deduce from looking at this literature. Clinicians should consider:

1. Networks for chronically mentally ill persons should be carefully enlarged to include new segments (or clusters).

2. Family members should be counselled or educated to be involved in other activities that will take their focus off of the patient in order to diminish the amount of expressed emotion in their relationship.[25]

3. Long term relationships should be established with an integrated spectrum of service providers, but also with permanent socialization segments in the community so that chronically mentally ill persons are not entirely dependent on the service sector to provide support.[39]

4. Chronically mentally ill persons can be helped to assume some responsibilities and activities that they can perform for other people in their network (including family), to enable them to build reciprocity and multiplexity into their relationship gradually, which process ultimately improves self-esteem and the likelihood of maintaining longer term relationships.

AN APPROACH TO NETWORK-BUILDING
FOR THE CHRONIC PATIENT

It would seem appropriate from what we now know to assume that in order to fit the social-skill and living-skill deficits of the chronic mental patient, the network should be augmented as a multisegmented one with special segments designed to enhance social skills, living skills, leisure skills, and work skills. Patients may then be evaluated in terms of their skill deficits in different segment areas and efforts can be made by therapists and case managers to help the patients enlarge certain network segments which they can then use to enhance the deficits they have in the various skill areas. For example, if a patient lives in a group home, this is where he should be learning daily living skills such as personal hygiene, food preparation, tidiness, and so forth.

Social skills may be taught in natural or nonservice settings such as church socialization centers, recovery incorporated groups, and other self-help organizations. Mental health workers should learn to take advantage of leisure activities already available in most communities that can be used to help patients develop leisure and recreational skills. Parks departments, bowling alleys, YMCA activities, and the like, are places where leisure training already occurs in the community and should therefore be used to help chronic patients. Patients may have to be taken to such places by staff or volunteers since they are not likely to risk showing up on their own.

The work or productive activities segment is one which is perhaps the most complicated to develop but is also extremely important for many patients. It is not true that all chronically mentally ill persons can not work. Many of them can and opportunities should be developed to enable them to work. This can generally begin with community college involvement or volunteer work activities, moving on to sheltered work or perhaps to graduated work, job sharing, or temporary employment such as the Fountain House model.[47] Work is, nonetheless, risky and stressful, and may stimulate relapse without continued support.

Lastly, the service sector must be dealt with more effectively by the patient. Chronically mentally ill persons definitely will need contact with the service sector for much of their lives outside the hospital. They will need at least some kind of ongoing medication supervised by a psychiatrist, they will usually need supportive psychotherapy, case management, welfare, pensions, social security, and so forth. Delivery of all of these kinds of services should be integrated and coordinated so that the patient does not "slip through the cracks in the system."

It is important to recognize that the clinician always has two major resources that he or she can tap into when planning treatment with a network orientation. The first, of course, is the patient himself, who usually wants to get better. By translating the findings into problems which are understandable to the patient, often the expected resistance does not materialize. On the other hand, social skill training, leisure training, work training, use of transportation always is done in a context. The clinician should consider holding planning-linking sessions with the members of these segments with the aim of developing treatment goals and objectives acceptable to all. Maintaining this perspective and working in this manner helps to relieve the burden the clinician experiences and makes his job more enjoyable and challenging, and himself less subject to burnout.

New findings from the research literature will, it is to be hoped, appear to support these notions. Yet it is clear that networks are no cure for schizophrenia. There is evidence, however, that network-oriented methods in conjunction with biologic treatments can help to transfer the "therapeutic community" from the hospital to the community.[48] More efforts are needed to answer the long-term question of whether these augmented networks can sustain themselves. Programs such as COPE in Tucson, Arizona were designed as augmented folk network programs[33] yet seem to have developed more in the direction of alternative services as opposed to additional groups of new friends.[49] Is the national evolution of all networks around chronic patients an institutional one? The risk, according to Collins and Pancoast,[32] certainly exists. New knowledge about the nature of networks should prevent that.

REFERENCES

1. Talbott JA: Deinstitutionalization: Avoiding the disasters of the past. *Hosp Community Psychiatry* 1979;30(9): 621–624
2. Greenblatt M, Becerra RM, Serafetinides EA: Social networks and mental health: An overview. *Am J Psychiatry* 1982;139:977–984

3. Bachrach LL: Overview model programs for chronic mental patients. *Am J Psychiatry* 1980;137:1023–1031
4. Llamas R, Pattison EM, Hurd G: Social networks: A link between psychiatric epidemiology and community mental health. *International Journal of Family Therapy* 1981;3:180–192
5. Beels CC: Social support and schizophrenia. *Schizophrenia* 1981;7(1):58–72
6. Jones M: *The Therapeutic Community.* New York, Basic Books, 1953
7. Cummings J and Cumming E: *Ego and Milieu.* New York, Atherton Press, 1962
8. Caplan G: *Principles of Preventive Psychiatry.* New York, Basic Books, 1963
9. Caplan G: *Support Systems and Community Mental Health: Lectures on Concept Development.* New York, Behavioral Publications, 1974, p 6
10. Bateson G, Jackson D, Haley J, et al.: Towards a theory of schizophrenia. *Behav Sci* 1956;251–264
11. Minuchin S: *Families and Family Therapy.* Cambridge, MA, Harvard University Press, 1974
12. Satir V: *Conjoint Family Therapy.* Palo Alto, CA, Science and Behavior Books, 1967
13. Speck RV, Attneave CL: *Family Networks.* New York, Vantage Books, 1973
14. Pattison EM, DeFrancisco D, Wood P, et al.: A psychosocial kinship model for family therapy. *Am J Psychiatry* 1975;132:1246–1251
15. Rueveni U: *Networking Families in Crisis.* New York, Human Sciences Press, 1979
16. Pattison EM, Pattison ML: Analysis of a schizophrenic psychosocial network. *Schizophr Bull* 1981;7:135–143
17. Cutler DL, Madore E: Community-family network therapy. *Community Ment Health J* 1980;16:144–155
18. Tomm KM, Wright LM: Training in Family Therapy: Perceptual, Conceptual, and Executive Skills. *Fam Process* 1979;18:227–250
19. Joint Commission on Accreditation of Hospitals: Principles for Accreditation on Community Mental Health Service Programs. Chicago JCAH, 1979
20. Cutler DL, Madore E: Community network therapy in a rural setting, in Keller P, Murray D (eds): *Innovations in Rural Community Mental Health.* National Association for Rural Mental Health, 1984
21. Falloon IRH, Liberman RP, Lillie FJ, et al. Family therapy of schizophrenics with high risk of relapse: A pilot study. *Fam Process* 1981;20:211–222
tions of schizophrenia: A controlled study. *N Engl J Med* 1982;306(24):1437–1440
23. Vaughn CE, Leff JP: The influence of family and social factors on the course of psychiatric illness: A comparison of schizophrenic and depressed neurotic patients. *Br J Psychiatry* 1976;120:125–137
24. Brown GW, Birley JLT, and Wing JK: Influence of family life on the course of schizophrenic disorders: A replication. *Br J Psychiatry* 1972;121:241–258
25. Berkowitz R, Kuipers L, Eberlein-Fries R, et al.: Lowering expressed emotion in relatives of schizophrenics, in *New Developments in Intervention with Families of Schizophrenics. New Directions for Mental Health Services, vol. 12.* San Francisco, Jossey-Bass, 1981, 27–48
26. Beels CC, McFarlane WR: Family treatments of schizophrenia: Background and state of the art. *Hosp Community Psychiatry* 1982;33(7)541–550
27. Barnes JA: Class and committees in a Norwegian island parish. *Human Relations* 1954;1:39–58
28. Bott E: *Family and Social Networks.* London, Tavistock Publications, 1957
29. Boissevain J: *Friends of Friends: Networks, Manipulators, and Coalitions.* New York, St. Martin's Press, 1974
30. Todd Workshop: *Support Networks.* Franklin Hampshire Community Mental Health Center, Oct. 1977
31. Hurd G, Llamas R, Pattison EM: The structure and function of normal social networks. Unpublished manuscript, 1983
32. Collins A, Pancoast DL: *Natural helping networks: A strategy for prevention.* National Association of Social Workers, Washington DC, 1976

33. Cutler DL: Volunteer support networks for chronic patients, in Stein L (ed): *New Directions for Mental Health Services.* San Francisco, Jossey-Bass, 1979, pp 67–74

34. Pattison EM, Llamas R, Hurd G: Social network mediation of anxiety. *Psychiatric Annals* 1979;9:56–67

35. Cohen CI, Sokolovsky J: Clinical use of network analysis in psychiatric and aged populations. *Community Ment Health J* 1979;15(3):203–213

36. Mitchell JC: The concept and use of social networks, in Mitchell JC (ed): *Social Networks in Urban Situations.* Manchester University Press, Manchester, 1969

37. Cutler DL: The chronically mentally ill, in Silverman WH (ed): *Community Mental Health: A Sourcebook for Professionals and Advisory Board Members.* New York, Praeger, 1981, pp 344–358

38. Hammer M: Social supports, social networks, and schizophrenia. *Schizophr Bull* 1981; 7(1):522–544

39. Lin N, Dean A, Ensel W: Social support scales: A methodological note. *Schizophr Bull* 1981;7(1):73–89

40. McFarlane AH, Neale KA, Norman GR, et al.: Methodological issues in developing a scale to measure social support. *Schizophr Bull* 1981;7(1):90–100

41. Sokolovsky J, Cohen CI: Toward a resolution of methodological dilemmas in network mapping. *Schizophr Bull* 1981;7(1):109–116

42. Sokolovsky J, Cohen C, Berger D, et al.: Personal networks of ex-mental patients in a Manhattan SRO hotel. *Human Organization* 1978;37(1):5–15

43. Tolsdorf CC: Social Networks, support, and coping: An exploratory study. *Fam Process* 1976;4:407–417

44. Hirsch BJ: Natural support systems and coping with major life changes. *Am J Community Psychol* 1980;8:153–166

45. Froland C, Brodsky MA, Olsen M, et al.: Social support and social adjustment: Implications for mental health professionals. *Community Ment Health J* 1979;15(2):82–93

46. Test MA: Continuity of care and case management in community treatment. Paper presented at the National Conference on Creating a Community Support System for the Long-Term Patient, Madison, WI, May, 1979

47. Beard J: The rehabilitation services of Fountain House, in Stein L, Test MA (eds): *Alternatives to Mental Hospital Treatment.* New York, Plenum Press, 1978, pp 201–208

48. Jones M: *Beyond the Therapeutic Community: Social Learning and Social Psychiatry.* New Haven, CT, Yale University Press, 1968

49. Nathan RG, Beigel A: Natural support systems: The development of socialization and residential networks for the chronic patient, in Cutler DL (ed): *Aftercare for the 80's. New Directions for Mental Health Services.* San Francisco, Jossey-Bass, 1983, pp 53–59

PART IV

Systems Issues

Jeffrey Rubin

18

Developments in the Financing and Economics of Mental Health Care

In recent years, mental health professionals have become more alert to and concerned about the important role of economic factors in the utilization of mental health services.[1] Over the same time period, economists have begun to apply their analytical constructs and techniques to problems of the mental health market.[2,3] In addition to the references noted, the evidence for both of these assertions is overwhelming. For example, in the five years since the American Psychiatric Association published the proceedings of its conference on the chronic mental patient,[4] the President's Commission on Mental Health published its report and offered a number of financing reforms,[5] the Department of Health and Human Services prepared a national plan for the chronically mentally ill that included a strong emphasis on financing changes,[6] and the Mental Health Systems Act with new funding and new programs was signed into law. The structure of federal financial support for mental health care was subsequently drastically altered through the consolidation of many programs into a block grant[7] and a tightening of eligibility conditions in the Social Security Disability Insurance (SSDI) and Supplemental Security Income (SSI) programs.[8]

In addition to these proposals and changes in the financing structure, many economic analyses of mental health programs and policies were published. The studies included analyses of the benefits and costs of special programs,[9,10] assessments of the economic impact of mental health litigation[11,12] and estimates of the effects of third-party coverage on the demand for mental health care.[13,14] There have also been studies on other factors influencing mental health policy. New

THE CHRONIC MENTAL PATIENT
ISBN 0-8089-1649-1

Copyright © 1984 by Grune & Stratton.
All rights of reproduction in any form reserved.

research was published on the role of housing supply[15] and boarding homes[16] in community placement, the effects of institutions on local economies,[17,18] and the impact of economic conditions and the work environment on the incidence of mental illness.[19,20]

The focus of this chapter is primarily on changes in the system of financing services for the chronically mentally ill. The findings of economic studies will be used to discuss the potential consequences of alternative financing structures and not as a subject of study themselves. The growing empirical and theoretical literature can be useful in evaluating different financing arrangements and in drawing conclusions about policy options.

An important caveat is in order before beginning. Care must be taken to avoid attaching excessive significance to the contributions of social science research to policy questions. The link between social science research and actual public policy is a tenuous one. Political factors, along with philosophic and ideologic shifts regarding the appropriate role for and size of the federal government, may be the determining elements in making policy choices. The significance of ideology in policy selection has, of course, been highlighted by the rationales offered by the Reagan administration to support such changes as block grants and a federalized Medicaid program. For example, arguing for a reorientation of responsibilities between the various levels of government, the President's Council of Economic Advisers concluded that it is "a basic tenet of the Administration that income redistribution is not a compelling justification in the 1980s for Federal taxing and spending programs" (p 92).[21]

These are not new arguments, nor is it true that past policy was conducted any differently, even though the ideology may have been different. For example, Aaron concluded from his review of several Great Society programs that "the findings of social science seemed to come after, rather than before, changes in policy, which suggests that political events may influence scholars more than research influences policy"[22] (p 9). Whether one would reach the same conclusion after a thorough review of the mental health field is uncertain. But it would appear that Aaron was correct when one compares recent changes in federal mental health financing with Aaron's conclusion that "neither the initial acceptance and enthusiasm for aggressive federal efforts to solve social problems nor the present rejection of and reticence about such undertakings are [sic] based on reliable information or on scholarly findings or indeed on the actual success or failures of the programs themselves" (p 10).[22]

We should thus harbor no illusions about the contributions of social science research to mental health policy. Yet as evidence mounts about the positive and negative elements of programs and policies, one can hope that the new information will be used in making future reforms. Certainly one goal of a block grant approach is to ensure that with many decisions under the aegis of state and local officials, the use of social science research in policy design can be increased. A maturing system of mental health advocacy may just be the mechanism through which research on such topics as the economics and financing of mental health services is utilized in the formation of public policy.

A CONCERN WITH FINANCING

In the last three years we have witnessed an extensive and rapid redirection in all realms of public policy. The extent to which a new administration in Washington could restructure much longstanding social policy serves as a warning against making naïve straight-line projections. Surely in 1978 no one could have predicted the shape of the 1983 budget. The current financing patterns for mental health are consequently not necessarily good predictors for 1988. A review of where financing for the chronically mentally ill (CMI) has been, where it is, and how it got there can offer some valuable lessons for those interested in achieving new reforms.

As recently as 1980, advocates who pressed for added public support of mental health care must have concluded that the furious pace of legislative and professional activity at the close of the last decade marked the culmination of years of turmoil. The forms and levels of financing in place today leave those advocates asking what went wrong. In only five years, the structure and extent of public mental health financing has gone through several dramatic changes. The speed with which these changes occurred is unprecedented in the history of American social welfare programs.

The selection of a financing structure traditionally depended largely on what one wished to achieve with respect to the services or individuals in question. A decision would be made to meet a need for income, medical care, or social services, and this would be followed by the selection of a level of funding and a program structure. Today it appears that ideology regarding the proper role of the federal government has replaced the distribution of services as the primary criterion by which financing decisions are made. With reduced federal spending and control, the important decisions about the level and type of mental health spending will be made at the state and local levels.

The impact of financing arrangements on the delivery of services for the CMI is best illustrated by considering three (of the many) ways to use a given sum of funds. One option is to allocate the money to individuals meeting eligibility criteria, but with no strings attached to use. Programs such as SSDI and SSI operate in this manner, although there are no ceilings on the total benefits paid. A second option is to offer reimbursement, up to the fund limit, for specific purposes for specific people. The reimbursement method is typical of medical insurance programs, though again there is no ceiling on total spending. A third possibility is to hire the staff and provide services directly. The Veterans Administration medical care system is the best example of this. In each case, the distribution of mental health services to individuals and the types of services people receive would be different, even though cost would be the same. Each case also represents a different pattern of control over decisions about the amount and type of care.

Another consequence of a financing choice is the distribution of benefits and costs. Service providers, consumers, and taxpayers will each be affected differently by the alternative financing systems. These distributional effects will, in turn, have an impact on political support for various financing arrangements.

Evaluating a financing system is more complex than simply analyzing the effects of public programs specially designed for a group or a problem. Sometimes mental health services are singled out and financed as separate programs, such as the CMHC program. Sometimes eligibility is tied to a related variable such as income, work disability, or veteran status. In these latter cases the CMI are part of the larger group of persons eligible for program benefits. One of the difficulties of not having a separate program, or at least separate eligibility criteria for the CMI, is evidenced by recent developments in SSDI. Definitional issues arise in the SSDI program because mental illness differs from physical impairments in the degree to which employability may be measurable. The usual tests applied by the disability examiner may require adjustment when applied to a person with mental illness.

Furthermore, the degree of program interrelationship, complexity, and overlap suggests that inquiries into financing have a wider scope than specific programs for a specific group. Cash payments, medical care, service programs, and such indirect assistance as advocacy, tax advantages, and research are all part of the financing system. Often overlooked are the private supports offered by individuals, voluntary agencies, and insurers. The system of financing support and services for the CMI and most disadvantaged groups is thus really a combination of multiple programs, each with its own objectives, eligibility criteria, funding level, and financing method. These attempts to analyze a (non)system of programs suggest that program evaluation be supplemented by analyses using individual or microdata. After identifying the population of concern, it would be feasible to work backwards and examine what benefits are received by which persons. Applying the method to a high quality microdata file, such as the Social Security Administration's Survey of Work and Disability,[23] would help identify persons "falling through the cracks."

Beyond the fact of individual social programs having an impact on the CMI, one could also consider how the CMI are affected by efforts to achieve a growing economy. Macroeconomic policies, though not as direct as specific programmatic efforts aimed at the CMI, can indirectly influence the availability of tax dollars by increasing taxpayer willingness to support additional public expenditures. An expanding economy, moreover, may reduce the stresses of unemployment and lead to more job opportunities for those CMI capable of productive work.

It is probably not a coincidence that as the economy blossomed in the 1960s, public spending grew rapidly. As "stagflation" with slow or no growth led to a fall in the growth rate of real income, efforts to restrict further expansion of the public sector seem a natural consequence. Mental health programs appear to be no more immune to this pattern than other programs; they are perhaps even more susceptible to it. Although the emphasis later in this chapter is on financing changes at the program level, it is important not to lose sight of the relevance of aggregate economic performance as a determinant of public spending for mental health care.

The concern over economic conditions is particularly relevant in the light of the Reagan administration view that "the Federal government can do more to provide lasting assistance to the disadvantaged by assuring strong and less inflationary economic growth than through income transfer programs"[21] (p 92). Although the emphasis on an expanding economy will benefit many of the disadvantaged who can participate in a market economy, it is not clear whether the CMI, especially the more severely impaired, will also get swept along on a wave of economic growth or will be left behind to depend on the diminishing array of federal social programs.

FINANCING—PAST AND PRESENT

Prior to 1963, public mental health care was largely a state function and largely institutional. Although such federal programs as SSDI and vocational rehabilitation existed, neither constituted a substantial reservoir of resources for the CMI. Even the 1963 Community Mental Health Center legislation had a strong state bias, with federal support designed largely as seed money.[24] Ultimately the states were to carry the fiscal ball. The passage of Medicare and Medicaid marked a major turning point in establishing the federal role in financing health care. Reagan's proposed "New Federalism" would extend the role even further by having the federal government take over Medicaid though there are unanswered questions about funding levels. Additional legislation establishing Title XX (Social Services) of the Social Security Act, the Supplemental Security Income program, and the Mental Health Systems Act indicated that throughout the 1970s there was an increasing federal role in providing categorical grants to states and cash payments to individuals to fund mental health services. At the same time, changes in the SSI and SSDI disability definitions and an increased awareness of these benefits led to an explosion in the number of beneficiaries (which has since slowed quite a bit) and an increase in the average benefit level.[25]

Corresponding with these programmatic changes, class action litigation in the 1970s put pressure on public mental health providers to improve the quality of care.[3] Though the long run consequences of litigation-induced policy changes are uncertain,[26] it appears that judicial activism led to increased mental health spending.[12]

By 1978, when the APA and the President's Commission on Mental Health co-sponsored a National Conference on the Chronic Mental Patient, it appeared that new and innovative financing and policy changes would be a hallmark of the Carter administration. As with other legislation, once established these programs would grow with the kind of momentum that carried along so many other programs.

Prior to the 1978 conference, the APA surveyed its members to obtain their sentiments on problems facing the chronically mentally ill. Not surprisingly, funding levels and the financing structure of public programs were identified as key issues. In his review of the survey, Talbott cited a litany of financing-related problems and proposals.[27] For example, he noted the need for benefit–cost studies to help establish priorities among treatment options. Many respondents also felt that there was a lack of funding, both public and private. Other related issues raised included the complexity of trying to meet the regulatory conditions imposed by different agencies and programs, the lack of a unified funding source, and the need for better benefits for the CMI in insurance programs.

In another paper in the same volume, Sharfstein et al. concluded "that existing funding patterns are a 'crazy quilt' of conflicting formulas, planning jurisdictions, eligibility requirements, etc. Both responsibility and resources for care of the chronically mentally ill are now fragmented among three levels of government and among a wide range of mental health and human service agencies . . ." (p 142).[28]

One proposal suggested by these authors and tested by NIMH is the comprehensive community support system. In this concept, a single agency is given resources and charged with the responsibility of insuring that their clients receive all necessary services. A case manager would act as a pathfinder through the thicket of regulatory and administrative problems the CMI might encounter in using cash transfer, service, and medical programs. The basic model has long been used with some success in the federal–state vocational rehabilitation program, though with an important difference: the rehabilitation program uses employment as its measure of outcome.

Professional opinion and legislation seemed destined to push the financing of mental health care toward the consolidation model, but with the advent of the Alcohol and Drug Abuse and Mental Health Services Block Grant, the prospects for complete implementation of the CSP model were drastically curtailed.

The push toward a comprehensive financing program with expanded benefits for the CMI seemed all but inevitable just six years ago. In 1978, the President's Commission on Mental Health issued a series of recommendations which later served as the blueprint for the Mental Health Systems Act, designed to produce "a comprehensive and integrated system of care that draws on the strengths of both the public and private sector" (p 16).[5]

In another section of the Commission's report, there was a call to establish a national priority to meet the needs of the CMI. In particular, the Commission recommended the development of a National Plan that would include a method to allocate resources.

A National Plan was issued in December by the Steering Committee on the Chronically Mentally Ill (Department of Health and Human Services).[29] In addition to providing background information and offering a detailed program of services, research, and advocacy, the Committee presented a review of the existing financing system and a series of reform strategies and recommendations. A summary and a critique of the entire national plan were published in *Hospital and Community Psychiatry* in October 1981.[6,30]

The financing proposals were designed to achieve a de-emphasis on institutions and a growth in community alternatives. The report surveys existing programs and documents the lack of a comprehensible and comprehensive financing system.

The programs surveyed in the National Plan include SSI, SSDI, Medicare, Medicaid, and Social Services. The first two programs involve cash payments and the next two reimburse the cost of medical services for eligible clients. While these four programs are the significant ones in terms of expenditures, Social Services offers some interesting insights into what may happen under a block grant system. Under Social Services, a given amount of funds (unlike the other programs which have no such ceiling) is allocated to the states, which in turn are required to satisfy certain conditions. The number and type of services are left largely to state discretion. Having only limited budgets, states must choose between providing fewer services per person, charging fees for some services, or setting eligibility conditions so that fewer persons become eligible. As noted in the DHHS National Plan, "the failure of states to target more monies to the service needs of the chronically mentally ill can thus be seen as a combination of scarcity of funds and competition for funds, which is an inherent feature of the Title XX program" (p 3/23).[29] The same can be said for the Alcohol and Drug Abuse and Mental Health Services block grant.

It will ultimately be a state and local decision whether federal funds should be supplemented, who the beneficiaries should be, and the specific form of the benefits. The prospects for extensive state spending for the CMI are not good. States are faced with federal budget cuts in almost all areas. Moreover, many states now face legislated limits on new taxes, and others are reluctant to raise what taxes they can to avoid putting their state at a competitive disadvantage in attracting new businesses and jobs.

There is no easy way to say which form of financing, block grants or categorical programs, is better. From an advocate's viewpoint, a series of categorical federal programs with additional support for a case management system would be the best form. State legislators and mental health administrators might disagree because of the lack of control over decision-making in federal categorical aid. It appears that the authors of the National Plan would have preferred less complexity and more money. With the programs instituted by the Reagan administration, it appears that they will get less of both.

FINANCING—A GLIMPSE AT THE FUTURE

In the National Plan, a series of incremental reforms (largely affecting Medicaid) were proposed. Most of the proposals fell short of being changes in financing structure and instead involved changes in client and service eligibility and reimbursement. Services would still be financed or paid for through the same structure: a categorical state-federal system with open-ended (no ceiling) matching, where the federal matching rate is inversely related to the state's capacity to finance services itself. An alternative is to establish a separate program with its own funding base, such as vocational rehabilitation, where the case manager would have wide discretion over the way funds are used.

As suggested previously, plans for comprehensive reform imposed by federal mandate appear unlikely at this time. Instead, the new system of block grants and restricted eligibility for cash and medical benefits seems certain to survive for at least another year. As categorical grant programs decline in number and as the purchasing power of new block grants is eroded in the future, it will fall to two systems of support to finance any expansion of mental health services for the CMI. Each will have different consequences for those who are served, in what way and with which services.

One method of financing services for the CMI, albeit somewhat indirect, is to make direct cash payments through existing disability transfer programs or through welfare programs. In the disability programs, qualifying for benefits requires a documented disability and either inadequate income (for SSI) or sufficient prior attachment to the labor force in covered employment (for SSDI). In either case, it is unlikely that the cash benefits alone would be sufficient to allow a recipient to meet normal expenses and purchase other services in the community. If associated medical benefits were not paid for, individual payments could be increased. Still, there is a need to avoid the private market when the consumer may be unable to select rationally from available benefit packages. Moreover, recent activities at the federal level have served to restrict eligibility under these programs by tightening the definition of disability and by holding down future increases in benefits.

The second system of support to which we might turn is state governments. With whatever block grants and categorical aid they receive, states have the option of supplementing these funds with their own revenues. While extensive expansion of state funding throughout the country is unlikely, for reasons noted earlier, some states may decide to use this opportunity to restructure their mental health system. The logic and ideology that guide the current administration suggest that returning these decisions on the type and amount of care to states, counties, and localities will help insure that citizens get what they want and are willing to pay for. The arguments for block grants are nowhere more succinctly stated than in the 1983 Budget. "The block grants will serve program purposes similar to the categorical programs consolidated, but will allow states the flexibility to coordinate and improve the effectiveness of services for their citizens. The block grants streamline program administration by reducing unnecessary Federal regulatory, legal, and reporting requirements previously imposed on the States and grantees. Duplicative and low priority programs can be eliminated, while gaps in needed local services can be filled" (p 5/135).[31] Focusing on the pros and cons of what block grants are designed to achieve really would miss the point. More important is that funding levels have been cut and that the likelihood of any extensive growth in the future is slim.

If, after block grants and other federal reforms are fully implemented, the result is fewer dollars for the CMI, then families and voluntary organizations will have to take up the slack. If they cannot, the problems of the CMI will go unanswered to a degree greater than ever before. It is a sobering thought and is indicative of just how much has happened in five years.

A FINAL WORD ON ECONOMIC RESEARCH

Whatever decisions are made regarding funding levels, there will still remain the issue of using those funds efficiently and equitably. Further economic research may improve our knowledge about such equity and efficiency issues as the impact of structural changes in the financing system, the cost effectiveness of alternative treatment programs, and the consequences of a growing economy for the CMI, but economic research does not change economic facts.

While the quality of economic evaluations of mental health policies and programs is good and getting better, the results do not constitute a ringing endorsement for one form of care and treatment over another.[10] Moreover, the distribution of costs and benefits from institutional closings suggests that the political economy of reforming mental health programs may continue to be an obstacle to achieving the desired goals. Unless the concentration of costs on institutional workers and the local economy can be distributed across other members of the public, we will continue to hear opposition to institutional changes. The economic effects of deinstitutionalization on families and on neighborhoods will also continue to be an issue.

By focusing attention on the economic (but not necessarily measurable) effects of mental health policies, we can better understand the responses of individuals to changes in policy variables. Unfortunately, there is yet no good model of the economics of mental health decision-making at the state level. It is difficult to know how state legislators will respond to block grants when we have so little empirical knowledge about the pattern of and rationale for state mental health policy decisions. The problem arises, of course, because so much of the mental health system for the CMI is not the typical market. Consumers are not choosing patterns of consumption to maximize their well-being, and producers are not arranging their affairs to maximize profits. Decisions about the way resources are used, who receives them, and how they are produced are grounded on factors difficult to quantify. Factors such as local political events and the extent of vocal lobbying efforts may influence decisions more than any economic evidence. Until better models of mental health decision-making are developed and tested, it is unlikely that the contribution of economic research to mental health policy can be much more than minimal. As I warned earlier in this chapter, the findings of program evaluations can contribute just so much to the decision-making process. Noneconomic variables may overwhelm any economic argument one can make for instituting change. In an environment such as this, perhaps the best one can hope for is to document the economic consequences of alternative policies, let the advocates of alternative views have their say, and hope that the end result is an improvement for the CMI and the taxpayer.

REFERENCES

1. Menninger WW: Economic issues involved in providing effective care for the chronic mental patient, in Talbott JA (ed): *The Chronic Mental Patient.* Washington, DC, American Psychiatric Association, 1978, pp 151–156
2. McGuire TG, Weisbrod BA (eds): *Economics and Mental Health.* Series EN, No. 1. Rockville, MD, NIMH, 1981
3. Rubin J: *Economics, Mental Health, and the Law.* Lexington, MA, DC Heath, 1978
4. Talbott JA (ed): *The Chronic Mental Patient.* Washington, DC, American Psychiatric Association, 1978
5. Report to the President from the President's Commission on Mental Health, Vol. 1, and Task Panel Reports Submitted to the President's Commission on Mental Health, Volumes 2–4. Washington, DC, US Government Printing Office, 1978
6. Rubin J: The national plan for the chronically mentally ill: A review of financing proposals. *Hosp Community Psychiatry* 1981;32:704–713
7. General Accounting Office: *A Summary and Comparison of the Legislative Provisions of the Block Grants Created by the 1981 Omnibus Budget Reconciliation Act.* Washington, DC, GAO, 1982
8. McGough PJ: Social Security Disability Insurance Program. Hearings before the Committee on Finance, US Senate, 97th Congress, 2nd session. Washington, DC, US Government Printing Office, 1982
9. Weisbrod BA: Benefit–cost analysis of a controlled experiment: Treating the mentally ill. *J Hum Resour* 1981;16:523–548
10. Rubin J: Benefit–cost analysis and the care of the chronic psychiatric patient in the community, in Barofsky I, Budson R (eds): *The Chronic Psychiatric Patient in the Community.* Jamaica, NY, SP Medical & Scientific Books, 1983, pp 457–474

11. Lambrinos J, Rubin J: The determinants of average daily census in public mental hospitals: A simultaneous model. *Med Care* 1981;19:895–906
12. Rubin J: Judicial standards and the financing of mental health services. *Inquiry* 1980;17:165–171
13. McGuire T: *Financing Psychotherapy: Costs, Effects, and Public Policy*. Cambridge, MA, Balinger, 1981
14. Craig TJ, Patterson DY: A comparison of mental health costs and utilization under three insurance models. *Med Care* 1981;19:184–194
15. Scott NJ, Scott RA: The impact of housing markets on deinstitutionalization. *Administration in Mental Health* 1980;7:210–222
16. Emerson RM, Rockford EB Jr, Shaw LL: Economics and enterprise in board and care homes for the mentally ill. *American Behavioral Scientist* 1981;24:771–785
17. Frank RG, Welch WP: Contracting state mental hospital systems. *J Health Polit Policy Law* 1982;6:676–683
18. Moore GA: Mental health deinstitutionalization and the regional economy: A model and case study. *Soc Sci Med [C]* 1981;15:175–189
19. Catalano R, Dooley D, Jackson R: Economic predictors of admissions to mental health facilities in a nonmetropolitan community. *J Health Soc Behav* 1981;22:284–297
20. Staten ME, Umbeck J: Information costs and incentives to shirk: Disability compensation of air traffic controllers. *American Economic Review* 1982;72:1023–1037
21. The Annual Report of the Council of Economic Advisers, in *Economic Report of the President*. Washington, DC, US Government Printing Office, 1982
22. Aaron HJ: *Politics and Professors: The Great Society in Perspective*. Washington, DC, Brookings Institution, 1978
23. Bye B, Schechter E: *1978 Survey of Disability and Work: Technical Introduction*. Washington, DC, Social Security Administration Pub No 13-11745, 1982
24. Dorris WL, McGuire TG: Federal involvement with mental-health services: An evaluation of the community mental health center program, in Altman SH, Sapolsky HM (eds): *Federal Health Programs*. Lexington, MA, DC Health, 1981, pp 83–101
25. Sunshine J: Disability payments stabilizing after era of accelerating growth. *Monthly Labor Review* 1981;104:17–22
26. Rubin J: A survey of mental health policy options. *J Health Polit Policy Law* 1980;5:234–249
27. Talbott JA: What are the problems of chronic mental patients—a report of a survey of psychiatrists' concerns, in Talbott JA (ed): *The Chronic Mental Patient*. Washington, DC, American Psychiatric Association, 1978, pp 1–7
28. Sharfstein SS, Turner JEC, Clark HW: Financing issues in providing services for the chronically mentally ill and disabled, in Talbott JA (ed): *The Chronic Mental Patient*. Washington, DC, American Psychiatric Association, 1978, pp 137–150
29. Department of Health and Human Services Steering Committee on the Chronically Mentally Ill: *Toward a National Plan for the Chronically Mentally Ill*. Washington, DC, DHHS, 1980
30. Talbott JA: The national plan for the chronically mentally ill: A programmatic analysis. *Hosp Community Psychiatry* 1981;32:699–704
31. Executive Office of the President, Office of Management and Budget: *Budget of the United States Government, Fiscal Year 1983*. Washington, DC, US Government Printing Office, 1982

Allan Beigel
Teddi Fine

19

Legislation

Patient's complaint: loss of direction, confusion, and depression resulting from
        decreased legislative impetus
Diagnosis: misguided myopia based on over-attention to Mental Health Systems
        Act
Prognosis: excellent chance of recovery, with appropriately corrected broader
        view of issue
Rx: corrective lenses providing wider perspective on legislative and regulatory
matters.

The foregoing hypothetical medical record belongs to a patient who, in his deep
and abiding concern for the chronically mentally ill, based his singular hope for
meeting the health, social, housing, and other needs of this population upon
passage of the Mental Health Systems Act.[1] This myopic view could indeed lead
to a sense of futility and depression.

The President's Commission on Mental Health,[2] which provided the initial
impetus for the Mental Health Systems Act (MHSA), met and deliberated for
18 months. In the ensuing two and a half years, Congress acted to draft a
response to the Commission's recommendations—many of which clearly identified the chronically mentally ill as an "underserved" population in need of
Congressional attention. The legislation itself, PL 96-398, was to have acted as a
springboard for federal, state, and local action to remediate the plight of the
chronically mentally ill, particularly the deinstitutionalized population.

This three-and-one-half-year struggle for implementation of a series of programs targeted to meet the myriad needs of the mentally ill (including a special
priority for the chronically mentally ill) was undone in less than one quarter of
that time, early in the Reagan administration. While strong interest group efforts

THE CHRONIC MENTAL PATIENT   Copyright © 1984 by Grune & Stratton.
ISBN 0-8089-1649-1   All rights of reproduction in any form reserved.

were successful in saving the initiatives of the MHSA and other (ADAMHA) programs from consolidation into one of four health block grants (themselves a consolidation of over 40 federal health programs), the MHSA was not wholly saved from repeal. It was, rather, deauthorized and relegated to inclusion in a special Alcohol, Drug Abuse, and Mental Health Services Block Grant, with many of the special features of the MHSA removed. Mental health and medical organizations were successful in retaining some mention of the chronically mentally ill in the block, but any specific federal impetus through program design or implementation was lost. States can now use the funds as they choose, within rather wide parameters. The funds themselves were radically reduced from those contained in the original MHSA.

Despite this development, if one steps back and looks not at the history of this one piece of legislation but rather reviews the gamut of legislative initiatives over the past five years, including State initiatives, the view of what government has been doing to enhance the life of the chronically mentally ill becomes substantially brighter, within the current framework of declining federal dollars and federal programmatic leadership.

From this perspective, therefore, it is more readily apparent that progress has indeed been made during the past five years in the legislative arena with respect to the needs of the chronically mentally ill. This paper will examine many of these, with an eye toward future legislative directions, future local, state, and federal efforts not only to "hold the line" but to take substantial programmatic strides forward.

FEDERAL INITIATIVES

Community Support Program

The Community Support Program (CSP) established by the National Institute of Mental Health (NIMH) was begun in 1977, shortly after the convening of the President's Commission on Mental Health (PCMH). While its initial objectives were not tied to the recommendations of the Commission, its work has been consistent with both the articulated objectives and stated recommendations contained in the Final Report of the PCMH.[2]

The CSP was initiated as a pilot program to help states develop community-based health and social-support resources for the deinstitutionalized chronically mentally ill. Federal funds were targeted to support and encourage systematic changes allowing for better care for the chronically mentally ill, and not to support direct service delivery. In the past several years, almost 20 state pilots have been implemented. The overwhelming majority of them continue in operation today, notwithstanding severe federal budgetary restrictions.

Evaluation of these programs[3] has demonstrated a marked positive result, through both increased state awareness of and funding for community-based programs benefiting the chronically mentally ill, and in many instances the implementation of state legislation and state-level program units to initiate or continue pilot efforts in this area. Concomitant with the initial federal investment in this program, many states designated their own resources to support the programmatic effort and to initiate direct services in conjunction with the system changes and improvements which the program inaugurated. Some estimates indicate that for each dollar of federal CSP funds, states have "kicked in" an additional eighteen.[4]

There have been state-level activities to benefit the chronically mentally ill in states other than those 20 that have been formally involved in the CSP, such as the development of program models derivative of the original without direct federal support. This has been true not only at the state level, but also at the local level where communities have initiated their own CSP efforts based upon the federal program model.

Studies have found that in most of the programs, the target populations involved have been among the most disturbed and at-risk individuals—the chronically mentally ill.[3] Positive results from the implementation of the program and its associated efforts have been found. The most significant of the findings has been that patients in the program frequently decreased their rate of hospitalization by more than 50 percent (compared to the rate in existence prior to the program's initiation).[3]

The positive experience with the program has led to benefits not only at the state and local level, but also at the federal level, where during the past several years new initiatives have resulted. In an interagency agreement with the Rehabilitation Services Administration (RSA), for example, the CSP has become involved in a $1 million research initiative. Moreover, the significant evidence of its substantial positive effects upon the chronically mentally ill has "saved" CSP from extermination in the FY 1983 budget. Congress in the lame duck session agreed to continue the program as a separate categorical program, funded at $6 million, in contrast to the administration's proposed termination or the Senate's proposed consolidation of CSP into the ADAMHA block grant.

A National Plan for the Chronically Mentally Ill

Partly as a result of the initiatives of the PCMH and partly based on the leadership of the NIMH, the latter began, in the final years of the Carter Administration, to develop a "national plan for the chronically mentally ill" which reflected broad-based input from numerous organizations and individuals involved in the field.

The document underwent substantial revision in order to achieve maximum consensus. Because of a sizable controversy within both the mental health community and in the administration regarding a number of the recommendations, the Carter administration was reluctant to release the document. As a result of mounting constituency pressure, however, the document was finally published in draft form over the signature of Secretary Harris in the last days of the Carter administration.[5]

While neither the release of the document nor its contents received wide publicity, the plan for the chronically mentally ill has had and continues to have a significant policy impact as a resource document for federal, state, and local initiatives in meeting the needs of the chronically mentally ill.

At the same time, because many of its recommendations had significant fiscal implications for existing funding mechanisms—Medicare, Medicaid, and SSI—its impact on Federal legislative initiatives has been limited. Nonetheless, such a blueprint could be enormously useful in the future, particularly when greater federal, state, and local funding resources again become available to deal with the numerous problems highlighted in the plan.

Patients' Rights

While, as noted earlier, the service provisions of the Mental Health Systems Act were repealed and ultimately incorporated in the administration's "block grant" approach to service delivery, the "patients' rights" section of the MHSA remains. This includes a model "bill of rights" for the mentally ill, which may be implemented by the states at their discretion. In fact, as a result of this legislation and local pressures, most states have now implemented a section on the rights of the chronically mentally ill and other mentally disordered individuals in their various mental health acts.

Furthermore, while the Reagan administration had proposed radical cutbacks in the regulations associated with Section 504 of the Rehabilitations Act, these efforts have met with relatively little success and this "Civil Rights Act for the Handicapped" has continued to have an enormous positive impact on the chronically mentally ill. As a result, handicapped individuals, including the chronically mentally ill, have begun to be able to assert a right to be included in programs that receive public funds and to assure their access to facilities which serve them. In conjunction with the Education for All Handicapped Children Act (PL 94-142), another piece of legislation that also recently withstood an administration attempt to radically and negatively alter its regulations, Section 504 has been responsible for opening schools to handicapped children and requiring these educational institutions to provide appropriate training and services. For handicapped adults, Section 504 has meant increased job and job-training opportunities, along with access to transportation, housing, and recreational services that were previously unavailable.

As a result of a November 1981 hearing, legislation was introduced in the 97th Congress to amend Section 1915 of the Public Health Services Act, replacing the concept of "least restrictive setting" with that of "optimal therapeutic setting." When and if this legislation is reintroduced and adopted in the 98th

Congress, individuals residing in public in-patient mental health facilities would be placed in an "optimal therapeutic setting," in-patient or outpatient, whichever is more appropriate. The intent of this legislation is to return the responsibility for patient placement to physicians, rather than the courts. The key provision of this legislation would allow for an increased balance between the rights of the patient and the responsibility of treating physicians and mental health professionals who are in the decision-making roles with regard to patient placement.

Nursing Home Regulations

Many of the chronically mentally ill have been placed in less than optimal settings, and regrettably, many of them include nursing homes. Over the past five years, considerable efforts have been undertaken to ensure that nursing homes become more responsive to the special needs of the chronically mentally ill.

As current Medicare law is written, there is no incentive for nursing homes to ensure appropriate diagnosis of and treatment for the mentally ill residing in such facilities. If, as some reports indicate,[6] well over 50 percent of those now in nursing homes are in fact mentally ill, many nursing homes (if such persons were diagnosed with primary mental illness) could lose their licensure, which provides eligibility for Medicare reimbursement. The current law specifies that no greater than 49 percent of patients may be so diagnosed, since if the population of mentally ill is over 50 percent of the total in the facility, the "nursing homes" would be recategorized as "mental institutions."

While no major effort has been undertaken to date by Congress to alter this statutory requirement, there were efforts under the Carter administration to ameliorate the plight of those diagnosed as chronically mentally ill and residing in nursing facilities.

Draft regulations were proposed which provided for training the staff of a nursing home (whether a skilled nursing facility or an intermediate care facility) to meet the special needs of the chronically mentally ill, appropriate psychiatric consultation for chronically mentally ill individuals residing in nursing homes, and increased attention by those nursing homes which contained a significant proportion of chronically mentally ill individuals.

While the above-mentioned regulations were withdrawn by the current administration in favor of a potentially damaging effort to reduce the number of regulations having an impact on nursing home operation, this course of action has been rebuffed by Congress, leading to the current "neutral" situation.

Nonetheless, recent press accounts[7] noted that for many older persons, what has been attributed as "senility" is actually depression, a reversible psychiatric illness, and may in the coming Congress provide an impetus for renewed effort to better staff nursing homes and other long-term care facilities with physicians and other professionals trained to provide treatment for mental illness.

As long as a significant number of chronically mentally ill individuals remain in nursing homes and as long as other housing opportunities for these individuals outside public institutions are limited, it is likely that close attention to the role of nursing homes in the care and treatment of the chronically mentally ill will continue.

Housing

Increasing the availability of appropriate residential alternatives for the chronically mentally ill apart from public institutions and nursing homes has been a major priority during the past 5 years. The American Psychiatric Association, in a recently published report,[8] outlined the spectrum of residential facilities which the chronically mentally ill may appropriately use. Such facilities are either few in number or absent altogether in most communities.

Nonetheless, two major legislative breakthroughs with regard to the problem of housing the chronically mentally ill have taken place over the past several years. Continuing efforts by numerous mental health organizations to "open up" the Section 202 Housing Program within the Department of Housing and Urban Development (HUD) to chronically mentally ill individuals were finally successful. While Congress had never intended to leave out this group (and, in fact, the 1978 Conference Report to the Housing and Community Development Act Amendments of 1978 affirms the intent that "the chronically mentally ill" were eligible handicapped individuals), they had never been specifically included by the Administration in the implementation of this program. Finally, in April 1982, HUD rewrote its regulations to include specifically the chronically mentally ill as eligible for Section 202 housing assistance.

Just as success was achieved with respect to the inclusion of the mentally ill under the section 202 program, however, the Reagan administration proposed to halve the funding allocation for the program and substantially increase the interest rate paid on loans to construct Section 202 housing. In Congressional action in the lame duck session of the 97th Congress, however, the $453 million included in the President's budget was increased to $634 million, providing an additional 4000 units of housing, and the proposed $11^5/8$ percent loan rate was rejected, with the current $9^1/4$ percent rate being retained. It will be critical to watch this program carefully to ensure that the mentally ill and other handicapped persons receive a "fair share" of the housing assistance funding, particularly since the program has pitted this population group against one of the most powerful voting blocks in the country—the elderly.

The second pertinent development relates to Section 802 of the MHSA another provision which was maintained in law even though a significant portion of this act was repealed. Section 802 mandated a continued report to Congress on the basic shelter needs of the chronically mentally ill. That report now has been completed by the NIMH and is scheduled for publication soon. The document will provide a further framework for housing applicants and others concerned about the residential needs of the chronically mentally ill to press for further action.

Training Initiatives

Despite substantial efforts on the part of the current administration first to reduce and more recently eliminate funds for clinical training, this NIMH program continues. With the sizable reduction in available resources, however, there has been a fundamental and comprehensive redirection of the psychiatric and related training programs to increase their clinical instruction and experience in dealing with the special mental health problems of identified unserved and underserved populations—particularly the chronically mentally ill (with a special emphasis on those who have been deinstitutionalized to community settings). Thus, the reduction in the availability of funds notwithstanding, the relative emphasis on the use of those funds for this population and other underserved or unserved populations has increased the amount of resources available for training initiatives in this area.

The redirected efforts for training programs in these areas include five major elements:

1. Teaching cost support to academic institutions (including medical schools) has been focused on the development of increased faculty capacity for instruction in the special mental health needs of underserved populations, including the chronically mentally ill.
2. Teaching support calls for more focused training of students so they are in a better position to meet the special needs of these identified populations.
3. Training funds available for those in primary care specialties have been redirected to enhance training and skill development in the management of those with mental illness with a redefined role for the psychiatrist to a consultative and referral relationship in the field of liaison psychiatry.
4. Support for state and local agencies to develop more effective methods for estimating and planning mental health manpower needs as they related to these special populations.
5. A requirement which obligates each trainee receiving an NIMH stipend to provide a payback in in-kind service in a setting which addresses the needs of an unserved or underserved population such as the chronically mentally ill.

Financing Initiatives

Despite initial optimism as a result of the efforts of the PCMH and the recommendations contained in the National Plan for the Chronically Mentally Ill, progress in this area has been especially slow. With "pro-competition" approaches now favored in both the administration and Congress, changes in either Medicare or Medicaid to benefit further the chronically mentally ill are unlikely at this time. Efforts to remove altogether the unique and discriminatory ceilings placed on the treatment of mental illness under Medicare have met with little success, notwithstanding the introduction of legislation as well as hearings in the 97th Congress. Furthermore, recent audits by the administration relating to the use of alternative institutional settings have suggested that previous flexibility in the use of existing financing mechanisms for the chronically mentally ill may be reduced or abandoned.

The outcome of funding under Medicare for the chronically mentally ill hangs in the balance, awaiting legislative initiatives in the upcoming 98th Congress as well as the results of a DHHS demonstration program which would provide outcome data on the effects of changing the outpatient Medicare psychiatric coverage in terms of both funds and providers. The most positive potential outcome in the area of providers might be the inclusion of community mental health centers (CMHCs) under appropriate physician/psychiatrist direction, as eligible Medicare providers.

The 98th Congress will provide a more clear indication of the direction which may be taken with respect to Medicaid. If the Reagan administration's "New Federalism" comes to pass and Medicaid is federalized in exchange for state assumption of other now federally-funded programs, the plight of the chronically mentally ill could substantially worsen. Optional services (including clinical services and in-patient psychiatric treatment in psychiatric facilities) currently provided by many states would likely be eliminated and greater restrictions on outpatient care could be imposed. We have learned already that the portions of the "New Federalism" already in place are indeed hurting the operation of CMHCs and other health and mental health programs for the chronically mentally ill—forcing the closing of programs, staff cutbacks, and coming reduced patient loads.

At the same time, most of these adverse initiatives have been successfully challenged, and while there has been no significant improvement in the financial resources for the chronically mentally ill at the federal level, there has also been no significant worsening except in the area of Social Security Disability Insurance (SSDI).

Social Security Disability Insurance

Using the 1980 amendments to the Social Security Act regarding mandatory continuing disability investigations of Federal Disability Program beneficiaries,[9] the current administration imposed (on top of the regular review process) a stepped-up effort designed to save several hundred million dollars in the first year by making drastic reductions in the disability rolls. While the principal purpose of this stepped-up review process was ostensibly to remove inappropriate beneficiaries, thereby decreasing fraud and abuse, the new reviews have also required recipients to meet new and more stringent non-statutory eligibility requirements, including their ability to work.

After several months of implementation, it became evident that this process was having a disproportionately negative impact on chronically mentally ill individuals. A significant number of psychiatric patients who clinically manifested an inability to engage in consistent and substantial gainful employment was being denied disability benefits by reviews conducted in an often perfunctory fashion, without adequate medical evidence or attention to individual patient problems. A large number of benefits to schizophrenics and other chronically mentally ill persons (who had been receiving these disability benefits for many years) were being terminated. Worse, though most of these terminations were being overturned subsequently by an Administrative Law Judge (ALJ), the law called for the discontinuation of benefits as soon as termination was recommended by the reviewer. Many CMI patients were therefore unable to support themselves until their disability benefits were reinstated—a process which could take as long as 18 months.

In addition, a greatly increased number of new applicants were being judged ineligible, thereby preventing many chronically mentally ill individuals from being discharged from institutions, and actually costing the federal and state governments *more* money as a result of continued institutionalization.

Congressional and interest group review of this situation indicated that the apparent culprit was the disability manual itself, which was being used for these reviews and which is not subject to public comment (as are regulations). Many individuals with serious residual symptoms (including chronic schizophrenics), who had nonetheless been able to make a marginal adjustment to the demands of semi-independent living outside of a facility, were being denied benefits because they were unable to meet the stringent new review requirements associated with their impairment. Using the existing disability standards, many of these individuals were being found capable of "unskilled work" despite the continued presence of severe psychiatric symptomatology that would worsen if the individual were subjected to a nonprotected work environment.

Procedural problems also arose, because many of the preliminary reviews conducted at the state level were being undertaken either by nonphysician claims managers or physicians with insufficient training to identify or determine what the exact level of emotional impairment was. Worse, purchased consultative reviews conducted at the request of the State Disability Offices were often of brief duration and without any prior review of medical history.

Strong response on the part of numerous mental health organizations to these developments has resulted in a slowing down of the review process by the administration. Several bills were introduced during the 97th Congress to address this problem, and a compromise bill[10] was passed during the lame duck session at the end of Congress, which contains the following provisions:

1. Extension of benefits through ALJ appeal completion (with payback if not reinstated to SSDI rolls) or through June 1984, whichever comes first, for all individuals undergoing comprehensive disability investigation (CDI) between date of enactment and October 1983. (Those individuals already in the process would begin receiving benefits on the date of enactment through the time remaining in their appeal process. If successful in appeal, any unpaid benefits withheld prior to enactment would be repaid in lump sum.)

2. A requirement that the Secretary slow down the CDI review process in states which have serious backlogs notwithstanding a good faith effort to process all CDI reviews and initial claims in a timely fashion.

3. Establishing a required face-to-face evidence hearing at the reconsideration review (first level review), with a clear enunciation of a beneficiary's right to counsel, a full review of medical records, etc. (The hearing record will *not* be closed as the result of the hearing—a provision of the original bill against which the APA argued.)

4. A semi-annual report to Congress by the Secretary regarding the CDI process, including number of terminations, appeals, etc.

At the same time, the Government Accounting Office has completed an in-depth evaluation of the impact of the SSDI/CDI process on the mentally impaired. The full report is available through the Senate Special Committee on Aging.

STATE AND LOCAL INITIATIVES

Targeted Appropriations

In much the same way that training initiatives have recently been redirected to unserved and underserved populations, including the chronically mentally ill, many states have taken advantage of the "block grant" program as well as their own funding initiatives to develop "targeted" appropriations, which require that a certain proportion of available funds be used to meet the needs of high-priority populations, including the chronically mentally ill.

These efforts are designed to make certain that available funding is not used solely for generic mental health care, which often runs the risk of serving only the "worried well" or less seriously mentally ill. States are increasingly concerned that with limited resources, the available funds reach those who are most in need and that they perceive the chronically mentally ill as among those having the highest priority.

New Financing Initiatives

While the introduction of new financing initiatives has been relatively unsuccessful at the federal level, it is interesting to note that in both a positive and negative manner, these initiatives are occurring at the state and local levels.

Several states, for example, have begun to examine seriously whether their public institutions should continue to be operated by the state or whether a part or all of their services should be "contracted-out" to the private sector. While it has been increasingly common for state institutions to contract for physicians' and other services, an increasing number of examples is now occurring where an entire state institution has been contracted for management to the private sector.

This is clearly a development which needs to be watched, both with regard to its frequency and its efficacy. It if proves that operation of public institutions by the private sector is more cost-efficient, this could then free-up additional funding resources for the development of other support programs that would address the needs of those people being deinstitutionalized.

In this latter regard, the State of California has recently implemented an initiative which would "mainstream" into a "single stream of funding" funds previously available for public sector support of the mentally ill, including those with chronic disabilities. In California specifically, the previous state- and county-funded "Short-Doyle" program is now being merged on a demonstration basis with the State's Medi-Cal Program, and both programs are being placed for competitive bid in order to reduce the cost of health care. The cost of funding Short-Doyle would thus be reduced by some 80 percent.

Integrated Programming

Legislative and administrative efforts to coordinate various programmatic elements that have an impact on the needs of the chronically mentally ill have met with limited success. Efforts are still under way, for example, to more actively relate work rehabilitation programs in general to the specific needs of the chronically mentally ill. While some successful pilot efforts have been described, this entire area has been less than fruitful, and executive and legislative initiatives to extend cooperation between diverse programmatic and bureaucratic elements have been less than successful.

FUTURE DEVELOPMENTS

Based upon the efforts and events of the past five years, it is somewhat difficult (if not impossible) to predict with certainty what will be the important future developments in the legislative arena dealing with the chronically mentally ill. At the same time, there are certain very apparent themes that will have a significant impact on legislative direction.

For example, who is going to control, from a professional perspective, the care and treatment of the chronically mentally ill is still a relatively unresolved issue. Will these individuals continue to be considered persons whose primary problems are medical in nature, or will they be perceived, as is increasingly the case in some quarters, as requiring essentially social intervention? An ultimate determination as to which of these two directions is more appropriate or whether some new model—a combination of the two—is required, will have tremendous implications for legislative and financing directions.

The judicial arena continues to have an important impact on legislative initiatives related to the chronically mentally ill. The recent Supreme Court decisions in both the cases of *Mills v Rogers*[11] and *Romeo v Youngberg*[12] will have tremendous implications for how chronically mentally ill persons are treated in different environments. At the same time, the renderings of the Court in these and other cases at the state level will play a major role in determining how much legislative action is taken to improve the availability of care to this population.

Because of the emphasis on declining resources, most states and local communities will become increasingly concerned about the efficiency with which existing resources are being used. One can consequently anticipate that future legislative initiatives, particularly at the state level, will be oriented toward a consolidation of existing resources and toward furthering a more unified system of care than has previously existed. The indirect results of some of the pro-competition initiatives will ultimately be to reduce the flexibility and diversity of choices which have been previously available to the mentally ill, including those with chronic disorders, rather than to expand those alternatives. This may not necessarily be an adverse development, particularly if it allows for more successful monitoring of programs and ensuring that all programs which are available meet certain basic standards. If this competition approach is allowed to go unchecked and unmonitored through existing legislation or regulation, on the other hand, it is possible that the quality of care will fall, along with the availability of diverse resources.

REFERENCES

1. PL 96–398, Mental Health Systems Act, 1980
2. *Report to the President from the President's Commission on Mental Health*, Government Printing Office, 1978
3. Division of Biometry and Epidemiology, National Institute of Mental Health: Collaborative data collection and analysis for community support program demonstration projects. NIMH Contract #278-79-0031 (CP), 1981
4. National Institute of Mental Health. Unpublished data, 1981
5. US Department of Health and Human Services, Public Health Service: Toward a national plan for the chronically mentally ill. Report to the Secretary by the DHHS Steering Committee on the Chronically Mentally Ill. Washington DC, 1980
6. Glasscote RM, Beigel A, Gurel L, et al: Old folks at homes: A field study of nursing and board and care homes. Joint Information Service of the American Psychiatric Association and National Mental Health Association, Washington, DC 1976
7. Depression often Masquerades as Dementia. *Washington Post*, 29 Nov 1982
8. Ad Hoc Committee on the Chronic Mental Patient, in Talbott JA (ed): *The Chronic Mental Patient: Problems, Solutions and Recommendations for a Public Policy.* American Psychiatric Association, Washington, DC, 1978
9. PL 96-265, Social Security Disability Amendments of 1980
10. PL 97-455, Disability Amendments of 1982
11. *Mills v Rogers*, 102 S. Ct. 2442 (1982)
12. *Romeo v Youngberg*, 102 S.Ct. 2452 (1982)

Paul S. Appelbaum

20

Legal Issues

Mental health law, relatively neglected until the last 15 years, has developed so rapidly of late that papers written just a short time ago often have a curiously dated sound. Thus, five years ago, when the predecessor to this volume appeared, it contained a chapter written by two attorneys for the Mental Health Law Project, entitled "The Rights of the Chronic Mental Patient."[1] With the assurance that was characteristic of advocates at the time, the authors of the chapter detailed the emerging rights of patients in five areas and confidently predicted the acceptance of the most liberal, extant court decisions and statutes as nationwide norms.

Contemporary approaches to mental health law have quite a different ring. No longer do discussions focus exclusively on patients' rights—the interest of the state and of third parties are likely to be given prominent attention—and neither do they assume that rights will be expanded indefinitely. Recent writings have recognized the competing interests inherent in most legal issues pertaining to mental health care, and have urged a balanced approach to reconciling them. Even the Mental Health Law Project, the most aggressive and successful of patients' advocacy groups, is counseling caution in pursuing litigation, fearful of losing the gains it attained such a short time ago.[2]

The reasons for this abrupt shift in tone are several and interrelated. In an era of fiscal restraints, the recognition that the promulgation of legal rights inevitably entails the expenditure of scarce public funds has considerably dampened enthusiasm for their proliferation. Further, the public at large (and thus courts and legislatures) is beginning to perceive that the rights model, which posits and

THE CHRONIC MENTAL PATIENT
ISBN 0-8089-1649-1

Copyright © 1984 by Grune & Stratton.
All rights of reproduction in any form reserved.

thereby encourages an adversary relationship between treaters and patients, impedes the provision of care and creates some very unexpected side-effects for those it was intended to benefit. Finally, as the appellate courts (particularly the U.S. Supreme Court) have been called upon to review the most liberal lower court decisions, they have recoiled from the degree of judicial intervention in institutional affairs required to enforce an extensive set of rights.

This chapter will review the legal issues affecting the care of chronic mental patients, with an emphasis on their evolution during this recent transitional period. The discussion will be organized sequentially from the clinician's perspective, beginning with hospitalization and proceeding to consider in-hospital treatment and community-based care.

INITIATING HOSPITALIZATION

The last 15 years have seen a striking departure from traditional American practices regarding involuntary commitment of mental patients. From the inception of an organized system of mental health care in the second quarter of the nineteenth century, based in large part on the massive state hospital system, the criterion by which a patient's suitability for admission was measured was the patient's need for care. Even as the locus of treatment and the procedures governing commitment varied, this standard remained constant.

Recent changes in the conception of the rights of the individual *vis à vis* the state, however, have led many state and federal courts to reject a "need for treatment" standard for civil commitment on constitutional grounds. One of the earliest of these decisions, and a prototype for many of the others, was *Lessard v Schmidt,* a 1972 Wisconsin case.[3] Beginning with the observation that "the power of the state to deprive a person of the fundamental liberty to go unimpeded about his or her affairs must rest on a consideration that society has a compelling interest in such deprivation," the *Lessard* court proceeded to restrict the grounds for involuntary commitment to behavior that indicated an acute danger to oneself or to others.

Many courts and legislatures, influenced by analogous considerations, acted similarly to tighten the requirements for involuntary hospitalization. By 1982, all but two states (New York and Delaware) had statutorily replaced their treatment-oriented commitment criteria with "dangerousness" criteria,[4] and even in the two exceptional states, actual practice corresponded to a dangerousness standard. At the same time, the procedures by which commitment could be effected were being substantially revised. Protections similar to those granted criminal defendants were introduced, including (as in *Lessard*) the right to a speedy adversary hearing, representation by counsel, to be notified of the allegations and to be present at the hearing, to remain silent, and to have the state assume the burden of proving its case beyond a reasonable doubt.[3]

The empirical evidence on the effects of these changes is weak; many of the opportunities to conduct well-controlled investigations were lost when the new statutes were enacted. Some evidence suggests that the new statutes have made little difference to psychiatrists and judges, who continue to commit those who appear to be in need of care.[5] But many clinicians clearly believe that this "criminalization" of the commitment process has deprived a large number of patients of care they desperately need and are, by virtue of their illnesses, not capable of seeking for themselves.[6] There is reason to believe that a substantial segment of the public is coming to share this view, particularly as the effects of a poorly managed program of deinstitutionalization are becoming apparent nationwide.

The stricter commitment standards of the 1970s are still the accepted norm throughout the country. Yet the trend of the last five years has been to limit the more extreme manifestations of the movement to criminalize the commitment system, and in some cases to reverse its direction. This process began with the 1979 US Supreme Court decision in *Addington v Texas*.[7] The appellant in *Addington* asked, in terms that reflected the reasoning in *Lessard* and similar cases, that the Court require the adoption of a standard of proof of "beyond a reasonable doubt" in commitment hearings. The Court refused.

Writing for the majority, Chief Justice Burger rejected the analogy between commitment and criminal proceedings. ". . . [A] civil commitment proceeding can in no sense be equated to a criminal prosecution," he noted, since "state power is not exercised in a punitive sense" (p 424). Further, the probable inability of the state to prove either the fact of mental illness or the likelihood of dangerous behavior beyond a reasonable doubt meant that adoption of the stricter standard would force courts "to reject commitment for many patients desperately in need of institutionalized psychiatric care." Rejecting both the then current Texas standard of a preponderance of the evidence (the usual standard in civil cases) and the criminal standard of "beyond a reasonable doubt," the Court settled on the intermediate guideline of "clear and convincing evidence" (p 425).

This refusal to apply criminalized rules of procedure to civil commitment cases was echoed later the same year, as the Supreme Court rendered its decision in a case dealing with commitment of children, *Parham v J.R.*[8] Again the Court was asked to impose rigid adversary procedures that would have altered the practice of parents consenting to their children's "involuntary" psychiatric hospitalizations, just as they did to medical hospitalizations. In another opinion by Chief Justice Burger, the Court declined to disturb the status quo. The Chief Justice noted that the constitutional requirement for due process, in this case to protect the child against unwarranted hospitalization, was not always synonymous with a formal judicial hearing. Psychiatric review of parental admission decisions, he concluded, which occurred as a matter of course, was likely to be more meaningful than judicial oversight, and to provide an adequate check on maleficent parental motives.

The response of lower courts to the Supreme Court's leads in this area has been mixed. Some courts' opinions have continued to extend the criminal model. Among the most notable of such decisions was the California Supreme Court's opinion in *Doe v Gallinot,* which required probable cause hearings for emergency committees within 72 hours of admission.[9] On the other hand, even the *Doe* court did not require judicial hearings, but allowed less formal procedures conducted by hearing officers who might not even have legal training. Other courts have generally endorsed the criminal model, but have stopped short of accepting its most radical components, such as the requirement that all patients be informed prior to a psychiatric examination that might result in their commitment of their right to avoid "self-incrimination" by remaining silent.[10]

A recent decision in a closely watched New York case, however, largely rejected the need for criminal-style procedures.[11] The federal district court in *Project Release v Prevost,* faced with requests for adoption of what were essentially *Lessard*-type standards, rejected them in toto. The court ruled that the constitution did not require due process hearings after 48 hours of hospitalization or automatic judicial review within five days; patient access to copies of their hospital records before hearings; or the right to remain silent. Although the court interpreted New York's statute, in which commitment criteria are phrased in terms of patients' need for treatment, as requiring a finding of dangerousness, the need for an overt act to prove dangerousness for purposes of commitment was rejected. *Project Release* was subsequently upheld on appeal, and may signal the beginnings of a retreat from the procedural rigors imposed by *Lessard* and similar rulings.

Although some courts, as in *Project Release,* have cut back on procedural requirements, the judiciary has been reluctant to endorse any modification of the dangerousness criteria themselves. Some legislatures, however, have taken steps in this direction. Washington State now permits commitment on the grounds of a likely severe deterioration in a patient's condition, or because of the likelihood of serious harm to property.[12] Pennsylvania now allows *threats* of harm to self as well as *acts* (as long as there was "an act in furtherance of the threat") to serve as grounds for involuntary commitment.[13] One of the recent changes in the North Carolina statute broadens the definition of danger to self to include an inability to exercise self-control, judgment, and discretion in daily responsibilities or social relations; grossly irrational or inappropriate behavior, or other signs of severely impaired insight and judgment create a presumption that the patient is unable to care for himself.[14]

It is too early to characterize the trends of the last five years as constituting an abandonment of the changes of the previous decade. In many respects, the more recent statutory amendments and judicial opinions represent partial adjustments to what was clearly an initial overreaction. Yet it seems likely that the next decade will see an easing of some of the most rigorous substantive and procedural requirements for civil commitment. Given that the chronically mentally ill are often released despite a clear-cut need for care, this may mean a greater opportunity to use hospitalization earlier in the course of patients' decompensation, without waiting for patients to become dangerous to themselves or others.

TREATMENT IN THE HOSPITAL

The Right to Treatment

Treatment of chronic mental patients has often been impeded by the absence of sufficient staff and facilities to undertake the effort. One suggestion for remedying this situation, and for circumventing legislatures reluctant to appropriate the needed funds, was to create a constitutional right to treatment. Five years ago, enthusiasm for such a right was understandably running high. The evolution of the right to treatment began with a 1960 paper by Morton Birnbaum, in which the term was first used.[15] Birnbaum proposed that committed mental patients were entitled to treatment under a vaguely described constitutional doctrine that approximated the notion of basic fairness. Initial judicial recognition of a constitutional basis for this right came with the landmark Alabama case of *Wyatt v Stickney* in 1971.[16] As the right evolved, it came to be rooted in fourteenth amendment rights to substantive due process, which were considered to be infringed upon when the conditions of confinement (i.e., the absence of treatment) bore no relation to the purpose of hospitalization.

Not only had one court after another accepted this notion by the mid-1970s, but the outcome of right-to-treatment suits was considered such a foregone conclusion that many states began settling them by consent decrees rather than awaiting a judicial ruling.[17] These decrees obligated the states, as had the previous judgments in *Wyatt* and other cases, to expend sufficient funds to provide acceptable levels of staffing and physical facilities, and to attempt to implement active treatment for all patients. Also sensing the trend, a number of legislatures guaranteed a right to treatment statutorily, without waiting for what seemed like the inevitable suit.[18] No wonder writers in the late 1970s could claim that ". . . the rights to treatment and to protection from harm have become well-established" (p 54).[1]

The issue no longer looks that clear-cut. It has become apparent that there is substantial distance between the issuance of a judicial order, or even the signing of a consent decree, and actual implementation of the desired changes. Although considerable improvements have apparently occurred in the Alabama state hospitals, for example, the system is still not in compliance with the *Wyatt* order (nor is compliance considered likely), well over a decade after the initial ruling.[19] A similar story can be told about almost every leading right-to-treatment case.[20-22] The mere issuance of a judicial order has proven insufficient to compel legislatures to allocate adequate funds to unfavored state hospital systems. These are the same bodies, after all, that pursued a policy of deliberate underfunding of the institutions in question for nearly a century. Even when the state departments of mental health have agreed to a consent decree, legislatures have not always been willing to back up those commitments with the required appropriations.[22]

A number of ingenious devices have been suggested, whereby the federal courts could compel the states to allocate needed funds.[23] As a rule, however, those strategems that have been tried have proven ineffective. Further, the courts themselves, led by the US Supreme Court, have been shying away from the intensive involvement in institutional affairs required to administer many right-to-treatment orders. This growing legal backlash has rejected courts' involvement in day-to-day operations of institutions as an appropriate use of judicial powers.[24]

Although every lower court to consider the issue has acknowledged the existence of a constitutional right to treatment, until 1982 the US Supreme Court had assiduously avoided the question. The Court declined the opportunity to affirm a right to treatment in the 1975 case of *O'Connor v Donaldson*[25] and denied the existence of a statutory right in the 1981 case of *Halderman v Pennhurst.*[26] Even the Court's 1982 decision in *Youngberg v Romeo* framed the issue somewhat more narrowly.[27] *Youngberg* arose from a complaint about conditions in a Pennsylvania state school for the retarded, in which the plaintiff had suffered physical abuse at his own hands and those of his fellow residents, and consequently had been physically restrained for substantial periods of time. Although the original decision in the case had spoken broadly of a right to treatment, by the time the case reached the Supreme Court the arguments focused on the case's peculiar factual setting.

Drawing an analogy from cases in the criminal area dealing with prison conditions, the Court (in *Youngberg*) held that the involuntarily committed mentally retarded have the rights to freedom from restraint and protection from harm and to whatever minimal amount of training was necessary to protect those rights.[27] The Court did not explicitly reject a more broadly conceived right to treatment (as did Chief Justice Burger's concurrence), but the narrow base for its opinion suggested a certain reluctance to embrace the idea. Further, the court indicated that individual mental health professionals and administrators could not be held responsible for legislative failures to appropriate necessary funds—a limitation that will probably impede the development of future litigation. In addition, as will be discussed in greater detail below, *Youngberg* allowed the abrogation of even the narrow set of rights it created, if it could be shown that such an action reflected a judgment by a qualified professional. This, too, promises to limit application of right-to-treatment arguments.

The Supreme Court's failure specifically to endorse or to reject a right to treatment leaves the numerous lower court decisions undisturbed. The concept will therefore continue to have some impact on state mental health systems. There is also, clearly, leeway for lower courts to read into *Youngberg* their own more expansive notions of individual rights. The first post-*Youngberg* right to treatment decision, the North Dakota case of *ARC v Olson,* resembled many of the earlier opinions in this area in both its tone and the scope of rights granted.[28] Of interest was the *Olson* court's reliance on new justifications for these rights, including the equal protection clause of the federal constitution, and North Dakota state law. State statutes and state constitutional provisions may become increasingly important sources of law in this area.[29]

The Right to Refuse Treatment

Among the conceptual innovations that accompanied the development of the mental patients' rights movement in the mid-1970s was the idea that all patients, even those involuntarily committed, ought to have the right to refuse unwanted treatment. This attempted elevation of treatment refusal to a constitutionally guaranteed right was intimately related to the previously discussed changes in the law of commitment and to the dispute over a right to treatment.

As long as the basis for involuntary hospitalization was the patient's need for treatment, as it was in most states until the last two decades, it would have made little sense to suggest that patients committed for the purpose of treatment should have the right to refuse it. With the shift to the use of dangerousness criteria for commitment, it seemed natural to some legal advocates to ask whether the state still retained a legitimate interest in the therapy of those it had hospitalized against their will. These civil libertarians argued that the state's avowed interest in preventing dangerous behavior was satisfied by the patient's detention in a mental facility. With the public thus protected, the argument went, the right of the individual patient to autonomous decision making about what was done to his mind and body took precedence over any residual societal interest in treating the patient's illness.

Also underlying much of the agitation for a right to refuse treatment was the recognition that, in many state facilities, patients were receiving less than optimal care.[30] The right to refuse treatment essentially represented an alternative strategy of change to the establishment of a right to treatment. Either would protect the patient from psychiatric malfeasance; advocates of a right to refuse treatment were simply less optimistic about the extent of the change that could ever be anticipated in many state hospital systems. As difficulties became apparent in the enforcement of a right to treatment, the right to refuse treatment attracted further support.

The initial test of a right to refuse treatment came in Massachusetts, in the case of *Rogers v Okin*.[31] Lawyers representing patients at Boston State Hospital alleged that a number of their clients' constitutional rights were being violated when medication was administered over their objections. From the justifications offered by the plaintiffs, the federal district court selected two bases for a right to refuse treatment: the first amendment right to freedom of speech, which the court thought was implicated by the "mind-altering" effects of psychotropic drugs; and the right to privacy. The initial decision, which was affirmed in its essentials by the appellate court on privacy grounds,[32] granted to all patients a right to refuse treatment (except in narrowly-defined emergencies) who had not been found incompetent in a judicial hearing. Although *Rogers* aroused considerable protest from psychiatrists,[33] it served as an important precedent in similar cases in other states.[34,35]

Almost simultaneously with the proceedings in *Rogers,* a similar case was being litigated in New Jersey, *Rennie v Klein.*[36] Although the *Rennie* court also found a constitutional basis for a right to refuse, Judge Brotman, who was motivated largely by concerns about the quality of treatment in New Jersey state hospitals,[37] provided substantially more leeway for overriding the patient's decision. An independent psychiatrist was granted the power to conduct a hearing and—after taking into account the patient's dangerousness and degree of competency, the possibility of less restrictive forms of treatment, and the risk of permanent side-effects—to order involuntary medication. *Rennie* was substantially modified in the Third Circuit Court of Appeals, which upheld the right to refuse treatment, but essentially allowed a clinical decision about the patient's need for treatment to override the refusal.[38] As might be expected, *Rennie* was greeted with favor by many psychiatrists, who recognized that whatever sop it contained to those who favored a right to refuse, the procedures it mandated effectively negated any application of the right that might impair long-term patient care.

Rogers and *Rennie* were both appealed to the US Supreme Court. As the Court's ruling was awaited, the psychiatric profession and others responded to the lower courts' actions. Monitoring of the situation at Boston State Hospital,[39] where *Rogers* originated, and preliminary empirical data from elsewhere[40,41] suggested that granting a right to refuse treatment would result in a substantial number of patients rejecting treatment. In one unit at Boston State Hospital, at times up to 20 percent of the patients were refusing medication.[39] Data also suggested that many long-term refusals were associated with delusional ideas about medication[40] and with an increased severity of illness.[41] In response, attempts were made to formulate clinical responses to patients' refusals.[42]

The courts meanwhile continued their activity in the area. The right to refuse was upheld on state law grounds in Colorado,[43] and other states considered legislative promulgation of a right of refusal. A federal court in Utah upheld that state's statute which, in limiting commitments to patients who were determined at the commitment hearing to be incompetent to decide about treatment, freed inpatient clinicians to treat all those under their supervision.[44] A statute designed to allow a similar process in Florida, however, was overturned on state constitutional grounds.[45]

When the right to refuse treatment ultimately reached the US Supreme Court, the results surprised many observers. After mulling over *Rogers* (now called *Mills v Rogers*) for nearly half a year, the Court declined to decide the constitutional issues in the case.[46] The case was instead remanded to the First Circuit Court of Appeals for determination of whether a Massachusetts state case, *In re Roe,*[47] established independent state grounds for a right to refuse treatment, thus obviating the need for a constitutional ruling. The issue was ultimately resolved by the Massachusetts Supreme Judicial Court on state law grounds, based on an idiosyncratic set of Massachusetts precedents. Thus, the case that many thought would decide the issue once and for all seems likely to have an impact only in its own state. On the other hand, shortly after remanding

Rogers, the Supreme Court accepted *Rennie* and, without the benefit of oral arguments, vacated the previous decisions in the case and remanded it for reconsideration in light of *Youngberg v Romeo.*[48]

Youngberg allowed patients' constitutional rights to freedom from restraint and from harm to be subordinated to decisions made by mental health professionals. The Court implied that these rights could be overridden either because institutional imperatives required such action, or because the patient's treatment needs necessitated it. If *Youngberg* is interpreted broadly by other courts considering the issue, the right to refuse may be moot. Although involuntary patients may nominally retain the right, the power of psychiatrists to treat them involuntarily when such is required to effect their treatment would all but eliminate its practical import. The sole remaining effect of the right to refuse would be to guarantee some reasonable process of reflection before involuntary treatment took place. It should be noted that there is near-universal agreement that *voluntary* patients have and will continue to have a right to refuse treatment.

Although the reconsideration of *Rennie* by the Third Circuit Court resulted in a confusing and ambiguous decision, there are some indications that this interpretation of *Youngberg* will be adopted by the lower courts. In *Project Release v Prevost,* the New York opinion that rejected criminalized commitment procedures, the court, applying *Youngberg,* found New York's administrative procedures to be adequate in overriding patients' refusals.[11] New York law allows patients to object to treatment, but also permits facilities then to compel treatment if the institution's director authorizes such action.[49] Additional, limited appeal is allowed within the bureaucracy of the Office of Mental Hygiene. The *Project Release* court found that this procedure more than met the requirements of *Youngberg.* An Arizona state court ruled similarly that that state's administrative procedures to guarantee that proper care was delivered provided adequate review of patient objections.[50]

For a time, commentators and textbook writers spoke of a near-absolute right to refuse treatment as an acknowledged constitutional reality. Although it is too early to rule out that possibility entirely, it seems more likely that the right to refuse will end up as the patient's right to have a competent determination made as to the reasonableness of the disputed treatment decision. In the absence of a comprehensive right to treatment, ironically, only patients who initially refuse treatment may have access to such careful review of their care.[30]

TREATMENT IN THE COMMUNITY

It is commonly observed with respect to funding of mental health programs that although the majority of patients are now in the community, the majority of funding is still given to in-patient institutions. A similar comment would be accurate with regard to mental health law: although the neglect of patients' needs and rights now appears to be much greater in the community than in institutions, the largest amount of legal capital is still invested in issues of institutional care.

The key questions in each locus of care are nonetheless the same: how to get sufficient resources for the task of treatment, and how to treat those who are reluctant to accept the care they need.

The status of a right to treatment for outpatients is even more tenuous than for in-patients, in large part because it was not as fully developed before the retreat from a broad concept of the right began. A number of cases urged the courts to accept the right to the "least restrictive alternative" as a component of the right to treatment. As employed in cases such as *Dixon v Weinberger*,[51] which dealt with conditions at St. Elizabeth's Hospital in Washington, DC, these arguments constituted a demand that only those patients who absolutely required in-patient care be subject to involuntary hospitalization. For the others, the plaintiffs requested that the federal government be compelled to create alternate, nonhospital-based services that would meet their needs in the community.

Dixon, coming as it did at the peak of right-to-treatment litigation, was settled by a consent decree in which the federal and District of Columbia governments agreed to the creation of community treatment alternatives and to the transfer of most in-patients to those facilities. As with the other right to treatment cases described earlier, unfortunately, the reality has fallen short of the promise.[20] It is not clear whether substantial numbers of additional community facilities have been created. As federal and district governments trade the blame, the population of St. Elizabeth's remains roughly stable and those in the community are left without adequate care.

Later attempts to achieve even the degree of success afforded the plaintiffs in *Dixon* have met with greater resistance. In the Kentucky case of *KARC v Conn.,* for example, a federal district court agreed that there was a right to treatment in the least restrictive alternative, but refused to order the creation of new facilities to accommodate that right or prevent the construction of a new in-patient facility.[52]

Even more significant has been the litigation in *Halderman v Pennhurst,* which dealt with residents in a Pennsylvania state school for the retarded.[53] The district court's decision in the case, among the most expansive of such rulings, ordered the state to close Pennhurst completely, on the grounds that an institution could never be the least restrictive form of care for the retarded. In addition, the state was ordered to create the requisite community facilities to which residents could be transferred. This order was never implemented, and repeated appeals have limited progress in this direction. The Third Circuit Court of Appeals endorsed the right to the least restrictive alternative, but on statutory rather than constitutional grounds.[54] The US Supreme Court rejected this interpretation, but left the issue of a constitutional right unanswered.[26] The Third Circuit then found the right to be based on state law, but its power to issue such a ruling is currently being challenged at the Supreme Court level.

The endless complexities of *Pennhurst,* the most closely watched case in the area, have left the question of a constitutional right to the least restrictive alternative somewhat up in the air. Indications that the US Supreme Court does not favor granting such a right, taken from dicta in *Pennhurst* and in *Youngberg v Romeo*, may cool lower courts' enthusiasm for rulings of this sort. Still it should be noted that the district court in *ARC v Olson*,[28] the North Dakota case discussed above, was able to rely on a state statute that granted the right to the least restrictive alternative as grounds for an order nearly as sweeping as the original decision in *Pennhurst*. As with in-patients' right to treatment, state law may become increasingly important in this area.

The issue of obtaining adequate treatment in the community has, of course, been complicated by the continuing deinstitutionalization of our large state hospital systems.[55] With thousands of discharged, chronically mentally ill patients living in most major cities, the capacity of even comparatively well-funded systems to cope with the patient load is limited. The status of deinstitutionalization as an official policy of most states has also contributed to a peculiar ambivalence toward those who are in need of care but cannot or will not request help directly. This was highlighted by the case of Rebecca Smith, "the woman in the box," who froze to death on a New York sidewalk, as municipal agencies argued about the legitimacy of efforts to save her life.[56] The tragic death of Smith pointed out the need for means of providing assistance to those who may not meet dangerousness criteria for involuntary commitment, but who are nevertheless unable to make reasoned decisions about their own care.

The traditional means of caring for the incompetent person involved the appointment of a guardian empowered to control the property and personal life of the ward. Guardians were ordinarily recompensed from the estates of those under their supervision; in the absence of sufficient funds for the purpose, guardians could usually be recruited only from family and close friends. The flood of deinstitutionalized mental patients in need of such services has demonstrated the inadequacies of the traditional system of guardianships. Usually without family or friends, and invariably penurious, these chronically mentally ill patients, whose affairs were once managed by the institutions in which they lived, are now often left to struggle on their own.

In a number of states, efforts have been made to meet this challenge. Public guardians have been appointed in some states for those who have no recourse to a private guardianship.[57] These positions are often part of the existing social welfare bureaucracy, and thus tend to suffer from the same shortage of funds and surplus of clients that afflict the welfare system. Other states have experimented with contracting guardianship services out to nonprofit agencies, or with the creation of adult services divisions, which provide the supervisory benefits of guardianship without the power to control patients' personal decisions.[57] All of these solutions have their limitations, some derived from inadequate appropriations to accomplish the task, others from the lack of a personal guardian–ward relationship that is necessary if one person is to be entrusted with making the most personal and far-reaching decisions about the life of another.

Even as experimentation continues with new forms of guardianship, efforts are being made to restrict the scope of guardians' powers.[58] In some cases, as with the movement toward limited guardianship, this reflects the laudable desire to confine the loss of autonomy to that absolutely necessary to the well-being of the incompetent. A recent Massachusetts case, however, *In the Matter of the Guardianship of Richard Roe III,*[47] established more problematic limitations on guardians' powers. The decision, rooted in a distrust of the goals of psychiatric treatment, as well as of the motives of family members who become guardians, held that only courts, and not guardians, could consent to treatment with psychotropic drugs over the objections of an incompetent ward. The court also established a complicated set of procedural and substantive guidelines for the decision process. If the precedent of this much-discussed case is widely adopted, it could further complicate efforts to provide treatment to those who once would have been institutionalized for care.

CONCLUSION

A detailed examination of all the legal issues likely to have an impact on the care of the chronically mentally ill would require much more than a single chapter for its completion.[59] Among the important issues that are not addressed here are efforts to limit the number of mentally ill who qualify for federal support under the social security system[60]; zoning laws that restrict attempts to provide group residences for chronic patients in the community[61]; and legal efforts to reduce education and housing discrimination against the mentally ill.[62,63]

It should nonetheless be clear that the last five years have not been a period of dramatic expansion of the legal rights of the mentally ill. It has instead been a time of consolidation, some retrenchment, and generally a period in which competing interests, which may have been ignored in the initial wave of enthusiasm for mental patients' rights, have been acknowledged and accommodated. It is unclear what lies ahead. Judging from recent trends, courts will be increasingly reluctant to affirm new rights for the mentally ill, particularly if those rights are likely to entail substantial costs to the states, to require extensive judicial supervision of institutional operations, or to significantly interfere with treatment of the mentally ill.

On the other hand, this period may represent only a temporary interlude of consolidation before new legal ground is marked out and new rights avowed. If this latter is the case, it will result not from an elaboration of the legal argumentation of the 1970s, but from the development of new legal theories in mental health law and an increasing resort to state statutory and constitutional grounds for decision. In either event, the current interlude provides those directly involved in the care of the chronically mentally ill with an opportunity to reflect on the meaning of the developments of the early and mid-1970s for their practices and to learn to accommodate them while still providing the best possible level of care.

REFERENCES

1. Friedman PR, Yohalem JB: The rights of the chronic mental patient, in Talbott JA (ed): *The Chronic Mental Patient: Problems, Solutions, and Recommendations for a Public Policy.* Washington, DC, American Psychiatric Association, 1978, pp 51-63
2. Ewing MF: The *Pennhurst* case—the Supreme Court fails to find a right to community services for mentally retarded people. *Clearinghouse Review* 1981;15:256-258
3. *Lessard v Schmidt*, 349 F Supp 1078 (ED Wis 1972)
4. Schwitzgebel RK: Survey of state commitment statutes, in McGarry AL, Schwitzgebel RK, Lipsett PD, et al: *Civil Commitment and Social Policy: An Evaluation of the Massachusetts Mental Health Reform Act of 1970.* Rockville, MD, NIMH, 1981, pp 47-83
5. Munetz MR, Kaufman KR, Rich CL: Modernization of a mental health act: I: Commitment patterns. *Bull Am Acad Psychiatry Law* 1980;8:83-93
6. Chodoff P: The case for involuntary hospitalization of the mentally ill. *Am J Psychiatry* 1976;133:497-501
7. *Addington v Texas*, 441 US 418 (1979)
8. *Parham v JR*, 442 US 584 (1979)
9. *Doe v Gallinot*, 486 F Supp 983 (CD Cal 1979)
10. *Suzuki v Yuen*, 617 F2d 173 (9th Cir 1980)
11. *Project Release v Prevost*, 551 F Supp 1298(EDNY 1982); 772 F2d 960(2 Cir 1983)
12. Durham ML, Pierce GL: Beyond deinstitutionalization: A commitment law in evolution. *Hosp Community Psychiatry* 1982;33:216-219
13. 50 Pennsylvania Statutes Annotated §7301 (1978)
14. Miller RD, Fiddleman PB: Involuntary civil commitment in North Carolina: The result of the 1979 statutory changes. *North Carolina Law Review* 1982;60:985-1026
15. Birnbaum M: The right to treatment. *American Bar Association Journal* 1960;46:499-505
16. *Wyatt v Stickney*, 325 F Supp 781 (MD Ala 1971), 344 F Supp 373 (MD Ala 1972)
17. Mills MJ: The right to treatment: Little law but much impact, in Grinspoon L (ed): *Psychiatry 1982: The American Psychiatric Association Annual Review.* Washington, DC, American Psychiatric Press, 1982, pp 361-370
18. Lyon MA, Levine ML, Zusman J: Patients' bills of rights: A survey of state statutes. *Mental Disability Law Reporter:* 1982;6:178-201
19. Drake J: Judicial implementation and *Wyatt v Stickney. Alabama Law Review* 1981;32:299-312
20. Armstrong B: St. Elizabeth's Hospital: Case study of a court order. *Hosp Community Psychiatry* 1979;30:42-46
21. Kihss P: Parents reject proposal in Willowbrook dispute. *New York Times* 13 Oct 1981, p B-4
22. Mass deinstitutionalization decree produces continued litigation. *Mental Disability Law Reporter* 1982;6:318-319
23. Fletcher WA: The discretionary constitution: Institutional remedies and judicial legitimacy. *Yale Law Journal* 1982;91:635-697
24. Horowitz DL: The judiciary: Umpire or empire? *Law and Human Behavior* 1982;6:129-144
25. *O'Connor v Donaldson*, 422 US 563 (1975)
26. *Pennhurst State School and Hospital v Halderman*, 451 US 1 (1981)
27. *Youngberg v Romeo*, 457 US 307 (1982)
28. *ARC of North Dakota v Olson*, 561 F Supp 473 (D.N.D. 1982); 713 F2d 1384 (8th Cir 1983)
29. Meisel A: The rights of the mentally ill under state constitutions. *Law and Contemporary Problems* 1982;45:7-40
30. Appelbaum PS, Gutheil TG: The right to refuse treatment: The real issue is quality of care. *Bull Am Acad Psychiatry Law* 1981;9:199-202
31. *Rogers v Okin*, 478 F Supp 1342 (D. Mass. 1979)
32. *Rogers v Okin*, 634 F2d 250 (1st Cir 1980)

33. Appelbaum PS, Gutheil TG: The Boston State Hospital Case: "Involuntary mind control," the constitution, and the "right to rot." *Am J Psychiatry* 1980;137:720–723
34. *Davis v Hubbard*, 506 F Supp 915 (D Ohio 1980)
35. *In re the Mental Health of KKB*, 609 P2d 747 (Okla 1980)
36. *Rennie v Klein*, 462 F Supp 1131 (DNJ 1978), 476 F(Supp) 1294 (DNJ 1979)
37. Brotman SS: Behind the bench on *Rennie v Klein*, in Doudera AE, Swazey JP (eds): *Refusing Treatment in Mental Health Institutions—Values in Conflict*. Ann Arbor, MI, AUPHA Press, 1982; pp 31–41
38. *Rennie v Klein*, 653 F2d 836 (3rd Cir 1981)
39. Gill MJ: Side effects of a right to refuse treatment lawsuit: The Boston State Hospital experience, in Doudera AE, Swazey JP (eds): *Refusing Treatment in Mental Health Institutions— Values in Conflict*. Ann Arbor, MI, AUPHA Press, 1982, pp 81–87
40. Appelbaum PS, Gutheil TG: Drug refusal: A study of psychiatric in-patients. *Am J Psychiatry* 1980;137:340–346
41. Marder SR, Mebane A, Chien CP, et al: A comparison of patients who refuse and consent to neuroleptic treatment. *Am J Psychiatry* 1983;140:470–472
42. Appelbaum PS, Gutheil TG: Clinical aspects of treatment refusal. *Comp Psychiatry* 1982;23:560–566
43. *Goedecke v State*, 603 P2d 123 (Colo 1979)
44. *AE & RR v Mitchell*, No. C78-466 (D Utah June 16 1980)
45. *Bentley v Florida ex rel Rogers*, 398 So.2d 992 (Fla App 1981)
46. *Mills v Rogers*, 457 US 291 (1982)
47. *In the Matter of Guardianship of Richard Roe III*, 421 NE 2d 40 (Mass 1981)
48. *Rennie v Klein*, 458 US 1119 (1982)
49. 14 NYCRR 27.8
50. *Anderson v State of Arizona*, 663 P2d 570 (Ariz App 1982)
51. *Dixon v Weinberger*, 405 F Supp 974 (D DC 1975)
52. *Kentucky ARC v Conn*, 510 F Supp 1233 (WD Ky 1980)
53. *Halderman v Pennhurst State School and Hospital*, 446 F Supp 1295 (ED Pa 1978)
54. *Halderman v Pennhurst State School and Hospital*, 612 F2d 84 (3d Cir 1979)
55. Bassuk EL, Gerson S: Deinstitutionalization and mental health services. *Scientific American* 1978;238:46–53
56. Herman R: Cold kills woman city was trying to rescue. *New York Times*, 27 Jan 1982, p A-1
57. Axilbund MT: *Exercising Judgment for the Disabled: Report of an Inquiry into Limited Guardianship, Public Guardianship, and Adult Protective Services in Six States*. Washington, Commission on the Mentally Disabled, American Bar Association, 1979
58. Appelbaum PS: Limitations on guardianship of the mentally disabled. *Hosp Community Psychiatry* 1982;33:183–184
59. Gutheil TG, Appelbaum PS: *Clinical Handbook of Psychiatry and the Law*. New York, McGraw-Hill, 1982
60. Bower B: Judge orders 20,000 returned to SSA disability rolls. *Psychiatric News* 4 Feb 1983, pp 1,10
61. Appelbaum PS: The zoning out of the mentally disabled. *Hosp Community Psychiatry* 1983;34:399–400
62. Appelbaum PS: Do the mentally disabled have the right to be physicians? *Hosp Community Psychiatry* 1982;33:351–352
63. Stolberg M: Housing opened for handicapped. *Pittsburgh Press* 8 Feb 1983, p A-6

Agnes B. Hatfield

21

The Family

It is important to understand the phenomenon of mental illness from the perspective of all those affected. This, of course, means the patient first of all, but it also includes the family, the mental health professional, and the community. The purpose of this chapter is to present the points of view of families as they live with a relative who is severely and chronically mentally ill. It is a perspective that has developed from research in which the family experience was elicited, from first-person accounts written by families, and from the documents of the consumer-advocacy movement of families, the National Alliance for the Mentally Ill.

It has become increasingly clear that the success of the movement toward care of the mentally ill in the community might well depend upon the capacities of families to sustain a large portion of the burden. As deinstitutionalization got underway, it was initially expected that the full array of services formerly received in the hospital would be available in some form in the community. This, of course, did not happen, and hospitals discharged large numbers of patients to their families. It is difficult to get an accurate estimate of how many patients do go home. After analyzing a number of reports, Goldman[1] concluded that about 65 percent of patients are discharged to their homes with one fourth of those still severely ill. There is an expectation that the numbers of families involved will increase, for the baby boom population is now reaching the vulnerable age at the same time that the cohort of vulnerable elderly is increasing. All of this is occurring at a time of fiscal restraint and reduction of social programs. Even those not living at home can make heavy demands on a family for financial

THE CHRONIC MENTAL PATIENT
ISBN 0-8089-1649-1

Copyright © 1984 by Grune & Stratton.
All rights of reproduction in any form reserved.

support, case management, rescue when in difficulty, and a temporary haven when the system fails.

While economic limitations partially explain the increased involvement with families, there is also an increased tendency to value the family and to question our overreliance on professionals to solve all human problems. Caplan[2] stressed the availability of families during times of crises and noted their contribution as sources of information, practical service, and concrete aid, and havens for rest and recuperation. Uzoka[3] has noted that persons usually turn to their families before using available social agencies. He feels that clinical workers have been too eager to label families as dysfunctional if they do not fit the clinician's stereotype of the adequate family.

The Report to the President of the President's Commission on Mental Health[4] reflected this new awareness of the family and the natural caregiving network. It stated that "people are usually better off when care is provided in settings that are near families and friends, and supportive networks" (p 12) and that "whenever possible, people should live at home and receive outpatient treatment in the community" (p 16). The Report recommends identifying the natural caregiving network and establishing linkages with them.

In recent literature, some therapists have spoken positively about the families of their patients and the contributions that the family makes.[5-9] Falloon et al.[5] criticized practitioners who reject families as overprotective and overintrusive, thus losing a valuable ally. Spitzer, Weinstein, and Nelson[8] note the family's role in identification of symptoms, determining the type of help sought and the type of hospital commitment, the length of hospitalization and the timing of discharge. Harbin[6] states that "many hospitals now work to include the patient's natural support system, and families are increasingly vocal about their right to stay involved with their hospitalized family members."

Taking everything into account, it is safe to predict that in the decade ahead the worlds of the families of mentally ill persons and the worlds of mental health providers will be increasingly brought together. How harmonious and fruitful this relationship will be may depend upon the worldview that each holds. A worldview is a sociologic term for a way of looking at people, events, and situations. One learns to see the world in a particular way, to interpret situations or define reality in terms of a particular point of view. It is logical to assume that to the degree that there is congruence between views of the world, there is mutuality of goals, collaboration, and mutual satisfaction.

THE WORLDVIEW OF THE FAMILY

The literature on mental illness to date has not provided us with an adequate picture of the scope of the family's burden.[1] Even though there is ample evidence to show that a severe or chronic physical illness or disability can have devastating effects on the family's capacity to cope,[10-13] there has not been a comparable effort to learn how a severe and chronic mental illness affects the family. There is some research, however, in which the family viewpoint has been directly assessed and some insightful observations made by mental health professionals.

Psychosocial Costs to the Family

Kreisman and Joy[14] made an extensive review of the literature in 1974 and concluded that the burden experienced by families caring for persons with mental illness had been poorly assessed and as a consequence the mental health community was not meeting the needs of these families. They felt that the ambiguous nature of such an illness and its episodic eruption required constant adjustment which was highly stressful. Lamb[15] also stated that the burden was very great, noting that "for those whose mentally ill child has been discharged from the hospital and come home, there has been more than a discernable impact; there has been a major upheaval in their lives and the lives of all family members" (p 35). Using a series of interviews with families, Kreisman, Simmens, and Joy[16] concluded that families of deinstitutionalized persons were significantly less happy than a comparison group. The difference was marked enough that they thought these families "at risk" for symptomatology or role impairment. The burden of care was only part of the explanation. Just the knowledge of the patient's impairment brought on anger, worry, frustration, and hopelessness.

Doll[17] used a sentence completion test to tap the subjective burdens of the family caregiver. He, too, found that these families were in an emotionally untenable and highly demanding situation which they feared could go on forever. Thompson, Doll, and Lefton[18] found that the burden was especially heavy when a single adult was coping alone. In their concluding statements, these researchers observed that there are forces that are "pervasively, silently, corroding the stability of these families" (p 12) and that by neglecting these forces the whole community-centered mental health treatment experiment may be threatened.

Emotions such as constant anxiety, depression, guilt, disappointment, frustration, and anger may be normal reactions to a confusing, incomprehensible, and apparently unmodifiable situation.[19] Raymond, Slaby, and Lieb[20] observed that for many families "the diagnosis of a mental illness, particularly schizophrenia, can be as tragic as the announcement of impending death" (p 497). They likened the stages of reaching emotional adjustment to that of the stages of adjustment to death, a predictable cycle of denial, anger, and mourning. Some families, they note, cope well or even rise to a new level of adjustment; others cannot come to terms and are left with lasting scars.

Hatfield[21] surveyed 89 members of a self-help group in which 57 percent of the families had a disabled relative living at home. Many of these patients were reported as displaying psychiatric disturbances of considerable severity; over a third had threatened suicide, four had succeeded. Families said that they lived in a constant state of tension, always on guard, and, as one beleaguered mother said, she "was constantly concerned about what would happen next." Some families felt that their other children suffered too much hardship and sometimes neglect. One mother attributed this to being "mentally and emotionally exhausted and therefore having little patience to cope" (p 356). Siblings typically could not understand the patient's irrational and bizarre behavior, blamed him for misbehaving, and resented their parents for what they considered failure to exercise proper control over him. Marriages suffered as a result of this severe problem and family members felt keenly the loss of time and energy for leisure activities and interpersonal relationships.

Respondents in the Hatfield study found the stress of living with a schizo-phrenic person "nearly unbearable at times," fraught with "severe physical and emotional drain" and resulting in "feelings of utter defeat" (p 358). Anxiety was high and aggravated by the unpredictability of events. The parents in the group expressed grief over the loss of a once-promising child who now seemed like a stranger to them. They found it difficult, because of the cyclic nature of the illness, to work through feelings of grief and disappointment.

Arey and Warheit[22] gathered survey data on the mental health of 4202 adults and established that there was a significantly higher percentage of psychiatric symptoms as a consequence of caring for a person with mental illness. They found that early age of onset seriously exacerbates the problems faced by these families. High rates of anxiety, depression, and psychosocial dysfunction were reported.

Families identify a wide range of painful emotional responses that from their perspective are a result of a person in their family becoming mentally ill: loss, grief, and mourning; guilt, frustration, and anger; anxiety, stress, and hopeless-ness; even mental and physical exhaustion. Several personal accounts of living with mental illness corroborate this distressing picture: Park,[23] Vine,[24] and Wasow.[25]

The Families' Needs for Help

There is a deep, sometimes unstated existential question that looms up when someone becomes mentally ill: Why did this have to happen to us? What did we do to deserve this terrible blow? This is asking much more than a question of personal guilt. It is raising a universal question of why there is tragedy and death in a world that is expected to make sense. It is the kind of question Job asked when so many disasters were visited on him. To be human is to be vulnerable, to be at risk for severe illness and disability, premature death, or mental illness. Families need help in accepting this.

In spite of the chronic sorrow that family members feel, life goes on, and there are a myriad of problems presented by mental illness with which they must cope. Hatfield[26] approached families directly to get their views on what they felt they needed to meet their problems effectively. Top priorities for these families were knowledge and understanding of the patients' symptoms, specific suggestions for coping with patients' behaviors, and people to talk to who had known the illness.

A further study was conducted by Hatfield[27] in which 138 family caregivers using mental health services indicated their needs and goals in therapy. Participants in the study were all members of self-help groups located in nine states and affiliated with the National Alliance for the Mentally Ill. They were given a list of 21 possible needs or goals for therapy and were asked to check off those that corresponded to their purposes in seeking service. Items in Table 1 have been arranged to show the frequency and rank order with which families prioritized their needs. Families indicated that they needed relief from the heavy anxiety that was weighing them down. Beyond this, perhaps needed to relieve their anxiety, was the need to learn how to motivate the patient, how to set appropriate expectations, where to find help during crisis, and how to understand the nature of mental illness better.

A final need of families coping with mental illness is to find ways for its members, in spite of constant burdens and tensions, to meet their own needs for

Table 21-1.
What families want of therapists (N = 138).

Goals of Therapy*	Frequency With Which Chosen	
	N	%
Reduction of anxiety about patient	96	70
Learning to motivate patient to do more	89	64
Understanding appropriate expectations	89	64
Assistance during times of crisis	83	60
Learning about the nature of mental illness	81	59
Help caregiver in acceptance of illness	78	57
Locating resources for patient in the community—housing, treatment, income maintenance, etc.	76	55
Understanding medications and their use	76	55
Learning potential side effects of medication	74	54
Reduce friction over patients' behavior	71	51
Alleviation of guilt and blame	66	48
Learning to respond to such psychiatric symptoms as hearing voices, talking to self, and paranoia	62	45
Help in gaining order and control over household	61	44
Reduction of nonproductive arguments	60	43
Achieving compliance with medication	54	39
Learning how to handle threats of violence	52	38
Getting acceptance of patient by spouse	51	37
Getting better hygiene with patient	47	34
Gaining time for personal life	47	34
Help in control of substance abuse	42	30
Getting other family members to share responsibility	39	28

*In order of frequency

growth and satisfaction in life. Families feel keenly the loss of time and energy for leisure and interpersonal relationships.[21] Parents of the adult disabled, for example, find it difficult to live in an age-appropriate way, in a way that is comparable to their late-middle-aged friends, for these parents are still tied down to the responsibilities of a parenting role which others have shed. These families are limited by financial considerations as to how they can educate their other children, what kinds of recreation they can have, and what plans they can make for retirement: mental illness is a costly disease. Families need relief from some of these burdens so that the quality of their lives is not totally compromised.

THE WORLDVIEWS OF PROFESSIONALS

In preceding sections we have attempted to present the world view of families of persons with mental illness. We have tried to show how they define the problems, how they see the reality of mental illness. In their search for help with their dilemmas they frequently turn to mental health professionals for assistance. There they find considerable diversity in viewpoints about what mental illness is, what causes it, how families are perceived, and how they can be helped. They each agree that families have difficulty, but they define the difficulty in a variety of ways. We will examine several of them.

Hierarchical Incongruity

Haley[28] feels it most useful to define the problem that is troubling the family as misbehavior of their young person. It is in a category with other such misbehaving youths as drug addicts, delinquents, and cultists. They are failures in life. He prefers the adjectives "mad," "eccentric," or "problematic," and believes the terms mental illness or schizophrenia are not useful. He rejects the possibilities of genetic or organic bases of the disorder and feels that the cause is in the present rather than in the past.

What lies behind the eccentric behavior that others call mental illness is an effort on the part of the young person to hold the family together. Basic to the problem are the marital difficulties of the parents which make it difficult for the young person to "leave the nest." Strange alliances develop within the family, causing the authority of one parent to be undermined; the child, then, begins to take charge and to dominate with his symptoms and his failure to achieve independence. His disorganized behavior and bizarre language is a reflection of, rather than a precursor to, family disorganization. Families, of course, see it as quite the reverse.

The goal of treatment is to keep the patient out of the hospital and help him overcome his propensity for failure. He is to become independent by working and living apart from the family. To achieve this, the therapist joins with the family to create a new hierarchy with the parents in charge. Parents must have the power; the young person is required to obey. Parents must push the child into normal behavior. No excuses are made for his behavior; he can behave like normal people of his age. Medication is reduced and the young person must go to work as soon as possible. The hospital is to be used sparingly because it removes the patient from the community and does not force the family to solve its problems. Haley does not believe, as do many families, that the person's psyche is ill, nor does he believe the notion that the problem is due to fragility, inner anxiety, or inability to tolerate responsibility.

From a family's perspective, it is important to know if the treatment works. Does the person, then, drop his symptoms, go to work, and move out? Haley says his concerns are not for research but to demonstrate a technique. He has no outcome data except those that show about 26 percent return to the hospital.

Madanes[29] concurs with Haley that the family problem is one of inappropriate organizational structures. The therapist uses his or her power to direct the family members as to how they should relate to each other and how the parents should exert more power over their children. Although the therapists identify the problem in the family, they do not explain the problem to them. Only the therapist needs to know what is going on; families can change without knowing what is occurring. One might assume that families would feel helpless, confused, and manipulated in this kind of a situation, that there would be little transfer of learning. Families would need to return to professional help for each new problem, for they do not learn the skill of problem solving.

Even in an event such as a potential suicide, Madanes does not show great concern for the anxiety and stress of the family. The therapist decides (and presumably takes responsibility for the consequences) whether to hospitalize the patient or to force the family to institute a 24-hour suicide watch. "This," she notes, "usually tests the limits of the parents' patience and helps them take a firm stand in demanding normal behavior from this youth" (p 135).

Central to the treatments of Haley and Madanes is the issue of power. First of all is the power of the therapist to control the situation by being in charge of medication, hospitalization, and the total treatment. They use a one-way mirror to gain an advantage over the family members by having a supervisor behind the mirror who telephones directions to the therapist. They refrain from sharing knowledge, for knowledge is power. Therapists uses their power over the parents to force them to make their children obey.

Disordered Communication

Wynne et al.[30,31] see disordered communication as the core problem of families with mentally ill relatives. These families' transactions are characterized by fragmentation, disjunctive quality, and blurring of attention and meaning. They fail to acknowledge each other, are easily distracted, and lack closure. Even verbalizations that appear normal to the casual observer, in their family context, are revealed to be a thought disorder like that found in most disorganized schizophrenic persons. Believing that the formal aspects of communication are relatively stable, these researchers feel that they have identified a trait that predates hospitalization of the schizophrenic family member. Wynne acknowledges that schizophrenics may show extreme response patterns, that is, they may have special stimulus sensitivity, a tendency to augment or reduce stimulation, and display other psychophysiologic disturbances. These, he hypothesizes, may be genetically determined.

Beels and MacFarlane[32] are critical of the kinds of treatment that grow out of communication theory. They feel that it would aggravate guilt feelings and would not provide the kinds of practical help families need, nor would it deal with families' many painful problems of feeling stigmatized and their confusion at seeing a loved one become schizophrenic.

Terkelsen[33] reviewed various studies relating to family communication disorders and found alternative ways of explaining them. He concluded that many communication aberrations are adaptive to two therapist attributes: failure to absolve the family of causal responsibility, and failure to inform the family about the nature of mental illness. Many of the responses in the clinic were not ongoing attributes of the family, but were responses of a beleaguered family to an accusatory authority. Whether or not this interpretation is acknowledged by professionals, it has much in common with the worldview of families.

Emotionally Disturbed Families

Lidz and his coworkers' theories[34,35] grew out of psychoanalytic tradition and were first based on the intensive study of 17 families whom they saw in their clinic. In their view, all schizophrenics come from families where there is severe emotional strife. One or both parents are extremely egocentric, with communication styles manifested by this egocentricity; this familial disturbance is a precursor to the severe disturbance of thinking in the children.

Mothers tend to be impervious to their children's needs, to be either too restrictive or too insufficiently firm, and they tend to live their lives through their children. Fathers tend to be insecure in their masculinity, in need of constant bolstering of their self-steem, and are often mildly paranoid. Schizophrenics' families have unclear sexual and generational boundaries and often behave seductively with their children.

Arieti[36] in 1974 shared many of Lidz's views of the family. He found families to be sick, unhappy, disharmonious, anxiety-ridden and loaded with unconscious guilt, which he felt existed before a member became schizophrenic. In every case studied, he noted there was serious family disturbance. By 1979 Arieti[37] seemed to have altered his view somewhat. He found that families can participate in the care of their relative and that "for many years schizophrenia was seen from a particular, probably biased stance and the participation of the family in reintegration and rehabilitation was viewed with skepticism" (p x). In his 1979 work, Arieti declared the need to avoid reductionism and to recognize a combination of causal factors, biologic, psychologic, and sociologic. He saw families less as a source of pathology and more as a major instrument of restoration.

High Expressed Emotion

Practitioners in this country have been strongly influenced by the work of Brown, Birley, and Wing,[38] followed by that of Vaugh and Leff[39] and their contention that the level of expressed emotion can affect the course of mental illness in a member. In these studies the family caregivers are rated on their level of expressed emotions at the time of the patient's hospitalization; it is a composite score based on the number of critical comments, tone of voice, and emotional overinvolvement. The behavior in the clinic is presumed representative of the family's general attitudes at home. In families with high expressed emotion (high EE), relapse rate was 56 percent; the rate of relapse was only 21 percent for those with low EE. Brown et al. emphasized that the behavior of relatives is not in general abnormal or excessive, nor is it causative. They saw the person with schizophrenia as exquisitely sensitive to his environment. Wing[40] saw the common factor in patient breakdown or relapse to be stress without opportunity for protective withdrawal. He felt that the role of the relative is a difficult one, since it is unnatural for a family to maintain the degree of detachment and neutrality required; it is easier for the professional to develop that stance. It is extraordinary, he notes, that so many families manage to find a way to live with a patient and provide him with a supportive and nonthreatening home.

Goldstein[41] observed that the families of persons with schizophrenia are "disordered" and "disrupted," but he acknowledges that they also have strengths. Family therapy and maintenance drugs are prescribed as a means to reduce the levels of stress. Goldstein and Kopeiken[42] recognized that the return of a patient to the family can produce inordinately high levels of tension. They use problem-solving approaches with the patient and the rest of the family, and do not encourage exclusive accommodation to the patient.

It is the view of Anderson, Hogarty, and Reiss[43] that schizophrenic persons are especially vulnerable to stress, but also that they live in families that have communication styles that exacerbate the problems. They recognize the need to be sympathetic to the troubles that families suffer and to help them overcome their guilt in order to establish an alliance helpful to the patient. It is the role of the therapist to provide information about the illness, about medication, and about behavioral management. They encourage families to establish interests of their own as a way to reduce overinvolvement with the patient.

Falloon et al.[5] were relatively successful in absolving the family of causative roles. They noted that any communication problems families have may be due to prodromal features of schizophrenia in a relative or as a reaction to stress. In assessing family behavior "it is assumed at all times that each member of the household is performing at his or her best possible level of function given the psychological and environmental constraints that they experience," and further, that "coping mechanisms that may appear somewhat undesirable to an observer—for instance withdrawal, intrusiveness, and criticism—represent each person's best efforts in that environment and at that particular time," (p 64). Families are offered therapy and round-the-clock availability for crisis management.

MacFarlane[44] was critical of "unsophisticated family therapy [that] has tended to worsen the situation by implying that family disturbance alone has caused the psychosis," (p 105). MacFarlane did, however, see families as highly dysfunctional. He found them to be enmeshed, a key factor in at least aggravating the condition. They also had poor social relationships, probably preceding the psychosis. Presumably, this view does not tend to worsen the situation for the family. He reported that most families are quite disturbed, with major structural and communication problems and a strong tendency to be overwhelmed with anxiety. Families, he found, tend to reject individual, group, and family therapy as unpleasant and stressful and rarely helpful. MacFarlane recommended the use of multiple family groups in which the families can support each other, correct each other's difficulties, and give positive feedback.

Severely Strained Adaptive Capacities

A number of theorists have recently made a decided shift in problem definition of families of the mentally ill and have come to view them in the same way any other family devastated by a traumatic event is viewed—the birth of a severely handicapped or retarded child or the onset of a terminal illness. The behaviors of all of these families are interpreted as the efforts being made to solve problems that are highly complex and also highly relevant to the family's well being, thus taxing the family's adaptive capacities. They go through similar cycles of denial, mourning, anger, and anxiety, and family life becomes disorganized and confused.[45-48] This is considered a normal and expected reaction rather than an indication of pathology. In this framework there is no need for such terms as "enmeshment," "double bind," "learned helplessness," "treatment resistant," "pathogenic," "dysfunctional," and myriad others bound to seem pejorative and rejecting by the families so labelled.

When a family's usual repertoire of knowledge and skills is not adequate to meet the exigencies of new problems, they flounder and act maladaptively until they learn how to solve the demands presented. What they need, then, is information, problem solving skills, and support; they need the help of someone who will focus on their competencies and coping skills, who knows how to deal with tangible problems in a realistic way, who recognizes and respects the family as the expert on its own member.

The advantages of using an educational approach to families with problems has been stressed by several writers.[49-53] Hatfield[54] has prepared a basic manual, *Coping with Mental Illness in the Family: The Family Guide* (together with *The*

Leader's Guide), so that mental health professionals can cond
seminars for families. These materials focus on the nature of men
various treatments for it, and practical techniques for dealing wi
problems. A variety of other materials addressed to families has t
by Kantor,[55] Bernheim, Lewine, and Beale,[56] and Torrey.[57]

CONGRUENCE BETWEEN WORLDVIEWS

The foci of this chapter have been families of persons with a mental illness, how families view the problems involved, and what they see as their needs for help. We have also looked at the view of a selected group of therapists in order to ascertain their perspectives and how they define the problems. At issue, of course, is the degree of congruence between their two worldviews. To the extent that there is congruence, there is empathy, cooperation, and satisfaction in service; to the extent that there is a large gap between these worlds, there will be alienation, "treatment resistance," and a restless search for something more harmonious to family needs.

Families have frequently expressed their need for understanding mental illness and for the practical help that can make coping more effective. Literature reviews show there is an increasing recognition on the part of professionals that they should respond to these needs, with concrete help a central part of their programs. In a recent study[27] no relationship was found between what families identified as their needs and what they felt professionals provided. It will clearly take time for mental health professionals to develop their own expertise in family management of patients so that they can be a teacher to families. The idea is quite new.

Families undergo painful emotional upheavals as a consequence of mental illness in a loved one. Since the goal of most family therapists is to use the family to help the patient, little attention is paid to other family members and their needs. Although an occasional reference is made in the literature, for example Atwood and Williams,[58] in which special groups are created just to help the family with their feelings, this is rare. In fact, in most experimental approaches to family therapy, no assessment is even made of outcome for other than the patient.

It is quite probable that most family therapy has some negative consequences for families who are treated. Inherent in the idea of family therapy is the notion of inadequacy, dysfunction, peculiarity, and pathology, which will inevitably be viewed as negative by families. Family therapists apparently recognize the problems, for many of them that we reviewed[28-31,41-43,45] were adamant in their criticism of other therapists who blamed families and produced painful dysfunctional guilt, but, predictably, they used terms just as critical of families and just as likely to exacerbate family problems. What is not recognized is that as long as the focus is on deficiencies of families, they will *feel* blamed, even if the therapist has not directly blamed them. Few, in fact, do that. Families do not feel absolved from blame if they are told that they unintentionally caused or prolonged the disorder; intent is not the issue. That so many therapists harbor such contradictory points of view suggests that there is a less than full understanding of these families. It also suggests that much of the problem lies in the concept of therapy, for in it there is no way to absolve the family from being at fault in some way.

Concern for the family as a whole and its well being is rarely expressed in the literature. Perhaps the most realistic hope for these families lies in the rapid emergence of self-help groups across the country.[59] Their first and most immediate goal is invariably to give emotional support to the family without judgment or criticism.

However distraught they are about the patient, most family members still have a deep need to live out their lives as meaningfully as possible. Although they are urged to develop an outside interest or go to work in order not to be harmfully overinvolved, there is little attention to the growth needs of members in and for themselves. Again, we are reminded that the word "family" in relationship to treatment or therapy is a misnomer, since the well being of only one member is considered, and sometimes at the expense of the rest of the family.

Probably least satisfactory is professional understanding of the existential dilemmas families face. Families need to know that someone understands their search for meaning in what is otherwise inexplicable—a loved one, the victim of a horribly destructive disease. Their frequent cry of "why did it happen?" is not necessarily a search for a cause in themselves. It is a search for a larger meaning; too often what is a deep and profound question is trivialized by assigning to it an implication of guilt. The clergy traditionally gave comfort to persons suffering unexplainable loss; we presently expect therapists to do this job, for which they may not be equipped either by training or by temperament. Families now transcend their traumas on their own, as best they can, and move toward acceptance with little help from anyone.

We are forced to conclude that there is considerable gap between the worldview of the family and that of the professional. Families and professionals define the problems differently, thus it is difficult to establish productive alliances between them. Professionals need training to develop their role-taking capacities. Unless training begins to address this issue, the schism is bound to widen.

OTHER MAJOR ISSUES FOR FAMILIES

While the major issue for families is their sense of alienation from providers of services in mental health, a number of other issues is also demanding attention. One of these has to do with lack of clarification between what should be the public's responsibility and what the family's responsibility in giving care to the mentally ill. A second, related issue has to do with what might best be called "family rights," and the last with the ways in which the growing consciousness of being consumers is going to be implemented.

The Role of the Family Versus the Role of Society

When care for persons with mental illness was provided in institutions, states provided the care, often at state expense, and the question of rights and responsibilities of families rarely came up. When deinstitutionalization got underway, there was an unstated assumption that care would be provided by the community, but adequate services for all have never become a reality and with the new fiscal conservatism it probably never will. If society doesn't provide the care, presumably families are expected to. This is not clear, however, for adult children and their parents have no legal claims on each other and can presumably choose to take this responsibility or not. Some patients are cared for by the public at present, some by their families, and some by a combination of the two, but there is no apparent rationale that determines who gets service and who does not.

The initiative for setting priorities may need to come from families. They may have to decide whether priorities should be based on the age of patient and family caretaker, on the degree of disturbance and disturbing behavior, or on the potential for becoming independent and self-sufficient. Or, perhaps, family income should be a deciding factor. Unless the community plans and sets priorities, families are handicapped in planning their personal resources to help the patient best and meet other members' needs.

The Rights of Families

The lives of families have changed irrevocably as they have taken on the burdens of caregiving. Since they are dealing with adults, some of whom are severely disturbed and disturbing, they have little leverage with which to require better behavior. With the growth of patients' rights, most families feel that their hands are tied, and many families spend exhausting lengths of time when the patient is on a downhill course, until he becomes sick enough to be hospitalized. Families feel that their rights have diminished; they have been caught in the squeeze between bureaucrats' zeal to empty beds and patients' rights to be free from involuntary treatment.

With professionals having less power over difficult patients, they have turned to families, expecting them to be able to control the patient and prevent a relapse. To this end, some professionals have begun to use highly persuasive tactics—bordering on the coercive—to get families to consent to therapy. Just to cite one example, Harbin[60] advises that if family treatment is crucial for positive outcome for the patient, "the threat of possible discharge" could be raised with the family and if that doesn't get a response, "ending the patient's disability payments" (p 22) might be threatened. He recommends discretion in using these measures. Now questions of "family rights" arise. Must families receive an adult mentally ill person back in their homes? Can professionals use coercive tactics to require family therapy if in the judgment of the family that is not desirable?

In the next decade we will hear much more about "family rights" and perhaps, even, the question of "involuntary treatment" of families. The success of the community care movement hinges on the willingness of families to provide care for the majority of patients. They have much more power and leverage than they have yet come to use.

Developing A Consumer Orientation

In 1979 the National Alliance for the Mentally Ill was formed to serve as an umbrella organization for the large number of family self-help and consumer-advocacy groups springing up all over the country.[61] The impetus for this movement was, in part, the frustration of users of mental health services in getting their voices heard and their needs known. Mental health professionals have sought little consumer information and monitored the market infrequently, and have therefore lagged in service development.[62] A vigorous consumer movement should change that.

At its 1982 annual convention, the National Alliance for the Mentally Ill chose as its theme "Empowering Consumers of Mental Health Services."[63] Its emphasis was on consumer education. Consumer education can arm individuals with the knowledge and self-confidence needed to make choices which can increase individual satisfaction, marketplace efficiency, and the public good, and according to Willett,[64] can be a change agent on the model of the Civil Rights and the Women's Movement.

REFERENCES

1. Goldman HH: Mental illness and family burden. *Hosp Community Psychiatry* 1982; 33:557-559
2. Caplan G: The family as a support system, in Caplan G, Killilea M (eds): *Support Systems and Mutual Help*. New York, Grune & Stratton, 1976, pp 19-36
3. Uzoka A: The myth of the nuclear family—historical background and clinical implications. *Am Psychol* 1979;34:1095-1106
4. Report to the President from the President's Commission on Mental Health. I. US Government Printing Office, Washington DC, 1978, pp 16-17
5. Falloon IR, Boyd JL, McGee CW, et al.: Family management training in the community care of schizophrenia, in Goldstein MJ (ed): *New Developments in Intervention with Families of Schizophrenics*. San Francisco, Jossey-Bass, 1981, pp 61-78
6. Harbin HT (ed): *The Psychiatric Hospital and the Family*. New York, Spectrum Publications, 1982
7. Goldstein MJ (ed): *New Developments in Intervention with Families of Schizophrenics*. San Francisco, Jossey-Bass, 1981, pp 1-4

8. Spitzer SP, Weinstein RM, Nelson HL: Family reaction and the career of the psychiatric patient: A long term follow-up study, in Harbin HT (ed): *The Psychiatric Hospital and the Family*. New York, SP Medical and Scientific Books, 1982, pp 173–186

9. Withersty DJ, Kidwell RE: Measuring the effects of family involvement on a psychiatric inpatient unit, in Harbin HT (ed): *The Psychiatric Hospital and the Family*. New York, SP Medical and Scientific Books, 1982, pp 173–186

10. Debuskey M (ed): *The Chronically Ill Child and his Family*. Springfield, IL, Charles C. Thomas Publishers, 1970

11. Travis G: *Chronic Illness in Children—Its Impact on Child and Family*. Stanford, CA, Stanford University Press, 1976

12. Bugen L: Human grief: A model for prediction and intervention, in Power PW, Del Orto AE: *The Role of the Family in the Rehabilitation of the Physically Disabled*. Baltimore, University Park Press, 1980, pp 489–501

13. Voysey, M: Impression management by parents with disabled children, in Power PW, Del Orto AE: *The Role of the Family in the Rehabilitation of the Physically Disabled*. Baltimore, University Park Press, 1980, pp 380–393

14. Kreisman D, Joy V: Family response to the mental illness of a relative: A review of the literature. *Schizophr Bull* 1974;10:34–57

15. Lamb H: Empathy and advice: Counseling families of the mentally ill. *Behavioral Medicine* 1979; 6:35–38

16. Kreisman D, Simmens S, Joy V: Deinstitutionalization and the family's well being. New York, New York State Psychiatric Institute, 1979, pp 1–17

17. Doll W: Family coping with the mentally ill: An unanticipated problem of deinstitutionalization. *Hosp Community Psychiatry* 1976;27:183–185

18. Thompson E, Doll W, Lefton M: Some affective dimensions of familial coping with the mentally ill. Paper presented at the 54th annual meeting of the American Orthopsychiatric Association, April 1977, New York

19. Creer C, Wing J: *Schizophrenia at Home*. London, Institute of Psychiatry, 1974, pp 1–75

20. Raymond M, Slaby A, Lieb J: *The Healing Alliance*. New York, WW Norton, 1975, pp 10–55

21. Hatfield A: Psychological costs of schizophrenia to the family. *Social Work* 1978;23:355–359

22. Arey S, Warheit G: Psychological costs of living with psychologically disturbed family members, in Robins L, Clayton P, Wing JK: *The Social Consequences of Psychiatric Illnesses*. New York, Brunner/Mazel, 1980, pp 158–165

23. Park D, Shapiro L: *You Are Not Alone: Understanding and Dealing with Mental Illness*. Boston, Little, Brown, 1976, pp 195–220

24. Vine P: *Families in Pain*. New York, Pantheon, 1982

25. Wasow M: *Coping with Schizophrenia: A Survival Manual*. Palo Alto, CA, Science and Behavior, 1982

26. Hatfield AB: Help-seeking behavior in families of schizophrenics. *Am J Community Psychol* 1979;7:563–569

27. Hatfield AB: What families want of family therapy. In MacFarlane WR (ed): *Family Therapy in Schizophrenia*. New York, Guildford Press, 1983, pp 41–63

28. Haley J: *Leaving Home: The Therapy of Disturbed Young People*. New York, McGraw-Hill, 1980

29. Madanes C: *Strategic Family Therapy*. San Francisco, Jossey-Bass, 1981

30. Singer MT, Wynne LC: Principles of scoring communication defects and deviances in parents of schizophrenics: Rorschach and TAT scoring manuals. *Psychiatry* 1966;290:260–288

31. Wynne LC: Family relationships and communications. Concluding comments in Wynne LC, Cromwell RM, Matthysse S: *The Nature of Schizophrenia*. New York, John Wiley, 1978, pp 534–542

32. Beels CC, McFarlane WR: Family treatments of schizophrenia: Background and state of art. *Hosp Community Psychiatry* 1982;33:541–549

33. Terkelsen K: Schizophrenia and the family: Adverse Effects of Family Therapy. *Family Process* 1983;22: 193–200
34. Lidz T: *The Origin and Treatment of Schizophrenic Disorders*. New York, Basic Books, 1973, pp 3–50
35. Lidz T, Fleck S, Cornelison A: *Schizophrenia and the Family*. New York, International Universities Press, 1965
36. Arieti S: *Interpretations of Schizophrenia* (2 ed). New York, Basic Books, 1974, pp 71–145
37. Arieti S: *Understanding and Helping the Schizophrenic*. New York, Basic Books, 1979, pp ix–xi
38. Brown GW, Birley JL, Wing JK: Influences of family life on the course of schizophrenic disorders: A replication. *Br J Psychiatry* 1972;121:241–250
39. Vaughn CE, Leff JP: The influence of family and social factors in the course of psychiatric illness. *Br J Psychiatry* 1981;139:102–104
40. Wing JK: The management of schizophrenia in the community, in Usdin G (ed): *Psychiatric Medicine*. New York, Brunner/Mazel, 1977, pp 427–471
41. Goldstein MJ: Editor's notes in Goldstein MJ (ed): *New Developments in Interventions with Families of Schizophrenics*. San Francisco, Jossey-Bass, 1981, pp 1–4
42. Goldstein MJ, Kopeiken HS: Short- and long-term effects of combining drug and family therapy. In Goldstein MJ (ed): *New Developments in Interventions with Families of Schizophrenia*. San Francisco, Jossey-Bass, 1981, pp 5–26
43. Anderson CM, Hogarty A, Reiss DJ: The psychoeducational family treatment of schizophrenia, in Goldstein M (ed): *New Developments in Interventions with Families of Schizophrenics*. San Francisco, Jossey-Bass, 1981, pp 79–94
44. McFarlane WR: Multiple family therapy in the psychiatric hospital, in Harbin HT (ed): *The Psychiatric Hospital and the Family*. New York, Spectrum Publications, 1982, pp 103–129
45. Bugen LA: Human grief: A model of prediction and intervention, in Powers PW, DelOrto AE: *Role of the Family in Rehabilitation of the Physically Disabled*. Baltimore, University Park Press, 1980, pp 489–501
46. Kiely WF: Coping with severe illness, in Power PW, Del Orto AE: *Role of the Family in Rehabilitation of the Physically Disabled*. Baltimore, University Park Press, 1980, pp 94–105
47. Wikler L, Wasow M, Hatfield E: Chronic sorrow revisited: Parents vs. professional depiction of the adjustment of parents of mentally retarded children. *Am J Orthopsychiatry* 1981; 51:63–70
48. Turnbull AP, Turnbull HR: *Parents Speak Out: Views from the other Side of the Two-Way Mirror*. Columbus, OH, Charles E. Merrill, 1978
49. Krauss JB, Slavinsky AT: *The Chronically Ill Psychiatric Patient in the Community*. Boston, Blackwell Publications, 1982, pp 255–279
50. Maluccio AN: Competence-oriented social work practice: An ecological approach in Maluccio AN (ed): *Promoting Competence in Clients: A New/Old Approach to Social Work Practice*. New York, Free Press, 1981, 1–24
51. Goldstein EG: Promoting competence in families of psychiatric patients, in Maluccio AN: *Promoting Competence in Clients: A New/Old Approach to Social Work Practice*. New York, Free Press, 1981, pp 317–341
52. Howell M: *Helping Ourselves: Families and the Human Network*. Beacon Press, Boston, 1973
53. Guerney B, Stollak G, Guerney L: The practicing psychologist as educator—an alternative to the medical practitioner's model. *Professional Psychology* 1978,3:76–282
54. Hatfield AB: *Coping with Mental Illness in the Family: The Family Guide and The Leader's Guide*. University of Maryland, College Park, MD, 1983
55. Kantor J: *Coping Strategies for Relatives of the Mentally Ill*. Bethesda, MD, Alliance for the Mentally Ill, 1982, pp 4–39
56. Bernheim KL, Lewine RRJ, Beale CT: *The Caring Family*. New York, Random, 1982
57. Torrey EF: *Surviving Schizophrenia: A Family Manual*. New York, Harper and Row, 1983

58. Atwood N, Williams ME: Group support for the families of the mentally ill. *Schizophr Bull* 1978;4:415–425
59. Hatfield AB: Self-help groups of families of the mentally ill. *Social Work* 1981;26:408–414
60. Harbin JT: Family treatment of the psychiatric inpatient, in Harbin HT (ed): *The Psychiatric Hospital and the Family*. New York, Spectrum Publications, 1982, pp 3–25
61. Advocacy for Persons with Chronic Mental Illness: Building a Nationwide Network. Proceedings of the 1979 National Conference, Washington, DC: National Alliance for the Mentally Ill, 1979, 1–117
62. Hornstra R, Lubin B, Lewis R, et al: Worlds apart: Patients and professionals. *Arch Gen Psychiatry* 1972;27:872–883
63. Empowering Consumers of Mental Health Services. Proceedings of the 1982 Annual Convention, Washington, DC, National Alliance for the Mentally Ill, 1982, 1–144
64. Willett S: Consumer education or advocacy—or both? *Social Policy* 1977;8:2–8

Judith Godwin Rabkin

22

Community Attitudes and Local Psychiatric Facilities

This chapter is organized in two sections. In the first, the cumulative research evidence is presented, including new findings published in the past five years concerning public attitudes toward the mentally ill and the issue of "stigma". In the second, studies in a newly emerging research area are reviewed. These studies are designed to assess public attitudes and responses to local facilities serving the mentally ill, an issue highlighted as a research priority by the authors of the President's Commission on Mental Health in their 1978 recommendations.[1]

OVERVIEW OF PUBLIC ATTITUDES

Secular Trends

Public attitudes about mental illness have been the subject of systematic inquiry since the late 1940s.[2,3] The number of publications in this area is now large but uneven in quality. Until very recently, most investigators focused on one broad issue: how do members of the general public view mental illness in the abstract, and what do they think of hypothetical mental patients? A less popular strategy for assessing public attitudes was to inquire about respondents' dispositions to use mental health services themselves or to recommend them to others.

THE CHRONIC MENTAL PATIENT   Copyright © 1984 by Grune & Stratton.
ISBN 0-8089-1649-1   All rights of reproduction in any form reserved.

Over the past 30 years, more than 100 studies have cumulatively demonstrated a temporal trend toward greater tolerance of mental patients, accompanying a more general flexibility in social attitudes. Openly expressed rejection of the mentally ill has noticeably declined over time. It is no longer socially acceptable to avoid and exclude those labelled as mental patients only on the grounds of their illness. People continue to be apprehensive about having to deal with the impaired mental patient, however, and their anticipated unpredictable and possibly dangerous behavior. Further, patients who have been hospitalized are often still concerned about their reception when they are ready to return to their communities, jobs, and friends.[4]

Along with a trend toward more receptive attitudes toward mental illness in general, there has been a shift in willingness to acknowledge the need for mental health services, and to use them. In 1957, Gurin et al.[5] conducted a national survey and concluded that Americans did not readily seek treatment for emotional problems. As Mollica[6] points out, the recent followup of Veroff et al.[7] reveals "a marked increase in the public's acceptance of mental health professionals and agencies and a willingness to accept the view that emotional problems should be referred to mental health specialists" (p 368). Much of this attitudinal change is attributed to the impact of the community mental health center movement.

Despite these generally positive attitudinal shifts, there remains considerable diversity in expressed attitudes about mental illness and mental patients. This diversity is associated with characteristics of respondents, of patients, and of their treatment situations. Older people, those with less education and lower social status, poorer people, and males in general are more intolerant in their expressed attitudes toward mental illness, as are recently-arrived ethnic groups and those who report less social contact with someone who has received psychiatric treatment. The patients considered least acceptable are those who are assaultive, of lower social, economic, and educational status, members of ethnic minorities, male, with few social or family ties, whose behavior is visibly disturbed, and who display behavioral rather than physical symptoms. Treatment situations associated with more negative attitudes are likely to be in-patient facilities, public rather than private, and specialized psychiatric rather than general hospital settings.

The relationships between these variables and attitudinal statements have been demonstrated repeatedly with different samples in different places, so there is little question about their reliability. The magnitude of the relationships, however, is consistently small, so that even in those rare studies where multiple regression techniques have been employed, their combined predictive utility has been low. Not only have investigators found it difficult to predict attitudes toward mental illness and mental patients, but they found attitudes to be weak predictors of actual behavior toward them. In fact, attitudes by themselves never have been very useful predictors of behavior, in this or any other area. Personal factors such as other attitudes, competing motives, past experiences, and social resources, together with situational factors such as the influence of other people, social expectations, and the number of options available in a given setting, are together far stronger influences on actions than is an expressed attitude. In this field, attitudes are sometimes even negatively correlated with behavior. A good example is the high level of acceptance of mental patients routinely articulated by the well educated and well to do, paired with the historical exclusion of local psychiatric facilities and residences from their prosperous neighborhoods.[8]

In view of the foregoing observations, one of the primary research recommendations of the Task Force on Implementation of the Report to the President from the President's Commission on Mental Health[9] addresses the need for research concerning the actual behavior of people regarding mental health facilities, as well as their expressed attitudes. Related issues include assessment of the impact of facilities on their neighbors' attitudes, and the extent to which psychiatric facilities compared to other public services are selectively opposed and resisted.

Labels, Stigma, and Rejection

Several studies comparing public reactions to the label of mental illness and to descriptions of disturbed behavior itself suggest that it is the behavior and not the label that evokes the negative response.[10] Those with episodic disorders whose symptoms remit are usually able to resume ordinary social activities, jobs, and lifestyle, despite their psychiatric histories; we all know patients and indeed friends and colleagues of whom this is true. Huffine and Clausen[11] followed for 20 years a cohort of married male patients hospitalized in the 1950s at NIMH. In this longitudinal study, they found that the "great majority" who had been employed for at least one year prior to their hospitalization returned to these jobs. They also reported that ex-patients and their families reported few actual experiences of rejection in other spheres, despite apprehension that this would occur.

Clausen's work supports the observation that it is deviant behavior, not a history of illness or treatment, that leads to labelling and/or rejection. It also supports his contention that while mental illness is generally "devalued," the term "stigma" is misleading. "Stigma," defined in the dictionary as a "mark of disgrace or infamy," is not an appropriate term if one is referring to negative attitudes induced by manifestations of psychiatric illness. As Clausen put it, "to blame the devaluation of mental illness on stigma is to ignore the nature of mental illness. I have not heard of any society which in general regards madness to be as acceptable as responsible self-control"[4] (p 32).

Clausen's view is generally beginning to prevail among those engaged in work in this field. In 1980, NIMH sponsored a workshop intended to address issues of stigma of mental illness and what could be done about it, at which Clausen presented the paper quoted above. At the end of the two-day meeting, the participants and the sponsoring NIMH division agreed that the term "stigma" was not a useful contribution to the goal of enhancing community acceptance of the mentally ill, and decided not to use the term in the title of the proceedings.[12]

Even the term "rejection" has been criticized as misleadingly negative. Roman and Floyd[13] argue persuasively that "rejection," by definition, "implies a prior condition of 'acceptance,' with 'rejection' stemming from ego's observation of *changes* in alter's behavior" or status as a function of some form of treatment experience (p 23). Accordingly, the usual measures of public attitudes toward hypothetical strangers who are described as mental patients cannot assess rejection but only low desire for social interaction. These authors suggest that the incorrect use of the pejorative term "rejection" may lead to exaggerated interpretations of data.

Roman and Floyd's observations are bolstered by considering the nonpsychiatric characteristics of those identified in the public view as mental patients. Those most apt to be visible to the community tend to be handicapped not only by deficiencies in social judgment and social supports, but often by the further burdens of low social status and meager personal resources. Further, the chronically mentally ill are often conspicuously lacking in social graces, indifferent to their appearance, and eccentric in their public behavior. Patients recently discharged from public facilities include an overrepresentation of poor, uneducated, single, minority males, and those with prior arrest records.[14] On those grounds alone, apart from any consideration of their mental status per se, they would not be welcomed as prospective neighbors. Desire for social distance, then, is not necessarily equivalent to rejection of the mentally ill.

Many former mental patients have recounted distressing experiences of rejection following hospitalization or treatment, and these were publicized during the years that Mrs. Rosalynn Carter held hearings on the subject across the country. There is, however, no way even to estimate the proportion of patients who encountered discrimination because of their illness or illness history, compared to those who did not. Few investigators have systematically studied the issue. While there is no question that some recovered, well functioning people have been sorely tried by blatant discrimination on either institutional or individual levels,[15] it seems in general that there is a gradient between rejection expressed toward patients or former patients, and the extent of their disabilities.[16] An earlier study by Serban[17] suggested that discrimination is not a major problem to the discharged chronically impaired ill who are far more preoccupied with the exigencies of daily living, including the procurement of shelter, food, disability payments, and other social services necessary for community survival. More recently, Nuehring[18] conducted a limited but interesting followup of patients and a "significant other" seen both at discharge from a southern state hospital and 6 months later. Patients were each asked 3 questions such as "being a discharged mental patient has made some of my friends avoid me." Each question was scored on a 4-point scale. The group mean score was 6, out of a possible total score of 12, and the scores clustered with little variation. Of this small amount of variance, only 11 percent was accounted for. Those predictors, weak as they were, included living in urban areas, being black, and living alone, all of which in turn were associated with greater psychopathology. These results tentatively support an association between degree of perceived social rejection and severity of impairment, as noted above.

In general, it seems that the label of mental illness continues to have negative connotations and negative consequences, although these consequences are certainly not universal and may be more of a problem in their anticipation than in their actual occurrence. Furthermore, the label is assigned primarily on the basis of current visible disturbed behavior. Relatively well adjusted, well educated people who develop a psychiatric disorder but then recover and return to good functioning are unlikely to suffer extensively from discrimination because of the history of illness. On the other hand, patients with chronic or progressive disorders, who never acquired vocational and social competencies or who do not return to their former adequate levels of adjustment, continue to be perceived as mental patients, with all the negative connotations that the label implies. It is the more or less permanently disabled people who are visibly different and less competent, and who require intermittent or long-term support from nonfamily sources to maintain themselves in the community, who are more likely to be the objects of aversion or avoidance.

To overstate the prevalence and intensity of stigma carries at least two hazards. First, it unduly exacerbates apprehensiveness about social rejection on the part of patients or those considering the possibility of obtaining psychiatric treatment. More insidiously, it has been suggested that talking about stigma may actually generate it.[19] Presenting a high level of rejection of mental patients as a social norm seems more likely to foster than reduce whatever latent prejudices continue to be harbored by members of the public.

In reviewing the available evidence in 1980, I drew the following conclusions: "overt discrimination against mental patients has diminished with the passage of time but seems to have reached a plateau in its descent . . . There is some risk that the current level of public acceptance will decline because of the presence of increasing numbers of chronically disabled mental patients who are returned to or maintained in the community . . . While the friction thus engendered is frequently attributed to lack of social and psychiatric services to meet the needs of these patients, there is reason to doubt the sincerity of this argument in view of the strong opposition by many communities to the establishment of local psychiatric facilities in their midst"[3](p 20). Since 1980, a new research area has developed, consisting of studies about community reactions to "local psychiatric facilities." These studies, presented below, cumulatively suggest that the public may be considerably more distressed by patients who are not served by formal facilities and who are seen wandering around the streets than those who are indeed enrolled in local psychiatric programs, or the local psychiatric facilities themselves.

COMMUNITY REACTIONS TO LOCAL PSYCHIATRIC FACILITIES

Within the past five years, a new area of research has begun to appear in professional journals. Several teams of investigators have studied the attitudes and behavioral responses of residents living near an existing community psychiatric facility, together with some form of matched comparison group. This research focus was one of the priorities recommended by members of the President's Commission on Mental Health Task Force, and represents a useful approach in the implementation of policies intended to maintain the chronically mentally ill in community settings.

Toronto Field Study

An extensive survey of community responses to local facilities has been conducted in Toronto by Dear and Taylor.[20-22] Their comprehensive design included, among other variables, consideration of attitudes toward mental patients and mental health facilities, effect of distance from facilities on attitudes, and the correspondence between general attitudes about mental illness and attitudes and dispositions to act with respect to local facilities.

Because existing attitude scales were either out of date or too narrow in focus, Dear et al. combined the strongest components of old scales and added new items. Their revised and amended 4-factor, 40-item instrument, the Community Attitudes toward Mental Illness (CAMI) Scale, is the best general instrument available.[21]

A total of 1090 respondents, representing an economically stratified random sample of urban and suburban Toronto residents, were selected for interview. One third lived within a quarter mile of a residential or outpatient psychiatric facility; the rest did not live near any facility.

This rich data set generated an array of findings which can only be highlighted here. First, measures of individual demographic, socioeconomic, and belief dimensions of respondents were found to be significantly correlated with general attitudes about mental illness in a statistical sense, but together accounted for less than a quarter of the variance in predicting attitudes: as such, their practical utility is limited. Aggregate measures of social class and distance from existing psychiatric facilities were weakly associated with attitudes. Their combined effect accounted for no more than 3 percent of the variance in predicting attitudes toward the mentally ill. High-status neighborhoods successfully excluded mental health facilities even though low-status neighborhoods were more rejecting in their expressed attitudes.

In general, respondents expressed sympathetic and benevolent attitudes toward the mentally ill, in contrast to the expectation that community reactions to the mentally ill are negative. They were also generally sympathetic toward hypothetical mental health facilities said to be planned for the neighborhood, although the desirability of the facility was reportedly greater if it was not hypothetically scheduled for construction on the respondent's own block.

A curious finding in this study was that only 36 percent of respondents chosen for interview because they lived within a quarter mile of an existing psychiatric facility were actually aware of its presence. Of these "aware" residents, only 4 percent (5 out of the 1090 interviewed) reported actually taking some kind of action to oppose the facility. Because this behavioral response was so low, the authors were unable to see whether an association existed between general attitudes toward mental illness or perceived desirability of mental health facilities and propensity for action.

Overall, the Canadian team concluded first that public attitudes to local psychiatric facilities were generally favorable, and that opposition to them was limited to "a vocal minority whose views are not representative of their community as a whole."[20] They also delineated dimensions of community concern: how well the facility fits physically with its surroundings, and how well the facility users fit socially into a neighborhood. Those respondents aware of a local facility were more optimistic about the possibility of fit than those who were not aware. In summary, surprisingly few neighbors were aware of local psychiatric facilities, attitudes were generally neutral, and facility presence had, if anything, a positive impact on the attitudes of its neighbors.

New York City: Telephone Survey

With colleagues, I conducted a more circumscribed attitude study of urban and suburban residents who lived in the immediate vicinity of a free-standing facility serving a chronically mentally ill clientele.[23] In the New York City study, we located two large public outpatient clinics, two residential facilities for discharged patients, and two single room occupancy (SRO) hotels known to serve a large number of ex-patients and whose proprietors were receptive to this clientele. All were in residential areas with no other health or mental health facilities within a 4-block radius. Using reverse telephone directories in which entries are ordered by address, we randomly selected in each of these "facility areas" 15 residents who lived on the same block as the facility. We then selected 6 nearby "no facility" control areas, matched in terms of residential-commercial mix and census measures of social class. Fifteen residents in each of these six areas also were surveyed.

A suburban study parallel in design to the urban study, with the same total sample size of 90 "facility area" respondents and 90 control area respondents, was conducted in 6 Westchester communities. Here some facilities served recovering substance-abusers as well as discharged mental patients.

We conducted a 10-minute telephone interview consisting of specific questions with a multiple choice answer format which covered, in part, assets and problems in the respondent's neighborhood, perceived desirability of hypothetical local social and health services, awareness of local psychiatric facilities and transient hotels, and attitudes toward their presence. We had originally planned to study responses by type of facility and clientele, but no differences were observed between those who lived near one type of facility or another so that responses were pooled to compare "neighbors" and "controls."

The most striking of our findings in both urban and suburban samples is the remarkably large number of people living in the same building or on the same block as a facility serving chronically disabled mental patients who were oblivious to the presence of the patients and the facility serving them. More than half the respondents selected because of their actual proximity to such a facility did not know it was there, just as Taylor et al. found in Toronto.

In general, awareness of such facilities was not related to attitudes about community services for the mentally ill. Unlike the Toronto results, the variable of geographic proximity did not emerge as a statistically significant attitudinal predictor. We did, however, replicate their finding that most respondents expressed no objection to or intolerance of the facilities or clientele. Not only were 90 percent of respondents unprepared to take personal action to block establishment of a "mental facility" near their home, but the large majority expressed no concern about the effect of local facilities on property values, personal safety, or neighborhood reputation.

We also were interested in the relative concern expressed by respondents about "crazy people in the streets," compared to eight other possible neighborhood problems, such as burglary, loitering, rundown buildings, alcoholics, or drug sales. None of the 9 problems was considered serious by even one third of the respondents, nor were there differences between facility and control areas respondents except for the problem of burglary, about which more concern was expressed by control areas respondents. A total score was computed for all problems combined. There were no significant mean differences between respondents in facility and control areas, between those aware of a nearby psychiatric facility and those not aware, or between those who objected to the presence of a local facility and those who did not object. Evidently, in the context of other problems, the presence of disturbed people in the streets is not an issue of central concern, even for people who live immediately adjacent to facilities carrying as many as 600 active cases at a time. One might even conjecture that, because these patients were receiving psychiatric services, or lived in hotels where the proprietors accepted them, they did not behave in a visibly disturbed or disturbing manner in public places.

While our findings would seem to apply to other urban areas with local psychiatric facilities, there is one distinctive characteristic about the areas we studied. Each contained only a single freestanding health facility; such spatial separation is, at least in New York City, the exception rather than the rule. It is far more common for facilities to cluster in specific neighborhoods; at times the density of such facilities is so great that the presumed normalizing effects of community settings are dissipated. Given this limitation, we concluded that the presence of community psychiatric facilities are not perceived as significant community burdens to their neighbors.

Oklahoma Survey

Another recent community study of the effect of proximity to a psychiatric facility on community attitudes was conducted by Smith[24] in a midwestern college town. Seventy-two women who lived on a block adjacent to the public mental hospital and local mental health center, and 68 women who lived a half mile away each were given a vignette describing either a severely or moderately ill mental patient, and were asked to indicate the degree of social distance that would be acceptable with respect to such a person—e.g., would be willing to work with such a person, to have her join one's favorite club, would rent a room in one's house. This design differs from the previously described studies in that the local facility was a very visible hospital of which the neighbors could scarcely be unaware.

Smith's results are slightly more ambiguous than those of the preceding studies. He found hospital neighbors to be more tolerant than control respondents regarding patients described as severely ill in the vignette presented to them, but no attitudinal differences were found for the patient described as moderately ill. The effect of geographic proximity was also nonlinear: respondents at a middle distance expressed greatest tolerance. While cautioning about the preliminary nature of his findings, Smith concluded that proximity to a psychiatric facility has a positive influence on attitudes toward the severely ill.

SUMMARY

Several common themes emerge from these studies. Neighbors are frequently unaware of local psychiatric facilities in their immediate proximity. When aware, they are usually not distressed about their presence. Hypothetical or proposed neighborhood facilities evoke much more expressed resistance than do existing facilities, suggesting that direct experience has, if anything, a positive effect on attitudes.

This same pattern has been reported in community responses to residential facilities for severely and profoundly retarded patients whose transfer from Willowbrook Hospital to neighborhood group homes in New York City was court mandated. When initially proposed, the modal response from the neighbors was one of vocal protest, often including self-serving expressions of concern that the area would be unsafe for the prospective residents. Despite the articulation of such objections at community meetings, over 100 group homes for Willowbrook residents by now have been established in New York City, and not a single one has been closed because of subsequent local opposition.[26]

These studies cumulatively suggest that freestanding psychiatric services spread out in predominantly residential areas do not necessarily constitute a recognized community burden. Further, they do not seem to detract from the quality of life of the neighbors to any substantial degree.

The available evidence does not support the notion that communities are united in their rejection of the mentally ill and the facilities that serve them, or that a special stigma characterizes them. It seems, rather, that people are no more strongly opposed to local services for mental patients than they are to any other public service facility. This is not to say that they are welcomed: no public facility is solicited or desired in any residential neighborhood unless it directly serves local needs (as do playgrounds or libraries). Neighborhoods do not welcome any groups brought in from the outside, whether they are social service recipients, students sharing quarters in a university town, or unrelated single people jointly renting vacation homes. Wolpert[26] has commented on this general "anti-group sentiment" which is particularly evident in neighborhoods where the traditional family unit is the prevailing mode. All forms of aggregate living by unrelated adults are regarded with doubt by the neighbors.

In this context, it is not surprising that the announcement of a planned public service facility of virtually any kind initially evokes resistance. In the course of a single recent week in New York City, for example, newspapers reported that 12,000 residents of Chinatown protested at City Hall about plans for a new jail in their neighborhood: 2000 Harlem residents held a street protest to block conversion of an unused school into a shelter for homeless men, and Hasidic Jews in Brooklyn rallied to oppose the establishment of a sewerage processing plan nearby (NY Times 19 Dec 82). Seen in this perspective, community opposition to psychiatric facilities has less the quality of prejudice than of a general attitude of resistance to the intrusion of any public service in a cohesive community. This "tendency for spatial exclusion" seems to vary primarily in terms of the stake people have in their neighborhood, and the extent of their political influence, rather than attitudes about jails, the homeless, sewerage processing plants, or mental patients per se. In this sense, the research findings may be misleadingly optimistic. Pragmatic politics may require the offer of community trade-offs (such as simultaneous introduction of a psychiatric facility and a new playground) as well as reliance upon good will for the successful establishment and management of local services for the chronically mentally ill.

REFERENCES

1. DHHS Steering Committee on the Chronically Mentally Ill. Toward a national plan for the chronically mentally ill. Washington, DC, US Government Printing Office, DHHS (ADM) 81–1077, 1981

2. Rabkin JG: The role of attitudes toward mental illness in evaluation of mental health programs. Guttentag M, Struening EL (eds): *Handbook of Evaluation Research,* II. Beverly Hills, CA, Sage, 1976, pp 431–482

3. Rabkin JG: Determinants of public attitudes about mental illness: Summary of the research literature, in Rabkin JG, Gelb L, Lazar JB (eds): *Attitudes Toward the Mentally Ill: Research Perspectives.* Washington, DC, US Government Printing Office, 1980, pp 15–26

4. Clausen JA: The family, stigma and help-seeking in severe mental disorder, in Rabkin JG, Gelb L, Lazar JB (eds): *Attitudes Toward the Mentally Ill: Research perspectives.* Washington, DC, US Government Printing Office, 1980, pp 31–34

5. Gurin G, Veroff J, Feld S: *Americans View Their Mental Health.* New York, Basic Books, 1960

6. Mollica RF: From asylum to community: The threatened disintegration of public psychiatry. *N Engl J Med* 1983;308:367–373

7. Veroff J, Kulka RA, Donvan E: Mental Health in America. New York, Basic Books, 1981

8. Segal SP, Baumohl J, Moyles E: Neighborhood types and community reactions to the mentally ill: A paradox of intensity. *J Health Soc Behav* 1980;21:345–359

9. Report of the HEW Task Force on Implementation of the Report to the President from the President's Commission on Mental Health. Washington, DC, US Government Printing Office. DHEW (ADM) 79–848, 1979

10. Segal SP, Aviram U: *The Mentally Ill in Community-based Sheltered Care.* New York, Wiley, 1978, pp 63–78

11. Huffine C, Clausen JA: Madness and work: Short and long-term effects of mental illness on occupational careers. *Social Forces* 1979;57:1049–1062

12. Rabkin JG, Gelb L, Lazar JB (eds): *Attitudes Toward the Mentally Ill: Research Perspectives. Report of an NIMH Workshop.* Washington, DC, US Government Printing Office, DHHS (ADM) 80–1031, 1980

13. Roman PM, Floyd HH: Social acceptance of psychiatric illness and psychiatric treatment. *Social Psychiatry* 1981;16:21–29

14. Steadman H, Melick M, Cocozza J: Arrest rates of persons released from New York State Department of Mental Hygiene psychiatric centers. *Report to the New York State Commissioner of Mental Hygiene,* 1977

15. Houghton J: One personal experience: Before and after mental illness, in Rabkin JG, Gelb L, Lazar JB (eds): *Attitudes Toward the Mentally Ill: Research Perspectives.* Washington, DC, US Government Printing Office, 1980

16. Weinstein RM: Stigma and mental illness: Theory versus reality. *J Orthomolecular Psychiatry* 1982;11:87–99

17. Serban G, Thomas A: Attitudes and behaviors of acute and chronic schizophrenic patients regarding ambulatory treatment. *Am J Psychiatry* 1974;131:991–995

18. Nuehring EM: Stigma and state hospital patients. *Am J Orthopsychiatry* 1979;49:626–633

19. Herbert W: Stigma, she said . . . but some aren't so sure. *APA Psychology Monitor* 1978;9:4–8

20. Taylor SM, Dear MJ, Hall GB: Attitudes toward the mentally ill and reactions to mental health facilities. *Social Science and Medicine* 1979;13:281–290

21. Taylor SM, Dear MJ: Scaling community attitudes toward the mentally ill. *Schizophr Bull* 1981;7:225–240

22. Dear MJ, Taylor SM: *Not on our Street: Community Attitudes to Mental Health Care.* London, Pion, 1982

23. Rabkin JG, Muhlin G, Cohen PW: What the neighbors think: Community attitudes toward local psychiatric facilities. *J Psychiatr Treatment and Evaluation,* in press

24. Smith CJ: Residential proximity and community acceptance of the mentally ill. *J Operational Psychiatry* 1981;12:2–12

25. Rothman D, Rothman S: *Willowbrook Wars.* Unpublished manuscript

26. Wolpert J, Seley JE: Community response to the deinstitutionalized population. *J National Assoc Private Psychiat Hosp* 1980;11:31–35

Index